MOROCCAN OTHER-ARCHIVES

Moroccan Other-Archives

HISTORY AND CITIZENSHIP AFTER STATE VIOLENCE

Brahim El Guabli

FORDHAM UNIVERSITY PRESS NEW YORK 2023

Fordham University Press gratefully acknowledges financial assistance and support provided for the publication of this book by Williams College.

Fordham University Press also publishes its books in a variety of electronic formats. Some content that appears in print may not be available in electronic books.

Visit us online at www.fordhampress.com.

Library of Congress Cataloging-in-Publication Data available online at https://catalog.loc.gov.

Printed in the United States of America

25 24 23 5 4 3 2 1

First edition

To the memory of my mother, Nna Zahwa n'Hmma M'bark (1945–2017), and father, Mbark Ould L'Houssaine Ould Abdellah (1928–2010)

To Shaina, Ilyas, and Naseem

Contents

Preface ix

Note on Transliteration xiii

List of Abbreviations xv

Introduction 1

1. (Re)Invented Tradition and the Performance of Amazigh Other-Archives in Public Life 26

2. Emplaced Memories of Jewish-Muslim Morocco 63

3. Jewish-Muslim Intimacy and the History of a Lost Citizenship 89

4. Making Tazmamart a Transnational Other-Archive 115

5. Other-Archives Transform Moroccan Historiography 150

Conclusion 177

Acknowledgments 189

Notes 193

Bibliography 253

Index 281

Preface

I am a child of the Years of Lead. I breathed the air of the period and internalized its atmosphere of distrust. A period of political violence that lasted from Morocco's independence in 1956 to the passing of King Hassan II in 1999, the Years of Lead left a lasting imprint on my generation. Like my peers who were born in post-independence Morocco, I had to navigate the fears, silences, and ambiguities that were quintessential characteristics of living under Moroccan authoritarianism.

Until age seven, Tamazight was my only language. The day I inadvertently enrolled in the village public school by following older children to this intimidating place was the day my mother tongue lost its privilege as the only medium through which I understood the world around me. By enrolling in school, I left one world and entered another. It was not like entering the "wolf's mouth," to borrow Kateb Yacine's famous phrase about his French colonial education in Algeria,[1] but it was a process that, while it added another literate member of the family to my illiterate parents' home, confined my Amazigh language and culture to daily life in the village. The value of my language depreciated. When I opened my mouth to answer a question in my mother tongue, the Tamazight-speaking teacher ordered me to shut up if I did not know the answer in Arabic. Moroccan nationalists and the monarchy had already decided on behalf of Moroccans that they were an Arab-Muslim country, and the schools worked to produce generations of Arabized youth in conformity with this top-down definition of the nation. The complexity of the broader structures that shaped me as a child were only made apparent when I gained consciousness of language and identity politics in Morocco and Tamazgha—the broader Amazigh homeland in North Africa. However, one thing was certainly clear from the beginning: my Tamazight was not welcome in school, the first space in which rural children encounter political authority.

This book is my attempt to make sense of how Moroccan cultural producers grappled with the forbidden pasts that repressive political forces prevented from being written about and circulated in the public sphere for almost fifty years. *Moroccan Other-Archives* offers a theorization of "other-archives." Other-archives are neither academic history nor firsthand memory, nor are they conventional archives. Rather, they are loci at which the stories of those who were left out of history and traditional archives reside, from where they return to rewrite history by haunting the predominant conceptions of identity and citizenship. Thanks to the creators of other-archives, rewriting history has become synonymous with exercising the right to citizenship in Morocco. Being a Moroccan citizen today means being able to reimagine the country's post-independence history, which has been mired in repression, disempowerment, and silence.

Moroccan Other-Archives examines how Moroccan cultural producers turned history into a space for civic engagement through the reconstruction of a pluralistic history that challenges taboos, silences, and omissions, none of which academic historians or political stakeholders were able to overcome before King Hassan II's death in 1999. Thanks to the production and wide dissemination of other-archives, formerly erased constituencies of Moroccan history—namely Imazighen, Jews, and political prisoners—reemerge in stories that reveal a traumatic history of disappearance and loss during the Years of Lead.

The Years of Lead came to a de facto end in summer 1999. I had just graduated from Ouarzazate Teacher Training School, and I was headed to Rabat for a well-deserved vacation with my maternal uncle's family. My uncle, a Black man, had joined the Royal Guards in 1958 and served in this elite army corps under both King Mohammed V and King Hassan II until his retirement in 1997. On July 23, 1999, as I was sipping mint tea in the upstairs kitchen, I heard a loud shriek from the downstairs living room, where a few minutes earlier I had left my uncle watching the news. I do not remember how I got down the two flights of stairs, but my uncle's tears as he mournfully announced the passing of King Hassan II are engraved in my memory. What followed were feelings of orphanhood, insecurity, and collective catharsis, as people took to the streets across Morocco to mourn the only king the vast majority of them had known. Torn between the urge to partake in this cathartic moment and my basic, albeit trenchant, knowledge about the deceased king's troubled human rights legacy, I decided to stand with thousands of others on Moulay Abdellah Avenue to watch the funeral procession.

As I began my teaching career in September 1999, in the village of Tizgui N'Barda, one of the most isolated areas of the High Atlas, the Rabat-based *al-Ittiḥād al-Ishtirākī* daily newspaper started serializing the memoirs of Mohamed Raïss. Sentenced to life in prison in 1972, Raïss was one of the fifty-eight soldiers forcibly "disappeared" to Tazmamart prison camp between 1973 and 1991 in the aftermath of the *coups d'état* against Hassan II in 1971 and 1972. Entitled *Min Ṣkhirāt ilā Tāzmāmārt: tadhkiratu dhahāb wa iyyāb ilā al-jaḥīm* (*From Skhirāt to Tazmamart: A Roundtrip Ticket to Hell*), this memoir was only the first trickle in the coming flood of revelations about Hassan II's reign. It was startling to learn, between 1999 and 2005 specifically, about secret detention centers in Agdz, Kelâat M'Gouna, and even Tamddākht. These locations are less than one hour away from where I grew up, which made me realize that Hassan II's authoritarianism had played out in places close to home. A few years later, I discovered that some of my teachers had passed through these detention centers but had kept silent about these painful episodes. Retrospectively, I can still visualize the bodily effects torture had on some of them. This was a transformative realization, prompting major questions that became central to my academic work in the years that followed.

Tifoultoute, my childhood home, is a touristic Amazigh village situated outside the city of Ouarzazate—the Hollywood of Africa, as it came to be known. My family home, which was adjacent to Thami El Glaoui's famous Kasbah, overlooked Aït Baroukh, a Jewish holy site. Made of two adobe rooms surrounded by an age-old cemetery, Aït Baroukh (named for Rabbi Yehia Ben Baroukh, as I learned later from research in the United States), was built on the right side of the road that linked Marrakesh to Zagora. Throughout my childhood in the 1980s, *udayn* (Jews in Tamazight) arrived and departed from Aït Baroukh during specific times in the fall and early spring, but I never understood why they came or left when they did. My childhood experience with Moroccan Jews until this day evokes a gray Bedford truck, a couple of sedans, and nicely dressed people who spoke a variety of languages, including Arabic, Tamazight, and French. Aït Baroukh is most strongly associated in my mind with melodious religious chants in a language I did not understand that went late into the night. Only the whirring of overloaded trucks transporting dates and other merchandise between Zagora and Marrakesh interrupted the Hebraic melody in these quiet evenings. I learned a great deal about Moroccan Jews during the years 1999 to 2009, which I spent teaching in the communes of Telouet and Ighrem N'Ougdal, two former hubs of Jewish life. Instead of school curricula and history books, it was older men and women who taught me the history they carried in their memories and entrusted it to me in the hope that it would not fall into oblivion.[2]

As I reflected on these events and their connections to the larger context of the Moroccan nation, loss emerged as an essential theme. Thus, I use loss as a conceptual framework to ponder the historiographical implications of the forceful cultural resurgence of the three categories of Moroccan citizens who symbolized this deprivation for Moroccan society for five decades: Imazighen, Jews, and political prisoners. Although much scholarship has focused on the impact of enforced disappearance and arbitrary detention on specific individuals or groups of prisoners, loss as a fundamental result of political repression and ensuing trauma has not been discussed in the current scholarship on this period. But authoritarianism took a costly socioeconomic and cultural toll throughout the Years of Lead. Cultural production stalled, investment in the economy failed to achieve its potential, education deteriorated, some regions housed secret prisons which, for security reasons, exacerbated their socioeconomic isolation, and the country lost the most vibrant segments of its population to either emigration or political imprisonment. Morocco suffered civically as well, as mistrust between society and state turned into a fear of institutions.

The Years of Lead may have ended in 1999, but their impact on people, space, and culture continues to shape the attitudes of the Moroccan people even today. *Moroccan Other-Archives* is just one of many possible ways to engage with the variegated, historiographical, and mnemonic legacies of a past that is not yet past.

Note on Transliteration

I have adapted the IJMES transliteration style to transliterate names and titles from Tamazight and Arabic into English. Accordingly, I have refrained from using a silent "h" at the end of the words that end with a "*ta marbūṭa*" (tied t) in Arabic, so I write *al-amāzīghiyya* instead of *al-amāzhīghīyyah* and *al-riwāya* instead of *al-riwāyah*. All Maghrebi names are written in their Latin spelling.

Abbreviations

AKM	The Academy of the Kingdom of Morocco
AMREC	*L'Association Marocaine de Recherche et d'Échange Culturel*
CBRM	The Committee Battling against Repression in Morocco
CCHR	The Consultative Council on Human Rights
CMCLA	The Council of the Moroccan Community Living Abroad
ERC	The Equity and Reconciliation Commission
FDCI	The Front for the Defense of Constitutional Institutions
IHP	The Institute of the History of the Present
MACM	The Moroccan Amazigh Cultural Movement
MCP	The Moroccan Communist Party
MMLM	The Moroccan Marxist-Leninist Movement
NCHR	The National Council for Human Rights
NCSR	The National Center for Scientific Research
NUPF	The National Union for Popular Forces
OPDA	The Organization of Popular Democratic Action
RIAC	The Royal Institute for Amazigh Culture
RIRHM	The Royal Institute for Research on Moroccan History
UIA	The Universal Israelite Alliance

MOROCCAN OTHER-ARCHIVES

Introduction

This book offers a theorization of what I choose to call "other-archives." In contrast to brick-and-mortar archives, other-archival power emanates from the life of cultural production in society. Other-archives are part of everyday life, not simply places in which diligent historians uncover and narrate stories destined for other professional historians.[1] Other-archives are texts, artifacts, alphabets, embodied experiences, toponymies, and inherited memories where stories of the excluded, the silenced, and the forgotten live in a ghostly state, ready to articulate loss even as they are situated outside the margins of what is considered canonical. While traditional archives are detained, consigned, housed, house-arrested, and confined to a closed, heavily-guarded space—ultimately endowing them with their official character because they belong to a dead past[2]—other-archives are part of an unfolding memory and history, existing to bridge the gap between a past that is not yet finished and a society still impacted by the consequences of this unfinished past. The forms that other-archives take in the public sphere—journalistic articles, memoirs, history-themed novels, activist gray literature, imaginary testimonies, to name just a few—democratize access to recent histories that are not solely of interest to the history specialist, but to lay citizens as well. As a result, their transformative force is lost when they are canonized and shelved in official holdings, since their life lies in social circulation and in the controversies that emanate from their existence in public life.

Thanks to the production and wide dissemination of other-archives, Imazighen (Amazigh people), Jews, and political prisoners—formerly "invisibilized" constituents of Moroccan history—reemerge in stories that reveal a traumatic history of disappearance and loss during the Years of Lead,

Morocco's period of state-sanctioned violence spanning the time from the country's independence in 1956 to the passing of King Hassan II in 1999.[3] Characterized by arbitrary detention and forcible disappearance, these four decades witnessed the repression of any form of civic and political participation that diverged from the monarchy's security- and technocracy-based vision of the nation.[4] State repression was directed at the constituencies that presented or were likely to present a challenge to the despotic regime that the monarchy gradually put in place, beginning in 1960 with the humiliating removal of Abdallah Ibrahim's socialist government.[5] Nationalist figures, Liberation Army leaders, the Moroccan Marxist-Leninist Movement (MMLM), Sahrawi nationalists, Amazigh activists, Islamists, Communist Jews, Bahais, members of the National High School Union, military insurgents, and ordinary citizens (who happened to be in political "hot spots" during the bloody events of 1973) were tortured, "disappeared," and assassinated.[6] Assured of their immunity, state officials deployed their boundless power to erase recalcitrant Moroccans from "the cartography of the nation."[7] Amnesty International highlighted these "serious and wide-ranging human rights violations," which included "the long-term imprisonment of prisoners of conscience, torture and unfair trials of political opponents."[8] Some victims overcame these ordeals and lived to tell the tale while others remain missing to this day. But their stories survive in the narratives of those who carry the burden of their memory.

After the collapse of the Berlin Wall and the demise of the Soviet Union, Hassan II began adapting his governance to a newly emerging world, in which respect for human rights became an important part of bilateral and multilateral relations. International aid was increasingly tied to human rights standards, and universal jurisdiction became a Sword of Damocles for dictators and human rights abusers. In 1990, Hassan II established the *Conseil consultatif des droits de l'homme* (Consultative Council on Human Rights [CCHR]).[9] CCHR's board members made significant recommendations that helped Moroccan authorities address international criticism of their human rights record, and they encouraged the release of assassinated General Mohamed Oufkir's family from their forced disappearance and twenty-eight other survivors from eighteen years of arbitrary detention in Tazmamart prison.[10] This first royal amnesty also benefited other political prisoners, including Sahrawi prisoners of conscience held in secret prisons in Agdz and Kelâat M'Gouna.[11] The most important amnesty, however, came in July 1994, with the pardon of 424 prisoners of all political and ideological persuasions.[12] Exiles were also allowed to return. While several Moroccan human rights and political organizations rejoiced at this news, the *Comité de lutte contre la répression au Maroc* (Committee Battling against Repression in Morocco [CBRM]) urged its members to continue the struggle "for a total and non-exclusionary amnesty" and demanded the trial of torturers and the payment of reparations to victims and survivors.[13]

King Mohammed VI was enthroned in July 1999, and in August 1999 established the Independent Arbitration Commission for the Compensation of Moral and Material Harm Suffered by Victims of Disappearance and Arbitrary Detention, and by their Beneficiaries (hereafter the Arbitration Commission). In Mohammed VI's words, the Arbitration Commission was to work with the CCHR "to determine the reparation of the victims and their beneficiaries who were subjected to disappearance and arbitrary detention."[14] The designers of the Arbitration Commission wanted it to be—in John Borneman's words in a different context—a "single happening" that brought about closure.[15] However, the commission was faced with significant obstacles that stemmed from the state's desire to protect torturers. Its mission was reduced to the more technical function of determining the amount of financial reparations, which required assessing damages by quantifying pain. In contrast, the general mood among the civil society organizations representing the victims and survivors of state violence favored holding wrongdoers accountable more generally for the crimes they committed during their tenure in public office. By the time the Arbitration Commission ended its work in 2003, it had received only 5,127 applications for reparations, which is a very small number of dossiers compared with the number of victims who would later submit their applications to the *Hay'at al-inṣāf wa-al-muṣālaḥa* (Equity and Reconciliation Commission [ERC]). After its deliberations, the commission paid almost a hundred million dollars to 5,300 claimants, a very limited success that led to increased demands (even among the partisans of the state within the CCHR) for a transitional justice process in line with the South African model.[16] Moroccan authorities were forced to bow to the pressing demands for a robust truth and reconciliation commission. Since the early 1980s, these commissions had been one of the ways in which states transitioning toward democracy chose to reckon with their traumatic pasts by adopting a holistic approach to reparations, rehabilitation, and reform similar to that of Brazil, Argentina, and South Africa.[17] Susan Slyomovics's groundbreaking book *The Performance of Human Rights in Morocco* notes that the period of 1999–2004 was characterized by various forms of performance focused on foregrounding and preserving the memory of the Years of Lead. Whether as "public hearings regarding past atrocities, indemnity hearings, actual transnational human rights trials, unofficial courts, [or] demands for truth commissions," performance extends to the rituals of office and is central to political transition and collective anti-punishment.[18]

On January 7, 2004, King Mohammed VI announced the establishment of the ERC. Made up of sixteen commissioners and a president, the ERC had a temporal mandate that extended from 1956 to 1999, the longest mandate of any transitional justice commission.[19] The ERC was tasked with "assessment, inquiry, investigation, arbitration, and formulating proposals concerning the grave violations of human rights" that fell within its jurisdiction.[20] The final object of this commission, the first of its kind in a Muslim country, was to contribute to the "construction of a state based on the rule of law, and to spread the values and culture of citizenship and human rights."[21] The ERC received a total of 20,046 files.[22]

Scholarship has not yet examined the multilayered ways in which these years left almost intangible marks defined by absence rather than presence on Morocco. More specifically, loss as a central driver of discourse around the Years of Lead has yet to receive the consideration it deserves. In *Political Crime and the Memory of Loss*, anthropologist John Borneman argues that "loss is always accountability's object."[23] As time passes, however, accountability focuses on the memory of loss, not the loss itself. The ERC's rhetoric remained within the literal bounds of transitional justice, which is characterized by "the recognition of the dignity of individuals, the redress and acknowledgment of violations, and the aim to prevent them from happening again."[24] Its methods of redress focused on arbitrary detention and enforced disappearance but excluded forms of loss that also changed the landscape and Moroccan people's sense of self: economic, educational, and human losses attributable to authoritarianism.[25] Loss cannot be reversed, but its traces can be historicized and refigured in light of the archival efforts that have become consubstantial to the practice of citizenship in Morocco today.

Histories of Loss: Imazighen, Jews, Political Prisoners, and the Years of Lead

Leïla Kilani's documentary film *Nos lieux interdits* (*Our Forbidden Places*, 2008) provides a glimpse into the pivotal role loss and disappearance occupy in Moroccan history, beyond the issues of arbitrary detention and enforced disappearance.[26] Hired by the newly established ERC to document its proceedings, the Paris-based Moroccan filmmaker and her crew followed senior ERC members as they worked to carry out their mission.[27] One of the families featured in the film is that of Abdeslam Harrafi, who disappeared sometime between 1965 and 1974. Harrafi was a southern Amazigh political militant, and his disappearance was linked to his underground political activism, specifically his presumed links to the Sheikh al-'Arab revolutionary group,[28] stamped out by General Oufkir in 1964.[29] Like all the forcibly disappeared prisoners in post-colonial Morocco, Harrafi disappeared without any written proof to indicate his whereabouts, or indeed his very existence. The only tangible evidence of his life is his illiterate grieving wife, traumatized daughter, and truth-seeking granddaughter, who carry the intergenerational burden of proving their loss and reconstituting the life of their beloved relative from the void of the archives and silence of witnesses. Confronted with the customary archival silence over Harrafi's fate, ERC executive Abdeslam Moussadik instructs the family to seek witnesses who can corroborate their story. A man named al-Ḥājj al-Maʿṭī is the only witness who agrees to come forward. When asked "Who would you advise us to contact among the elderly as potential witnesses?," he responds:

> The Seniors are almost all dead. . . . There was Mustapha Chemseddine, the treasurer of the Moroccan Workers Union, who is dead. There was a Jew named ʿĀzar. He left for Palestine for good. There was another Jew known by Ben Sahel. Driss Medkouri is dead, may God bestow his mercy upon him. There was Mohammed Tibari who is also deceased. May he rest in peace. There was Zouhir Abdelkarim. He also passed away. May he rest in peace. There is El Moufakir Mustapha of the Chemical Industry. He died too. I doubt there is anybody who would still remember him.[30]

This very ordinary act of witnessing, one that brings out information helpful in determining the whereabouts of this activist, veers inadvertently into a litany of disappearances combining death, political repression, and emigration. Al-Ḥājj al-Maʿṭī knew that all the Muslim witnesses had passed away, but all he knew about ʿĀzar and Ben Sahel is that they left Morocco for good. Whether they are still alive or dead, the heart of the matter is that they carried part of Moroccan history with them to Israel/Palestine. Instead of dealing only with the initial forcible disappearance, *Our Forbidden Places* elucidates another disappearance, carried out through emigration, and pieces together scattered fragments of Moroccan history. At this pivotal moment when Morocco tried to revisit its post-1956 history of state violence, an Amazigh, two departed Jews, and a story of enforced disappearance converge to shed light on loss and historiography.

Amazigh identity, Jewish emigration, and political imprisonment during the Years of Lead may seem distant and disconnected topics, but they are linked through themes of disappearance and absence from post-independence Moroccan history. Silencing was the common denominator between Imazighen, Jews, and political prisoners after Morocco's independence. Besides academic silence, there was a de facto ban on Amazigh identity in the public sphere. Similarly, the majority of Moroccan Jews (up to 1.6% of the Moroccan population until 1960) emigrated, disappearing from both the geography of the nation and its official history even while remaining an object of social memory, as Aomar Boum has compellingly theorized in his intergenerational model.[31] Boum does not explicitly connect Jewish emigration to state politics in the Years of Lead, but Jewish departure from Morocco occurred in a larger frame of reference in which political and cultural repression actively worked to eliminate real and potential "political and ideological opponents of the royal regime."[32] The causes and implications of these disappearances are different, but they represent facets of the loss which, in the words of former president of the National Council for Human Rights (NCHR), Driss El Yazami, contributed to Moroccans' "amputated and impoverished" knowledge of their "Amazigh and Jewish" history.[33] While much has been written about the political and human rights consequences of the dictatorial rule during the Years of Lead,[34] no one has yet undertaken a comparative investigation into the disappearance of different constituencies during this internal time of political struggle in Morocco. *Moroccan Other-Archives* examines how cultural production writes histories of loss that center Amazigh activism, the emigration of Moroccan Jews, and state violence unleashed on political opponents. Most importantly, *Moroccan Other-Archives* investigates how loss itself becomes an other-archive, which foregrounds cultural production's central role in rewriting a multifaceted history of Morocco's recent past.

The first two years of Morocco's independence (1956–1958) saw unbounded aspirations for both democracy and a political structure that recognized the Moroccan people's rights to citizenship. Building on this democratic enthusiasm and positive spirit born out of independence, a group of nationalist Jews and Muslims formed *Jam'iyyat al-Wifāq* (the Concord Association) as an "expression of national unity and solidarity regardless of religion,"[35] a move that also indicated a desire to foreground citizenship in a shared country. Kosansky and Boum have demonstrated that despite the goodwill shown toward Moroccan Jews during these early years of independence, *dhimma*, which refers to the status of non-Muslims within the Islamic state, remained the framework that governed them.[36] To further expand Kosansky and Boum's argument, it is possible to argue that citizenship—not in its strict understanding as a matter of passports and travel documents, but rather as a sense of having the right to envision a different polity and to act to implement that vision without fear—was called into question for both Muslims and Jews. Jews and Muslims were *ra'āyā* (the king's subjects), a status that continues to inform state discourse today. The question of citizenship was whether political participation was going to be meaningful and open or whether the culture of *ra'īyya* (being the ruler's subject) would prevail. If the latter, all Moroccans, Jews and Muslims, would be stripped of citizenship in its modern understanding.[37]

Ra'īyya culture was threatened by educated Jews and Muslims after Morocco's independence.[38] Conceptions of citizenship had been transformed by the impact of the Protectorate among Muslims and by almost a hundred years of heavy Gallicization of middle-class Moroccan Jews.[39] There was an effort among Jewish, Muslim, and French figures to recreate and build bridges between their different communities in order to build the new nation-state together on the fundamentals of citizenship developed through their encounter with colonialism. *Les Amitiés Marocaines* (1950–1956), an association that brought together French liberals with their Moroccan Muslim and Jewish counterparts, worked for a peaceful co-existence of these communities in the independent state.[40] Reflecting a collective desire to work toward a shared future, Carlos de Nesry, a Jewish lawyer from Tangiers, authored two books that acknowledge the transformations this wrought on Jewish life in Morocco; he formulated a road map for a future democratic Moroccan state that would retain its Jewish population and made a case for a new relationship between the ruler and the ruled in independent Morocco.[41] *Le Juif de Tanger et le Maroc*'s subtext underlines the crucial importance of redefining post-independence Morocco in order to accommodate the transformed native Jewish population.[42] At the core of de Nesry's writing was the need to see Jews and Muslims as citizens, not merely subjects.

Despite these aspirations, the dream of a democratic, citizenship-based state was dashed when King Muhammad V dismissed Abdallah Ibrahim's popular government on May 21, 1960, a final sign that the monarchy was intent on arrogating all state powers. With the weakening of the *Istiqlal* party as a result of the secession of *al-Ittiḥād al-Waṭanī li-al-Quwwāt al-Sha'bīyya* (the National Union for Popular Forces [NUPF]), the monarchy had a wide-open path to pit political camps against each other. The sacking of Ibrahim's popular government coincided with Hassan's secret negotiations with Alexandre Easterman, an envoy of the State of Israel who sought to lift the Ibrahim government's passport restrictions on Moroccan Jews.[43] The royal authoritarian regime would become official in February 1961 after Mohammed V's sudden death. Maâti Monjib, a rare historian of contemporary history, concludes in his precocious book *La Monarchie marocaine et la lutte pour le pouvoir* (*The Moroccan Monarchy and the Battle for Power*) that May 1960, the year the king abruptly terminated Ibrahim's mandate, is "perceived by the democratic movement as the end of a sweet political dream and the beginning of a new era punctuated by suffering, repression and assassinations."[44]

The ensuing years of struggle between the monarchy and its opponents culminated in total control by King Hassan II over the "democratic" process and civic initiatives. Royal authoritarianism dissolved the *intercommunal* organization of citizens and the modernist polity that would have instituted a new understanding of the relationship between state and citizen after independence. Instead of taking the route of modernity and citizenship, Morocco was re-traditionalized to counter other civic reimaginations of the state:[45] Islam, Arabness, and revived pre-colonial traditions became the pillars of a conservative political regime, undoing the forty years of progress toward political and social modernity that had been achieved under the French Protectorate. Even education was re-traditionalized by the revival of *al-taʿlīm al-aṣīl* (classical education), despite the advice of experts to the contrary.[46] Conservative and traditionalist forces that cooperated with the French Protectorate were reestablished.[47] Meanwhile, nationalist parties and modernist figures that helped establish the monarchy as a symbol of the Moroccan nation were sidelined, and former French Protectorate collaborators filled key positions in the army, security forces, and civilian administration.[48] The revival of the old protocols of *bayʿa* (Islamic allegiance to the ruler), partially halted under the French Protectorate, set the political clock back to the pre-colonial era, as did all the implied threats toward the nascent political and societal modernization of the country.[49] The entangled nature of these issues was pointed out as early as 1965, when writer and political activist Saïd Ghallab published an article, "Les Juifs vont en enfer" ("Jews Are Going to Hell"), in which he articulated how anti-Semitism was entwined with the politics of Jewish emigration in Morocco.[50] Ghallab's thought-provoking article draws on urban residents' allegations about Morocco's "sale" of its Jews to demonstrate how the Moroccan state became the final beneficiary of the Jews' dislocation:[51] Ghallab claims that Hassan II consolidated his dictatorial rule with American donations granted in exchange for eased travel restrictions on Jewish emigration candidates, effectively exchanging Jews for wheat. According to Ghallab, these donations were used to rig the 1963 elections, which placed the newly constituted, pro-monarchy Democratic Front for the Defense of Constitutional Institutions (DFDCI) at the helm of Moroccan politics.[52]

The leftist tendencies of most politicized Jews—the threat of an educated minority to Morocco's dictatorial future, their staunch support for the retention of their coreligionists in their ancestral homeland of Morocco—must have been the main incentive to let them leave *en masse*.[53] When the name of Meyer Tolédano, a leftist confidant of Mahdi Ben Barka, was mentioned by the Israeli envoy Easterman, Crown Prince Hassan called Tolédano "opportunistic, a man without God, a man deprived of religion, of belief and honor. I am disgusted by him and I only have disdain for him."[54] Marc Sabbah, a Jewish communist teacher from Rabat, also experienced Prince Hassan's distaste for the left during a meeting in Casablanca.[55] It is easy to imagine how the future king would rather deal with a "Jewless" and "leftless" Morocco than fight hundreds, if not thousands, of Jewish and Muslim activists who would advocate for the construction of a democratic, citizenship-based state. Jewish-Muslim cooperation in the transformation of the country's politics seems to have been at the core of Prince Hassan's fears, driving his decision to ease the travel ban on Jews and facilitate their acquisition of collective passports, and suggesting a motivation to accelerate their peaceful "disappearance" and prevent cooperation with modernist Muslims in their bid for an egalitarian and democratic state.[56] Some of Prince Hassan's future intentions can be easily discerned from his conversation with Easterman: He went so far as to declare that Moroccan Jews would be "a burden more than an advantage for the country."[57]

Parallel to its much-studied systematic repression and outmaneuvering of political opposition, Hassan II's regime facilitated the emigration of Moroccan Jews to Israel/Palestine, the United States, Canada, and France. Doing so achieved two important goals: preventing further confrontation with American Jewish organizations, and depriving Moroccan political parties of their politically engaged Jewish allies. Jacques Dahan, a longtime president of the *Conseil des Communautés Israélites du Maroc* (Council of Israelite Communities of Morocco [CICM]), revisits this crucial period in Moroccan history in his memoir, arguing that there was a direct connection between the facilitation of Moroccan Jews' emigration and Hassan II's desire to weaken the political parties and impose royal absolutism.[58] The Jewish population of Morocco dwindled from 250,000 in the early 1960s to 60,000–70,000 by 1967.[59] The Jewish community's falling numbers and increasing dependence on the monarchy led to the depoliticization of the remaining Moroccan Jews. To paraphrase Victor Malka, they started to look inward, focusing on civil society and civic initiatives within their community, rather than on political activity, as they had done in the past.[60] Having inherited a national landscape that sustains an abundance of Jewish signs and imprints, younger generations of Moroccan Muslims who neither lived with Jews nor learned their history in school curricula have created a "mnemonic literature" in which they recover and reimagine the Jewish-Muslim life that bustled, but which no longer exists, in these sites.

The state's fears of the participation of Jewish youth in politics materialized in the radical work of Abraham Serfaty, a nationalist figure exiled to

France because of his resistance to colonization, who became the ideologue of the MMLM.[61] The failure of the monarchy and traditional political parties to win over the increasingly disillusioned Moroccan youth led to their search for revolutionary options.[62] The goal of the avant-garde Marxist-Leninist movement *Ilā al-Amām* (Forward!) was to "sow revolutionary ideas, and to craft the beginning of a Morocco in which workers and peasants could be masters of their own destiny, all conceived with the certainty that such ideas would chart their path beyond us."[63] *Ilā al-Amām* was the crucible in which disillusioned Moroccan youth gave voice to their revolutionary aspirations.[64] Before they created *Ilā al-Amām*, the core members of this secret organization had congregated around the cultural journal *Souffles/Anfās* (1966–1972), a project that brought together creative writers, poets, visual artists and literary critics under the editorship of Abdellatif Laâbi to create a new dynamic in the Moroccan Francophone and Arabic cultural scenes.[65] Laâbi was the cultural dynamo of the magazine, but Serfaty was *Ilā al-Amām*'s ideologue par excellence. The prominent role of a Jew in an extreme-left organization that sought to overthrow the monarchy speaks volumes about the staying power of secularizing and citizenship-based ideals of the early years of independence, principally among Moroccan youth in the 1970s.

By the time of Hassan II's ascent to the throne, the enthusiasm of the independence years had waned, and arrests, torture, and political disappearances became systematic.[66] After the elections of 1963, which the FDCI lost to the NUPF and the Istiqlāl parties, important leaders of the opposition were arrested, held *incommunicado*, and then sentenced to long periods of imprisonment for spurious accusations. Mahdi Ben Barka, the best-known Moroccan socialist leader, was accused of supporting Algeria against Morocco during the Sand War (1963) and was sentenced to life in prison for treason. Two years later, he would be kidnapped while in Paris, never to be seen again.[67] Only nine years into the country's era of independence, King Hassan II declared a state of emergency that would remain in effect from 1965 until 1970. Political trials targeting different dissident groups took place in Casablanca (1964), Marrakesh (1971), and Casablanca again (*Ilā al-Amām, 23 Mārs*, and *Linakhdum al-Sha'b* 1977).[68] But the regime's internal conflicts, which Ben Barka predicted in 1962,[69] erupted in two *coups d'état*: the Skhirat coup on July 10, 1971, and the airplane coup on August 16, 1972. These two coups served as the impetus for the creation of the globally notorious prison camp in Tazmamart, which gave its name to the most traumatic set of enforced disappearances in the history of Morocco. After the trial of the coups' ringleaders by the military tribunal, the majority of the soldiers were released at the end of their jail time, except for sixty-two prisoners who were sentenced to three years or longer. Fifty-eight of these prisoners were kidnapped from the "legal" jail where they were serving time under the supervision of the Ministry of Justice on August 7, 1973. Thirty of the prisoners who were forcibly disappeared to Tazmamart perished in hellish conditions. The twenty-eight who survived have since created a dynamic testimonial prison literature that opened Moroccan people's eyes to how, from 1973 to 1991, the secret prison was an unbridled manifestation not only of the state's ability to erase people from the surface of the earth, but also to deny that they ever existed. Tazmamart would later represent the epitome of human rights violations during the Years of Lead, as well as an inexhaustible source of transnational and multilingual fictions that continually refigure its meaning.

This examination of the intersection of histories of Imazighen (Amazigh people), Jews, and political prisoners within the trajectory of the Years of Lead rehabilitates the holistic and multidimensional approach that cultural producers have used in their works to address disappearance and loss and foreground their historiographical resilience. Indeed, ʿAbd al-Qādir al-Shāwī, a litterateur and former Marxist-Leninist prisoner, has authored two novels that are successful examples of the imbrication of these histories. An Amazigh revolutionary with the *Munaẓẓamat 23 Mārs* (March 23 Organization), which was a component and rival of *Ilā al-Amām*, al-Shāwī was sentenced to twenty years in prison in 1977. His novel *Bāb Tāza*,[70] which he set up as an investigative journalistic mission into the sudden death of a character named Muhammad al-Māghūti after the failure of his rumored visit to the city of Kenitra in search of his disappeared son, pilot al-Mufaḍḍal, connects the political history of the MMLM with the plight of the soldiers and officers who were forcibly detained in Tazmamart after the two consecutive coups against King Hassan II. In fact, the leaders of both coups were Imazighen, and part of the marginalization of Morocco's Amazigh identity is attributable to the ensuing distrust of Imazighen. Al-Shāwī continued this tendency in his third novel, entitled *Al-Ṣāḥa al-sharafiyya* (*The Square of Honor*).[71] The five characters in this multivocal and multiperspectival narrative attempt to reconstitute their lives after their release from a lengthy period in jail. The novel enacts the connectedness of the histories that are told in other-archives by giving a female Jewish character a significant space in the narrative. When Saʿd al-Abrāmī returns to his hometown of Branda, Khāna, the only Jewish person who was left in the village dies. Khāna's death reminds the community of the existence of this forgotten Jewish woman, but in the eyes of the narrator, the passing of the last Jewish villager was "the end of the soul that inhabited this village and went hand in hand with its traditions."[72] This same interconnectedness is reflected in the memoirs of Aïda Hachad, who discusses the role of

Omar El Khattabi, a nephew of Muhammad ibn Abd al-Karim al-Khattabi, the Amazigh hero of the Rif War (1921–1926), in mediating between politicians and the army before the 1972 coup.[73] Al-Shāwi and others' work also indicates that any methodological distinction between Imazighen, Jews, and political prisoners does not mean that these categories do not overlap or bleed into each other, blurring any separation between them. In reality, political prisoners were Jewish, Muslim, and/or Amazigh, which adds to the richness and complexity of the links between the histories that I seek to uncover.

Archives, Power, and the Production of Historical Silences

Archives are loci of power. The authority vested in them maintains and perpetuates hegemony through the stories they allow to be told and the ones they suppress.[74] Jacques Derrida has drawn attention to the notions of *commencement* and *commandment* that underlie archives as both beginnings and sources of authority.[75] The power of archives, in their universal understanding, lies not merely in the material evidence they provide, but also in the legitimacy they confer upon historiographical statements, a fact that Michel Foucault captured in his well-known expression that archives are "the law of what can be said,"[76] meaning that lack of archival evidence limits the possibilities of the *dicible* (sayable). The sayable is not only prescribed by laws and statutes of limitations governing archival content, but also by the nature of archiving itself.[77] Archives are not sites of preservation, as is commonly understood, but sites of loss, governed by a double impossibility: first, the impossibility of complete access to the truth about the past, and second, the impossibility of recovering all the archives available about a given event.[78] This loss is compounded by varying degrees of access, regulated entry, and guarded use, all of which perpetuate silence.

Archival authority is obviously not some natural condition. Rather, it is carefully contrived and sustained through rituals of officialization: "the rituals, surveillance, and discipline serve to maintain the power of the archives and the archivist."[79] From bestowing legitimacy on power to furnishing provisions and "disciplin[ing] the population," archives have proven to be instruments of government.[80] It is not surprising, then, that power-holding institutions such as churches, states, security apparatuses, and law enforcement have all been the ones to own and control archives.[81] However, this overlap of power and archives has not been left uncontested. The rise of memory studies, "colonial ethnography," testimonio, queer theory, postmodernism, and post-structuralism has provided the intellectual framework to dispute both discursive and material power structures that perpetuate the erasure of the colonized, the enslaved, and the vulnerable.[82]

Michel Rolph Trouillot suggests an answer to the problem of exclusionary practices prevailing in archives and the instrumentalization of archival authority by governments, proposing a focus on "the process of historical production" rather than on the "nature of history." Thus, Trouillot taking the reader inside the different loci in which historiographical silences are produced.[83] Rather than seeing silence as accidental, Trouillot calls attention to its active, transitive construction at four crucial moments in the historical production process: "the moment of fact creation (the making of *sources*); the moment of fact assembly (the making of *archives*); the moment of fact retrieval (the making of *narratives*); and the moment of retrospective significance (the making of *history* in the final instance)."[84] Of these, archive and source creation are the key moments for the infiltration of silence into the process, because they are the pivot points for decisions regarding which stories or events are deemed worthy of being saved for the future. Trouillot is not centrally concerned with what motivates the silencing of certain stories, but it is important to extend his theoretical framework to contexts in which the state-nation relationship is plagued by mistrust, and where taboos about the past prevail.[85] Silencing the past is not a mechanical operation. The case of the petty criminals that Foucault analyzes in his essay *La Vie des hommes infâmes* (*Lives of Infamous Men*) shows how the same power that predestined these individuals to forgottenness by "*invisibilizing*" them in society created documentary evidence of their very existence. Foucault attributes the archival existence of these marginal people to their "encounter with power," which grants them a possible future in history at the cost of losing their own voices: What is available to us is "what was said about them" while "nothing remains of who they were or what they did except for a few sentences."[86] As a result, archives can both enable the emergence of stories of hitherto unknown individuals and groups in society as well as simultaneously prohibit them from becoming willful, historical actors in the narratives told about them.[87]

Despite the assumption that all societies possess archives in the form of a guarded building where documents of authority reside, the biggest deterrent to Moroccan historiographical research is not Moroccan historians' access to archives. It is, in fact, an even more serious problem: the absence of *any* organized archive between independence and 2011 when the Archives du Maroc was created.[88] Unlike the Khmer Rouge in Cambodia, the Stasi in East Germany, or the Apartheid regime in South Africa, each of which left large numbers of meticulously kept archives, the Moroccan Years of Lead are distinguished by the dearth or outright non-existence of documents and documentation.[89] Thus, even Aleida Assmann's distinction between "political archives," which are still mired in power, and "historical archives," which are obsolete for the exercise of authority in the present, does not apply in this context.[90] In 2011, Driss El Yazami, then President of the NCHR, confirmed that no archive exists in Morocco concerning the systematic violations of human rights that occurred in the post-independence period, telling reporters interviewing him: "There was a [mis]conception [. . .] that all those events were documented and that this documentation exists somewhere waiting to be discovered. However, our biggest discovery throughout the ERC's work was that the country had no archives. It means that there was nothing."[91] Eric Ketelaar renders archival erasure powerfully, noting that archives have so much power that external reality can be denied if it does not conform to archival material: "What is not in the records does not exist."[92] It did not matter whether the experiential knowledge of Moroccan academic historians supplied information that was not to be found in the archives. Disciplinary conventions and the political climate made documentary evidence into a white whale: simultaneously essential and out of reach.[93] How does one write histories for which there are no archives? Rather than asking what the inherent incompleteness of archives has excluded, *Moroccan Other-Archives* attends to the even more fundamental concerns of creating archives where there are none and writing histories in which loss and silence occupy the place of archival sources.[94]

Toward a Theory of Other-Archives in Moroccan Cultural Production

Truth and reconciliation commissions, which have flourished globally since the early 1990s, have put archives, history, and archive creation at the heart of transitional justice rituals and processes. A similar impulse comprised a central part of Morocco's much-anticipated transition to democracy. Asmaa Falhi, the ERC's former archivist, has underlined the link between democratization, citizenship, and reconciliation with the past, writing that the ERC needed to create and use archives because they were necessary for "establishing the truth," "repairing and rehabilitating the victims," "reconciliation," and appropriation of a painful past.[95] For Falhi, "when they survive, archives document societies' histories, their existence, and evolution, and establish the proofs that guarantee citizens' rights."[96] The ERC was aware of the importance of "creating a written and audio-visual archive of some of the subjects and places related to the grave violations of human rights, which may help to preserve the memory."[97] This archival enthusiasm is more speculative than retrospective, geared toward future outcomes instead of the past. Slyomovics has analyzed the ERC's archival work and traced the different ways Morocco developed an archiving practice. Most important are her questions regarding the credibility of the documents, their ability to "capture the pain of violations" as well as the issues they pose in terms of accessibility to scholars and ordinary citizens.[98] Her analysis of post-ERC archives demonstrates that the ERC has neither revolutionized nor transformed what it means to archive: both the practice and conceptions underlying archiving conform to the notion of archives, best summarized by Achille Mbembe, as a building that houses written documents produced by one of the organs of the state.[99] This conventional understanding of archives has instituted an archival transformation that could be "the point of departure and the condition for a new history,"[100] which again begs for a more radical definition of archives that emerged from this period.[101]

On the margins of this official archive, Moroccan cultural producers have instituted an other-archive contesting both silence and hegemony. Slyomovics articulated the importance of this other-archive, writing that "artistic expression—articles, books, magazines, broadsides, graffiti, and cartoons—comprised most of the evidence of their [i.e., the regime's] 'crimes.'"[102] Susan Gilson Miller, a historian of Morocco, has also highlighted the significance of these unconventional archives in "contest[ing] the restrictive pro-makhzanian discourse that has monopolized the field since independence."[103] This cultural production, unlike brick and mortar archives, is focused on documenting and refiguring the meaning of Morocco's recent past, and is a ubiquitous part of everyday life. Again Miller captures the importance of the "plurality of perspectives" that other-archives make possible in understanding Moroccan history.[104] Instead of solely undoing amnesia and breaking the silence on a particular taboo topic—infiltrating the traditional archive, which was a demand of many survivors of state violence during the Years of Lead—producers of other-archives have shifted their attention to using their historiographical agency to articulate individual and collective traumas and democratize access to multiple histories of the Moroccan nation. There are no gatekeepers or architects of power that stamp them with their official seal. Their legitimacy and authority stem from the veracity of the stories they tell and the traumas their authors attempt to work through.

In addition to the journalistic and interview-based archives in the National Library in Rabat,[105] three significant other-archives have taken shape since the middle of the 1990s. First, the activism of the Moroccan Amazigh Cultural Movement (MACM) in the public sphere has formed an other-archive that enacts the re-Amazighization of the Moroccan public sphere and puts into writing the history of silence and erasure that suppressed Morocco's Imazighen for almost fifty years. Amazigh activists have interrogated geographies and reconceived historical sources to assert their indigeneity to North

Africa, which they renamed Tamazgha or the Amazigh homeland. Second, Moroccan Muslim novelists' reconstructions of an imagined history of the erstwhile Jewish-Muslim shared communities in Morocco has transformed inherited memories into a written source that reactualizes a past that is generally conceived of as irrevocably lost.[106] Moroccan Muslim novelists write "mnemonic literature" to remember their departed Jewish co-citizens and fill the voids of historical silences in a way that radically transforms the vacuum of amnesia into a locus for memory. Unlike the memory aiding devices that the adjective "mnemonic" evokes in English, mnemonic literature here refers to the literary output that is anchored in individual, collective, and intergenerational memories of loss. Third, testimonial prison literature, either in the form of memoirs or fictionalized accounts of lived experiences, addresses the traumas of state violence.[107]

Other-archives chronicle repression, disappearance, and silence, alongside of the affective reactions to all of these. MACM's struggle for recognition of Morocco's Amazigh identity is in itself a documentation of the emotional as well as historical charge of *ḥugra* (disdainful humiliation) and exclusion within one's own indigenous country. Rather than simply reading MACM's achievements in the Moroccan public sphere as realizations that crowned its members' struggles, it behooves us to ponder the emotional histories encapsulated by MACM's own history in a context wherein fear, intimidation, and overt denial of Amazigh identity reigned.[108] Similarly, the void left by departed Moroccan Jews, and the broken destinies of Jewish spouses and neighbors in the nation-scape, demonstrate the emotional scars of a nationwide loss that have yet to be investigated and historicized. The inscription of these emotions in other-archives will allow them to be rewritten; this study of emotions and their attendant losses is outside the purview of Moroccan academic historians, and other-archives are the locus that register and preserve the full emotional cost of the Years of Lead.

The emergence of a history and historiographical consciousness devoted to post-independence Morocco has required the concomitant emergence of other-archives to fill a void left by the dearth of historical studies about the Years of Lead.[109] Moroccan academic historians typically prefer a traditional understanding of archives as *al-wathāiq al-makhzaniyya* (state documents) or *al-arshīf al-makhzanī* (state archives), developed by historian Germain Ayache as a way to counter colonial historiography on Morocco, over oral histories and ethno-historical data.[110] Ayache's notion has instead had a negative impact on later historians: written evidence-based history has fossilized over the years, drawing criticism from historians themselves,[111] and careerism among some influential historians has also served to thwart Moroccan historiographical interest in the problematic question of post-independence history.[112] After the passing of King Hassan II in 1999, however, Moroccans had a chance to read detailed accounts of enforced disappearance and arbitrary detention.[113] The countless interviews with historical victim-actors and survivors in the post-independence period also shed light on different aspects of Moroccan history not hitherto available to the public. Amid this societal interest in the past, Moroccan academic historians were finally compelled to engage in methodological discussions on the writing of recent history—meaning the history of post-independence Morocco.[114] The academic historians involved in these debates sought to subjugate memory to the critical examination of history as a scientific discipline. However, there is an implicit assumption that history written from the cross-examination of archival documents is truer than memory. This undermines survivors' agency and runs the risk of invalidating their experiences.[115] In resisting the conceptualization of the significance of what I call other-archives, many historians have failed to see memory's potential to generate a renewal of the academic discipline of history itself.[116]

The existence of other-archives predates the establishment of the ERC, which found its *raison d'être* in the testimonial prison literature that chronicled, detailed, and provided its own history of the Years of Lead through the firsthand accounts of survivors of state violence. Ahmed Chaouqi Benyoub acknowledges the importance of other-archives in initiating the Moroccan version of a transitional justice process while calling attention to memory's pivotal place in the writing of new histories: "Writing and its implications, regardless of its forms and literary genres, was the justification, the need and the motive for us to know and analyze what happened, how it happened, and how to overcome it. Today international experts can conclude that [Moroccan] transitional justice started historically with a fundamental cultural given—the memory of individuals and victims."[117] Instead of simply emphasizing how other-archives provide information that the state erased or did not have, Benyoub attributes a transformative agency to testimonial writings, echoing philosopher Jacques Rancière's famous argument that while the political conditions the thinkable, aesthetics are always ahead of society and political constraints.[118] In the same way, other-archives have made it possible to rethink the nation thanks to the way other-archivists have reimagined the portrayals of losses that have marred the Moroccan recent past. In addition to stressing cultural production's ability to preserve memory and chart a path for the writing of history, Benyoub highlights its important role in representing the collective ownership of the Moroccan past,[119] giving cultural production's mnemonic work a collective dimension beyond the individual experiences that it recounts. Providing testimony, real or imagined, about past events thus becomes a civic act—in total opposition to the political culture that produced the traumas the nation was trying to overcome through reconciliation and historical truth. This appeal to the values of citizenship for the reappropriation of history subverted the official hegemony, which, through the elimination of historical archives, presented itself as the sole source of truth about Morocco's recent past.

The makers of other-archives have placed pain and loss at the center of the history-to-be-written. In contrast to the expected responses to loss, i.e., mourning and depression,[120] other-archives discover the potential for loss to be generative and transformative. Recent scholarship from Judith Butler, David Kazanjian, and Rosalind Shaw has called for the investigation of trauma's positive potential.[121] Meera Atkinson claims that investigating women's transmission of intergenerational trauma as "lived experience and literary testimony" allows "the political potency" of a poetics of "an innately feminist practice" to be theorized.[122] Expanding this argument for trauma's liberating potential, she proposes a crucial distinction whereby those who write about transgenerational traumas are not producing "the victim narrative, the straightforward sob story, the accusatory rant, or the sanctimonious declaration of survival. Theirs is a poetics driven and informed by a productive witnessing-testifying-introjection drive."[123] These show engagement with trauma and loss not merely as inhibitive, but instead as a force of liberation allowing survivors, victim-actors, and those erased from the record to regain their historiographical agency, reclaiming citizenship through other-archives and the histories they produce.

Testimonial prison writings specifically meet this challenge through their detailed descriptions of the atrophied bodies of political prisoners in detention centers and the mental and physical degeneration of vanished soldiers in the desert town of Tazmamart.[124] Similarly, mnemonic literature's depictions of Jewish-Muslim families, the fragmentation of intergenerational relationships, the vanished Jewish-Muslim shared communities, and the void left by the disappearance of Jews from Morocco provide insights into a past that professional historiography is still leery of investigating. Despite anthropological work conducted among Muslim Moroccans in both rural and urban areas,[125] the question of the historical significance of Jewish emigration since 1956 remains unsettled. Histories of this loss are inscribed and reimagined in mnemonic literature, but the disciplinary divide and academic practices in Moroccan history have allowed little work on this literary corpus at present. Most academic histories published in Morocco thus far have limited connections with literary studies and shun trauma theory, nor has the nationalist approach to positivist, archive-based history prepared Moroccan historians to study trauma or examine how literature engages with history. And so mnemonic literature, immersed in trauma and loss, has remained outside the purview of historical research. Literature's ability to represent multiple perspectives, condense extended periods of time, resuscitate the dead, shorten physical distances, and bring disparate events together is a major advantage in engaging with history and historical events, particularly in ways that the exigencies of academic history cannot accommodate. These successes have motivated some prominent historians to make a case for a heteroglossic, multi-perspectival history that borrows literary techniques, one that has the potential to "express both personal and cultural truths and reveal connections between individual memory and social memory, culture, and history."[126] Literature is also intertwined in webs of mnemonic and textual relationships that allow it to mediate memories, memorialize other texts, and refer to their various intertexts, thus offering unlimited possibilities for history writing.[127]

Other-archives thus transcend the focus on individual experiences to provide a sophisticated historical context for structural aspects of Moroccan history, including structures of oppression and their internal mechanics. Survivors' descriptions of the systematic use of kidnapping, torture, and intimidation reveal that the collective trauma Moroccans experienced during the Years of Lead was part of a larger structure, a system of oppression of which the ERC has only been able to scratch the surface, extending from the head of the state to the prison guards in Tazmamart, including an alliance formed by the police, the justice system, and the administrative apparatus.[128] Cultural producers document, comment on, and record in accessible forms the acts of those in power that formed the core of the collective traumas.[129] This exploitation of sources that academic historians would not typically cite has great significance for writing "history from below,"[130] as these sources refine the quality of academic history and democratize access to the histories of marginalized classes, all while enabling communities to recover the silent history of subaltern groups' experiences.[131] History is also central to the formation of cultural and national identity, and, when written from the perspective of marginalized people, it reminds us that "our identity has not been formed purely by monarchs, prime ministers, and generals."[132] The voices of the *petites gens* then open up new possibilities for the silenced to exercise agency as history-makers, and so the social significance of historiography makes writing it from below even more revolutionary. Indeed, history's "social purpose" is what justifies society's investment in historiographical research and teaching.[133] In Morocco, this social purpose of history can be clearly observed in the 2006 royal decree whereby the Institut Royal pour la Recherche sur l'Histoire du Maroc (Royal Institute for Research on the History of Morocco [RIRHM]) was created to respond to the needs of a post–Hassan II society. The decree states that the institute invests in historiographical work so as to "anchor Moroccan identity and strengthen collective memory by opening it up to the different actors involved in [the creation of Moroccan] identity and character throughout [different] eras."[134] The very creation of the RIRHM recognizes memory's place in writing a pluralistic history and acknowledging the contributions of formerly silenced historical actors to the formation of Moroccan identity. Again, this founding decree is silent on the fact that RIHRM's creation was a direct response to the ERC's recommendations, and thus a restorative act for victims of state violence. This makes the role of other-archives all the more essential for democratizing access to multiple versions of Morocco's traumatic pasts.

Mnemonic literature's recovery of a Jewish-Muslim past also shares many similarities with microhistory, which focuses on individual and collective stories at the microscopic level of the village, household, and community, as well as on the ways in which historical events impact the object of study. The focus on minutiae of historical events rehabilitates individual stories that would otherwise fail to make it into the larger historical narratives.[135] Microhistory's rehabilitation of the "daily, the ordinary, [and] the marginalized" allows us to see the microhistorical aspect of the multiple pasts resurrected in other-archives, pasts that had been prevented from circulating in official Moroccan memory and history.[136] This restoration builds upon myriad possibilities offered by narrative and fictionalization so as to reimagine the experiences of Jewish and Muslim life in rural and urban spaces in Morocco. As with microhistories, other-archives allow the quotidian to offer a way to examine dilemmas, frustrations, and anxieties engendered in Moroccan life by the unexplained emigration of Moroccan Jews. Other-archives, in their various dimensions, foreground ordinary people as they frame the bigger story of a reimagined nation—a *possible* nation that is premised on a *new* history.

Rewriting the Nation: Other-Archives and the Reimagination of Morocco

History has had a strategic role to play in the formation of the "imagined community" of Moroccans, supposedly united by an imaginary allegiance to an immemorial monarchy, the practice of Islam, and the Arabic language that is spoken throughout the geopolitical space known as Morocco.[137] This historical narrative, which foregrounds the monarchy as the backbone of

Moroccan history and was once tightly controlled by the state, has become a contested territory in which alternative conceptions of Moroccan identity have already taken shape. The existence of other-archives and their life in the public sphere has, to borrow Miller's words, "trumped the bland official accounts that screened out popular grievances. [. . .] The resurgence of civil society in all its forms is another manifestation of change that enriches historical discussion and constitutes a continuous theme."[138] A different Moroccan identity slowly emerged from these alternative imaginations—and in departing from authoritarianism, required a *new* history.

Typically, history alone is not enough to create a shared ethos, since its work is combined with other disciplines, including geography, linguistics, and various forms of acculturation, in order to transform subjects into citizens.[139] However, in its final report, the ERC made the rewriting of history a crucial marker of Morocco's rupture with subjugation and authoritarianism, recommending reforms in history, education, the economy, social justice, archive production, and the preservation of literature. The ERC's report underlined the need to:

> promote the importance of school in society and to inculcate a culture of human rights, beginning from the first stages of studies, and concentrating on educating people in human rights and creating university courses in areas related to human rights, especially since Morocco has accumulated significant experience in this field in recent years. Our country has witnessed a dynamism that has resulted in significant original productions, both novels and films, that handle issues that may further the entrenching of increased originality and develop the process of satisfying the Moroccan citizen's desire for a human rights culture.[140]

The ERC's approach to history converged with that of other-archivists, expressing willingness to move away from the traumatic past and promising a future without state abuse. History curricula are one place where the concrete effects of other-archives can be noticed.[141] For this reason, a new national identity emerging from other-archives cannot be formed without being incorporated into school and university curricula. Disagreements between the Makhzen—the state, including the monarchy and the security apparatus—and the ERC have had an important impact on the success of this endeavor.[142] These divergences speak volumes about other-archives' power to impose an agenda on the nation and force the state to co-opt that agenda, albeit discursively, in the course of rewriting the nation.

The ERC devoted the fourth volume of its final report, *The Components of Reform and Reconciliation*, to rewriting history as a key component of redefining the nation. The new history required recognizing overlooked, if not oppressed, identities, such as Amazigh, Black, Sahrawi, and Jewish, and recognizing the country's multilingualism, all with the goal of "strengthen[ing] national unity and reinforc[ing] national identity" and "enshrining cultural pluralism,"[143] goals that would later be taken up in the 2011 Constitution. Drafted in the heated atmosphere of the Arab Uprisings of that year, this document constitutionalized the ERC's recommendations and translated them into a solemn preamble in which Morocco admits that it is a state "forged by the convergence of its Arab-Islamist, Berber [*amazighe*], and Saharan-Hassanic [*saharo-hassanie*] components, nourished and enriched by its African, Andalusian, Hebraic and Mediterranean influences [*affluents*]."[144]

Revisiting the past through the rewriting of history is now a condition for a democratic present, and it is likewise a guarantee for a future devoid of state violence.[145] A citizenship "based on the rule of law and institutions, to protect freedoms and to help to ensure non-repetition" will hopefully emerge from this history-to-be-written.[146] This ostensible institutional desire to move away from the traumas of the past fosters historiographical justice, but it also hinges upon a collective *abreaction*, a reliving of the traumatic past in order to facilitate "putting an end to fear and re-establishing the relationship between citizens and the state, and making citizens feel that politics must become a concern of theirs," making political participation and testimony a "legitimate practice and a patriotic duty."[147] These newly espoused principles require the reconfiguration of the subject/citizen-state relationship even as the state co-opts the same conceptions of citizenship and imaginations of an all-embracing Morocco that its servants perceived as a threat to its security during the Years of Lead.

The clearest transformation in the redefinition/rewriting of the nation can be seen in the shift in focus from the center, which is historically associated with the Makhzen, to the periphery, which was wrongly associated with *siba* (dissidence) and disorder. This demonstrates the regained potential of marginalized peoples to transform this center of power: the ERC, in its final report, writes that "the history that was written in the past was the history of the center, nowadays the margins and the periphery are coming to the fore with their own histories, and these margins have become a partner in the rewriting of this history."[148] The process of rewriting the nation's history is not intended to create a new entity, but rather to force the current state leaders to confront the wrongdoings committed by their predecessors and undertake concrete steps to redress them. This rewriting of Morocco, with its "normalization" of previously uncomfortable (hi)stories in which the state and its agents were negatively implicated, is to be found in the state promise to take a different approach to power by holding officials accountable, disseminating a culture of human rights, and recognizing the memory and history of groups and communities who were disappeared from social and cultural memory and history. Moreover, rewriting the nation entails the emergence of a "civic history," which posits the rereading of the traumatic past as a condition for understanding the present state-citizen relationship.[149] This re-calibrates the story of the nation and holds the potential for a new sociopolitical contract between state and nation.[150] While state promises are what they are—promises, which may be kept or broken—other-archive producers have endowed their works with a transformative force that daily propels both history and memory into the nation's consciousness, marking the dawn of a new understanding of history and memory as equivalents to citizenship. Only a multi-pronged analysis of other-archives will reveal the full extent to which Moroccan history has been rewritten from this conscientizing position.

Rewriting the nation is also a crucial opportunity to reassess the role of cultural production in sustaining or undoing historical silences in Morocco. Although former prisoners, activists, and filmmakers practiced a rich intersectionality in their creation of other-archives post-1999, scholars, mainly influential ones, maintained an astounding distance from the issues discussed here. For instance, although historian Abdallah Laroui would write in 2007 that the "existence of a Christian minority in a Muslim society, in addition to the Jewish or any other minority, is the guarantee of the success of the democratic project in the land,"[151] he never fleshed out these ideas in his academic publications prior to the 2000s. Similarly, Abdelkébir Khatibi, who was a global figure and a connoisseur of Moroccan cultural production, supported Amazigh activists, but, to my knowledge, refrained from writing about political detention and Jewish emigration from an endogenous perspective. Revisiting his legacy one year before his death in 2009, Khatibi wrote proudly about his work alongside sociologist Paul Pascon to introduce postcolonial sociology studies, including a different understanding of Amazigh language, into the curriculum offered at the Institut de Sociologie in Rabat in the 1960s.[152] Yet the closest Khatibi comes to articulating an opinion about the emigration of Moroccan Jews happened at the instigation of Jacques Hassoun, his Franco-Egyptian friend and co-author of their epistolary book *Le même livre*, who asked him about his feelings regarding the departure of Moroccan Jews.[153] Staying within a strictly personal experience, Khatibi seemed to consider Jews gone once and for all, without any contextualization of that emigration and its impact on society. Apart from being an object of his culinary and olfactory memory,[154] the sudden disappearance of the local

Jew does not seem to present any political or historical dilemmas for Khatibi, who was otherwise very perceptive of the movement that was taking place in Moroccan society. Nonetheless, Khatibi's work contains several significant references to Moroccan Jews, which I argued were trail-blazing for his own theoretical work and for the advent of mnemonic literature.[155]

Chapter 1, "(Re)Invented Tradition and the Performance of Amazigh Other-Archives in Public Life," draws on MACM's work, specifically the work of Brahim Akhiyyat and Ali Sidqi Azaykou, to probe how this movement ushered in *Tankra Tamazight* (*al-nahḍa al-amāzīghiyya*/the Amazigh Renaissance). This chapter investigates how MACM preserved, restored, invented, and reinvented Amazigh traditions against the background of state repression and silencing of Amazigh identity during the Years of Lead, and it contends that Tifinagh's use in public signage is an other-archive that embodies Morocco's re-Amazighization. By examining the histories and historiographical agencies that are projected onto Tifinagh, this chapter posits that this alphabet now adorning official buildings throughout Morocco has transformed Morocco's visual and historical identity by recounting histories of loss and suppression of Amazigh culture from the public sphere.

Chapter 2, "Emplaced Memories of Jewish-Muslim Morocco" investigates mnemonic literature's recovery of memories and microhistories of place in portraying the history of loss of Jewish-Muslim Morocco. Strongly embedded in the intergenerational transference of memories, mnemonic literature by Muslim novelists draws on inherited memories to reimagine Morocco with its Jews. *Le Captif de Mabrouka* (*The Captive of Mabrouka*, 2009), *Zaghārīd al-Mawt* (*Ululations of Death*, 2010), *Shāmma aw Shtrīt* (*Shāmma or Shtrīt*, 2013), *Anā al-mansī* (*I Am the Forgotten*, 2015), *Casanfa* (2016), and *Cintra* (2016) recreate Morocco before the 1948–1967 dislocation of its Jews. Combining a close reading of mnemonic literature with theoretical reflections on microhistory, home-as-archive, and distinctions between space and place, this chapter demonstrates the centrality of memories of place in the reimagining and recounting of the taboo history of the Moroccan Jews' exodus five decades after their negotiated relocation to Israel/Palestine, Europe, and the Americas.

Chapter 3, "Jewish-Muslim Intimacy and the History of a Lost Citizenship," argues that mnemonic literature's depictions of the end of Jewish-Muslim intimacy represent the loss of a community-based citizenship that, given different historical circumstances, Jews and Muslims might have forged together through that synchronous intimacy. Drawing on recent ethnographic work and theories of intimacy and citizenship, it probes mnemonic literature's representations of interfaith Jewish-Muslim border crossings, shared Jewish-

Muslim childhoods, and Jewish and Muslim women's transgressive solidarities as forms of community citizenship, lost with the emigration of Moroccan Jews. Close readings of the mnemonic novels *Zaghārīd al-mawt*, *Shāmma aw Shtrīt*, and *Ḥārith al-nisyān* (*Tiller of Forgetfulness*, 2003) demonstrate that the departure of the majority of Morocco's Jews in two short decades tore the Moroccan Jewish/Muslim relationship and temporality asunder and dealt a severe blow to the Jewish-Muslim citizenship that could have been.

Chapter 4, "Making Tazmamart a Transnational Other-Archive," uses testimonial prison literature about Tazmamart's eponymous jail to theorize how scandalous, embodied, and fictionalized other-archives have arisen from the disappearance of fifty-eight soldiers to this prison in 1973. Drawing on *Notre ami le roi* (*Our Friend the King*, 1990), *Tazmamart une prison de la mort au Maroc* (*Tazmamart: A Prison of Death in Morocco*, 1992), and *Kabazal—Les Emmurés de Tazmamart* (*Kabzal: Tazmamart Prisoners*, 2005) as well as *Cette aveuglante absence de lumière* (*This Blinding Absence of Light*, 2001), *Rapt de voix* (*Voice Theft*, 2004), *Ṭā'ir azraq nādir yuḥalliqu ma'ī* (*A Rare Blue Bird Flies with Me*, 2016), and *Farag* (*Blue Lorries*, 2009), the chapter probes how Tazmamart has evolved to encapsulate the histories of political detention in Morocco. Both the extraordinary nature of Tazmamart and the state's eighteen-year denial of its existence generated a human rights movement whose advocacy on behalf of the prisoners paved the way for various literary adaptations. The chapter also shows how global activism and local political transition yielded different kinds of other-archives that incorporated Tazmamart into a global vocabulary of human rights violations, thus opening other-archives to questions of translation, authorship, literary appropriation, and circulation.

Chapter 5, "Other-Archives Transform Moroccan Historiography," delves into the historiographical debates that took place in Morocco from 1999 to 2012. The chapter explains how the proliferation of other-archives has infused a new life into Moroccan historiographical thinking. Analyzing academic historians' use of *tārīkh al-zaman al-rāhin* (the history of the present) alongside literary-historical writing experiments, such as collaborations between academic historians and novelists, as well as the Moroccan state's investment in the institutionalization of history outside academia, this chapter teases out how other-archives' existence and accessibility have begun to transform the discipline of history. From spurring methodological debates about memory and the history of the present to repurposing human rights institutions to sponsor history-focused projects, this chapter demonstrates how the consequences of rewriting the nation play out in history.

1

(Re)Invented Tradition and the Performance of Amazigh Other-Archives in Public Life

> The Amazigh cause is a deep cultural revolution. As a result, it is a civilizational and political revolution [that] seeks to make change from within; change of mentalities and reconsideration of concepts and behavior.
>
> —AKHIYYAT, *al-Nahḍa al-amāzīghiyya* (2012), 383

The Moroccan post-independence state repressed Amazigh culture and identity for almost fifty years between 1956 and 2001, effectively denying Imazighen (Amazigh people) both citizenship and access to the public sphere. The establishment of the *Institut Royal de la Culture Amazigh* (Royal Institute for Amazigh Culture [RIAC]) in 2001 and the newly official status of the Amazigh language in the revised 2011 Constitution marked a shift in this official, if unstated, policy. The exclusion of Morocco's Amazigh identity from the *cité* was undergirded by an even more consequential historiographical and archival silence, one that has further marginalized Moroccan Imazighen. Instead of sapping Amazigh agency, though, this complex historiographical and political silencing of Morocco's Amazighity served as a catalyst for the Moroccan Amazigh Cultural Movement (MACM), which grew and prospered despite an active disregard for the country's indigenous populations. Aware of history's pivotal role in gaining both civic and political recognition, MACM's institutional and individual members worked to uncover and popularize a parallel history as well as an innovative other-archive that put Amazigh people and their culture at the center of Moroccan and Maghrebi history. Since the early 2000s, thanks to its consistent work in reimagining Moroccan history and how it is studied, MACM has succeeded not only in reclaiming a silenced

Moroccan history, but also, and most importantly, in placing history and other-archive creation at the core of a new and public reconceptualization of Moroccan identity and citizenship.

When Morocco won its independence in 1956, the monarchy and the nationalist bourgeoisie that inherited power from the French Protectorate adopted an irredentist approach to the country's cultural identity. Combined with the Jacobin state model, this philosophy obscured Amazigh identity and its manifestations, primarily language, from all areas of the public sphere, including education, media, and administration.[1] Moreover, the lingering legacy of the so-called Berber Dahir, which was passed by the French Protectorate on May 16, 1930, in order to attempt to divide Arabs and Imazighen in Morocco, prevented Moroccan leaders from seeing the benefits of cultural and linguistic pluralism.[2] Similar to the "assimilationist" Kabyle myth in Algeria, which Patricia Lorcin discussed amply,[3] the establishment of French-Berber schools and the application of ancestral customary law to Amazigh areas sought to remove them from both the Moroccan nation and the ummah of Islam. The more significant exception that in Morocco this Amazigh myth was enacted into policy. This colonialist decision, which the Imazighen themselves were not consulted on, has informed the Moroccan Arab-Salafist, nationalist position vis-à-vis Moroccan Imazighen ever since.[4] To make things worse, the distrust of Imazighen deepened after the two consecutive *coups d'état* against King Hassan II in 1971 and 1972. The top leaders of these coups, namely Colonel Ababou, General El Madbouh, General Oufkir, and Colonel Amkrane, hailed from Amazigh areas, and their attempt to take power from the king led not only to their individual punishment but also to the marginalization of entire Amazigh-speaking regions.[5] This multiform and multidecade marginalization notwithstanding, educated Amazigh youth in the mid-1960s were not deterred from advocating for their right to citizenship, developing a cultural and political program that shaped much of the 2011 Constitution.

MACM, a heterogeneous network of individuals and non-governmental organizations, has been advocating since the mid-1960s for the recognition of the Moroccan Amazigh people's political and cultural rights. Created in 1967 and 1978 respectively, *al-Jam'iyya al-Maghribiyya li-al-Baḥth wa-al-Tabādul al-Thaqāfī* (*Association Marocaine de Recherche et d'Echange Culturel* [*Moroccan Association for Research and Cultural Exchange*], AMREC) and *Munẓẓamat Tamaynūt* (formerly *al-Jam'iyya al-Jadīda li-al-Thaqāfa wa-al-Funūn al-Sha'biyya* [*New Association for Culture and the Popular Arts*]) spearheaded Amazigh cultural and political activism. While AMREC was entirely dedicated to building and preserving Amazigh identity through cultural action and advocacy within the prism of *al-thaqāfa al-shaʿbiyya* (popular culture),[6] *Munẓẓamat Tamaynūt* adopted an action plan that wedded cultural activism with political work and, later, with global human rights activism.[7] The leftist and legal background of *Tamaynūt*'s founders was evidenced in the organization's statutes, which emphasize principles of equality, modernity, democracy, and independence vis-à-vis the state.[8] Nowadays, MACM includes hundreds of organizations that have emerged throughout Morocco and which continue to advocate for full citizenship for Morocco's Amazigh population.[9] To reflect this proliferation of Amazigh organizations and their political and cultural achievements, Brahim Akhiyyaṭ, AMREC's founder and lifelong president, has coined the phrase *al-nahḍa al-amāzīghiyya* (Amazigh renaissance) to describe the multidimensional "deep cultural revolution" that led to the revival of Amazigh language and culture.[10] Akhiyyat's use of *Nahḍa* (renaissance) as the title of his memoirs conveys MACM's success at exhuming Amazigh language and culture from official oblivion, establishing a remarkable parallel between this Amazigh revival in the twentieth century and the Levantine Nahḍa in the nineteenth century. In fact, Akhiyyat's reference to Nahḍa, whose linguistic dimensions are reminiscent of the revival of Hebrew during the Jewish Haskalah, references the deeper and longer-term impact of MACM's work in Morocco and beyond.[11]

Lest it be thought that MACM was confined only to culture, it should be stressed that the actors involved oftentimes straddled the cultural and political arenas. Although AMREC was clearly apolitical, which probably fed dogged rumors about its association with the Makhzen-state, some of its founding members oscillated between cultural and political activism.[12] Moreover, the pro-monarchist political parties *Mouvement Populaire* (The Popular Movement, [PM]) and *Mouvement National Populaire* (The National Popular Movement [NPM]) presented themselves as representatives of the marginalized Amazigh areas.[13] Additionally, the short-lived *Parti Démocratique Amazigh* (The Democratic Amazigh Party, [DAP]) was a radical political party that enjoyed brief legal recognition by the Ministry of Interior between 2005 and 2007 before its judicial dissolution in 2008.[14] While some of these proponents of political action, particularly the leaders of the PM and the DAP, did the important work of paying lip-service to the language on national television during electoral campaigns,[15] such initiatives were forestalled by the inherent limits of the political arena itself, thus emptying their rhetoric of any ability to make concrete change. Unlike political parties, whose maneuverability was restricted for both objective and subjective political reasons during the Years of Lead,[16] cultural activism focused on history and citizenship and challenged the Moroccan state's silence on and repression of the country's Amazigh identity. Specifically, MACM's cultural and linguistic advocacy created an Amazigh-centric other-archive of Amazigh citizenship, which has given the culture historiographical and archival dimensions heretofore unexamined by scholars. Whether in analyzing the revival of symbols of Amazigh past or the use of Tifinagh in the public sphere, MACM's historiographical and other-archival work has been undergirded by a subversive memory that contests Morocco's official history and its sources and unearths broader, Amazigh-focused histories that undermine the narratives sanctioned by the state.

Because these historiographical and other-archival practices have not yet been studied, the links they establish between history, archive creation, and the reclamation of Amazigh citizenship in Morocco have also escaped scholarly attention. Social sciences and linguistics have certainly produced a very rich and valuable body of scholarship about Tamazight (the Amazigh language) in Morocco. Social scientists have traced MACM's historical trajectory in response to the marginalization of Imazighen, presented crucial arguments about gendered spaces and the preservation of Tamazight and its art, and even theorized racial dynamics in the performance of identity among MACM's activists.[17] Linguists, meanwhile, have delved into Tamazight's linguistic history and tackled issues of standardization and revitalization.[18] Both social scientists and linguists agree on the fact that Moroccan Tamazight, which is composed of three dialects (Tashlhīyt, Tamazight, and Tarifit) and spoken by approximately 45 percent of Moroccans, has suffered significantly from government marginalization, enough to become a minority language. However, the arguments presented in these important anthropological and linguistic works leave ample space to analyze the significance of MACM's commemorative practices, history rewriting initiatives, and archive creation strategies to affirm Amazigh people's citizenship in the public sphere.[19]

King Mohammed VI's establishment of RIAC in 2001 was the culmination of MACM's lengthy journey toward the rehabilitation of Morocco's Amazigh identity by way of access to both school and the public sphere.[20] The creation of RIAC was a crucial step toward the official recognition of the linguistic and cultural rights of Morocco's indigenous Imazighen. RIAC was tasked with the "preservation of [Amazigh] culture and the promotion and consolidation [of] its position in the national social, cultural, and media environment as well as in the local and regional affairs."[21] In explaining the necessity of its establishment, the founding decree inscribes RIAC's creation as part of the democratic practice within a law-abiding state that seeks to "achieve equality in rights and duties between Moroccan citizens."[22] Referencing the king's Throne Day speech on July 30, 2001, the preamble inscribes RIAC's mission within the definition of Morocco's "plural identity," which is "built around diverse confluences: Amazigh, Sub-Saharan African, Andalusian."[23] This sentence, which later found its way into the preamble of the revised Constitution in 2011, embraced MACM's long-resisted approach to Moroccan identity as both plural and multiconfluenced.[24] *Al-waḥada fī al-tanawwuʿ* (unity in diversity) has been MACM's founding motto since the first summer university organized in Agadir in 1980.[25] Rather than excluding Morocco's other identities, "unity in diversity" espoused a plural and democratic identity in which all dimensions of Morocco are recognized and treated equally. As such, MACM's project was not just to end the suppression of Tamazight but also to liberate other groups who were erased by the Jacobin, Arab-Islamist state. Although RIAC's founding decree acknowledged the country's diverse identities and lists the institute's scholarly, pedagogical, linguistic, and cultural mission,[26] its meticulously written articles remain silent on Morocco's Amazigh history and that history's significance. Amazigh activists incorporated into RIAC have, however, seized this silence as an opportunity to work from within this institution to promote MACM's subversive memory practices—practices that emphasized history and archive creation through the symbolic usage of the Amazigh Tifinagh alphabet in public.

The standardization of Tifinagh alphabet script and the ubiquity of its use in the public space are two of RIAC's most remarkable achievements; this reconnects Morocco to both its repressed Amazigh identity and the histories underlying it. It is true that MACM itself was plagued by widely publicized disagreements over RIAC's mission.[27] Moreover, RIAC members had to work from within an institutional framework that caused deep divisions among MACM's leaders and the rank and file. It became clear that the shared struggle for the recognition of the Amazigh people's civic, cultural, and linguistic rights would not eliminate diverging individual interests and positions within the movement. Yet RIAC has succeeded over the course of its twenty-year existence in making Amazigh language and culture a tangible reality in Moroccan people's visual and linguistic landscape. The Tifinagh alphabet in particular has become a manifestation of the silenced history and nonexistent archives of Morocco's Amazigh identity, as well as a marker of Morocco's re-Amazighization.

Adopted by RIAC's board on January 31, 2003, as the official script for the writing of Tamazight in Morocco, Tifinagh now adorns school curricula, public transportation signage, and the facades of many official buildings (Figures 1 and 2).[28] Seventeen years after the infamous 2003 *maʿrakat al-ḥarf* (war over the alphabet), Tifinagh is used as an iconic marker of Morocco's Amazigh identity in the public arena. Tifinagh has fulfilled a strategic and historical function in the public sphere as a tool for the re-Amazighization of

Figure 1. The Court of Auditors, Rabat. Photo by author.

Figure 2. The Archives of Morocco, Rabat. Photo by author.

Morocco's history, notwithstanding the lack of consensus over its adoption as the official script for Tamazight.[29] Re-Amazighization is an apt description for this project, because MACM activists consider the recognition of Morocco's Amazigh identity to be a return to the country's roots, which the state's disregard for "cultural and linguistic diversity" has sidelined for so long.[30] Mohammed Boudhan, an Amazigh intellectual and activist, has written that MACM should "consider the Makhzen an Amazigh entity that underwent a [. . .] perversion."[31] For Bhoudhan, the solution lies in "re-Amazighizing [the Makhzen . . .] and returning it to its natural, original Amazigh stock."[32] Re-Amazighization does not posit that Imazighen were extinct and are now being revived. Instead, the confluence of colonization, Arabization, and Islamization has resulted in the erasure of Tamazight and its culture over time, not only in Morocco, but also in Tamazgha (the larger Amazigh homeland), which Amazigh activists argue extends from southwest Egypt to the Canary Islands.[33] Re-Amazighization is an intellectual and cultural project that combines cultural production with the deployment of reinvented symbols of Amazigh identity so as to enfranchise this identity and its cultural expression, placing its civic structure at the core of an overly Arabized and Gallicized public sphere. The current re-Amazighization of the Moroccan public space seeks to undo historical erasure and centers Tamazight within Moroccan public life. The powerful work of memorialization and (re)invention of tradition that allowed MACM to advance its cultural and linguistic demands can be clearly assessed in the revival and dissemination of the Tifinagh alphabet, which has now been established as an other-archive as well as a symbol of Amazigh activism.

(Re)Invented Amazigh Traditions and Subversive Memory

Eric Hobsbawm's "invented tradition" applies to the long-term work MACM has undertaken since the mid-1960s to re-Amazighize Morocco through the rewriting of its history. Hobsbawm has distinguished between traditions that are "actually invented, constructed and formally instituted" and "those emerging in a less easily traceable manner within a brief and dateable period—a matter of a few years—and establishing themselves with great rapidity."[34] One characteristic of invented traditions, according to Hobsbawm, is the fictitious temporal continuity they establish between the past and the present.[35] Moreover, invented traditions require repetition, ritualization, and formalization in order for the link between the past and the present to be entrenched and for a repurposing of the past to serve the goals of the present.[36]

In Morocco's post-independence context, both the monarchy and its opposition invented and ritualized traditions that foregrounded Morocco's Arab-Islamic identity, thereby relegating other expressions of this identity, including Tamazight, to oblivion.[37] An amnesiac official collective memory excluded Imazighen and reinterpreted Moroccan history from the perspective of the post-colonial wielders of power.[38] This is not surprising, though, because pivotal moments, like a country's independence, tend to rally support around a "master commemorative narrative," which, according to Yael Zerubavel, "contributes to the formation of the nation, portraying it as a unified group moving through history."[39] Series of single commemorations crystalize into what she calls "commemorative narratives."[40] While Zerubavel has explained how master commemorative narratives function, her work does not provide a straight answer to how they are challenged and subverted by the groups that are left out. This absence creates space for the theorization of what I conceive of as subversive memory, which is characterized by the (re)invention of real or fictitious traditions that challenge, undermine, or even replace official master narratives. Post-independence Morocco's master commemorative narrative established the monarchy, Islam, and Arabness as *thawābit al-umma* (fixtures of the ummah) to the exclusion of other components of the country's identity, namely blackness, Amazighity, and Judaism, which have millennial historical roots in the country. MACM has sustained and revived excluded identities through commemorative acts that (re)invented Amazigh traditions, creating symbols that unsettle official canons and reopen space for Morocco's Amazigh histories. Creating a subversive memory undergirded by (re)invented traditions has allowed MACM to repurpose the pre-existing or revived Amazigh heritage to put an end to the marginalization of Tamazight and its culture.

The process of Morocco's re-Amazighization speaks to MACM's will to deploy this subversive memory to take ownership of a (re)invented past. MACM drew on a great deal of (re)invented traditions in order to confer legitimacy on Imazighen's long-denied linguistic, cultural, and Amazigh identity–centered demands. In rewriting history, revisiting toponymies, reviving a new version of Tifinagh, and adopting the *Académie Berbère*'s Amazigh flag,[41] MACM wedded public activism via petitions and media statements with an ongoing effort to create distinctive history-based markers for Amazigh identity. One such (re)invention is the use of Tifinagh to serve as a connection between the Moroccan present and its ancestral past. Although Tifinagh's origins are still debated among scholars, between those who foreground its indigenous origins and those who defend its Punic roots,[42] MACM used this alphabet as a distinctive symbol of Imazighen's obscured history and a source of historical legitimacy for demands to rehabilitate Morocco's

Amazigh identity. The (re)invention of tradition has also been paralleled by the creation of a subversive, historical memory, which makes accessible a history that until the 2000s was out of reach for the majority of Moroccans. Both this recovered history and the newfound citizenship that accompanies it are supported by robust intellectual production and odonymic (public signage) practices that have yielded a complex public space, posing crucial questions about the significance of Amazigh activism and Tifinagh in the Moroccan public arena.

This subversive memory and the (re)invented traditions underlying it have taken various forms that are in healthy dialogue with similar experiences elsewhere in the Maghreb. Like their Algerian counterparts, who resorted to "catalogues," "academic production," "gray literature," and "Berber websites" to lay down the foundations for Amazigh cultural and political work,[43] MACM deployed the past in order to legitimize its demands and debunk unfounded claims about Imazighen's lack of a history or their Yemenite origins, which prove their original Arabness. Subversive memory, woven through with strong references to the Amazigh people's indigeneity to North Africa, serves therefore as both a source of pride and temporal, spatial, and historical continuity in a land for which Tamazight has been the language for millennia.

As part of this broader subversive memory, MACM (in conversation with other Amazigh movements in Tamazgha) developed a strong discursive practice that focused on the life stories of historic and prominent Amazigh figures. Amazigh activists throughout North Africa delved into the pre-Islamic period to rehabilitate intellectuals, philosophers, priests, and fighters who figured prominently in the alternative memory they were constructing in lieu of or parallel to the Arab-Islamic-centered official history.[44] These recovered Amazigh figures served as role models for Imazighen, their past having been denied and represented from the point of view of foreigners.[45] The past here is resuscitated to embody the regained Amazigh historical consciousness and "reconstruction of [Amazigh] historical memory."[46]

A significant portion of the effort to solidify this new historical memory went to documenting Amazigh oral heritage. In this regard, AMREC has played a crucial role in launching the first modern effort to document Amazigh literary, poetic, and musical patrimony in Morocco.[47] The association invented its own writing method, known as "*ṭarīqat arrātn*" (the method of journal *Arrātn*), to write Tamazight in Arabic script.[48] Despite the difficulties involved in this documentary endeavor, AMREC saw it as a "point of departure for a new history" that would grant Amazigh culture prominence as an "intellectual and tangible reality in the intellectual scene."[49] Before the founding of AMREC, however, Mukhtār al-Sūsī, a 'ālim and a former

Minister of Endowments and Islamic Affairs, created an impressive compilation of Amazigh heritage in his publications. Unlike the modern efforts of AMREC and other Amazigh civil society organizations, al-Sūsī's approach was based on an Islam-centric vision that did not align with the leftist and indigeneity-informed ideas of the emerging Amazigh activists.[50] Nowadays, associations like *Tirra* (Tirra League for Amazigh Writers), which means "writing" in Amazigh, have drawn on the legacy of their predecessors in Amazigh activism to create a powerful outlet for an Amazigh aesthetic and literary sensibility, connecting it to MACM's long-term work toward winning public recognition for Amazigh citizenship.[51] Publishing in Tamazight is no longer surprising nor is awarding the National Award for Creation in Tamazight to books and studies written in this language.[52]

(Re)inventing the Tifinagh alphabet was a foundational aspect of this subversive history. Despite its continued use by the Tuaregs, the script was not widely disseminated among North African Imazighen.[53] However, the Paris-based *Académie Berbère*, which developed a modernized version of this system of writing based on the Tuareg Tifinagh, paved the way for its reclaiming as a symbol for Tamazight and the histories of exclusion of North African Amazigh people.[54] Although the leadership of *Académie Berbère* was made up of Algerian Imazighen, its founder, Mohand Arav Bessaoud, attributes the adoption of Tifinagh to Mahjoubi Aherdane, who challenged his preference of the Latin alphabet and underlined the civilizational significance of Tifinagh.[55] In Aherdane's words, Tifinagh "are not, for us, just an alphabet like others, but witnesses of a large part of our history. They, anyhow, attest, to the existence of a civilization and express the indentity that you [i.e., Arav] intend to defend."[56] Aherdane goes on further to underline how Jews were able to revive old Hebrew, establishing connections that later would become significant for the overlaps between Amazighity and Jewish indigeneity.[57] In a matter of years, this neo-Tifinagh has not only been standardized and officialized under the aegis of RIAC, but it has been transformed into "a visual representation of the Amazigh language."[58]

Reviving and transforming Amazigh musical memory was part and parcel of the reinvention of Amazigh musical tradition. The case of the musical band Usmān (Lightning) is educational in this regard. Committed and poetic, combining old Amazigh rhythms and melodies with new musical sensibilities (including the introduction of the guitar), Usmān, under the leadership of musician Ammoury Mbark, rejuvenated Amazigh music and created a style that was equally appealing to the younger and older generations.[59] In the words of one of its founders, Usmān was a "real epic" that represented MACM's "will and perseverance against marginalization and exclusion in order to sensitize Moroccans towards their Amazigh self through art and sincere lyrics."[60] This musical renewal, which happened in conjunction with the rise of urban bands like Nas El Ghiwane and Jil Jilala, was also marked by the phenomenal ascendance of Izenzaren (The Sun Rays) under the leadership of the incomparable Abdelhadi Iggout.[61] These groups, among others, made Amazigh-illiterate populations aware of the Amazigh struggle and brought histories of exclusion and marginalization to thousands of villages and isolated communities across Morocco. This recreation of Amazigh music was also accompanied by a strong innovation in sung poetry. In addition to modernizing inherited poetry, a new generation of poets composed poems that widened Tamazight's poeticism and its expressive potential, which gained new audiences for the new Amazigh music.

Unity within diversity, the MACM's now emblematic motto, also took the form of the invention of a new idiom within the Amazigh language itself. Not only did the MACM members create a poetic sensibility that targeted the needs of the new generations of Amazigh educated people, but they also focused on the language itself to develop a learned idiom that would furnish the metalanguage needed for intellectual and literary discussions that the marginalization of Tamazight for over fifty years did not allow to develop. Hence, experimentation with the novel and short story genres, translation of world literature (meaning, from dominant languages) and the development of the genre of literary essay, particularly in the 1980s, were all manifestations of this new idiom that bridged the gap between the language spoken in people's daily lives and the one needed for learned analyses and critical examination of cultural and societal issues. As a result, Imazighen now use *ungāl* to refer to the novel genre, *tullist* to short stories, *amzgūn* to talk about theater, and *amzrūy* for history, narrative genres that have been central to the emerging indigenous literary field that the MACM members worked to create.[62]

A no less foundational aspect of this subversive memory was the creation of an Amazigh flag. Made of three horizontal stripes (blue for water [*amān*], green for land [*akāl*], and yellow for sand [*ajmmār*]), which represent the three topographic elements of Tamazgha (North Africa), the flag was the brainchild of an Algerian immigrant named Da Yūsuf Amazigh.[63] Da Yūsuf defied the reservations of the senior members of the *Académie Berbère*, who feared the political implications of having a flag, and drew on his own resources to create one.[64] When the World Amazigh Congress adopted the flag as the Amazigh flag on August 30, 1997, this iconic blue-green-yellow emblem, with a large Yaz (Z in Tamazight) at the center, acquired transnational, emotional, and symbolic significance. The Amazigh Flag Day is celebrated every year on August 30 as a "supreme symbol of Amazigh identity as well as a symbol of unity, resistance, and struggle for the rights and fundamental freedoms of the Amazigh people."[65] The phenomenal embrace of the Amazigh flag speaks volumes about the force of (re)invented traditions and their myths in feeding the revival of Amazigh identity. Although the flag dates back merely to the 1960s, it acquired such iconic status that its provenance, contrived and recent, is forgotten by its admirers.

This new history is also entrenched in a solidified notion of indigeneity, land, and geography. Conscious of the importance of geography as an anchor of identity, Amazigh activists redefined Tamazgha to refer to the Amazigh homeland in North Africa. Extending from the Siwa oasis in southwest Egypt to the Canary Islands in the Atlantic Ocean, Tamazgha, in this recovered past, subversively reintroduces an indigenized history that returns to a supposed original toponymy of North Africa. By using Tamazgha to refer to the vast lands that were formerly inhabited by Amazigh people, the new toponymy injects an alternative history into the geography of silence that treated North Africa as an Arab-Islamic land. As Amazigh scholar Mohand Tilmatine has argued, although there is no proof that the premodern inhabitants of this land were "conscious of any ethnic, linguistic or, *a fortiori*, historical unity,"[66] Tamazgha has allowed modern Amazigh activists to reclaim North Africa as an indigenous homeland whose inhabitants are united by their Amazighity. This reclamation has given an even deeper significance for Amazigh identity through the use of the motto *akāl* (land), *awāl* (language), *afgān* (people),[67] which tethered the native Amazigh people and their language to the land (Figure 3). Topography, toponymy, and language are intertwined to re-envision the entire North Africa and larger portions of the Sahara, where Tamazight is/was spoken, as a millennial Amazigh homeland.

A no less significant development in this reinvented tradition is the ritualized extension of the notion of autochthony and indigeneity to Moroccan Jews. Israeli state narrative considers Israel/Palestine to be the homeland of the Jews, which they left after the destruction of the temple.[68] However, anthropologist André Levy has shown the limitations of this approach among Casablanca Jews themselves.[69] Among Amazigh activists too, Tamazgha is considered an Amazigh-Jewish homeland. Not only does this idea place both Imazighen and Jews on the same level of indigeneity and autochthony to Tamazgha, but it also adds another layer of complexity to the very idea of Israel/Palestine as a Jewish homeland for Amazigh Jews.[70] Boudhan has recently made a distinction between two types of *waṭaniyya* (nationalism) based on a reading of the difference between *partie* and *nation* in French.[71] While the former refers to being from *hunā* (here), which refers to *tamazirt* (the land of origins/indigenous homeland), the latter is more along the

Figure 3. Amazigh Mascot By Maggie Boum.

lines of Benedict Anderson's "imagined communities," which cements together people who might not even have any shared origins or language.[72] According to this distinction, patriotism extends to all those, including Jews, who are from Tamazgha and whose connection to it is based on the feeling of belonging to *tamazirt* (the indigenous homeland). Not only do these notions of autochthony and patriotism open up space for generative ways of understanding the homeland-diaspora issues regarding Moroccan Jews, but they also pose questions that MACM members have yet to answer or clarify. Most significant is the question of whether their fascination with the Israeli model of linguistic and cultural revival is contingent on condoning occupation, a question that influential Amazigh activists have thus far chosen to dodge. One thing is certain, however: Amazighitude, which I have defined elsewhere as "a process that allows us to gain consciousness of our Amazigh indigeneity and work to restore our critical, decolonized self," is anti-colonial and supportive of other indigenous people's struggles for liberation.[73]

These various (re)invented traditions, which combined the historical, the symbolic, the scriptural, and the musical, took place as the MACM gained more ground domestically and began to integrate transnational,[74] indigenous networks globally, particularly after the Vienna World Conference on Human Rights in 1993. There was a complementarity between the global deployment of these (re)invented traditions, such as the design of the flag and the recovery of the geopolitical term Tamazgha to rename North Africa, and their local use to exert pressure on the Moroccan state. Global pressure was also a consideration in the move to rebrand the Amazigh question as "a fundamental human rights [problem] in Morocco and internationally."[75] Thus conceived, this invented subversive memory created the missing cultural and symbolic infrastructure for the re-Amazighization of Morocco and endowed Amazigh language and culture with the symbolic power to be recognized in an overly-Islamized, Arabized, and Gallicized public sphere after decades of institutionalized marginalization. The rewriting of history in particular was foundational to this Amazigh citizenship project.

Writing an Amazigh-Centered History of Morocco

These broader gestures to reclaim the Amazigh history and memory of Morocco found their clearest manifestation in Ali Sidqi Azaykou's historiographical work. Azaykou, who passed away in 2004, was an Amazigh activist and historian, and he was also quite an accomplished poet in the Amazigh language.[76] Working on a dissertation at the Sorbonne University on the cultural and social history in the region of Saksawa under the supervision of the prominent historian Jacques Berque, Azaykou had already been exposed to new ideas about questions of power in the field of 1970s historical studies. Although Azaykou has yet to receive the academic recognition his pioneering historiographical work deserves, it is almost impossible to discuss other-archives and rewriting of Moroccan history as they pertain to Amazigh identity and citizenship without mentioning his prescient work. Azaykou, who is also considered the first political prisoner of the Amazigh cause, was arrested, tried, and sentenced to prison after the publication of his article "Fī sabīl mafhūm ḥaqīqī lithaqāfatinā al-waṭaniyya" ("Toward a Real Conceptualization of Our National Culture") in the newly-created *Amazigh: Revue marocaine d'histoire et de civilization.*[77] In this article, Azaykou refuted the overlap between Arabic language, Islam, and national culture in Morocco by driving a wedge between the prevalent association of Arabness with Islam and demonstrating that discussions about Arabization were only meant to sideline Amazigh language while the Moroccan elites appropriated French for themselves.[78] Azaykou undermined the argument that Arabic, as the language of the Quran, took precedence over Amazigh language. Following his argument, which clearly targeted one of the tenets of the post-independence Moroccan state, in order to illustrate that claiming Amazigh culture and being Muslim were not mutually exclusive, Azaykou showed that the advent of Islam did not produce a new Arabic language specifically for the Quran.[79] According to historian Bruce Maddy-Weitzman, "[Azaykou's] article constituted a frontal attack against the advocates of Arabization, who falsely linked the primacy of Arabic to Islam and preached incessantly the need to replace foreign languages with Arabic in order to promote a national culture while acting in an entirely contrary manner in their own lives."[80] However, the price for the introduction of such a forceful argument was a year and seventeen days in jail as well as the suspension of the journal that had published the article. The historical marginalization of Morocco's Imazighen was also up for debate at the trial, thanks to Azaykou's lawyers' arguments on the falsification and distortion of Amazigh history.[81] Thus, his trial was transformed into a trial of the state of Amazigh "linguistic and cultural rights."[82] Though it presented an opportunity to shed light on the repression of Amazigh language and culture, Azaykou's arrest ushered in a period during which the "Amazigh cultural movement was deprived of any [public] activity" until the early 1990s.[83]

The distinction that Azaykou sought to draw between language and religion took an even more dramatic turn with the translation of the Quran into Tashlḥīyt by El Houssaine Jouhadi. While Azaykou sought to undermine the religious argument, which excluded Amazigh language by stripping Arabic language of the sacredness wrongly associated with it, Jouhadi chose the even more subversive act of rendering the meaning of the holy scriptures into Tamazight. This move demonstrated that although the Quran was revealed in Arabic, it is able to speak all the languages of Muslim communities worldwide. Reminiscent of similar debates in West and South Asia, the stakes of this discussion in the Moroccan context are multifold and have the potential, in the words of *The Economist*, "to shake the Moroccan establishment."[84] The king is the Commander of the Faithful, and protecting the Islamic and Arabic nature of the state is one of his constitutional duties. By translating the holy text into Amazigh, this non-Arabic language, Jouhadi had achieved three goals. First of all, he demonstrated that Islam and Arabness are not the same thing. Moroccan Imazighen are equally Muslim without being Arab. Second, the absence of any collective heretic tendencies among Imazighen in the aftermath of his translation proved that all arguments claiming that reading and interpreting the Quran in a language other than Arabic might lead to deviation were politically motivated, thus demonstrating the instrumentalization of Islam to repress Amazigh rights. The third and most significant effect of this translation, which is still unknown to many Amazigh secularists, is the way it reconnects Amazigh Islam with its historical roots by recalling the Almohad and Bourghwata eras, during which Amazigh language was used as frequently as Arabic in sermons and interpretation of the Quran. In fact, under the Almohad dynasty, knowledge of Amazigh was a requirement for anyone who wanted to be an Imam.[85]

Unlike what one might expect in a translated holy text, the reader cannot but notice the argumentative nature of Jouhadi's introduction. To rationalize his translation, Jouhadi has underlined the Quran's own history of borrowing words from other languages as well as its injunction to exchange ideas between civilizations:

> Following [this Quranic injunction], Amazigh language, in its turn, borrowed—after a give and take—from other languages from other neighboring nations in the Mediterranean basin.
>
> This is not surprising since Amazigh language is one of the oldest languages in the world. As old as the age of its homeland in North Africa. Despite the foreign invasion inflicted on its homeland and regardless of its centuries-old marginalization, it did not die like other languages died because its vocabulary was registered in its topography as a human, plant, animal, naval, or spatial encyclopedia, or in the dialects of its expansive homeland, and in the accumulations of its popular literature.[86]

Jouhadi addresses his potential interlocutors to demonstrate that the Amazigh language is as capable of conveying the meaning of the Quran as is Arabic. He makes crucial connections between topography and language and urges his readers to make an effort to learn Tamazight the same way they learn foreign languages. Thus, Jouhadi, albeit belatedly, continued in the footsteps of Azaykou, who charted a very critical intellectual path beginning in the late 1970s.

In 1968, Azaykou had published an article in a small journal called *Ṣawt al-Janūb* in which he warned against the destruction of popular culture due to the hegemony of Orientalizing and Westernizing projects that were shaping Moroccan national identity. As usual, Azaykou adopted a critical position and called for the rehabilitation of Amazigh literature which, in his words, is "the best expression of the emotions of the children of this land."[87] In this same article, Azaykou reviewed journalist Ahmed Amzal's edited poetry collection *Amanār* (A Shining Star), which many still consider the first contemporary literary work written in the Amazigh language, and underlined how, regardless of its shortcomings, this book marked a rupture between "the period of silence over and marginalization of Berber literature" and what he called "the return to the popular authenticity that lies in our literature, mythology, and tales."[88] This early work would later permeate Azaykou's historiographical project and serve as a beacon for his innovative thoughts about archives and history.

Azaykou's transformative historical thinking would become even more provocative and fully fledged in an essay that he published in 1971 while he was still a graduate student living in Paris. Entitled "Tārīkh al-maghrib bayna mā huwwa 'alayhi wa mā yajibu an yakūna 'alayhi" ("The History of Morocco between What It Was and What It Should Be"), this article presented three foundational elements that would later be the distinctive imprints of Azaykou's Amazigh-centered historiographical project.[89] First, a new conceptualization of history as a "tool for understanding and guiding the present based on conscious comprehension of and consciousness about the past."[90] By using history to guide the present, Azaykou seemed to warn against repeating the same errors that led to Morocco's colonization and continued economic backwardness. This is made clear every time he says that historical consciousness is crucial for social and intellectual development. He distinguishes the era of "al-tārīkh al-wā'ī" ("conscious history") from the history of chroniclers and official historians who were merely invested in compiling rather than explaining historical events and investigating questions of causality as they pertain to the present.[91] In this area, Azaykou advocated for the training of Moroccan youth, so that they could learn to understand history as a part of the present. However, he warned that it was impossible to impart this kind of training if historians themselves did not have the tools to do it. The conclusion for Azaykou is that Moroccans need historians who are "conscious of our situation and understand our present deeply in order for their departure [from it] to be built on solid foundations."[92] Once he establishes the need to rewrite Moroccan history, which was the second pillar of his historiographical project, he cuts to the heart of the issue by saying:

> Our primary problem is rewriting our history, because the way it has been written was not intact. Also, because the specific circumstances in which it was written imposed the form in which it is today. Moreover, this history came to us from the outside; meaning that the history that we read, teach, and are influenced by was written by foreign hands and with a mentality that is different from ours, and for goals that are different from or are even in total opposition to the aspirations and goals that we entertain.[93]

It is important to underline the fact that "foreign" in this context refers to both Europeans and Arabs, whose dominant narratives shaped the perceptions of Moroccan and Maghrebi history.

The third pillar of Azaykou's historiographical project is the central role history plays in the recognition of a pluralistic Moroccan society. This history is not free from "foreign" alienation, which had until that moment in time (1971) interpreted Moroccan history through its own lens and, as a consequence, pushed Amazigh people to "see ourselves through the eyes of the other and strive to conform to their image of us."[94] Azaykou's dis-alienating history has to "start from us," meaning it had to be Morocco-centered, written by Moroccans, and from "a pure Moroccan spirit."[95] Although Azaykou's words might seem ultra-nationalistic today, readers have to be aware that his thought is rooted in discussions of Moroccanization in the post-independence period and ongoing debates on decolonizing history.[96] Moroccanization was Azaykou's segue into rewriting Moroccan history from within the discourses that excluded Imazighen at the time. He used the discursive framework that was prevalent in the 1970s to draw attention to the status of Amazigh language and culture, which he only introduced through his discussion of history and the need to rewrite it.

Azaykou's pioneering work to rewrite a pluralistic Moroccan history from an Amazigh vantage point evolved gradually in conversation with the works of both historians and social scientists. In his 1971 article, "Min mashākil al-baḥt fī tārīkh al-maghrib" (Some Problems of Research in Moroccan History),[97] Azaykou tackled, among others, the issue of archives and documentary evidence, which he would later develop into one of his most original contributions to the centering of the Amazigh people in Moroccan history and citizenship. Unlike his foreign colleagues, Azaykou argued forcefully, in agreement with Moroccan historian Germain Ayache, that there was no shortage of archival documents in Morocco. In opposition to Robert Montagne, who asserted in 1930 that "historical sources that are really worthy of this name are rare in this country," Azaykou asserted that it was not so much a question of documentation as a question of access, organization, and the content of the documents themselves.[98] Unlike many of his colleagues, who were dedicated to producing written-evidence-based histories in the 1970s,[99] Azaykou suggested using sources and methodologies that would require the "intersection and collaboration of the scholar of religion, the litterateur, the historian, the geographer, and the specialist in popular culture, among others."[100] Azaykou was laying the foundation for what I have theorized in this book as other-archives. In addition to this interdisciplinary approach that, in his opinion, would yield the pluralistic history for which he advocated, he called for constant attention to be paid to organizing the available archives, reorganizing the discipline of history, establishing the discipline of social history, and documenting popular heritage.[101] At this early stage of his research, Azaykou did not talk explicitly about Amazigh language and culture, but subsumed them under *al-turāth al-sha'bī* (popular patrimony). It is also important to note that he posited historical knowledge as a path toward development, stating that "as long as we don't know our history as a total unit, we cannot pretend that we have indeed taken the path of real development."[102]

In the following years, Azaykou's historiographical project established an alternative history and blazed a clear trail for a historical imagination that was based on novel thinking about archives and the past. He contested the prevalent genealogical approach to the history of Morocco and North Africa, proposing instead a history that takes into account people's "material environment and its deep impact on societies' adaptation."[103] In Azaykou's opinion, transcending the limits of genealogical history would incentivize scholars to "search for other documentary ways that enrich our knowledge about a past whose deep dynamics remain unknown to us."[104] In showing that North African and Moroccan topographies were deeply shaped by Amazigh toponymies and onomastics, Azaykou inscribed the history of North Africa within the continuity of Amazigh histories, which predate the arrival of Arabs and Islam. In this case, it is the land itself that serves as an other-archive for the reconstruction of occulted Moroccan histories. Interrogating the landscape would not be possible without the examination of the native language of the people who inhabited it for millennia, hence the subversive importance of this method. Genealogical evidence as to whether Imazighen (Amazigh people) were descended from Yemen or not did not matter to Azaykou; what mattered was the fact that North Africa was an Amazigh land that had its own history before the arrival of the Arabs. He went on to say that "it seems that language, among other tools, is considered one of the best documents that could help open this field for research because language, more than anything else, reflects most often the human groups' deep and everlasting reactions vis-à-vis nature as well as the results of their impact on their behavior and mentality."[105] This project on language and history culminated with the publication of two books entitled *Tarikh al-maghrib aw al-ta'wīlāt al-mumkina* (Morocco's History and the Possible Interpretations) and *Namādhij min asmā' al-a'lām al-jughrāfiyya wa-al-bashariyya al-maghribiyya* (Samples of Names of Moroccan Geographic and Human Landmarks,[106]),[107] which all introduce new, Amazigh-focused histories of Morocco and North Africa.

Working in a cultural and sociopolitical context in which Amazigh language and culture were not even recognized, Azaykou rereads histories and reinvents archives that situate these unacknowledged aspects of Moroccan identity at the heart of its past. As is the case with several other historians, Azaykou's trailblazing ideas were unfortunately shunned by his academic colleagues, including at Mohammed V University in Rabat, during his lifetime, and his work remains entirely open for more academic examination. Therefore, it is not surprising that even such a long-term Amazigh activist as the aforementioned Boudhan was unaware of the "intellectual and philosophical value of his thoughts, analyses, and methodology in terms of thinking and analysis, and their impact on the level of formation of the Amazigh awareness"[108] until 2020.

Azaykou's historiographical work, which was unfolding in tandem with MACM's endeavors to achieve the recognition of the Imazighen's right to citizenship, made two contributions to Amazigh activism. Firstly, he succeeded in providing a scientific approach on the basis of which the entire history of North Africa, not just Morocco alone, could be contested. Although it might seem like an exaggeration, in the words of his friend and classmate Ahmed Tawfik, the current Minister of Endowments and Islamic Affairs, Azaykou "searched for a history of reconciliation or a reconciliation of history."[109] Tawfik does not explain the elements nor the parties of this reconciliation, but it is clear from the context that the reconciliation he meant was between the state and Amazigh people. Secondly, Azaykou turned the Amazigh language itself into an other-archive, which has an effect both on history writing and language preservation. By conferring archival importance on the repressed Amazigh language, Azaykou turns it into an object of historical reflection and a site for the recovery of undocumented information about historical events, which, in turn, contributes to its preservation. Additionally, the paradoxical nature of something as fleeting as language being the container of historical data would further intrigue researchers and serve the endeavor to document and preserve the language and the identity embedded in it.

The historical consciousness that Azaykou's academic writings constructed was foundational to MACM's approach to winning Amazigh citizenship in the public sphere. AMREC, for instance, established what it called a "history and anthropology workshop," which it tasked with the mission of correcting the historical injustice done to Amazigh civilization not only in Morocco but in North Africa as a whole.[110] This not only puts Amazigh people on equal footing with their Arab co-citizens, but also has a psychological effect, "since awareness of oneself releases [Amazigh individuals] from the inferiority complex" that was widespread among them.[111] In order for this rehabilitating and freeing historical consciousness to be achieved, AMREC mapped out a long-term program that included creating other-archival sources, compiling bibliographies, and even appropriating digitized copies of colonial archives from France and other foreign countries.[112] Notwithstanding the importance of these measures, AMREC's other-archival work was most represented by its endeavor to create a "toponymic dictionary" as well as well as a "biographic dictionary of forgotten Amazigh historical figures."[113] Again, the focus on toponymy is really central to the connection between citizenship, identity, and land, which acquired an even deeper significance after the officialization of Tifinagh as a script in 2003. This historiographical trend started by Azaykou culminated in the organization of an international summer school on "Imazighen's History" in 2000.[114] The essays included in the proceedings deconstructed the many facets of Amazigh history from an Amazighitude perspective. However, the observer of discourses about Amazigh history will notice that even the word history has been Amazighized through the use of the Amazigh term *amzrūy*. Derived from *izri*, which means to pass or elapse, *amzrūy* enacts a new, Amazigh-centic understanding of both time and narrative. This conceptualization of the past from an Amazigh perspective demonstrates how significant history has become in the process of recognition of Imazighen in their homeland.

The focus on history as a space for recognition and civic acknowledgment was reflected in the revised 2011 Constitution. Article 5 of this new Constitution stipulates that "Tamazight [Berber/Amazigh] constitutes an official language of the State, being common patrimony of all Moroccans without exception."[115] In addition to granting Amazigh language an official status, the Constitution enriches and reuses the preamble of RIAC's founding decree, which now states that Morocco's unity is "forged by the convergence of its Arab-Islamist, Berber [amazighe] and Saharan-Hassanic [saharo-hassanie] components, nourished and enriched by its African, Andalusian, Hebraic, and Mediterranean influences [affluents]."[116] In the span of forty years, Morocco's re-Amazighization went from being a niche project of activists who had to work within the ambiguous and obviously less confrontational phraseology of *al-thaqāfa al-sha'biyya* (popular culture) to providing the state with much-needed language in the midst of the February 20th Movement's calls for constitutional and political reforms in 2011.

Tifinagh Is Not Just a Script: It Is an Other-Archive

The now well-known arrest of seven members of the Tellili Association in 1994 was a triumphal moment for MACM's subversive memory.[117] Seven male teachers from Guelmima and Errachidia were arrested in the aftermath of the 1994 May Day celebrations for brandishing protest signs in Tifinagh.[118] The men were accused of, among other things, posing a threat to public order and using an unconstitutional language,[119] and these arrests and the ensuing trial stirred a global human rights outcry. The desire to ban Tifinagh in the public space led to major backlash, which forced Hassan II to make a historic speech on August 20, 1994, in which he announced the need to teach dialects in order to protect national identity.[120] After Hassan II's education promises were not implemented, Mohammed Chafik, a leading figure of Amazigh activism, released his 2000 Amazigh Manifesto, which enumerated the different historical injustices perpetrated against Imazighen and made nine crucial demands. These demands include the recognition of Amazigh language and culture in the Moroccan Constitution, the allocation of development projects to Amazigh regions, the rewriting of Moroccan history to include Amazigh contributions, and the rehabilitation of the Amazigh culture.[121] Chafik stated that "thousands of Berber speakers live like foreigners in their own country. The resentment they feel from it is stronger than what it would have been if they lived in a real exile."[122] In other words, Imazighen have been stripped in de facto fashion of their citizenship rights.

MACM's endeavors constructed the foundation for the more human-rights-oriented activism that emerged in the 1990s.[123] MACM became bolder and more politicized thanks to the creation of an alternative imaginary of North Africa and the construction of discursive, visual, and intellectual tools for the defense of its project. In addition to affirming that Amazigh language and culture are the oldest in Morocco, the six signatory associations of the 1991 *Mīythāq Agadir* [the Agadir Charter] presented demands that ranged from constitutional codification of Tamazight to developing pedagogical tools for its teaching.[124] The boldness and comprehensiveness of MACM's demands in the 1990s were reflective of Morocco's increasing political openness, which was conducive to the emergence of a subversive memory and the (re)invented traditions that made the stipulations of the 2011 Constitution possible. Interestingly, King Mohammed VI's speech in which he announced the establishment of RIAC on October 17, 2001, took on both the tone and the rhetoric of Tamazight activism in emphasizing that Amazigh identity is "property of all Moroccans."[125] The king also stressed the fact that the rehabilitation of Tamazight is "a national responsibility, because no national culture can disown its historical roots."[126] With RIAC's inauguration, the road for Amazigh subversive memory and (re)invented traditions to enter the Moroccan public sphere was wide open; their now-pervasive existence initiated a transformation of the way this public arena had been perceived since Morocco's independence in 1956.

The debates leading up to RIAC's thirty-three-member board's decision to adopt Tifinagh script for the writing of Tamazight in Morocco were the clearest demonstration that this script was not merely a technical issue.[127] As previously mentioned, Tifinagh only emerged in the 1960s, when the Paris-based *Académie Berbère* adopted it, but it quickly acquired an iconicity and symbolism that give the impression that its use in North African public life dated back to time immemorial. In the absence of a unified script, Moroccan Amazigh activists have historically used all three scripts (Arabic, Latin, and Tifinagh) in their publications.[128] Sometimes, these alphabets have been used alongside each other, depending on the activists' affinities. However, the longest-serving Amazigh association in Morocco, AMREC, has consistently used the Arabic alphabet in its publications, *Arrātn, al-Tabādul al-Thaqāfī*, and *Amūd*, since the 1970s.[129] Moreover, AMREC held workshops in which its members reflected on the different aspects of developing a convenient script to write Tamazight.[130] By 2003, however, MACM had changed dramatically; it became more transnational, more radical, and ideas about modernity and progress permeated its discourse, which erupted in the infamous *ma'rakat al-ḥarf* (the battle over the alphabet). While the pro-Arabic script positions of the Islamist Justice and Development Party (PJD) and pan-Arabist groups were an open secret, the divide within MACM revealed its members' profound disagreements.[131] As MACM faced accusations of being anti-Arab and anti-Islam, as well as being a tool of colonialism,[132] a cliché accusation that has been brandished against it since its beginning, the polarization within MACM's ranks over whether to use Latin or Tifinagh script to write Tamazight threatened the unity of the movement. Of utmost interest in this regard is the generational divide between AMREC veterans, who all advocated for Tifinagh despite the fact that their publications were in Arabic/Aramaic script, and the younger generations and newcomers to Amazigh activism, who signed the "Meknes Declaration" in favor of Latin script.[133]

Beyond the technical and functional aspects of the alphabet, these divides were symptomatic of the transformation of imaginaries about Morocco's

Amazigh history and the place of modernity in its identity. The war over the alphabet was in fact a battle over Morocco's Amazigh citizenship and the most efficient way to reject or reclaim it.[134] By having Tamazight written in Arabic script, proponents of the Arabic alphabet sought to contain Imazighen within the fold of their Arab-Islamic worldview of Morocco as a primarily Arab-Muslim country.[135] Amazigh activists from all walks of life understood that the proponents of Arabic script wanted "Tamazight to remain under the banner of Arabness, as a language, culture and civilization," which led to the "unanimous rejection of the Arabic script."[136] Those who advocated for the Latin script were more concerned about modernity, communication, and the future growth of the language, but they inadvertently gave the Islamists and pan-Arabists more ammunition to attack MACM's project as a whole.[137] Analyzing AMREC's pro-Tifinagh position, Akhiyyat writes:

> We, at the Moroccan Association for Research and Cultural Exchange [AMREC], have had a clear position vis-à-vis this issue since the beginning of the 1990s. Our choice had been made since we organized a workshop on writing and the dictionary in Maamoura in 1992, which adopted a holistic approach to Tamazight; Amazigh language should not be divorced from its Tifinagh alphabet. We considered the Tifinagh alphabet to be a fundamental element in Amazigh identity, since by writing Tamazight in Tifinagh our language liberates itself from subordination to other linguistic systems, either Oriental or Western. Therefore, we say that Tifinagh is the symbol of our liberation both symbolically and civilizationally.[138]

The civil and symbolic recognition of Amazigh language and identity as a historical substratum of Moroccan identity mattered the most for the pioneers of Amazigh activism. For AMREC, issues of standardization, functionality, computerization, and dissemination (important for the proponents of Latin script), were moot compared to Tifinagh's symbolism and iconicity as a token of Amazigh identity.[139] This movement is tied to the importance of subversive memory and the historiographical imaginations it makes possible in the public sphere.

In tracing its trajectory as a crucial (re)invented tradition within MACM's push for recognition, Tifinagh emerges as a vital force in the work of Amazigh subversive memory. By not heeding the scholarly debates about Tifinagh's origins and by favoring its civilizational importance, MACM activists, even with their deep internal disagreements, turned this alphabet into a transformative tool in their endeavor to consecrate Morocco's historically diverse Amazigh identity. From its (re)invention by the *Académie Berbère* in Paris to its adoption by RIAC in 2003, Tifinagh has resignified artifacts and mnemonic devices, juxtaposing a subversive worldview with a master commemorative discourse of codified truths and historical narratives in the Moroccan public space. Tifinagh script has therefore played a crucial role in iconizing an alternative Amazigh past, one that reshuffled the "visual identity" of the Moroccan public arena.[140] This transformation of the Moroccan people's visual identity has not been without hurdles and bureaucratic obstacles. As activist and academic Ahmed Assid has written, the opponents of Tifinagh "don't accept that Moroccan visual identity becomes Amazighized through its symbol, Tifinagh alphabet, after the official recognition of Tamazight."[141] However, what really matters here is the fact that Tifinagh has become a potent public marker of subversive memory by reclaiming Morocco's Amazigh identity openly. The use of Tifinagh in official signage and in all manner of governmental literature has placed this very subversive memory at the center of Moroccan people's societal consciousness, principally by reshuffling the order of languages and adding a new visual marker to Moroccan public life.

The Civic and Historical Significance of a Re-Amazighized Public Sphere

Beginning in 2011, the incorporation of Tifinagh as a language of public signage in Morocco complicated Arabic-French bilingualism, which had dominated Moroccan public life since independence. The addition of Tifinagh has created a visual dissonance and added more textual elements to an already complicated linguistic landscape, further complicating the legibility and the navigation of the Moroccan public sphere. It took fifty years for Moroccan government buildings to display trilingual panels (Arabic, Amazigh, and French), thus becoming sites in which Amazigh "locational citizenship" is re-actualized and performed.[142]

Access to the public sphere is a marker of citizenship or lack thereof. Andrés di Masso equates "locational citizenship" with "the right to have a place in the public space."[143] Derived from "the right to the city," which emphasizes the "entitlement of any urban dweller to freely access and use public space," locational citizenship is about the politics of place and the codification of access to it.[144] Moroccan Imazighen have been denied for a long time the right to the city through intensive Arabization, the folklorization of their language and culture, and the non-recognition of their existence.[145] The absence of Amazigh culture from official public life was such that the drafters of the Agadir Charter requested that Tamazight be granted "the right

Figure 4. Tramway Station in Downtown Rabat. Photo by author.

to the city in mass and audiovisual media."[146] Between its marginalization in the first Constitution in 1962 and the repression of its expression in public space, Amazigh identity was essentially excluded from locational citizenship from Morocco's independence until the creation of RIAC in 2001. However, Tamazight's resurgence on the facades of official buildings, in tramway stations (Figure 4), and on institutions of higher education is an indication that Amazigh cultural and linguistic citizenship is now located, and has full potential access to the public arena. It is certainly ironic that the same buildings where the aforementioned decisions to marginalize Tamazight were issued are now adorned with the Tifinagh alphabet. Even if this is only a symbolic change, the contrast is stark between 1994, when Amazigh activists were denied locational citizenship on the basis that they wrote their protest banners in Tifinagh, and 2021, when this marker of Amazigh subversive memory now graces the facades of ministries and courts of justice.

Public signage is crucial for daily life. Signage can be a source of both orientation and dis-orientation, hence the transformative nature of the inclusion of Tifinagh in these trilingual signboards. Public signs "help us to structure physical space, to mark it, to give it meanings and thus to create particular places and landscapes in which we live and act, which have a practical and emotional value for us, and which are sources of our identity."[147] Public signage is a complicated network of connections that all intersect in concretizing the identity of a place and its values. While post-independence Morocco suppressed expressions of Amazigh identity, it Arabized the public sphere with utter disregard for the emotional and cultural needs of its Amazigh citizens. Hence, French and Arabic, two non-indigenous languages, conveyed Morocco's chosen Arab-Islamic, post-colonial identity, which relegated Amazigh language and culture to oblivion, making its resurgence in public buildings all the more meaningful.

The use of Tifinagh in the public sphere raises new questions about the legibility and functionality of this (re)invented script in public signage. Tifinagh, a conspicuous marker of MACM's subversive memory, has a fourfold transformative value for Moroccan society. First, beyond their functional role, the inclusion of Arabic, Tamazight, and French (in this order; Figure 5), is a translation of the constitutional text and a performance of the spatial hierarchization of languages based on their official status, albeit divorced from their varied economic power, a domain where the French language still dominates. Second, by having a corporeal existence in spaces from which it was once excluded, Tamazight destabilizes the normalcy of the predominantly Arabic-French public space and reclaims its place therein. While Arabic and French scripts have been a normal presence in Moroccan public life since 1956, Tamazight is the latest to acquire a *droit de cité* in the public sphere. Third, educated Moroccans' perceptions of literacy are destabilized by the new linguistic reconfiguration, because the majority of them have no mastery of their ancestral language and its neologisms. Amazigh speakers themselves experience a disconcerting unfamiliarity within a language that is supposed to be familiar, but is not anymore. Fourth, Tifinagh is an aesthetic script, which vulgarizes the Amazigh sense of beauty even as it creates a visual dissonance in the Moroccan public space. Regardless of the fact that educated readers default to Arabic or French to read street signs, they will think of their inability to read Tifinagh as a handicap, which is in itself reflective of the impoverishing impact the repression of Amazigh language and culture has had on Moroccan society.

Tifinagh's subversive memory in public life disturbs any as-usual reading of the Moroccan public sphere. The space it occupies between Arabic and French on signboards inserts an additional visual and historical layer into the already bilingual palimpsest of Moroccan identity, thus disrupting the linguistic order and driving a wedge between languages of foreign powers that colonized North Africa. The introduction of the indigenous language of North Africa in the space MACM has managed to reconquer drives a wedge between Arabic and French. In fact, Tifinagh is not there to reorient, but to remind the public of a hidden past and an occulted Amazigh history. Indeed,

Figure 5. Bab Rouah Gallery, Rabat. Photo by Maroua Cherkaoui.

contact with Tifinagh is meant to encourage Moroccans to move beyond surface-level observations of these incomprehensible Tamazight neologisms in order to penetrate the layers of silence and ignorance that excluded this language and its history from Morocco's official visual space for decades. Furthermore, the presence of Tifinagh on signboards in front of courts, hospitals, schools, and even police headquarters can be read as the Moroccan state's attempt to reconcile Amazigh subversive memory with the legacy of the violence perpetrated against Amazigh language and culture. Finally, compared to earlier scholarship that rightly suggested that Tamazight survived only as a form of art practiced at home and in gendered spaces,[148] Tifinagh's conquest of public facades is proof that Moroccan Amazigh identity has been normalized. Normalization does not, however, mean that MACM holds no grievances or that the Moroccan state is not constantly attempting to chip away at these gains when the circumstances are opportune for such regression.

Tifinagh's conspicuous and constitutionally protected status in the public sphere now functions as an other-archive that holds and tells multiple histories of Imazighen's exclusion and perseverance. As a sign that Tamazight has gained its *droit de cité* across Morocco, Tifinagh's presence in public life holds within it a story of marginalization and triumphant survival despite systematic de-Amazighization policies that were enacted in the post-independence period. The sudden appearance of Tifinagh in streets and city squares and official buildings is reminiscent of the same sudden process that excluded Amazigh identity from the Moroccan public sphere for fifty years. The very recognition of Tamazight, then, is also a reminder of historical injustice. Tifinagh is as much a source of historical transformation as of historical injustice. Moreover, Tifinagh connects the emerging histories of this public sphere with stories of MACM's activism since the country's independence. Rather than seeing Tifinagh script and the public sphere it has refashioned as just another top-down change, we should focus our attention on how it rewrites the Amazigh people's stories of indigeneity, belonging, homeland, and pride after five decades of active silencing and marginalization of Imazighen. Tifinagh rewrites history even as history unfolds in the Moroccan public sphere.

Afterlives of MACM's Subversive Memory in the Field of Publication

Tamazight has always been the throbbing heart of the Amazigh civilizational project. Language was the core of Amazigh subversive memory and the subsequent work to end the marginalization of Amazigh culture. The examination of RIAC's publications' catalogue and the recent emergence of bookshelves dedicated to Amazigh cultural production in Tamazight in Moroccan bookstores represent some of the deeper dimensions of MACM's seminal work in the Moroccan public sphere.

Dalīl manshūrāt al-ma'had al-malakī li-al-thaqāfa al-amāzīghiyya *[RIAC's publications catalogue/guide]*

Since its founding, RIAC's mission has been to collect and document Amazigh heritage, conduct research on Amazigh culture, promote cultural and artistic production in Tamazight, and produce knowledge on Amazigh language and culture.[149] With the establishment of RIAC, this official institution took on the activists' "cataloguing and inventorying" mission to anchor Amazigh culture and preserve it.[150] Beyond the mere function of inventorying a pre-existing knowledge or patrimony, though, RIAC's publications catalogue perpetuates MACM's subversive memory from a position of power. Many researchers and members of RIAC's board of directors were activists within MACM, and the institute furnished them with a space where they could influence the making as well as the implementation of decisions about the revitalization of Tamazight. The continuity of this activist spirit can be noticed in the institute's publications guide. Although RIAC is an official institution funded directly from the budget of the royal palace, its catalogue reveals that it has inaugurated a publishing culture influenced by the subversive memory that informed MACM's activism.

Published in 2017, sixteen years after the RIAC's establishment, *Dalīl manshūrāt al-ma'had al-malakī li-al-thaqāfa al-amāzīghiyya* (Figure 6) displays a long list of the institute's publications. The introduction is written first in Tamazight and then in Arabic, thus inverting the constitutional order of languages in the country in order to foreground Tamazight's primacy. This mere displacement of Arabic to the second line on an official publication is a powerful, although subtle, subversive act, as it breaches established linguistic hierarchies. Moreover, the catalogue emphasizes the fact that RIAC has "become a referential and pioneering pole in the field of Amazigh studies through its subscription to the concretization of the strategic goal of promoting Amazigh culture."[151] Inside the catalogue, the reader discovers poetry collections, novels, children's literature, monographs, scholarly studies, and journal issues that discuss all aspects of Amazigh language and culture. These works, the authors underline, are a testament to RIAC's "enrichment of this [Amazigh] culture with numerous publications that contribute to the development of scientific research in and rehabilitation for Amazigh culture."[152] In a self-congratulatory tone, the authors add that these publications reveal the "depth and efficiency of the Institute's participation in the process of modernizing Amazigh culture and standardizing language." It is clear that a colossal effort went into the publication of over three hundred works in fifteen years, but the catalogue itself is an important object for the entrenchment of an Amazigh visual reality.

The catalogue is a piece of art. It was clearly designed to communicate the subversive memory that underlines a distinctive Amazigh publishing identity. The catalogue carries RIAC's circular Tifinagh blue logo, centered around a large Yaẓ (Z). Because of the iconicity of the letters, the reader cannot miss the fact that this is an Amazigh-branded publication. As was mentioned previously, most educated Moroccans' inability to read Tifinagh does not mean that they cannot access these publications in French or Arabic. The catalogue itself documents an existing, organized, meticulously prepared, and prolific Tamazight literature, further building on MACM's legacy and (re)invented

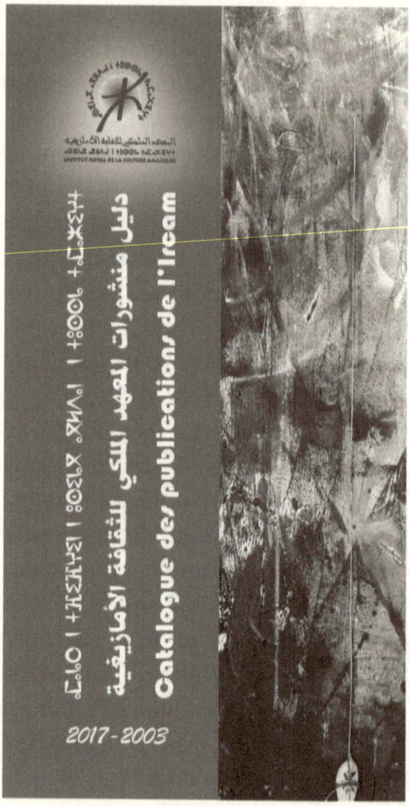

Figure 6. Publications Catalogue, IRCAM.

traditions. For instance, the perceptive observer will notice the camouflaged Amazigh flag on the cover of the catalogue. Despite the fact that they are not arranged in horizontal order, the mixture of blue, green, yellow, and red colors evokes the Amazigh flag, making the catalogue a mnemonic device. The catalogue's memorial function is even deeper than it would appear at first glance. For instance, the reprinting of some of the earlier publications gives the catalogue a chance to remember Amazigh activists and their writings, which also serves MACM's memory. Additionally, the use of bright-colored, polished, and highly artistic covers contributes to the distinction of Amazigh cultural production from the rest of Moroccan art and literature. It would be limiting to analyze RIAC's publications catalogue only as a commercial or promotional tool. It is in fact a testament to the continued impact of Amazigh subversive memory even after the open struggle with the state over recognition and acceptance of Amazigh people's rights.

Maktabat al-Alfiyya al-Thālitha (Third Millennium Bookstore): A Home for Cultural Production in Tamazight

Bookstores are commercial spaces, and their raison d'être is to make a profit. However, bookstores are also an important extension of the public sphere and as such are spaces where societal change can be felt. Before the beginning of the 2000s, profit-seeking bookstores dedicated their shelves to commercially successful books. Since Amazigh language and culture publications were not profitable, they were circulated, like all "gray literature," only in activist spaces.[153] The visitor will notice the transformation of Moroccan bookstores, which now feature entire shelves dedicated to Amazigh studies.

Located across the street from the Moroccan parliament in Rabat, Maktabat al-Alfiyya al-Thālitha has ultramodern shelves dedicated to cultural production in or about Tamazight. Not only does the bookstore display an entire section in Tamazight, but the works its shelves offer span generations of Amazigh thinkers and intellectual producers. The visitor will find Mohammed Chafik's three-volume Arabic-Amazigh dictionary, Muḥammad Hawzālī's religious exhortation *Baḥr al-dumūʿ*, Brahīm Iʿzzā's poetry book *Iskla n yiḍ*, Hassan Aourid's Arabic poetry collection *Taghūyt n tīn hinān*, Mohammed al-Jaafari's bilingual collection of proverbs and aphorisms *Swingm ṭamzt awāl* alongside Mohammed Mestaoui's complete works entitled *Smmūs idlisn n tmdiazin*, and Ali Sidqi Azaykou's collection of poems *Timitār*, among many others.[154] Combining centuries-old Tamazight literature in Arabic script with the newest publications in Tifinagh, the Amazigh section of al-Alfiyya al-Thālitha bookstore speaks to the spirit of the Amazigh renaissance that MACM has brought about in Morocco. Whereas in the past Tamazight was absent, now the customer can, in the space of a few shelves, see how rooted Amazigh cultural and linguistic heritage is in Moroccan history. In addition to bearing witness to Amazigh intellectuals' prolific production, the diverse quantity of works on sale indicates that Tamazight is increasingly gaining ground as a language of cultural production. It also shows that Tamazight has left the *gynécée*, which played a crucial role in its preservation for a long time, to exist in the larger world of education and intellectual debates about politics, culture, and aesthetics. A visit to al-Alfiyya al-Thālitha does indeed demonstrate that writing in Tamazight has become a "civilizational act" that has succeeded at "rehabilitat[ing] an ancient language that represents North Africa's inhabitants' shared civilizational legacy."[155]

Tamazight's creation of a lifeworld in street signage, bookstores, and even storefronts represents a stark contradiction to the days when poets Azaykou and Mestaoui had to struggle against their deprivation of *awāl* (voice/

speech/language/authority). In 1978, Azaykou wrote a poem titled "*awāl*" (language/voice), whose narrator conveys deep internal suffering as a result of the state of siege under which Amazigh language and culture were placed:

Awāl inu gān Amazigh	[My language is Amazigh
Urtn īsn yān	which nobody knows
Kra nnānd igā tāwārgīt	some say it's a fiction
Īddū flnākh	and left us—alone]

However, instead of being discouraged by the ridiculing attitudes and lack of recognition of his language, the poet stresses his endurance and resilience, determined to continue speaking his language despite the repressive and unaccepting environment:

Awāl nnakh ūgln	[our language hangs
Izakarn gh-umggarḍ	fetters around its neck
Ilsinū ddrn ukān	yet my tongue is still alive
Ar ūkān sāwāln	and is still talking
Gr īḍrḍār ūr rmīn	tirelessly, among the deaf][156]

Similarly, Mestaoui reflected this state of repression in his 1991 poem "*manzān awāl*?" (where is language/voice?), which is a lyrical narration of the intergenerational questions about the absence of Amazigh language from Moroccan television programs. Staging a contrast between the state television station's coverage of news, ranging from AIDS to American alliances in the world, and the exclusion of Tamazight, the poet notes:

Mīsgā āgmā tamāzīght ūrāt zrrāgh	[but Tamazight, oh my brother, is not shown
Isaqsa wād mzzīyn bābās d-innās	the little one asked his father and also his mother
Innāyasn tamāzīght ūrāt zrrāgh	he told them I don't see Tamazight on TV
Innāyasn bābās āmṭṭā ārd iṭṭār	his father responds in tears
Sāqsāgh bābā llighā nsawāl dnkkīn	I also asked my father when I was little too
Isaqsā bābās sāqsānd innās	he had asked his father and his mother too
Tsaqsā innān dnttāt	his mother asked her mother too
Āmnshk nyān isaqsākh ghīn dūfān	and countless others asked their elders
Ūsrāsn nīn ūhū ūlā yāh fssān	silent, they are, responding neither no nor yes
Wānāygh isllān iḍṣā ārd āllān	but whoever hears us will laugh-cry][157]

The difference between the repression Azaykou and Mestaoui decried in their poetry and the central stage their work occupies in the cultural scene today is grand. It almost seems like their cultural production has taken its revenge on decades of systematic exclusion of Tamazight. Nevertheless, Tamazight has changed Moroccan consciousness thanks to the space MACM's activism has carved out for it in the public arena. Amazigh poetry, because of its sung nature, was and is still one of the most efficient media for Amazigh culture to battle Tamazight's rejection from the public arena in post-colonial Morocco.

Conclusion

MACM employed multiple strategies to establish Morocco's Amazigh identity, most notably through the (re)invention of tradition and the creation of a subversive memory that displaced Morocco's official history and identity in the public sphere. Historiographical action combined with work in memory and archive creation practices has culminated in a forceful exercise of Amazigh locational citizenship in the public sphere. The ingenuity and creativity of MACM's leaders allowed them to tap into the powerful potential of memory and (re)invented traditions to anchor Amazigh cultural identity in the spaces of Moroccan daily life. Although MACM's activism has won some of the movement's most significant demands, the future of these achievements looks bleak in light of recent governmental projects to establish *al-majlis al-waṭanī li-al-al-lughāt wa-al-thaqāfa al-maghribīyya* (the National Council for Moroccan Languages and Culture). The adoption of the bill which organizes this new council by the Moroccan parliament has ended RIAC's autonomy and subjected its most significant achievement in the last two decades to an Arab-dominated entity.[158] This organization's very existence is dictated by the need to take away RIAC's ability to initiate projects in favor of Tamazight within the very limited space of maneuver it enjoyed as an autonomous institution. As all its prerogatives are subsumed within the National Council for Languages and Culture, RIAC has lost its financial and administrative autonomy, which heretofore allowed it to write its laws and bylaws, establish hiring processes, and manage its annual budget.[159] RIAC has now become a mere directorate, which means that its freedom of initiative is curtailed and its ability to make decisions is limited. It remains to be seen how MACM member associations will navigate the arduous challenges that lie ahead and, most importantly, how they will re-signify and repurpose their own activist past. They will have to combat the state's noxious efforts to take back the spaces Amazigh activists have spent years fighting for.

Connected to MACM's historical and other-archiving practices is the place that Moroccan Jews should occupy in the history of the nation. The next chapter examines the resurgence of Morocco's Jewish past in the rich novelistic output that constitutes what I theorize as mnemonic literature. In the same way that Azaykou called for the interrogation of topography and toponymies to rewrite Moroccan history, mnemonic literature has been the site of writing and rewriting Morocco's Jewish-Muslim post-colonial past.

2
Emplaced Memories of Jewish-Muslim Morocco

Boy 1: "What are those two guys doing walking around here?"
Boy 2: "It's obvious. They're looking for the Jews."
[. . .] Youness and I had not come to look for the Jews; we had come to look for the traces they left behind.

—MICHAEL FRANK, *In Morocco, "Exploring Remnants of Jewish History"* (2015)

This conversation took place in the city of Fez between two Moroccan children as *New York Times* journalist Michael Frank and his Moroccan guide, Youness, were visiting the Jewish quarters—also known as the *mellah*—in Fez in 2015. As the conversation clearly indicates, the two children assumed that Frank and Youness were looking for Moroccan Jews rather than for traces of their former existence. Whether the two children were right or wrong in their assumptions about Frank and Youness's visit, their conversation reveals their awareness of the memory of place that informs this chapter's analysis of mnemonic literature's representations of Morocco's silenced Jewish history.[1] Although the majority of Morocco's Jewish communities had not lived in their homeland for almost six decades, these two children talked about their vestiges in the country as though Jews were still physically part of the Moroccan present. This chapter investigates the ways in which mnemonic literature, as both a medium of remembering and a site for the observation of social memory, recovers and communicates memories of place to reimagine and other-archive the post-colonial Jewish past in Morocco.

Instead of reading novels about Moroccan Jews as historical fiction, I place them under the category of mnemonic literature. A translation of the

Arabic phrase al-kitāba al-dākhirātiyya, mnemonic literature is not about memory tricks as its name in English would indicate. It is rather a type of writing that draws on memory, whether experienced firsthand or inherited intergenerationally. It addresses loss and creates conditions for the recovery of insufficiently documented pasts and to account for severed relationships. Megan O'Grady has stressed the fact that historical fiction tells stories about a past that is "forged at the place at which the archives end and the author's imagination begins."[2] The insinuation here is that historical fiction is based on some sort of archives that the novelist enriches with their imagination. O'Grady does, however, make a significant point in underlining the unevenness of access to history. She writes that "[i]f history belongs to the victors, it's generally fallen to everyone else—the women, the colonized or enslaved, those on the other side of wars and walls—to subvert conventional understanding of it, to make up for the burned or redacted documents, the missing transcripts and the experiences that were never recorded in the first place."[3] Mnemonic literature, unlike historical fiction, addresses a situation where both absence and silence are the norm. Absence of the people whose stories are represented, and silence of historical records over the processes that created their absence in the first place. Accounting for traumas engendered by both silence and disappearance, mnemonic literature does not just fictionalize—it reinvents a history that, in the context of generalized fear during the Years of Lead, was considered taboo and too dangerous to uncover. Furthermore, mnemonic literature is inherently linked to memory, which means that the past recovered in novels still has a strong impact on living historical actors or their family members. After all, archives are not made available or accessible because silence protects the officials who were involved in the way this history unfolded. The way in which mnemonic literature fills the historical and archival voids while navigating repression and archival silences distinguishes it from historical fiction.

The number of Moroccan Jews decreased dramatically between 1956 and 2020. According to *The New York Times*, "as many as 240,000 Jews lived in Morocco as recently as the 1940s, [but] only around 3,000 remain in the country today [2015]."[4] Moroccan Jews had indeed started leaving the country even before the founding of the State of Israel in 1948, but the majority, meaning over 180,000 people, left only after independence in 1956.[5] The impact of this emigration was felt throughout Morocco, especially in areas inhabited by both Jews and Muslims. Simon Lévy, a Moroccan Jewish scholar and politician, observed a "notable [demographic] change" in "certain cities and rural villages," as "entire villages were emptied" of their Jews.[6] Omar Mounir, a scholar and jurist, has written that "as paradoxical as this may seem, the departure of Jews, which mostly happened in the 1960s, occurred in anguish for all."[7] As these testimonies indicate, the termination of a Jewish-Muslim Morocco whose existence lasted for millennia was one of the many losses inflicted on Moroccans by the dislocation of their Jewish co-citizens. This loss is exacerbated by local historiographical disinterest in the study of Moroccan Jews, thus pushing younger Moroccan novelists and filmmakers to return to the past in order to both uncover and recover the overlooked traces that have a national significance for this Jewish-Muslim Morocco.

Scholarly pessimism has been a corollary of the physical absence of thousands of Jews from Morocco and the prevalence of historical and national amnesia regarding their past. Scholars Samir Ben-Layashi and Bruce Maddy-Weitzman reflect this pessimism by writing that "one can only wonder how future generations of Moroccans will come to view the country's Jewish legacy," given the lack of institutional and social engagement with its memory.[8] Simon Lévy criticizes the institutional and historiographical void left by the loss of Moroccan Jews, going so far as to hazard that Moroccans have forgotten the meaning of the word "Jews."[9] Echoing similar concerns, historians Emily Gottreich and Daniel Schroeter lament younger Maghrebis' lack of knowledge about Jewish-Muslim life in the Maghreb.[10] Moreover, Aomar Boum, a scholar of Moroccan Judaism, has blamed the rise of antisemitism among younger Moroccans on the absence of any lived experience of Jewish-Muslim life.[11] While this justified pessimism over the future treatment of Moroccan Jews and Jewish-Muslim Moroccan history is well-founded, memory and cultural production attendant to it, such as mnemonic literature, a fast-growing subgenre of Moroccan literature entirely dedicated to reactualizing the life of Moroccan Jews over the last three decades, complicate issues of amnesia and historiographical engagement with this painful past. Creative writing and cinematography have opened breaches into the solid walls of thought that have cemented this scholarly pessimism, raising crucial questions about the role of literature as an other-archive that emplaces the departed Jews in both memory and reimagined sources of a history-in-becoming.

Indeed, mnemonic literature, which has uncannily escaped the attention of these very meticulous social scientists, has formed a clearly defined literary corpus within Moroccan literature in French and Arabic. Strongly embedded in the intergenerational transference of memories, the novels that constitute this literary subgenre recreate a Morocco that existed before the collective dislocation of its Jews between 1948 and 1967. The novelistic output that constitutes this corpus is larger and richer than what one chapter can hold. Thus, to create a more manageable volume of mnemonic literature to work with,

I draw solely on El Hassane Aït Moh's *Le Captif de Mabrouka* (*Mabrouka's Captive*), Mohamed Ezzeddine Tazi's *Anā al-mansī* (*I Am the Forgotten*), Driss Miliani's *Casanfa*, and Hassan Aourid's *Cintra*, which all recover and inscribe, albeit in fictional terms, a portion of Morocco's anecdotally known Jewish past.[12] These novels draw on emplaced memories to bring back to existence the sounds, voices, smells, and broken connections that have yet to interest Moroccan academic history.[13]

Although part of a larger literary and cinematographic trend that has been reshaping Jewish-Muslim pasts in the Maghreb and the Middle East,[14] mnemonic literature has emerged from Moroccan society's need to grapple with what I am calling "the forbidden zones" (*al-manāṭiq al-muḥarrama*)—that is, the taboo topics of post-independence history, which encompass Amazigh history, Jewish emigration, state violence, and race and racism, among other issues. As far as the Jewish dimension of these forbidden zones, every Moroccan coming of age after the 1960s is confronted with a paradox between the material existence of 167 entirely Jewish sites in the country's forty governorates and the silence about their significance in history classes.[15] Even a connoisseur of Moroccan history such as historian Ibrahim Boutaleb has had to underline that Moroccan historiography has not given the departed Jewish community the scholarly attention its contributions to the nation deserve.[16] Confronting both taboos and silence, mnemonic literature textually recuperates Moroccan Jews from oblivion and describes the contexts that allowed their mass exodus as well as the losses that resulted from their emigration. Memories of place in mnemonic literature restore forgotten Jewish pasts and create an other-archive—a midway between history and archive—of a Jewish-Muslim life that has long resided outside of official Moroccan and academic histories.[17] Whereas the rituals of powerful and self-restrained historiography have flattened the image of the Moroccan Jew to an immutable being who remains nearly unchanged by the passage of time, mnemonic literature complicates the story and depicts the multiple facets of this historical subject who acts, wills, and moves through time. Because academic historians have not been able to stay abreast of the societal and cultural awakening taking place in Morocco vis-à-vis its Jewish-Muslim past, mnemonic literature is charting new paths for historical research on this taboo topic, one that has for so long resided outside the purview of post-colonial academic historians.

Mnemonic Literature as Microhistory/Memory of Jewish Places

In the 1980s, French historian Pierre Nora argued that "there are *lieux de mémoire*, sites of memory, because there are no longer *milieux de mémoire*, real environments of memory."[18] That is, *milieux de mémoire* (authentic environments of memory) are places where memory is lived, experienced, and transmitted intergenerationally, while *lieux de mémoire* (sites of memory) are contrived spaces in which the desire not to forget finds its embodiment in objects of memory.[19] Moroccan mnemonic literature functions as a site of memory, and it aims to remedy the void left by the lack of an authentic Jewish-Muslim environment of memory as well as the absence of historical archives attendant to this lack of firsthand experience. Specifically, the disappearance of Moroccan Jews from the nationscape and the resulting quasi-impossibility of an intergenerational formation of Jewish-Muslim memories in the present day have turned place into a historical record.[20] In this context, the text is a site where both representation and recovery of histories of Jewish places occur. Literary texts are not only media and objects of remembrance, as Astrid Erll and Ann Rigney have argued, but also media "for observing the production of cultural memory."[21] In our case, mnemonic literature unearths an overlooked past, documents and unsilences it, and then makes a statement about the absence of Moroccan Jews from post-independence history, principally through its refiguring of the places that both Jews and Muslims inhabited before Jewish emigration between 1948 and 1967.

Mnemonic literature's reconstruction and reimagination of Moroccan Jews' existence across different times and places, specifically through *memories* of place evokes the work of practitioners of microhistory. Microhistorians unearth the anomalous, abnormal, and atypical aspects of the past in order to reveal realities that would have otherwise been excised from the historical narrative.[22] Their focus on topics that are marginal to traditional history allows microhistorians to rehabilitate individual stories without losing sight of the larger significance of the historical actors' "actions, behavior, social structures, roles and relationships."[23] Moreover, when novelistic endeavors take micro-level communities as their objects for writing history—be they villages, neighborhoods, nuclear households, or extended families—they benefit from place's disposition to convey "identity, character, nuance, [and] history."[24] Connections between mnemonic literature and microhistory are not only linked through the latter's origination in the former, but also, to borrow historian Beverley Southgate's words in another context, are characterized by "interrelatedness and interdependence and the borderlands they share."[25] Similarly to the microhistorian, the writer of mnemonic literature has to write a larger history from fragmented documents, if any, and abundant memories to create a fuller and more complicated picture of historical events.

Given the state of historical research, which has not made much progress regarding the history of Jews in post-colonial Morocco, literature serves as a space for the documentation of a topic for which there are no official or openly accessible archives. As microhistorian Giovanni Levi writes regarding the genre of the picaresque novel, it "raises the problem of documenting that which leaves no documents behind," alongside the potential to "present the previously unrepresented."[26] As already mentioned, the departure of Moroccan Jews and the losses that ensued from it have eluded professional historians' attention.[27] Moroccan academic historians have claimed a lack of archival documentation to justify their reluctance to write post-1956 history, which, however, is not merely limited to Jews.[28] In the face of this historiographical disinterest, literature creates other-archives, which can potentially make up for the absent or the not-yet-available official archive. Southgate has claimed that despite historians' disagreements, "fiction has always provided useful material, especially for social and cultural historians."[29] According to Southgate, fiction has always proven useful "to extend the parameters of history's interests and concerns."[30] So, in the absence of historical investigation, mnemonic literature producers have taken on the tasks of remembrance, documentation, and, in sum, other-archiving that are necessary to write a history of this erasure. Rather than wait for Moroccan academic historians to write evidence-based histories of Morocco's Jewish post-colonial history, authors of mnemonic literature retrieve memories of place to consign this imagined past to writings that occupy a space between history, memory, and archives—an other-archive for the present and the future history of the Moroccan nation. Even the nature of the document in this context is different. Rather than a paper-focused documentation, and similarly to Ali Azaykou's aforementioned theorizations in Chapter 1, landscape and place are interrogated to form the archives historians complain do not exist. In emplacing Jewish pasts across Morocco's variegated geographies, mnemonic literature draws attention to the potential histories that the examination of topographies and onomastics could yield.

Fictionalized Microhistories of Place of Jewish Morocco

Le Captif de Mabrouka, or Home as a Place to Remember and to Be Remembered

Because of its microfocus, mnemonic literature's retrieval of histories of place happens on a smaller, more familiar scale, turning domestic places into objects of memory and historical rehabilitation. Investigating home as the archive of a finished time in Indian history in *Dwelling in the Archive: Women Writing House, Home, and History in Late Colonial India*, Antoinette Burton suggests that, in the Indian subcontinent, the struggle between nationalists and colonialism over the home has transformed it into an archive.[31] The three women authors that Burton studies write memoirs and novels to record the history and produce an archive of a place that is about to disappear. Burton's primary goal in theorizing the house-as-archive is "to engage the problem of who counts as a historian, what archives look like, and why memories of house and home should be recognized as crucial to what we think of as the historical imagination."[32] Countering the predominant conceptions of archive and history, memories of home-as-archive deconstruct gendered and power-laden historiographies. Burton also rightly takes issue with the male-dominated definitions as to who counts as a reliable source on the past.[33] Thus, Burton carves out an important space for novels and homes to be approached both as archives and histories. Burton's propositions guide us to see how the historiographical agency of mnemonic literature's writers produces a history of loss of Moroccan Jews, among other communities, through memories of place.

Le Captif de Mabrouka, El Hassane Aït Moh's debut novel, tells the story of two Moroccan-born, foreign-raised individuals. Both Richard D. and Walter Baroukh Kinston were born in the city of Ouarzazate, but their parents relocated abroad when they were still children. Richard's parents were French cooperants who taught French language in the only high school in Ouarzazate and were forced to return to France due to Morocco's repressive political climate in the 1960s.[34] Walter was the child of Moroccan Jews who emigrated first to Israel/Palestine and then to the United States. In the novel, these two characters return to Morocco around the same time to reclaim their childhood house. The house that both Richard and Walter seek to buy had belonged to Walter's parents before they sold it to Richard's parents upon emigrating to Israel/Palestine in 1960s. Richard's parents, in turn, sold the house to a wealthy Muslim merchant named Lhaj Lahoussine.

Le Captif de Mabrouka interlaces the varied histories of the house into intergenerational memories of emigration, nostalgia, and longing. In doing so, the novel reveals the complex local histories of Ouarzazate, which is home to Greek nationals, French cooperants and soldiers, and a now-vanished Jewish population. Although Ouarzazate is a marginal city, located at the periphery of the Moroccan centers of Rabat, Casablanca, and Marrakesh, it emerges in *Le Captif de Mabrouka* as a converging point for destinies of Moroccans of different faiths. Basing the story of shared memory on the house allows the novel to resuscitate a web of relationships that the characters share with each other without necessarily having had any synchronous existence in the same place. The house, named Mabrouka (the blessed one), serves as a focal point for the intersection of histories of departure and return, involving descendants of Moroccan Jews and French colonizers. As the histories of the different families that owned and occupied Mabrouka in the past emerge in the novel, so too does another story, this time of overlooked entanglements between local memories and histories of colonialism, decolonization, and the struggle to cling to a past that is not yet past in the city of Ouarzazate.

Just as the mellah structures the memories and lives of the characters in Mohamed Ezzeddine Tazi's novel *Anā al-mansī*, as we will see later in this chapter, the house, Mabrouka, is the pivot where the lives of the characters converge and create a recoverable archive of Jewish-Muslim existence in Ouarzazate.[35] Only the connection to the house, which Lahoussine has transformed into an affordable motel for the homeless and poor, is the thread that links these characters together. Each character's claim to a piece or a period of history in the house rests on his personal or inherited memories about the place. In the eyes of the characters, neither its charitable status nor its dilapidated state has erased the house's mnemonic significance. In fact, Mabrouka is an archival site for the characters, who come back to find the ultimate thread that would allow them to reconnect with their roots. In doing so, they allow the telling of previously untold stories about the intertwinement of Jewish emigration, disappearance, failure, and trauma in Morocco.

Aït Moh's novel also records how globalization and neoliberalism impact historical intermediaries due to urbanization decisions that further peripheralize the impoverished sections of society. Erasure of local lore does not seem to present any issue for the authorities who decide to cleanse the city of its poor and marginalized population in order to accommodate the cinema and touristic industries for which the city is known. The expulsion of the dwellers of Café Mabrouka means that part of the knowledge about the city will be lost. Charjane, the former art teacher in high school, is a prime example of this loss. Not only was Charjane friends with Richard's parents, but he was bequeathed with a box of documents that will unlock a part of Richard's own past and the complex relationship between his now-deceased father and Morocco. While passing the box down to Richard, Charjane tells him, "I have been waiting for Bernard's return. For many years [. . .], I have kept this box scrupulously. This is the only remnant of him, but I never dared to open it."[36] Charjane functions in the novel as what psychologist Jacques Hassoun calls "smugglers of memory," these individuals who mediate between the past and the present.[37] Hassoun firmly states that all humans are carriers of concentric histories of a unique biography that is forged in a place or a civilization. In fact, the rich history that is the object of recuperation, recovery, writing, and rewriting into a manuscript in *Le Captif de Mabrouka* hinges on intermediaries, like Charjane, who occupy a position in the dregs of society. This is a conceptual space where historical narratives are made from below, but whose fragile existence leads to more loss.

The microcosm of the house also serves to recreate a nation-family in whose history both Richard D. and Walter Baroukh Kinston can belong. In the physical absence of any Jewish population, the oral histories about the house serve as proof of belonging, which allow Richard and Walter to rejoin a community of citizens from which they were severed during their childhood. Thus, both Richard and Walter's need to return to Morocco to reappropriate the physical house indicates the insufficiency of what ethnographer Joëlle Bahloul calls "symbolic roots," namely in their ability to come to terms with the memories and traumas of deracination in exile.[38] Houses do indeed hold the genealogical and biographical history of a family, but Mabrouka is a metaphor for the nation's history as well. This aspect of the house can be discerned in Richard's statement that he shares "this house, or to be more precise, the past of this house" with the other characters in the novel.[39] The shared house, then, transcends its purely physical existence and serves as a bond that buttresses memory and grants both familiarity with and belonging to the larger body of the nation. The house's symbolism is explicitly stated at the end of the novel: "O Mabrouka, Moroccan land, source of my life, you are the sacred place where ties have been interwoven, where destinies have intersected; you are the venerable land where lives intertwined, where destinies of men and women were united."[40] In contrast to these nostalgic words of praise, destinies were also dis-united, fragmented, and unraveled on this much-celebrated land. Nonetheless, the longing and recognition that Richard and Walter receive from their recovered co-citizens somehow leads to the dissipation of the forgetting that has prevailed over their existence in the recent Moroccan past. Both Richard and Walter end up being accepted as part of the local community, all without forgetting to allude to the impact the transformation of the house into a fancy guest house will trigger.

Public Micro-Places of Morocco's Jewish History

In addition to the house, public places play a crucial role in mnemonic literature's recovering of Morocco's Jewish past. Several of these novels, specifically *Anā al-mansī*, *Casanfa*, and *Cintra*, unfold in contained places, such as bars, cafes, synagogues, and neighborhoods. This allows the daily interactions of the characters to bear witness to those who used to inhabit or populate them but are no longer there. The mellah, or the Jewish quarters, is one of the main places mnemonic literature writers use to recover the infinitesimal details of the once-exuberant Jewish life in Morocco. Though historians agree that the mellah was only an exception in Morocco's integrative cartography, where both Jews and Muslims tended to live in the same neighborhoods,[41] *Anā al-mansī* makes the mellah a focal point of Jewish life in Fez in pre-1967 Morocco.

Anā al-mansī is an intergenerational saga that spans the colonial period to the June War in 1967. Plotted around the story of Hārūn bin 'Imrān Kūhīn's family, *Anā al-mansī* recounts stories of the Jews of Fez as they face internal and external challenges that lead to their emigration and ultimate vanishing from Morocco. The mnemonic agenda is all too clear in the novel's title: *I Am the Forgotten*. In foregrounding *al-mansī* (the one who is forgotten), Tazi anchors the narratives in the politics of history and memory in post-colonial Morocco. Depicting the intergenerational changes in the family throughout the colonial and post-independence periods, the novel follows its Jewish characters' trajectories as they slowly sever their ties with the mellah and embark on transnational emigration experiences beyond Morocco. In an act of metanarration within the novel, Ibn 'Amitha'īl, the novel's ageless and omnipresent narrator, remarks that despite the diversity of "their backgrounds, desires, and behaviors," the characters in *Anā al-mansī* "converge in the fulcrum of events lived by Moroccan Jews, in the mellah of Fez and in their shared past and living memory."[42] In fact, *Anā al-mansī* uses the forgotten (*al-mansī*) to recall a rich Jewish existence in Fez before depicting the long-term historical process that led to its attrition and the end of Jewish life in the mellah, namely: the creation of the state of Israel in 1948; the end of the French Protectorate in 1956; and the June 1967 War. Moreover, these processes are depicted as causing deep tensions between the older generation of Moroccan Jews, who remain attached to Morocco, and the younger one, who imagine their lives elsewhere and are ready to leave.

The use of the mellah as a microcosm inscribes the loss of Jews into this environment that is often associated with their life in Morocco. This reimagined mellah is contained enough to serve as a witness to the transformations that accelerated the depletion of Moroccan Jewry imprinted on the identity of the place. *Anā al-mansī* records the changes that took place in the mellah after 1967:

> Life in the mellah of Fez is not as it used to be after the departure of the Jews. The famous Hārūn Apartment Building is inhabited by Muslims who occupied all the apartments after they found them empty and used incense to expel the smell of Jews from them, as they said. The nails, chains, tar, and insecticides shop has become a snack shop

> that offers *ḥarsha* (cornbread), crepes, and curdled milk to those who stop by its doors to order something to eat or drink. Raḥamīm's bar in Dār Dbibagh has become a shop for men's and women's shoes.[43]

As a result of these transformations, the City of Fez renamed the Jewish quarters *Ḥayy al-Marīniyyīn*, the Merinid neighborhood, in reference to the "Merinid Prince who was the first to have advocated for the creation of special quarters for Jews: the mellahs."[44] According to Victor Malka, "by creating a distance between Jewish and Muslim agglomerations, this Sultan thought that he was acting on the best interest of the Jews, by isolating them in a neighborhood in which they would be safer."[45] *Anā al-mansī*, however, disrupts this official, amnesia-facilitating move and returns *Ḥayy al-Marīniyyīn* to its original name, *al-mallāḥ*. This re-renaming of the six-century-old urban landmark underscores place's crucial role in memorializing Jewish existence in Morocco.

Mnemonic literature's mobilization of histories of places is in dialogue with a rich theorization of landscape's historical functions. Landscape is not merely a material space where we, humans, evolve, but is also "the richest historical record we possess."[46] Place's malleability and transformability over time are in themselves the qualities that allow it to become a historical record. By tracing changes to policies and reconstructing the circumstances in which a place was renamed or a street erased from the cartography of a city, we are not only able to learn about place, but also to understand the broader dynamics in which transformations in the landscape take place. A prime example of how place both holds and responds to history can be found in the odonymic transformations that took place in Berlin after World War II to erase the traces of Nazism.[47] South African cities have also undergone a significant amount of renaming in the post-apartheid era.[48] Renaming is usually a sign of a major political change that institutes a *rupture* between two eras in a nation's history. Therefore, acts of naming and renaming that ensue from political change transform the landscape into a palimpsest, one into which histories of spatial politics and attitudes vis-à-vis constituencies of the nation are inscribed. Moroccan mnemonic literature is no different in that it captures a moment of liberation from historical taboos, and it further reflects a determination to terminate the psychological barrier that prevented Moroccans from openly engaging with a problematic portion of their history.

The mnemonic and historical stakes of place renaming are openly addressed in *Anā al-mansī*. The durability of Jewish existence in Morocco is written in stone, and no act of name changing can entirely induce its forgetting. As Ibn 'Amithā'īl recounts, "Even the name of the mellah was erased.

The quarter has been named Ḥayy al-Marīniyyīn. Despite this erasure, Jewish memory will not be forgotten because it is imbued with the tattoos that have left their imprint on it."[49] The use of the words *maḥw* (erasing), *dhākira* (memory), and *lā tunsā* (cannot be forgotten) all indicate the centrality of the dialectic between official *nisyān* (amnesia/forgetfulness) and *tadhakkur* (agentive remembering), which the novel undertakes. Historian Mohammed Kably writes: "The mellah, as a traditional Jewish space, has disappeared."[50] However, Jewish memory, expressed through place, is not fleeting. Indeed, Ibn ʿAmithā'īl insists that this memory is indelible because it is deeper than what authorities have attempted to erase. Thus, the act of remembering the past of this neighborhood and repopulating it with Jews subverts amnesia and re-places Jews as an important constituent of Moroccan urban topography. In doing so, it turns the re-renaming, recreation, and repopulation of the mellah with its original Jewish dwellers into an act of historiographical agency and mnemonic dissidence, all by opposing the act of official forgetting that is a corollary of the renaming. Landscape, according to anthropologist Alan Rumsey, is the "main locus of social memory, with both myth and history inscribed in [it]."[51] *Anā al-mansī*'s recreation of forgotten Jewish toponymies undertakes the project of both redefining Moroccan social memory and exhuming histories still hidden in city- and village-scapes. Place's ability to defy erasure is clearly observed by the two Moroccan children quoted in the epigraph that began this chapter. Jews seem locatable for these children as long as there is a place that refers to their former existence in the country, despite their physical dislocation from the post-independence nation-state.

The focus on place in *Anā al-mansī* also recovers the richness of life in the mellah. Instead of depicting the mellah as an insular, purely Jewish, closed universe, the novel reveals its multidirectional openness to its surrounding environment, a nexus of a vibrant social and cultural life.[52] The bar, because of its openness to both Muslims and non-Muslims, is a place of memory *par excellence* where Jews and Muslims shared pasts that are now fictionalized in mnemonic literature. For instance, Raḥamīm's bar, despite its location within the mellah, is described as being frequented by even more Muslims than Jews.[53] This multidirectionality is what allows Muslims to engage in activities that are prohibited by Islamic/Moroccan law, such as drinking alcohol and gambling, which again shows the mellah's ecumenical nature. The narrator of *Anā al-mansī* describes the mellah as:

> Having a complete social life. Stores, butcher's shops, and grocery shops as well as bars and brothels were opened. A pharmacy came later. There was security. The inhabitants of the Mellah included the

> noble and evil, the happy and miserable, the satisfied and greedy, the patient and complainers, the sick and healthy, the serious and nonchalant, the lovers of the soul and of the body, the usurers and indebted, those who frequent bars and those who frequent their [spiritual] inside, the employed and jobless, the crazy and sane, barren and fertile women, the sick and healthy, the old and fit. All this is normal. But urban life has also infused the quarter, and in every aspect it has achieved distinction among all the neighborhoods in Fez.[54]

In this sense, the mellah of Fez represents a microcosm of Moroccan life in which characters are depicted with all their successes, frustrations, defeats, betrayals, and internecine conflicts. Restaurants, cabarets, and cafes in the mellah are loci of Jewish existence as well as sites of memory formation between the two communities.[55]

Unlike *Anā al-mansī*, which unfolds in the larger space of the mellah, both *Casanfa* and *Cintra* take place in the iconoclastic space of the bar as a mnemonic site. Furthermore, both novels derive their names from colonial-era Casablanca bars, which play a counterintuitive role in these reimagined memories of place.

The larger urban space of Casablanca is the object of archiving in Driss Miliani's novel *Casanfa*. The novel recounts the story of Casablanca—and Morocco by association—from the early years of the Protectorate in 1912 through independence, from the perspective of a Moroccan Jew. Before his mysterious disappearance, the thirty-year-old Jewish character Isḥāq Abitbol bequeaths his older brother Ya'qūb a box, which he, in turn, passes down to his Muslim neighbor Yūsuf al-Fāṭimī. When al-Fāṭimī opens the box, he discovers a manuscript entitled *Casanfabar*, which serves as the meat of the novel narrated within *Casanfa*. *Casanfabar* unfolds mainly in the closed spaces of cafes and bars in Casablanca, including its namesake, and chronicles the author's thoughts and reactions to events in the outside world as he hops from one bar to another.

The significance of the *ṣundūq* (box) is amply discussed by al-Fāṭīmi before he dares to open Abitbol's *amāna* (something with which one is entrusted). In fact, *ṣunqūd* in Arabic usually evokes treasures and hidden things that become the subject of a quest to be discovered or found, and *amāna* is synonymous with integrity and moral rectitude, which are prerequisite for trust. Thus, as al-Fāṭimī ponders the box, he remembers other boxes that have historical significance and inscribes Abitbol's story in a larger Arab-Islamic history. Al-Fāṭimī suddenly realizes that the box was "a little coffin in which lay a living-dead and a dead-living [person] who has neither a tomb nor a shroud."[56]

Only his curiosity about the life that is hidden in the box warrants breaking its privacy and opening it, the narrator noting that it is not "just a normal box made of ebony, but a history that does not age, and a deep past and a present memory and an absent subjecthood identity."[57] The maker of the box is named Māḥī al-Ṣwīrī.[58] The word *māḥī* in Arabic means the person who erases something. Yet the paradox here is that it is the box made by Māḥī that holds the manuscript that becomes the novel. Between the act of entrusting the box, the curiosity it takes to open it, and the reminiscence on the interrelatedness of death and memory and history, *Casanfa* sets the stage for a powerful other-archive of Casablanca through a reimagined Jewish experience.

Casanfabar anchors a Moroccan-Jewish past in place. Not only does the Jewish author of *Casanfabar* register his observations of the city, but he inscribes his journal within the Jewish calendar, thus adding another temporality to the history that is recounted in his manuscript. The novel starts on 12 *Tīshrī* 5721, which is the equivalent of October 3, 1960. The Casablanca described in the novel is thus lived through Jewish time and calendar dates rather than Islamic or Gregorian ones. Not only does the reader of *Casanfa* have to read a portion of Moroccan history through a Hebraic temporality, but the novel also forces them to account for the voice of the Jewish author who addresses them from beyond their disappearance. Given the uncertainty about whether Isḥāq Abitbol wrote *Casanfabar*, the novel can be read as the voice of any Jewish resident of Casablanca of Abitbol's age. Whether it is Abitbol or someone else who authored *Casanfabar*, the ambiguity about its internal authorship allows the novel to speak to a collective experience of transformation and disillusion with the post-independence state, feelings that facilitated later processes of Jewish dispersion. Identity issues aside, the manuscript's author is multilingual, aware of Morocco's Amazigh and Arabic identity. He announces that the manuscript is only a blueprint for "the picture of 'tāddārt' (Amazigh for home), 'al-dār al-baydāt' [sic] (Casablanca), and 'tāmūrt' (homeland)."[59] The use of tāddārt and tamūrt specifically reconnect with Amazigh discourses about Jewish-Amazigh indigeneity to Tamazgha or the broader North Africa, revealing, in the meantime, how the novelistic medium is in conversation with and reflects the ongoing debates about *amzrūy* (history) from an Amazigh perspective.

Hassan Aourid's novel *Cintra* conjoins the story of Moroccan nationalism with Jewish emigration through the protagonist 'Umar Binmanṣūr's unconventional life story. The novel traces Binmanṣūr's trajectory from the time he was a young translator in the colonial administration through the 2003 terrorist attacks in Casablanca. The novel takes place in a hospital room, where a political scientist joins a physician to help Binmanṣūr regain consciousness after he slips into a coma. Vital to the story's development, Binmanṣūr's coma is brought on by his visit to Cintra Bar, a site of memory, which he had not visited in sixty years. The retrieval of Binmanṣūr's consciousness, which requires him to revisit his experiences of the 1940s, in fact also preserves the memories that he had never consigned to writing. As the novel evolves, we learn about Sulaika Uḥayyūn, Binmanṣūr's Jewish wife from decades ago. Uḥayyūn emigrated to Palestine in 1947, in the midst of Binmanṣūr's involvement in nationalist endeavors to achieve Morocco's independence, but his family knows nothing about her existence in his life. The parallels between Binmanṣūr's repression of this episode of his personal history and the existence of an unknown portion of Moroccan history cannot be any clearer. *Cintra*, however, builds on the silences to uncover the Jewish-Muslim past in Casablanca through the story of Cintra Bar.

In Arab-Amazigh cultures, alcohol and intoxication are usually associated with forgetting and with the desire to block out episodes from one's current or past life. However, bars in *Casanfa* and *Cintra* emerge as a catalyst of profound memories. In both *Casanfa* and *Cintra*, the bar helps to access and register the past. What makes bars even more interesting in terms of memory is their status as heterotopic spaces in Muslim lands[60]—no-man's-lands where all communities are welcome regardless of their religious and social backgrounds. This heterotopic nature of bars is described by Raḥamīm, a Zionist informant of the French authorities and owner of a successful bar in the mellah of Fez depicted in *Anā al-mansī*, who tells employees to be careful when they serve his clients because "Jews and Muslims, nationalists and traitors, come to the bar."[61] *Cintra* specifically digs into the history of Cintra Bar which, at first glance, may not seem to have any relevance to present-day Morocco, but in reality is enmeshed in memories of colonialism, nascent nationalism, and Jewish-Muslim collaborations across class, religious, and ethnic lines in the mid-1940s.

The Jewish narrator of *Casanfabar* is more eloquent in his description of the importance of the bars as sites of memory in Morocco.[62] Adopting a metanalytical position, Isḥāq Abitbol describes the importance of bars in Moroccan society during his time: "It should be mentioned that during these years bars and brasseries were the places that Casablanca residents and elites visited the most [. . .] Not only did these bars witness the formation of the most beautiful memories as well as the penning of these pages of memory, but it is also there that this amnesic narrator regained his consciousness."[63] The mnemonic importance of the bar is such that the author of *Casanfabar* writes the entire manuscript in different bars throughout the city. Bars are central to the manuscript's identity, since every chapter is entitled with the name of the bar in which it was written. Each bar—Maqhā Bāb Mrraksh, Sphinx Bar, Maqhā Les Arches, Maqhā La Presse, al-Dīyk al-Dhahabī, and others—inspires a story, a lost event, an incident that has fallen into oblivion, which the author tenaciously recovers in detail so as to portray a Jewish past that still eludes the majority of Moroccans in the present. Bars thus serve as a medium to reimagine a bygone past during which both Jews and Muslims evolved and shared the same space of the nation.

A state of inebriation enabled by the bar also amplifies the powerful political statements made by the author of *Casanfabar*. Inebriation, like Binmanṣūr's coma in *Cintra*, places a person outside the realm of law and creates a space in which they may say things a fully conscious person would be too inhibited to state publicly. Therefore, the bar in *Casanfa* acts as a pretext for scathing criticism of Moroccan authorities, society, and political parties for letting the Jews leave. This unrestricted criticism reaches its apogee in the last section of the novel. The narrator simply accuses Moroccan authorities of exchanging the departure of Moroccan Jews for American wheat and a modest amount of funds. Abitbol's manuscript states: "Many other Jews were in a 'state of expectation,' perplexed and regretful to see thousands of their coreligionists being taken into buses, planes, and ships in order to deport them in exchange for twenty-five dollars per each Jew. This didn't take place at the hands of Christian, crusader enemies but at the hands of Caids and Pashas and other ignorant administrators [. . .] The Jews were sold in exchange for barley and American wheat during the lean years of drought."[64] This passage is reminiscent of arguments Moroccan writer Saïd Ghallab proposed in the 1960s to bring attention to the far-reaching impact Jewish emigration would have on Morocco. In 1965, Ghallab made a precocious allusion to the Moroccan government's bartering of Jewish emigration for receipt of American donations, later used in the political struggle that pitted the monarchy against the leftist opposition, particularly the National Union of Popular Forces (NUPF). Ghallab has written that "this depopulation campaign [meaning Jewish emigration] and the total nakedness and impoverishment that came with it have helped the authorities establish a feudal and reactionary party FDCI—the Front for the Defense of Constitutional Institutions—thanks to the distribution of American wheat and milk to the poor populations of Tafilalet."[65] Ghallab's allegations would later be supported by Zakya Daoud, who wrote that Moroccan Jews' "departure agreement was negotiated against American wheat," a fact that historian Abdallah Laroui underlines is in total coherence with King Hassan II's "legitimist convictions."[66] Simon Lévy, the former director of the Museum of Moroccan Judaism and one of the last prominent Jewish figures in the country until his death in 2001, also alluded to a similar conclusion in declaring to Moroccan-Canadian filmmaker Kathy Wazana: "The King (Mohamed V) said: 'Don't leave; you are my children, stay.' At the same time, it was State-owned buses, trains, boats and airplanes that carried and had exclusive contracts to transport Jews away from their homeland."[67]

In addition to questioning any facile narratives about the emigration of Moroccan Jews, *Casanfabar*'s sharp and forthright criticism addresses the larger issue of who counts as a citizen in Morocco. For instance, the rambling narrator chronicles different types of discrimination faced by Jews, including their inability to serve in the army or hold a passport.[68] In attempting to rehabilitate the important aspects of Jewish memory in Morocco, the novel sometimes becomes a chronicle of the author's disillusionment as he bears witness to the rapidly disintegrating world around him. Ultimately, however, he resorts to the past as a source of legitimacy by reminding his readers about the contributions of the Jewish community to Morocco's recent history. The narrator, for instance, recounts the story of the founder of the Moroccan Communist Party, Léon Sultan, a Jewish lawyer, to remind his readers that Sultan sacrificed his life in the fight against Nazism and Fascism during WWII in Europe.[69]

Aourid's *Cintra*, on the other hand, is set in a marginal bar in the Old City of Casablanca. Congregating around music and alcohol, the working-class people of the city engage in rowdy behavior to camouflage their highly politicized, subversive discourses. The characters' mock craziness and Sufi prattle serve to prevent colonial authorities from discovering the anti-colonialist awareness gained and articulated by the ordinary people who visit Cintra Bar. The very centrality of the Cintra Bar to Moroccan nationalism lies in stark contrast to its peripheral location in relation to the places where nationalist activism is taking place. Bū'azīz, a trade union activist, speaks to this when he tells Binmanṣūr, formerly a translator within the French Protectorate regime in Morocco but now an emerging nationalist figure, "the center of gravity has shifted to marginal neighborhoods, in Kariān Centrā and Bin Msīk. Those who are transforming history are the city's proletariat and rural migrants, not the Chamber of Commerce or Paribas or Mas Group. The course of history has changed. It needs someone to explain its message and decipher its code, like diviners who explain God's word and will."[70] The institutions of French colonization, represented by the Chamber of Commerce, Paribas, and Mass group, are no longer the wielders of power, since a new anti-colonial and working-class consciousness has emerged in the country. Accordingly, *Cintra* rehabilitates those lower social strata of Moroccan society that were left out of the grand narrative of Morocco's independence and in doing so, it also brings to consciousness Moroccan Jewish communists who were part and parcel of this underground.

The work to restore Binmanṣūr's consciousness following his coma triggers a process of historical discovery. This historiographical work devolves to his medical doctor, named Dr. Vivānī, and a political scientist named Dr. Aourid, who collaborate to locate the key, albeit hidden, moments in Binmanṣūr's biography between 1946 and 1948 that would accelerate their effort to revive him. In the process, they shed light on the silences in Binmanṣūr's life, including those regarding Moroccan Jews involved in the formation of Moroccan nationalism, especially the Jewish members of the Moroccan Communist Party. Cintra Bar is revealed not only to be the location where Binmanṣūr absorbed his first nationalist ideas, but also the site of his traumatic separation from his Jewish wife, Sulaika. As a result, this bar serves as a background for Binmanṣūr's and Sulaika's story sixty years later. The bar is also a witness to a changed nation, symbolized by Sulaika's departure to Israel and her former husband's state of unconsciousness following his visit to this site, which continues to exist in a social and political context that ignores its history.

Taken in its metaphorical and historical dimensions, Cintra Bar is not just a bar. Its symbolism extends beyond any localized place. In the novel, one of the characters discussing this period in Moroccan history says "Cintra is not a place—it is indeed a phenomenon."[71] Another character calls for making "Cintra a symbol for regained consciousness."[72] In a collective song they chant at the bar, the nationalist activists sing, "Cintra is a state of mind,"[73] thus referring to the fact that Cintra has ramifications that encompass both Morocco's past and present. Binmanṣūr himself, after he is initiated into the nationalist discourse in Cintra, "realized that this place [Cintra] is a place of conscience; not a place for merrymaking and fun."[74] Indeed, Binmanṣūr is slowly "attached to Cintra and its world."[75] While the French authorities have tasked him with the mission to spy on Cintra Bar, which "is frequented by locals" and "has become a seat of rebellion,"[76] Binmanṣūr becomes possessed by Cintra's spirit and joins the endeavor to free Morocco from French colonialism instead of serving his French handlers. Indeed, the bar's patrons teach Binmanṣūr nationalism, and only sixty years later does his coma enable these formative years of Jewish-Muslim cooperation to reemerge in novelistic form.

Aside from the place as a mood, in the case of Cintra Bar, place as a physical space is pivotal to recovering details that will ultimately serve as a source for a history to be written. Public places, including synagogues like the Ibn Danan Synagogue in Fez, as well as bars and cafes, are crucial for remembering

Jewish life in Morocco. Not only do these places show how Moroccan Jews left their imprint in the public sphere, but they also represent the relationships formed among the many characters who shared these spaces. Regarding the Fez synagogue, Ibn 'Amitha'īl clearly declares his goal in telling its story in *Anā al-mansī*: "It does not matter who I am. I am a Jew, son of a Jew. After I have shown you both sweet and bitter aspects of Jewish life in the Mellah of Fez, I will, in the next scene, show you another aspect of Jewish religious life in the Danan Synagogue before its traces vanished and the place fell into ruin."[77] Ibn 'Amitha'īl here refers to the fact that this place is still there today and has a story to tell, but that there is also the danger that erosion and the passage of time will condemn these stories to oblivion.

Anā al-mansī depicts conversations that took place in Ibn Danan Synagogue between the Jewish leadership and their coreligionists about the formation of the State of Israel and the status of Jews in Morocco. In imagined dialogues between the rabbi of the synagogue and his disciples, *Anā al-mansī* delves into and portrays the contribution of religious discourse to the emigration of Moroccan Jews and the desertion of the synagogue of Fez. Rather than falling into the usual trap of overgeneralization and essentialization about Jews, the novel depicts the diversity of opinions within the Moroccan Jewish community, ranging from hardline Zionists to Communists and ordinary citizens. The private dialogues in the Ibn Danan Synagogue also reveal the complexity of a situation in which Jews had to choose between their homeland, Morocco, and what they believe is a biblical Promised Land in the newly formed State of Israel. At the end of the religious service, however, most Jews start "promising to see each other in Israel when emigration is possible."[78] Without judging their intentions, Ibn 'Amitha'īl portrays the variety of positions that permeated Moroccan Jewish communities regarding emigration to Israel, thereby placing the reader in the moments when Moroccan Jews were faced with the need to make the decision to leave or stay. Although not directly referring to it, *Anā al-māsī* reflects in a potent way what Jewish lawyer Carlos de Nesry had analyzed as Moroccan Jews' being at the crossroads.[79] In reliving these moments in a synagogue full of worshippers, *Anā al-mansī* provides a historical narrative that complicates the reader's understanding of the processes that led to the gradual disappearance of the majority of Moroccan Jews from their country of origin.

By remembering Jews and bringing them back into post-independence spaces, mnemonic literature rehabilitates departed Jews as part of the nation's history. Since the challenge has always been the difficulty of writing history based on written sources, Moroccan mnemonic literature has been successful at recreating, oftentimes in very realistic and compelling ways, events and situations that serve as a source for history. Moroccan mnemonic literature has indeed lived up to fiction's ability to represent and embody not only the "widely accepted social mores and intellectual propositions of its age," but also to "provide evidence, not so much for historical periods in which its stories might be set, but for the time in which it was actually written."[80] Because mnemonic repression and historiographical censorship have both prolonged and exacerbated the silence of Morocco's Jewish past, mnemonic literature works as a double-edged sword that, on the one hand, cuts through censorship to make stories available and, on the other hand, reflects the collective interest in knowing this inaccessible part of Moroccan history. Thus, mnemonic literature writers engage with the concerns of their time as they strive to recuperate the history of another era that most authors have not even experienced. Place figures prominently in this mnemonic literary endeavor to other-archive the complex history of Jewish migration and turns it into examinable history.

Functions of Place Memories in Mnemonic Literature

Memories of place play a crucial role in establishing connections between people and place, but memories are also the result of an affective relationship to place. Philosopher Janet Donohoe makes a distinction between space and place and writes that "space is more abstract, lending itself to mathematization and geometry, while place resists such attempts in the way in which it is imbued with value and meaning."[81] Moreover, according to Donohoe, "place grants a feeling of familiarity, strangeness and identicalness,"[82] thus creating a sense of connection and belonging between people hailing from the same place. Familiar places also trigger memories, anchor them, and facilitate their intergenerational transmission.[83] It only takes a visit to one's old neighborhood to remember stories about neighbors, store owners, and childhood friends. On a related note, in his book *A Place to Remember*, historian Robert Archibald writes that the neighborhood "store [of his youth] was more than a marketplace; it was also a place where relationships were initiated, reinforced, and buttressed by life on Division Street, the values of church, the parish school, and a shared ethnicity."[84] Place, as this story reveals, is not only a trigger of memories but also a medium and a shaper of memories.

In the novels analyzed in this chapter, place is deployed to anchor memories, produce recollections, and recreate the quasi-extinct world occupied by Jews and Muslims in pre-1967 Morocco. It is the only witness left to tell the story of what Morocco used to be before the Jews' mass emigration and the establishment of an authoritarian regime in 1961.[85] An endeavor to dissipate national and social amnesia is at work in mnemonic literature. However, not all the novels examined in this chapter do so in the same way. *Casanfa*, within its narrator's meaningful rambling, makes a strong, explicitly political demand that Moroccan Jews "enjoy the right of eternal nationality and complete citizenship."[86] This ties the writing of a new history to the need to support Moroccan Jews' access to and exercise of their citizenship. *Anā al-mansī* compares the booming life of the mellah during the Protectorate with the desolate state of the place after 1967. This comparison conveys the depth of loss through the void that Moroccan Jews' emigration left in place. *Cintra*, on the other hand, uses place to confront the Moroccan nation with open questions about its unresolved past through the silences in the biography of the nationalist character of Binmanṣūr. Juxtaposed with the state of historiography and memory in Morocco, Binmanṣūr's coma is a powerful metaphor for the state of amnesia that has settled on post-independence Morocco. Dr. Vivāni's and Dr. Aourid's focus on recovering Binmanṣūr's personal history between 1945 and 1947 gestures to the importance of these years in Moroccan history and the crucial importance of every detail for a collective history. In the final analysis, Binmanṣūr's failure to write his memoirs has a cost for the entire nation's understanding of its past.[87] However, it's Binmanṣūr's reluctance to write down the collective history he embodies that also empowers the literary text to recover the history of Cintra. Through this, it tells the story of separation and repression of memories of a Jewish-Muslim couple (Binmanṣūr and Sulaika) and the various possible histories that could have emerged from their severed destinies.

Place also functions as a site of liberation in which the silenced Jewish past in Morocco can finally be revealed. A visit to a bar or a house that had some significance in a character's earlier life in Morocco seems enough to open the floodgates of memory. In psychoanalysis, this process is called abreaction, which is a return to the site of one's trauma in order to make it available to memory.[88] For instance, abreaction occurs in *Le Captif de Mabrouka* with the return of the two main characters to the house that is associated with their childhood traumas. For Richard, his childhood home in Ouarzazate has haunted him like a curse that can only be broken by returning to live in Morocco. On the other hand, Walter returns to the site of his parental trauma to carry out his father's wish to return to his home. Walter says that "for many years, my late father wished to return to Morocco to spend his last days . . . If I come back here now, it is to fulfill my father's last wish."[89] For Walter, whose parents emigrated to Israel/Palestine before moving to the United States, the house is the symbol of an intergenerational wound, which he attempts to heal by buying back the place symbolizing the original dislocation of his family. Moreover, in *Cintra*, Binmanṣūr "lost [his] memory as a result of strong emotional trauma" when he visited Cintra Bar after sixty years of absence.[90] Cintra was not only a site of past trauma in Binmanṣūr's life, but it is also a *conditio sine qua non* for his healing. This speaks to the fact that no memory of loss can be resolved without the readiness to confront its pains and its buried pasts, including in the archival and historical terrains.

Connecting Memories of Place through Mythical Characters

An important device frequently found in mnemonic literature is the use of mythical characters, whose longevity and supernatural abilities bring together disparate emplaced memories and experiences.[91] The realism of place combined with the magical realism of mythical characters allows mnemonic literature to assemble Moroccan Jewish characters dispersed throughout the world in order to depict their erstwhile Jewish life in the country. Because Jews are not there anymore, their remembrances as well as their reflections on place can only be brought together through these mythical characters. Both Ibn 'Amitha'īl Zāz in *Anā al-mansī* and al-Mūtshū in *Cintra* are assigned a variety of supernatural abilities, which allow them to transcend the ordinary temporal and spatial boundaries and conjure up a collective past or futurity that has slowly fallen into oblivion.

In addition to allowing the narratives to go back and forth between different temporalities, spaces, and crucial events, mythical characters achieve two goals. First, they underscore the fact that revisiting the silenced histories of Jewish life in Morocco is a daunting enterprise. Both pan-Arabism and pan-Islamism have conflated Judaism with Zionism to make any recovery of the Jewish past a fraught subject, which then necessitates supernatural beings to confront these amalgamations. Second, in order to become aware of loss, one needs time to pass, for the comparison between what was and what is no more to happen. Only mythical characters have the capacity to juxtapose an extended past with the situation in the present, a fact that literary scholar Renate Lachmann suggests makes "fantastic literature" the most suitable literary genre for grappling with repressed pasts. According to Lachmann, fantastic literature "recovers suppressed knowledge, revives obsolete knowledge and reincorporates formerly rejected unofficial or arcane traditions of knowledge."[92]

As they do not experience time in the same way that other mortal beings do, mythical characters possess longevity, which enables them to form and compare memories across different time periods, to bear witness to the lives of different generations.[93] For instance, because of his extraordinary longevity, Ibn 'Amithā'il in *Anā al-mansī* "shared the life of Moroccan Jews, attended the construction of the Mellah of Fez about six centuries ago and saw with his eyes how Jewish life in all its social dimensions formed in the Mellah. He observed the emigration of numerous Moroccan Jews to Canada, the United States, and Israel. He happened to stay in his hidden location until he witnessed the departure of the last Jew who remained in the Mellah of Fez after the June War in 1967. His name is Mordekhai al-Sammār."[94] Here we are not just in the presence of a character who bears witness to contemporary history, but one who claims that his move to Israel/Palestine is to "observe the other life that Moroccan Jews will live in Israel."[95] Ibn 'Amithā'il's capacity to occupy multiple spaces and temporalities further deepens his ability to compare the past and the present of Moroccan Jews and their society.

Mythical characters are similarly unconfined by spatial boundaries. The supernatural ability to connect different places, generations, and eras allows these characters to reinscribe the loss of Moroccan Jews into space. For instance, having "lived in numerous eras and places as a witness of Moroccan Jews' history, which was characterized by many ordeals," Ibn 'Amithā'il bears witness to the changes that have happened in Jewish life over the centuries.[96] This ability to be simultaneously in Jerusalem to witness the current life of Moroccan Jews and in Fez to resuscitate their past is a feat that fosters comparison between the past and the present, inscribing the questions of history and memory into the novelistic other-archive. Inevitably, this process leads to the realization of loss of Moroccan Jews. Anthropologists Ruth Van Dyke and Susan Alcock have argued that the "construction of social memory can involve direct connections to ancestors in a remembered past, or it can involve more general links to a vague mythological antiquity, often based on the re-interpretation of monuments or landscapes."[97] Both of these elements—connection to antiquity and resignification of Jewish existence in Morocco—are at work in *Anā al-mansī*. The mythical character of Ibn 'Amitha'īl transcends space and time to bridge the distance between Moroccan Jews who emigrated to Israel/Palestine and their coreligionists and compatriots who stayed in Morocco, which again allows the subaltern Jews who left Morocco to compare their mostly fulfilled life in the mellah of Fez with their supposedly broken dreams in exile.

Ibn 'Amithā'il's powers allow him to reconstruct the vanished world of Jewish-Muslim life that was lost in the aftermath of the country's independence in 1956. Observing this, Isḥāq Bin Hārūn Mīmī, one the Jewish characters in *Anā al-mansī*, remarks, "You don't die, you don't fall sick. You don't forget. You doubtless hail from history. Also, from your seat, here at the

Café la Renaissance, you look like a statue."[98] Thus, the endowment of characters with transtemporal powers transforms them into a nexus or a point of convergence of different experiences that speak to overlooked histories and memories of Jewish life in Morocco, which, in turn, become an other-archive in the novel. Hence, Ibn 'Amithā'il uses his abnormal skills to serve the downtrodden elements in society whose voices would be otherwise lost to both archives and history. The void and silence of formerly Jewish places requires the depiction of their erstwhile life from the point of view of characters who can juxtapose and confront such places with their own extensive experiences.

Unlike Ibn 'Amithā'il, whose focus is the past, al-Mūtshū's supernatural abilities in *Cintra* manifest in his foreknowledge about a Moroccan futurity without Jews. Although al-Mūtshū wears no ragged clothing and speaks no elaborate rhetoric as is usual among *aṣḥāb al-ḥāl* ("people of spirit"—the people who are in conversation with spirits or the unknown), he is still endowed with undeniable abilities that allow him to straddle the present temporality, which he shares with the other characters, as well as a future temporality that only unfolds in the future—toward the end of the novel. This skill to inhabit the two temporalities is usually confusing to other characters, who cannot keep up with his indecipherable, laconic insights into a future that is not accessible to them. A prime example of this confusion is illustrated by his conversation with Binmanṣūr:

al-Mūtshū: How is Bushrā?
Binmanṣūr: Bushrā, who?
al-Mūtshū: Your granddaughter.
Binmanṣūr: I just got married, and my wife Sulaika hasn't given birth yet.
al-Mūtshū: May God be merciful to her.
Binmanṣūr: My wife?
al-Mūtshū: She died seven years ago.
Binmanṣūr: Sulaika?
al-Mūtshū: Indeed, indeed, she married a Polish man, and she gave birth to their son David, who died in the war of October in Sinai, and a daughter named Rebecca who currently lives in Boston, where she studies at Harvard. She is married there. Rebecca still owns her mother Sulaika's house in Ashdod.
Binmanṣūr: Ashdod?
al-Mūtshū: Indeed, indeed, in Israel.
Binmanṣūr: Israel?

al-Mūtshū: Sir, you are no different from these others. Stupid. May God bring you where you should be.[99]

As this dialogue between Binmanṣūr and al-Mūtshū reveals, the latter is able to foresee Sulaika's departure to Israel and how her life will unfold after she leaves Morocco in 1947. While Binmanṣūr is stuck in the present temporality of his marriage to Sulaika and their life together in Morocco, al-Mūtshū is able to see beyond that, which distresses Binmanṣūr. At the end of their encounter, Binmanṣūr's conception of the present and the past is confused, and his sense of a linear time is challenged from a future that will unfold in his life one year later with Sulaika's sudden disappearance.[100]

The use of mythical characters to converge various memories of place and their former Jewish inhabitants results in the rehabilitation of the places remembered as well as the voices of Jewish individuals and communities that could have been entirely lost, were it not for mnemonic literature's engagement with reconstructing and relaying their significance. However, even in the absence of mythical characters, as in the case of the novel *Casanfa*, mnemonic novels employ similar techniques to connect the disparate trajectories of their characters. In *Casanfa, Casanfabar*, Isḥāq Abiṭbol's supposed manuscript, is in itself a mythical object that records the prescient concerns of its visionary author. Both its dubious authorship and visionary qualities transcend the humanly normal. It is, in fact, a history of Casablanca and its Jewish community from the future, a future history whose archives are being constructed and refigured in other-archival forms by the day.

Conclusion

Moroccan novelists draw on memories of place to articulate the loss of the Morocco that was inhabited by both Jews and Muslims. By recovering memories of Jewish places, authors of mnemonic literature recreate the richness of ordinary Jewish life that has ceased to exist across Morocco. Attention to detail and the individual characters' capacity to reinvent the nearly unwritten Jewish-Muslim world indicate the authors' desire to consign to writing a crucial part of Morocco's past, which has long remained unarticulated, without falling into nostalgia or hagiography. The lack of historiographical engagement with the loss of Moroccan Jews has spurred Moroccan novelists to delve into microhistories of place not only to make up for the absent academic histories, but make history accessible and an object of hearth and home in Morocco.

Naming and re-renaming strategies, as well as the recovery of Jewish-

Muslim memories of everyday places, such as homes, bars, cafes, synagogues, and specific neighborhoods, are the sites where mnemonic literature recovers and reconstructs histories of the erstwhile Jewish-Muslim Morocco. By reinscribing the significance of places that are important to Jewish Morocco, mnemonic literature deploys fictional recreations of place as physical witnesses to a world that no longer exists but whose possible history relies on the production of other-archives. However, instead of merely registering absence, place speaks to desolation, erasure, and loss of a formerly prosperous life. Fictional memories of place inscribe Jewish-Muslim memories into a textual site of memory where this silenced past regains its full force as we wait for academic historians to engage with this risk-laden portion of Moroccan history.

Having examined the myriad strategies producers of other-archives use to reinscribe Jewish presence in the places and history of post-colonial Morocco, the following chapter probes mnemonic literature's depictions of the Jewish-Muslim citizenship that could have been.

3

Jewish-Muslim Intimacy and the History of a Lost Citizenship

Moroccan history books may wish to forget Jewish emigration and the societal losses that ensued from it for the Muslims they left behind, but mnemonic literature, which constitutes an other-archive through the recovery of Morocco's erstwhile Jewish past, refuses to condone amnesia. This chapter argues that mnemonic literature reimagines the possibility of Jewish-Muslim intimacy and community-based citizenship that was lost after Jews left the nation in a massive exodus between 1948 and 1967. After Morocco's independence in 1956, different constituents of Moroccan society, specifically Jews and Muslims, could have forged a citizenship grounded in their daily interactions. Yet Jewish emigration amid state violence directed at all forms of dissent during the Years of Lead prevented the emergence of this alternative Morocco. It is precisely because synchronous Jewish-Muslim intimacy ceased to exist that its reimagination became a pivotal topic in the mnemonic works examined in this this chapter. Abdelkarim Jouiti's *Zaghārīd al-mawt* (*Ululations of Death*), Ibrahim Hariri's *Shāmma aw Shtrīt* (*Shamma or Shtrit*), and Kamal El Khamlichi's *Ḥārith al-nisyān* (*Tiller of Forgetfulness*) all depict this lost intimacy in their representations of interfaith border crossings, shared Jewish-Muslim childhoods, and Jewish and Muslim women's transgressive solidarities.[1] In Hassan Aourid's *Cintra* and Mohamed Ezzeddine Tazi's *Anā al-mansī* (*I Am the Forgotten*), the final two books analyzed in this chapter, Jewish-Muslim intimacy acquires an even stronger political resonance through the stories of collaboration between Jews and Muslims against French colonialism.

The massive, albeit gradual, emigration of the majority of Moroccan Jews by the end of the 1960s was the culmination of a long historical process that combined both external and internal factors. The *Alliance Israélite Universelle* (Universal Israelite Alliance [UIA]), a philanthropic French organization that opened its first modern school in the northern Moroccan city of Tetouan in 1862, initiated the linguistic and cultural transformation of native Jews.[2] Since their inception, the UIA's schools opened the door to the Gallicization of Moroccan Jews, which in turn transformed their social status, widened the gap between them and their Muslim co-citizens, and exposed them to the suffering of European Jewry as well as the emergence of Zionism.[3] The result was the acceleration of Jewish departure after Morocco's independence in 1956.[4] The conflict in Israel/Palestine, especially during the 1967 and 1973 wars, likewise increased the number of Moroccan Jewish emigrants to the Holy Land.[5] The impact on both Israel/Palestine and Morocco was profound. As Israeli historian Michael Laskier writes, "when the state of Israel was established the largest Jewish community in the Muslim world was that of Morocco. Of the community's 250,000 members, 220,000 settled in Israel between 1948 and 1964."[6] This Jewish exodus irrevocably homogenized Morocco's religious and cultural landscape and terminated the possibility of Muslim-Jewish intimacy therein. Not only that—even the possibility of a democracy, which historian Abdallah Laroui asserts cannot be "produced in an ethnically, religiously, culturally, and linguistically monolithic country,"[7] was aborted as a result of the massive departure of Jews.

Whereas foreign historians have documented the different aspects of this speedy dislocation, as well as the behind-the-scenes multipartite negotiations that facilitated it,[8] academic historians in Morocco continue to shun a critical engagement with the topic of Jewish emigration due in part to the scarcity of archival sources but also because of the riskiness of researching this highly politicized issue. As a result, native Moroccan historical works on the topic are limited, and the prevalent explanations of Jewish emigration in Morocco remain anecdotal at best. Morocco has never had any systematic policy against Jews as such. It is rather one of the very few places in the Maghreb and the Middle East where Judaism is recognized and celebrated as an important element of national identity, particularly after the 2011 constitutional reform, which explicitly affirms Moroccan identity's Hebraic dimension, among others. Nevertheless, there is a distinction to be made between acknowledging Morocco's Jewish heritage and opening up space for historiographical work to engage with uncomfortable questions that remain unanswered about the process that led to Jewish emigration and its impact on Moroccan society. Moroccan Jews were not living in a void, and their speedy emigration between 1947 and 1967 disrupted entire regions and left many questions that academic history has yet to answer. In the absence of historiographical works that can examine the risky questions surrounding Jewish migration and the ways it internally benefited authoritarianism, mnemonic literature stands in for history. In this regard, Ahmed El Madini's forceful statement that "the novel surpasses history when it transforms absence into an intense presence" applies to mnemonic literature,[9] which reimagines how Moroccan society was impacted by the loss of its Jews. Foremost among these losses, this chapter demonstrates, was the potential for a Jewish-Muslim community-based citizenship that could have emerged from these two communities' synchronous intimacy.[10] In emphasizing the emplacement of community, I probe the various ways the novels analyzed here propose a local, community-based citizenship can be lived without necessarily being associated with a central nation-state.

Sociologist Harry Blatterer defines intimacy as "a non-instrumental relationship of trust based on affection, care and respect."[11] Blatterer's relational conception of intimacy places emphasis on positive sentiments, genuine concern for others' well-being, and the absence of instrumentality as cornerstones of intimacy.[12] Lynn Jamieson has revealed that intimacy is underlain by notions of equality, the recognition of the intimate's whole personhood, and the elimination of boundaries between the parties within an intimate relationship.[13] Put differently, intimacy in these renderings is tangled up in ideals of equality, mutual acceptance, reciprocal care, and respect: "intimacy involves feeling understood, validated, cared for, and closely connected with another person. It also entails lowering defenses and reducing self-doubts and self-reproach."[14] Anthony Giddens similarly theorizes intimacy as a democratic relationship that requires trust and equality to take effect and is highly dependent on both time and place.[15] Trust and confidence are built over *time*, as their concretization requires long periods of exchange between the different parties.[16] Temporal continuity in a shared place fosters intimacy; only through the synchronicity of the time lived together does one appreciate the worthiness of another to be their intimate—their equal and co-citizen. Any rupture in temporality disrupts this intimacy and potentially stirs opposite feelings of strangeness and enmity.

These understandings of intimacy inform my study of Jewish-Muslim relations in Morocco and its bygone Jewish-Muslim communities' practices of citizenship. I explore how interreligious relations, which can be characterized by conflict and antagonism, are reimagined in mnemonic literature's depiction of the positive feelings and reciprocal care brought about through synchronous intimacy between Jews and Muslims. The post-1948 disintegration of mixed communities and the ultimate mass exodus of Jews from

Morocco terminated the community-centered citizenship that I argue is an object of loss in mnemonic literature.

Morocco's Jewish-Muslim temporality has split asunder since the establishment of the state of Israel in 1948 and the ensuing emigration of over 200,000 Moroccan Jews between 1956 and 1967.[17] The departure of the majority of Morocco's Jews in short succession made intimacy between Muslims and Jews intermittent, interrupted, and discontinuous over time due to geographical distance, which in turn dealt a severe blow not only to their shared citizenship but also to remembrances and representations of Jews in Moroccan society.[18] Although the past cannot be recovered, mnemonic literature recreates the erstwhile Jewish-Muslim community that would have been possible if Moroccan Jews had not emigrated.

Place is also pivotal for the formation of the type of citizenship lost with the departure of Moroccan Jews. Indeed, Reis and Shaver have emphasized intimacy's connection to place, defining it, among other things, as "people's arrangement in space" with long-term "transactional process[es]," which "influence each other's feelings and behavior over time."[19] Accordingly, spatial contiguity over a long period of time not only facilitates intimacy but also fashions how the connection to the other is remembered and rationalized. Through her research among exiled Algerian Jews in France, anthropologist Joëlle Bahloul has confirmed that proximity in place not only fosters the formation of experiences and memories, but also retrospectively recalls for us that, in the minds of Jewish emigrants from Algeria, "past geographical proximity equals agreement whereas present distance equals hostility."[20] In other words, the spatial distance between Jews and Muslims has bred negative feelings, exacerbated their imagined enmity over time, and transformed the significance of citizenship in everyday life.[21]

The concept of intimacy does therefore allow us to understand the community-building practices that mnemonic literature vividly conjures up, practices of citizenship that ceased to develop with the disappearance of the world that had first fostered its existence. Citizenship, however, is a complicated concept that combines the social, the political, and the cultural. British sociologist Thomas Humphrey Marshall, the founder of a modern theory on citizenship, defines citizenship "as a status bestowed on those [who] are full members of a community."[22] Thus, in addition to conferring the legal status of a citizen, this membership also "implies the capacity to participate in both the political and the socio-economic life of the community."[23] According to this Marshallian definition, citizens benefit from the privileges their membership in the community confers upon them, but, in the meantime, they have the duty to use their independence in the public arena toward the collective, common good.[24] Taking this Marshallian definition into account, *citizenship*, in this chapter, refers to a set of intimate relationships that undergird a group's understanding of themselves as a community with shared struggles and a common destiny forged from synchronous encounters and community-building in a challenging, and maybe even conflict-laden, interreligious context.

The idea of a nation-state was still novel and unstable after Morocco's independence in 1956, and the community-building-based citizenship portrayed in mnemonic literature is that which was lost to Jewish emigration. In fact, almost one million Moroccan Jews in Israel/Palestine and the Moroccan diaspora still retain the right to claim their legal Moroccan citizenship. However, the community dimension of this citizenship is irrecoverable for the simple reason that the erstwhile intimates, both Jews and Muslims, are separated by decades of spatial and temporal distance, which mnemonic literature producers belatedly recuperate, revive, and inscribe into fictionalized histories of the nation that would have been created had Jews not been let go.

Portrayals of a Lost Jewish-Muslim Intimacy in Mnemonic Literature

Disintegrated Jewish-Muslim Households

Ibrahim Hariri's debut novel, *Shāmma aw Shtrīt*, is a representation of the destructive impact that the Arab-Israeli conflict had on Jewish-Muslim households. A story that spans Morocco, Israel/Palestine, and France during the June 1967 War, *Shāmma aw Shtrīt* is constructed as a journalistic investigation into Jewish-Muslim families whose stories have been forgotten or silenced in Moroccan society. In the novel, Ṣūfiā Aṣrrāf, a "Moroccan Jewish journalist [who] investigates the topic of emigration of Moroccan Jews during the 1950s, 1960s, and 1970s," asks: "What about Jewish-Muslim interfaith marriages? What about the children? What happens when half of the family emigrated to Israel and the other half stayed in Morocco?"[25] Covering events unfolding between 2002 and 2004, the novel depicts the lives of Immā Būkbbāt, a socialist hardliner Zionist pediatrician from Tel Aviv; Yūsuf Būkabba, a Muslim leftist anti-Zionist lawyer from Casablanca; and Shāmma/Shtrīt, their sixty-four-year-old Moroccan Jewish mother who has moved to Israel with her daughter Immā (whose Muslim name before emigration was Fāṭima) during the June 1967 War.

Ṣūfiā, herself the fruit of a Jewish-Muslim relationship, is passionate about interviewing these Jewish-Muslim families for a story she is working on for the widely read French daily newspaper *Le Monde*. However, conducting research on these families is rife with silences and obstacles, among them the "dearth of information and lack of interest on the part of Moroccan authorities, whether because of the nonexistence of information or of sheer nonchalance."[26] In the absence of archival material from which to reconstitute these stories, Ṣūfiā relies on oral interviews in order to retrieve stories of disintegrated Jewish-Muslim households. However, her Jewish interlocutors—professor and politician Simon Lévy and novelist Edmond Amran El Maleh, representations of two prominent figures of Moroccan Judaism—fail to satisfy her curiosity for the same reason: lack of information based on solid evidence. Simon simply tells Ṣūfiā that "there are no specific cases."[27] But Ṣūfiā does not give up; she persists until she learns of Shāmma and Muṣṭafā's family.

Structured as an investigative work into Morocco's vanished Jewish community, *Shāmma aw Shtrīt* is a multinational story about the loss of Jewish-Muslim intimacy. The more Ṣūfiā finds out about the family, whose characters are scattered across Casablanca, Marseille, and Tel Aviv, the more Jewish-Muslim intertwinement emerges as a reality that once existed but was eradicated from the lives of ordinary Moroccans as a result of separation and migration. Shāmma is the character who best exemplifies the process that led to such loss. An ordinary mother and resident of the al-Ma'ārīf working-class neighborhood in Casablanca, Shāmma converts to Islam to marry Muṣṭafā, but her Judaism "was never a problem neither for him nor me until the war [1967] erupted."[28] Shāmma reveals to Ṣūfiā: "I met Muṣṭafā in the 1950s, in 1952 to be exact, and we got married quickly to avoid our parents' refusal. We were poor, but happy."[29] However, the overpowering Israeli propaganda and the rise of Arab-nationalist discourse in Morocco, compounded by the complacency and even complicity of Moroccan authorities as demonstrated in the total freedom of Israeli agents to smuggle Jews out of the country, takes an irreparable toll on the family, leading to its intercontinental dispersal. Due to Shāmma's fears for her family in Israel/Palestine within the context of the war, she converts back to Judaism and decides to emigrate clandestinely with her children. It so happens that Muṣṭafā's mother falls sick, and Muṣṭafā takes Yūsuf with him to visit her on the day of Shāmma's scheduled departure with her Israeli smugglers. Shāmma takes Immā with her, and Yūsuf stays behind. In his attempt to find Shāmma and Immā, Muṣṭafā follows their itinerary to Marseilles in France, but he self-exiles and never returns to Morocco to raise Yūsuf or reconnect with his family. The Būkabba/Būkbbāt family, whose erasure is also indicated in the different transliterations of their last name between Morocco and Israel, is the victim of both global and local politics that cause a traumatic disintegration of their formerly tranquil existence, scattering them across three continents.

Traumatic dispersal is central to the family's story; these dislocations include family, home, and nation, as well as from the communal citizenship that bound them together to a place, a community, and a shared Moroccan ethos. A comparison between Shāmma, Immā, and Yūsuf reveals how emigration impacts their worldviews and who they become. For instance, Immā and Yūsuf have diametrically opposed positions vis-à-vis the state of Israel, Zionism, and the rights of Palestinian people. Yūsuf is a staunch anti-Zionist activist, whereas Immā is an anti-Arab hardliner. In the absence of a shared ethos within a shared home and family, Yūsuf and Immā, although brother and sister, have nothing in common other than the blood that runs in their veins. Their mother, Shāmma, on the other hand, has a stronger connection to people she knew in Morocco before her emigration to Israel/Palestine. The welcoming reception she receives upon her return visit to her old neighborhood provides a counter-example of how her locally forged citizenship with the people in her old life supersedes the boundaries of their current separation. During an outing in her former neighborhood, Shāmma meets Lalla Fāṭna, an old woman who remembers her immediately and starts asking about her husband and children:

> "Welcome Shāmma." Then she hugged her for a long time, and as if she was talking to herself, says: "It's been a very long time since you traveled to France with al-Hajāmī [Muṣṭafā]. How is he?" The old lady was asking: "How is your son, Yūsuf, and the daughter who was born in al-Ma'ārif, what's her name? How is she? Is everybody alright?"[30]

Even after years away, Shāmma retains her connection to home, and her place in its collective memory—however imperfect it may be.

In contrast to Shāmma's explicit sense of belonging in the neighborhood and among the people in Casablanca, Immā is "scared," declaring that she does not "feel in [her] place, in [her] country."[31] Even when Shāmma confronts her about her earlier desire and decision to visit Morocco, Immā insists that she "will return to Tel Aviv, to [her] homeland."[32] Immā has no connections to the people who might give her the crucial sense of community, belonging, and shared system of beliefs that can bond her to the people surrounding her during her short visit to Morocco. In other words, she lacks intimacy with the homeland of her birth and its people.

Shāmma and Muṣṭafā's family is a microcosm through which the novel attempts to "break the silence" about the "existence of many Jewish families that left Morocco and left their relatives behind."[33] The novel foregrounds awareness of silence, and the narrative is geared toward giving voice to experiences of those who suffered from the loss of Jewish-Muslim intimacy. However, instead of simply relaying lost intimacy, the novel explores the deeper ramifications for the sense of citizenship and belonging that characters develop. In this particular case, loss is not material, but familial, which makes recovery and closure all the more elusive. For instance, Shāmma and Muṣṭafā's community is destroyed and their family is fractured, thus creating space for unbridgeable antagonisms like the ones the reader witnesses between Immā and Yūsuf who espouse entirely oppositional ideologies. Instead of growing up together and being socialized as intimates into equals, as the reader observes in the aforementioned connection between Shāmma and Lalla Fāṭna, the spatial distance between the siblings creates a divide in their worldviews, which only deepens conflict and feeds loss.

With the narrative emphasis on silence and broken relationships, the novel also points to the historical nature of the loss depicted in this family story, thus reminding readers of the existence of these stories, whose excision from Moroccan history and social memory is brought to the fore. *Shāmma aw Shtrīt* magnifies the familial and historical dimensions of loss of Jewish-Muslim citizenship as a loss of potential in both family and community building, as exemplified in these erstwhile fictional households. There is a history of Jewish-Muslim families; but the combination of familial loss and historical silence has rendered any narrative of their existence inaccessible to younger generations of Moroccans.[34] Mnemonic literature's reimagining of these histories in fictional form helps to arouse social consciousness in young readers and to incite the historiographical community to transcend the limits of the discipline to probe loss as a topic of history.

Shāmma aw Shtrīt reimagines Jewish-Muslim life where children in the interreligious family are the pinnacle of community. Children symbolize both stability and continuity, so it follows that Immā and Yūsuf are symbols of a Morocco that could have been, had Shāmma not left for Israel/Palestine and Muṣṭafā not been forced into exile in Marseille. However, because of their separation, Yūsuf and Immā are acculturated to think in entirely antagonistic ways, and they each espouse values that further distance them from one another. The separation between Yūsuf and Immā and the impossibility of closing the thirty-year divide that splits their lives asunder speaks to intimacy's fundamental importance for a citizenship that is formed in daily interactions between people. While it is true that Yūsuf and Immā seem to negotiate ways to accept each other after they discover that they are related, this process of learning is fragile and requires the commitment of both siblings. The fragility of this newfound kinship is such that Immā declares to her mother that she "never had a brother or father."[35]

The collapse of Shāmma and Muṣṭafā's family is not only a disruption of a household; it is also the end of a way of being within the same nationscape, the same communal territory. The daily practice of citizenship that is symbolized by Shāmma and Muṣṭafā's love story, marriage, and childrearing is overtaken by loss, antagonism, and displacement when Shāmma and Immā leave Morocco, thus depriving all the characters of any sense of normalcy, even thirty years after the disruption of their happy life. The characters do, however, experience and respond to loss differently, depending on whether they are old enough to register what it is that was lost, or not lost. While Immā and Yūsuf seem to have accepted the fact that their parents' world is not theirs, both Shāmma and Muṣṭafā cannot move away from it. Shāmma and Immā return to Tel Aviv, Yūsuf resumes his life in Casablanca, but the father, Muṣṭafā, is doomed to exile in a foreign country. Even his location in Marseille remains unknown, and closure for the rest of the family is contingent upon his unlikely reappearance. In the larger implications of the novel, Muṣṭafā is not just a father; he is, one can venture to say, the symbol of the disintegrated fatherland who, in the context of the Six-Day War and the ensuing political ramifications, failed to protect his family whose future he lost to emigration to Israel/Palestine. Muṣṭafā's exile is therefore an allegory for a nation that has yet to recover from the loss of its Jewish family members. If we further accept that Muṣṭafa stands for Morocco, it is possible to interpret his continued absence at the end of the novel as a metaphor the impossibility for the nation to be whole again after the loss of its Jews.

Mnemonic literature as an other-archive not only registers the larger context in which Jewish-Muslim separation took place, but also adds an emotional dimension to understanding the way history unfolded for those who were either its actors or its victims. The novelistic other-archive in this case opens emotional history as a worksite for Moroccan historiography by providing a blueprint of what might have happened and the variety of sentiments it stirred. The familial dimension of this emotional history is complicated by the novelistic other-archiving of no-longer-existing experiences of synchronous Jewish-Muslim childhood.

Memories of a Vanished Jewish-Muslim Childhood

Kamal El Khamlichi's novel, *Ḥārith al-nisyān* tells the story of three children: a Muslim boy named Sāmī, and a Jewish brother and sister named José and Eléna. The three grow up in the northern village of Targuist, where Eléna, José, and their parents are the only Jewish family left in the region. Their mother works as a midwife in the only health center in the area, and their father is the owner of a shop. One day in the 1960s, the family vanishes from the village without any explanation, leaving their neighbors and friends at a loss as to their whereabouts. Sāmī is traumatized by his friends' unexpected absence from his life. With no one to help him understand their sudden disappearance, Sāmī goes about his life with many unanswered questions. However, Sāmī reconnects with his Jewish friends when he moves to Casablanca to finish high school.

Evolving against the backdrop of the famous March 1965 student strikes in Casablanca, *Ḥārith al-nisyān* hints at the severe political repression in Morocco in this era. The high school where Sāmī studies is the epicenter of a youth uprising against the government's decision to institute an age limit for high school students. Driven by the Moroccan state's desire to get rid of older, politically active students, this decision dashed many families' hopes for social advancement through their children's education, thus resulting in what historians and social scientists refer to as the first urban rebellion in post-independence Morocco in 1965.[36] During the siege of his high school, Sāmī wanders into the wealthy part of town surrounding his school and is saved from an attempted rape by Mrs. Simon, a Jewish widow who lives alone in the affluent neighborhood. This fortuitous connection leads Mrs. Simon to adopt Sāmī, thus opening the door for him to reunite with his childhood friends, José and Eléna, whose parents are good friends with Mrs. Simon. The rest of the plot hinges on magical realism and powerful insights into transformations in Jewish-Muslim existence in pre-1967 Morocco.

Ḥārith al-nisyān uses Jewish-Muslim childhood relationships to represent the community Jews and Muslims once shared in Morocco. Sāmī's deep entanglement in his Jewish friends' lives embodies a practice of citizenship as a shared belonging to a community. The three friends are portrayed not as supernatural beings who transcend religious boundaries, but rather as children who lived, played, and did the things children do when they are bound by a shared ethos that is constructed from their lived reality. Sāmī's, José's, and Eléna's worlds are interconnected through their play and also through the familial solidarities that unite them as a community regardless of their faith. With only 3,000 Jews left in some pockets in big cities today, this kind of interreligious childhood is impossible for most ordinary Moroccan children, so its literary representation underscores what has been lost with the disappearance of Jewish-Muslim intimacy.

Interestingly, and by way of comparison, José and Eléna's relationship with Sāmī is deeper than the newly discovered biological kinship between Yūsuf and Immā in *Shāmma aw Shtrīt*. While Yūsuf and Immā grew up separately in different cultural and political worlds, Sāmī, José, and Eléna grew up together, sharing the same set of values and united by the same bond to their village or city of citizenship, which they forged in their daily interactions over several years. The conspicuous religious and cultural distinctions between Yūsuf and Immā are only matched by the multilayered and porous identities inhabited by Sāmī, José, and Eléna. The power of this early, shared sense of belonging (in other words, the power of citizenship based on intimacy) sustains the three friends' relationship. Even years after his disappearance from their life, Eléna and José retain vivid memories of Sāmī, and the latter announces that he is "comfortable with Jews, and happy in their company, probably because they sympathized with me and considered me a stranger, like themselves, or maybe because I feel honesty and warmth in my interaction with them."[37] Even after Sāmī leaves Casablanca to study law in Rabat, while José and Eléna move to Paris and New York, respectively, they are able to reconnect without difficulty. Oftentimes, it seems like their citizenship—meaning their shared values and worldview as members of a community in both Targuist and Casablanca—is stronger than their respective religious affiliations.

The relationships one forms, nurtures, and builds during childhood are foundational to one's way of being in the world, including the type of citizen one becomes. When Masrūr, Sāmī's subservient jinn—the invisible being who has the power to do anything for those who master them—gives him the opportunity to make a last wish, Sāmī quotes from Kafka's *Letters to Milena*: "Everything must be earned, not only the present and future, but the past as well—something which is, perhaps, given every human being—this too must be earned, and this probably entails the hardest work of all."[38] As the novel ends, Sāmī, this man who is able to straddle and live in two worlds (Jewish and Muslim) coherently, seeks "liberation from [his] very distant exile, from [his] dear past."[39] It is not entirely apparent *how* Sāmī is exiled from his past, but it is clear from the narrative that neither José nor Eléna is there for him anymore. Eléna moves to the United States, while José decides to stay in France—both leave Sāmī in Morocco. However, even worse than being stuck in Morocco is Sāmī's memory blockage, which prevents him from accessing the Jewish-Muslim past that he shared with his two childhood friends.

In contrast, the childhood of Yūsuf and Immā in *Shāmma aw Shtrīt* reveals the citizenship that is lost in the aftermath of the dismemberment of one's family through migration. In addition to epitomizing the disruptive end of Jewish-Muslim intimacy, Yūsuf and Immā's failure to relate to each other even after they discover their kinship denotes the absence of relatable anchors for a Jewish-Muslim community in post-independence Morocco. Yūsuf and Immā have neither shared ethos nor memories; their estrangement from one another is such that their former antagonism comes more naturally to them than their newly recovered sibling relationship. As Yūsuf aptly articulates, "what divides us is bigger than what unites us."[40] As a result, biological kinship is represented as more limited in terms of bonding than shared memory and lived intimacy in the same nationscape. This representation further underscores memory's importance for the community and intimacy-based citizenship. After a long discussion with Yūsuf, Immā tells him: "We didn't choose our religions, not even our political opinions. I grew up in Israel and I found myself Jewish, and in politics all Arabs and Palestinians are enemies. Neither one of us can change the world."[41] The naïve and blatantly simplistic nature of this statement aside, it serves as a way into understanding how Yūsuf and Immā's lack of socializing prevented them from having a base minimum of shared beliefs about ideas of nation, community, or working toward a common goal. Their divided loyalties and allegiance to oppositional social and political models are the direct result of the disruption and dislocation of their childhood. Yūsuf and Immā had been apart for thirty years and unable to share the same temporality and space, which, in turn, deepens the hiatus that separates them.

Ethnographic work conducted in Morocco on Jewish-Muslim relations reveals related and relatable stories. For instance, recent scholarship by Aomar Boum, Emanuela Trevisan Semi, and Hanane Sekkat Hatimi has demonstrated that Jews and Muslims who shared the same nationscape formed mutual memories, fostered positive attitudes toward each other, and worked for the common good of the polity they were building together.[42] Polity, however, here does not refer to a national government, which may have existed only nominally beyond the borders of imperial cities; rather, it points to forms of local management that emerged from daily life and its challenges. According to this analysis, what I call *synchronous intimacy* provided both Jews and Muslims with a sense of belonging and allegiance to their shared communal space and to the collective project of building a community of citizens as they lived synchronously in the same nationscape. On the one hand, the bonds between Sāmī, José, and Eléna in *Ḥārith al-nisyān* exemplify this kind of community and are underlain by their treatment of each other as equals as a result of their shared childhood. On the other hand, Immā's and Yūsuf's relationship in *Shāmma aw Shtrīt* is imprinted by mistrust as well as the preconceived prejudices Jews and Muslims have about each other in the context of struggle in Israel/Palestine, which diminish their discovered kinship. Certainly, gender, class, geography, and literacy have a bearing on the way Jewish-Muslim intimacy is lived and remembered;[43] but the reimagined lives of Sāmī, José, Eléna, Immā, and Yūsuf show that the loss of childhood connections impacts the future relationships between the different characters. The antagonistic relationship between Yūsuf and Immā is particularly revealing of how blood kinship is weaker and less significant than relationships forged while living as a community of intimate citizens.

One of the clearest examples of the positive effects of synchronous intimacy can be gleaned in Abdelkébir Khatibi's discussion of his culinary and olfactory memories. Unlike the Westernized North African Jews, like Jacques Derrida and Jacques Hassoun, whom Khatibi is used to dialoguing with as "professional strangers" whose class and fame allow them to straddle multiple identities, his childhood Jews are more concrete and enmeshed in memories of food, including "*pain azim*" (matzah) and "*mā' al-ḥayāt*" (water of life/*eau de vie*), a Jewish alcoholic beverage distilled from figs or dates.[44] When Khatibi evokes his childhood memories of Moroccan Jews, he does not locate it within the mind. He instead opens up a very generative space to think about the mouth, nose, and ears as sites of this past Jewish-Muslim citizenship through the graspable senses that lived this memory.[45] The mouth remembers the delicious Jewish foods and the nostrils are filled with the smells of this displaced cuisine, while the ears remember the acoustics of Jewish songs and their Andalusian accents, especially their inability to pronounce the Arabic sound *Qaf* (ق), which they instead pronounced as a short *Alif* (أ). Even more important is Khatibi's underlining of the plural identity Jews and Muslims created in his hometown: "Now, I think that my childhood was more complex in its emotional formation. Biographically, I lived my youth in [. . .] a weft of cultural elements, simultaneously, Arab, Muslim, Berber, French, Jewish, [infused with] a Portuguese mythology."[46]

Depictions of Interfaith Border Crossings

In Abdelkarim Jouaiti's novel *Zaghārīd al-mawt*, the Jewish Blūlū family leave their southern village in the region of Agadir and migrate to the city of Meknes around 1916, the fourth year of the French Protectorate in Morocco. A combination of factors which include drought, lack of economic opportunities, and chronic fertility problems force husband Shīmūn Blūlū, his wife, Izzā, and their half-blind and developmentally delayed son, Issū, to make this dangerous trip to central Morocco. As the Blūlū family trudges through the mountains, the reader of *Zaghārid al-mawt* glimpses the world of a Jewish family at the turn of the twentieth century and the myriad dangers that lay in their path. The family is unable to complete their journey to Meknes due to the French War of Pacification (1912–34) on Moroccan insurgents in the region between Marrakesh and Meknes. Upon their release from the French army's custody to which they were taken to prevent them from continuing their trip, the Blūlūs settle down in the city of Béni-Mellal, where they are stranded without resources and ultimately rescued by a Muslim sheikh who adopts and provides for the family until his death three years later.

Shīmūn is forced to find another job after the sheikh's heirs take over his estate and divide their inheritance. Mr. Lanseau, a racist French colonist, hires Shīmūn to help him build a home where he can house his wife and children, who are joining him from France. When Madame Lanseau, a dilletante zoologist who is interested in studying animal sexuality, joins her husband in Béni-Mellal, Shīmūn becomes her bodyguard and assistant during her outings to conduct her observations in nature. During one of these trips, she asks Shīmūn to climb a tree to save a bird, but he falls and breaks his leg. No longer able to work jobs that require physical labor, he moves back into commerce, opening the doors to financial success and further anchoring the family in the city of Béni-Mellal.

By contrast, Izzā slips into a state of melancholy caused by repeated miscarriages. Hannū, a hundred-year-old Muslim midwife and traditional healer, becomes Izzā's mentor and saves her from depression. Thanks to Hannū's extraordinary longevity, she has been able to experience life with different generations of Jews and Muslims in Béni-Mellal, which explains the success of her interventions to support Izzā in her pregnancy-related troubles. Izzā's failure to carry a fetus to term, despite Hannū's traditional recipes and amulets, opens a space in the novel for Jewish and Muslim women's transgression of religious codes in solidarity with each other. Upon learning about the predicament of a single Muslim girl impregnated by her fiancé, a cousin who dies suddenly of cholera before the marriage can be legally recorded, Hannū orchestrates the adoption of the Muslim-born Samīḥa/Shamīḥa by the Blūlūs. As a result, Hannū helps the Blūlūs and spares the pregnant Muslim girl's family the shame of an illegitimate child. The connection between Hannū and Izzā and the process through which Samīḥa/Shamīḥa's adoption takes place thus depicts a community of Jews and Muslims who support each other in the face of French colonialism and Zionism, which were simultaneously working, albeit for different agendas, to pull their community apart.

More than anything, *Zaghārīd al-mawt* reveals interfaith border-crossing as an essential aspect of the lost Jewish-Muslim citizenship in Morocco. Although some characters demonstrate the ability to cross imagined boundaries between Jewish and Muslim communities more than others, their capacity to inhabit these two worlds blurs the imaginary lines of demarcation between Islam and Judaism. The ongoing back-and-forth movement between Jewish and Muslim spaces is mnemonic literature's clearest reflection of the bygone hybrid society that was lost to Moroccan Jewish emigration. For instance, Hannū refuses to declare whether she is Muslim or Jewish and in so doing consistently and consciously transgresses the social lines that separate Jews from Muslims and vice-versa.[47]

The formation of a homogeneous Muslim country at the cost of emigration of a significant Jewish population has impoverished Moroccan society significantly, specifically because there is no space left for characters like Hannū to straddle multiple identities within one nationscape. Homogeneous societies leave no room for ambiguity like the one depicted in *Zaghārīd al-mawt*. Despite her marginal presence in the novel, Hannū plays a crucial role by crossing interfaith borders and refusing to take for granted the distinctions between Jews and Muslims in her community. Hannū sees no difference between Judaism and Islam, between Jewish and Muslim households, as her orchestration of the Blūlūs' adoption of the illegitimate Muslim child Samīḥa/Shamīḥa clearly demonstrates.

Hannū's role in Samīḥa/Shamīḥa's adoption is an example of the ultimate gift enabled by community-building as citizenship depicted in mnemonic literature. On the topic of gift exchanges, Moroccan anthropologist Abdellah Hammoudi reinterprets Jewish-Muslim intimacy in the celebration of Mimouna based on two descriptions of the celebration from the nineteenth and mid-twentieth centuries.[48] A secular North African annual ritual that takes place at the end of Passover, Mimouna, according to Hammoudi, turns Jews and Muslims into one community through intimacy and gift-giving.[49] Mimouna, therefore, was a civic space in which Jews and Muslims renegotiated power relations and even reconfigured the cityscape through the fusion of their separated quarters for the period of the celebration.[50] Mimouna rituals, which included music, dance, and trance, among other forms of mingling between Jews and Muslims, were in fact egalitarian acts in which mutual recognition of the two communities was lived in practice.[51] In this sense, understanding Hannū's facilitation of Samīḥa/Shamīḥa's adoption by the Blūlū family as a gift opens up this transgressive act to an interpretation that foregrounds the well-being of the community as a whole. With a single act, Hannū grants the Jewish family the baby they so wanted while saving the honor of the Muslim family. It is a type of communal healing that Moroccans will not likely experience today due to the absence of Jews in their community, but which mnemonic literature recovers and foregrounds to further emphasize that which was lost.

Not only does Hannū use the healing power of gift-giving to deliver her Jewish client-turned-mentee, Izzā, from depression and madness, but she also plays the role of an interfaith leader in the Jewish-Muslim community.

The privilege that her pan-religious position confers on her explains both the authority and unique status she enjoys in the two communities. Her role as a nexus for community-building between Jews and Muslims is not limited to when she is alive, but extends to her death, when the Blūlūs pay for her funeral.

Hannū's fluid religious identity recalls that of Zakiyya, a character in Shimon Ballas's 1992 short story "Iyya," set in an Iraqi/Israeli Jewish-Muslim context.[52] In her analysis of the story, Lital Levy writes:

> As a hybrid character, Zakiyya occupies the most liminal of spaces: she is a Muslim living in a Jewish household, in a mixed Muslim–Jewish neighborhood, in a predominantly Muslim country. In her daily life, she crosses boundaries both literally and figuratively, moving between Jewish and Muslim space, speaking the Jewish dialect at home and with members of her adopted family's extended community, and reverting back to the Muslim dialect when visiting with her "blood" family, her nieces and nephews.[53]

Even though Zakiyya is much younger than Hannū, the ease with which they carry themselves in the two religious communities is indicative of the complex relationships, memories, and histories that can emerge from interreligious intimacy, and which are most likely lost to archives. Zakiyya is presented as someone who has internalized the secular and religious codes of both communities and is able to live comfortably in the two without any difficulty. In fact, Zakiyya seems to be entirely Jewish and completely Muslim at the same time. Like Zakiyya, Hannū practices an all-embracing citizenship that is forged in day-to-day interactions with her Jewish neighbors.

Bearing in mind our understanding of citizenship as community-building through intimacy, *Zaghārīd al-mawt* suggests that the subversion of accepted social norms is an important element of this citizenship. By helping to arrange Samīḥa/Shamīḥa's adoption, Hannū defies Islamic law, which prohibits the adoption of Muslim children by non-Muslims. Yet Hannū does not conspire alone. Indeed, the entire community of citizens works in cahoots to transfer Samīḥa from her biological Muslim mother to her adoptive Jewish mother, which effectuates a larger communal healing. This adoption and the efforts that go into supporting it raise questions and challenge preconceived ideas of blood purity and religious antagonism. The transference also shows that uterine relationships between Jews and Muslims are much more important than previously thought. This episode offers a glimpse into a history of mixing and miscegenation that remains taboo today, but mnemonic literature brings up, further complicating Morocco's yet-to-be-written history.

The subversive potential of this type of Jewish-Muslim community may explain the suspicion of both the Protectorate and the post-independence state vis-à-vis Jewish-Muslim cooperation. Moroccan Jewish nationalist Joseph Lévy recounts one such example in his discussion of the French Protectorate's recurring opposition to the celebration of Mimouna. Lévy describes how French authorities blocked Muslims from entering the Jewish quarter—the *mellah*—in Fez in the 1940s to prevent mingling between Jews and Muslims.[54] These actions undertaken by colonial administrators indicate that they were aware of the highly generative potential of Jewish-Muslim intimacy, solidarity, coalition, and community formation. It takes this powerful reimagination of Jewish-Muslim intimacy in mnemonic literature to fully understand the significance of its suppression, and to recognize its generative potential.

Transgressive Solidarities between Jewish and Muslim Women

Jewish-Muslim transgressive solidarities in mnemonic literature most clearly illustrate how a high level of intimacy undergirds their citizenship. Although the history of Jewish-Muslim solidarity—especially among women[55]—has yet to be examined, in representing instances of it, mnemonic literature paves the way for such work. The process of unearthing these solidarities effectuates a shift in our understanding of these underground relationships and their decisive importance for the type of citizenship that crystalizes from this intimacy. "Feminine solidarity transgresses even religious boundaries," writes Bahloul.[56] One example of this solidarity is Hannū's sacrilegious act of facilitating the adoption of a Muslim baby girl by a Jewish family. In violating an explicit Quranic rule, Hannū carries out a most profound act of solidarity with Izzā Blūlū. The complexity of these entanglements and the value systems that underlie them are deeply underscored by Hannū's lack of guilt and the Muslim family's acquiescence to this face-saving arrangement. Such endeavors to build community show how women are integral, if not the most important, partners in building and maintaining intimacy between Jews and Muslims in mnemonic literature.

In *Shāmma aw Shtrīt*, Shāmma's visit to Casablanca and the encounter between her and Khadīja, her former sister-in-law, reveal how this feminine solidarity works. While Ṣūfiā Aṣrrāf's investigation leaves no doubt that Yūsuf is Shāmma's son, Yūsuf, the anti-Zionist activist, is reluctant to acknowledge that his mother is Jewish and, even worse for his standing in society and in the political arena, an Israeli citizen. However, his aunt Khadīja's solidarity, or even collusion, with his Jewish mother leads to Yūsuf's acceptance of

Shāmma as his biological mother. Khadīja, Yūsuf's de facto mother, uses her need of medicine as a ruse to lure him home in order to start a conversation with the Israeli side of the family over lunch. Although this reintroduction necessitates Khadīja's facing her family's traumatic history, she bravely does so without hesitation, corroborating Shāmma's narrative about her identity. Without any vindictiveness toward Shāmma for all the pain that her flight caused the family, Khadīja urges Yūsuf to "forgive her, love your sister because, like you, she is a victim of this separation."[57] It is only because she knows Shāmma very well that Khadīja understands Shāmma's emigration was a result of forces beyond her control. During their reunion, Khadīja prioritizes healing the wounds of her family's traumatic separation over shortsighted revenge that would only protract their division.[58] Khadīja's endeavor to mend the relationship between Yūsuf and his mother does not, however, constitute a justification of occupation. It acknowledges the existence of wider structures that caused the separation while focusing on their impact on the microcosm of the family.

Reimagined Nationalist Activity against the French as a Site of a Lost Jewish-Muslim Intimacy

In Morocco, as in other formerly colonized countries, participation in nationalist resistance against the colonizer confers political and social legitimacy on those who could prove that they partook in the decolonization process. This legitimacy in and of itself becomes a source of both symbolic and financial capital that benefits those upon whom the term *muqāwim/muqāwima* (freedom fighter) is bestowed. However, even beyond the material gains it grants the members of this privileged category of *al-waṭaniyyūn* (nationalist fighters), contribution to nationalist activity, or resistance against the colonial forces, served as a benchmark to determine who belonged to the nation and who did not. At a later stage, the post-independence Moroccan monarchy would rely on these distinctions to promote hagiography and forms of nationalism that did not disturb the configuration of power in the country.

Moroccan Jews were not immune to the consequences of the enshrinement of nationalism as the expression of one's commitment to the nation. In a series of interviews with anthropologist Mikhaël Elbaz, Abraham Serfaty underscores how Dr. Leon Benzaquen, the first Jewish minister in the history of post-independence Morocco in 1956, wasted a historic opportunity.[59] For Serfaty, Benzaquen's rejection of the invitation to sign the Proclamation of Independence, although comprehensible in the context of the deep divisions within the Moroccan Jewish community in the 1940s, was an extraordinary blunder. "If he had signed, it would have meant the commitment of the Moroccan Jewish community to Morocco's independence."[60] Simon Lévy, one of the few Jews who stayed in Morocco after the mass departure of their coreligionists, on the other hand, has persuasively wondered who was considered a Moroccan nationalist during the colonial period. Addressing a large group of Moroccan academic historians at a conference in 2007, Lévy urged his fellow historians to pose difficult questions about nationalism in Morocco and the participation of Moroccan Jews in its formation: "Is the ownership of nationalism in this country Muslim only? [. . .] Is it enough for one to be Muslim to be nationalist? This was the question at that time. I imagine that being Jewish is sufficient for a Jew not to be [considered] a nationalist [. . .]. In reality, nationalism takes different forms and types."[61] By casting doubt on the prevalent assumptions about Moroccan nationalism, Lévy's pointed questions are a provocative call for a new reading of Moroccan history. Both Serfaty and Lévy's positions evoke Frantz Fanon's observations regarding Algerians Jews' attitudes vis-à-vis the struggle for independence. In Fanon's analysis, there was no doubt that many Algerian Jews supported Algeria's anti-colonial endeavor, but many factors, including class, education, and location between rural and urban areas, determined the degree of this support.[62]Again, the absence of archives and the silence on the role of Jews from the witnesses who lived this period position mnemonic literature to furnish other-archival portrayals of what possibly happened.

Hassan Aourid's novel *Cintra* contains paratextual as well as plot-level elements that acknowledge Jewish contributions to Morocco's independence.[63] Recounting the story of an obscure freedom fighter and nationalist figure named 'Umar Binmansūr, *Cintra* is about both memory and the history of Moroccan nationalism, and specifically the memory of subaltern Moroccans—both Jews and Muslims—who fought French colonization from the margins of society. *Cintra* reconstructs Binmansūr's life story after he slips into a coma during a visit to Cintra Bar in the early 2000s. During his youth, Binmansūr was assigned to spy on the working-class people who frequented the bar when he was a young administrator in the colonial security apparatus. His coma brings together Dr. Vīvānī, an emergency medical doctor; Dr. Awrīd, a political scientist; and Bushrā, Binmanṣūr's granddaughter, in an attempt to resuscitate him and bring his memory back. As the effort to help Binmanṣūr recover his consciousness unfolds, *Cintra* opens up a little-known and seldom fictionalized history of Jewish-Muslim cooperation in the Communist Party to defend the Moroccan people's right to independence.

Cintra's focus on Jewish-Muslim citizenship first occurs in the paratext of the novel. Aourid dedicates the novel to a coterie of deceased, progressive Moroccan Jewish and Muslim intellectuals, including historian Germain Ayache and his wife Freha Ayache, novelist Edmond Amran El Maleh, politician and university professor Simon Lévy, economist Driss Ben Ali, sociologist Mohamed Guessous, journalist Mohamed Larbi Messari, intellectual Farid Naïmi, and feminist sociologist Fatema Mernissi.[64] The epigraph states that all these intellectuals "believed in a Morocco that could accommodate everyone."[65] The author's desire was for his book to be an echo of that to which these Jews and Muslims had "dedicated their lives."[66] The novel itself depicts Muṣṭafā Bū'azīz, a charismatic union leader, 'Umar Binmanṣūr, the protagonist, and two Moroccan communist Jews, Edmond Amran El Maleh and Simon Lévy, in a meeting at the headquarters of the Moroccan Communist Party (MCP) in Casablanca during the height of French repression in 1947, after King Mohammed V's historic speech in Tangiers. The flight of Binmanṣūr's first (Jewish) wife, Sulaika, to Israel/Palestine precipitates his involvement in Moroccan nationalism. In a way, Sulaika and Binmanṣūr's opposite movements in this climacteric period reflect a historical reality facing Moroccan Jews: whether to stay or leave their homeland. It is (the fictional) Lévy who delivers Sulaika's farewell letter to Binmanṣūr. By depicting both those who emigrate—like Sulaika—and those who stay—like Lévy and El Maleh, the novel portrays the range of positions within the Moroccan Jewish community during these pivotal years. Even more important for their nationalist standing is the depiction of Lévy and El Maleh among the notables of the Moroccan Communist Party, specifically at a time when many Moroccan Muslim leaders were collaborating with the French and occupying official positions within the colonial administration. The situation echoes Lévy's statement during the aforementioned meetings of historians that the major traitors during the colonial period were Muslim.[67]

Jewish involvement in nationalist activities is also highlighted when they help smuggle Binmanṣūr from Morocco after the French authorities discover his support for the Moroccan nationalist movement. The party sends him to German Ayache's house in Saint Peter's Square in Rabat before he "join[s] Ayache's family in Berkane, and [goes] from there to Melilla, Madrid, and then Cairo."[68] In real life, German Ayache was the Jewish founder of contemporary Moroccan historiography and a former leader of the MCP.[69] Both his real existence and his fictionalized character in *Cintra* make a statement that reassesses the position of Moroccan Jews during the colonial period. By placing the fictional character of Ayache and his wife, Freha, at the center of Jewish-Muslim underground resistance to French occupation in Morocco, *Cintra* places Jews at the epicenter of Moroccan nationalism.

Unlike the direct and open cooperation between Jews and Muslims against French colonialism depicted in *Cintra*, the Jewish characters in *Zaghārīd al-mawt* are more ambiguous in their positions. This ambiguity can be explained by the ordinariness of the characters and their lack of any learned or educated ideological basis from which to articulate their struggle. The highly educated communists in *Cintra* find their contrast in *Zaghārīd al-mawt*'s rural, less politically organized characters. So, while the former's activism emanates from an understanding of the existence of an imaginary entity called the Moroccan nation, the latter are only loyal to each other based on their belonging to the same local community, which this chapter has conceptualized as community citizenship. However, the characters in *Zaghārīd al-mawt* are not completely apolitical. Shimūn Blūlū is said to have a direct connection to the heroic nationalist leader Aḥmad al-Ḥanṣālī, who waged a staunch war of resistance against the French colonial army. The narrative also insinuates that Blūlū informed al-Ḥanṣālī of the arrival of French soldiers who had come to arrest him. By having al-Ḥanṣālī, an icon of Moroccan nationalism, learn the news from Blūlū, *Zaghārīd al-mawt* puts a Jewish character at the heart of the risky and glorious nationalist enterprise.[70] Blūlū's role thus represents another facet of the complexity of the Jewish experiences of national liberation in the Maghreb in general and in Morocco specifically. Histories of liberation and nationalism written in the absence of Jewish actors have created homogenized narratives, which producers of mnemonic literature revisit and reassess, adding heretofore invisible dimensions to this particularly canonized history.

Although Blūlū does not openly resist the French, he acts to facilitate the nationalist endeavor. One example is Blūlū's collaboration with Muslim freedom fighters during a strike that al-ʿAllālī, a freedom fighter, calls for in the city of Beni Mallal. Even when the French civil government of Beni Mellal forces Blūlū to show up at his bus station during a general strike, his collusion with al-ʿAllālī renders the controller's pressure ineffective. Blūlū's loyalty to his Moroccan-ness is likewise expressed in his rejection of Zionist emissaries and in his refusal to leave his homeland. Again, the novelist questions the predominant narrative that tends to exclude Jews from the decolonization process by giving a crucial role to a Jewish character, who embodies what we might call shared values of Moroccan-ness.

Jewish-Muslim intimacy and shared citizenship in Tazi's novel *Anā al-mansī* serves as a space for nationalist activity. Through its reimagination of life in the Jewish quarters of Fez up until 1967, this saga of three generations of the Kūhīn family delves deeply into the contradictions that permeate the complex worlds inhabited by its characters. *Anā al-mansī*'s plot reveals the different forces that reshaped the characters' relationship to Morocco during the long process of their dislocation from the country. For instance, Raḥamīm, a Jewish bar owner in the mellah of Fez, is an informant for the colonial authorities who sends his son to the French Aviation Academy to become a pilot in order to join the Israeli army. However, his rootedness in the city of Fez prevents him from emigrating to Israel despite his unbounded support of the newly formed state. However, not all Jews share the same position in the novel. Unlike Raḥamīm, who supports colonialism, Mūshī Bin 'Imrān Kūhīn, one of the main characters in the novel, carries out a nationalist act. Witnessing an exchange between Mūshī, an ordinary Jewish man, and his informant 'Abd al-Raḥamān, who provides information about the national resistance in exchange for money, he tells resistance leader, al-Sharīf, about their exchange. As soon as al-Sharīf arrives at Raḥamīm's restaurant, Mūshī Bin 'Imran Kūhīn starts an argument with him about the resistance, asking why no Jews joined its ranks.[71] While al-Sharīf never confirms these allegations—and this lack of confirmation can be interpreted as a rejection of their veracity—Mūshī makes a strong statement about himself, avowing that he is neither a freedom fighter nor a traitor:

> I, for example, am not a fidā'ī but I am not a traitor either. A little time before you arrived, another Mūshī, who is not me, was sitting at this table with 'Abd al-Raḥmān. I said these words to the other Mūshī who is not myself.[72]

Al-Sharīf believes Mūshī's interest in the resistance and its nationalist activity is the first stage in his transformation into a committed nationalist by expressing his desire to tell on "traitors who sell the fedayeen to the agents of colonization,"[73] but al-Sharīf's project is short-lived. Raḥamīm informs the colonial authorities of his suspicions that al-Sharīf had killed someone that night, and they arrest him immediately after he leaves the table he shared with Mūshī Bin 'Imrān Kūhīn. Mūshī Bin 'Imrān Kūhīn's agreement to spy on the traitor for al-Sharīf in exchange for money can eventually be understood as his way of making a living while serving a higher purpose.

Mūshī Bin 'Imrān Kūhīn is also conscious of his rootedness in Fez, which may explain his readiness to take the risk of joining the nationalist movement. His ambiguous position questions the very reductive meaning that being a Moroccan nationalist has come to hold over the years. Rather than being an expression of high moral integrity, one's history of activism within the nationalist movement has become a source of privileges and prebends. However, Mūshī Bin 'Imrān Kūhīn's brand of nationalism opens the readers' eyes to his deep roots in, and love for, the country. Rather than proving that he has participated in nationalist activities against the French, he shows his love for Fez, his real homeland. For instance, when his son-in-law Emil tells him that their future is in Israel, Mūshī Bin ʻImrān Kūhīn responds with a rhetorical question: "And here in the mellah of Fez, do we only have the past and no future?"[74] He asserts: "Listen, Emil, I am not Israeli, I am a Moroccan Jew, from the house of Kūhīn. I was born in the mellah of Fez, like my father, his parents and our ancestors who were born in the mellah."[75] For Mūshī, the nation is Fez, and specifically the mellah, which serves as his anchor for belonging to a wider community in Morocco.

Mūshī Bin ʻImrān Kūhīn's historical awareness of the importance of Jewish-Muslim intimacy and the type of citizenship it facilitated also emerges in his description of his father's relationships with Muslims:

> What I am talking about happened in the '30s and the beginning of the '40s of the last century—it was during the period of French colonialism and the promulgation of the Berber Decree. It is a well-known fact that a significant number of Moroccan Jews were Amazigh,[76] but, like all Amazigh people, they rejected the Berber Decree because one of its goals was opening the doors for Amazigh people to abandon Islam and become Christian. Assuming the same situation would apply to Amazigh Jews, they showed their solidarity and, despite the diversity of their affiliations, made clear to the leaders of the nationalist movement that they rejected Marshal de Gaulle's conspiracy against Moroccan national unity.[77]

Mūshī Bin ʻImrān Kūhīn's story predates the creation of Israel and shows that what united Moroccan Jews and Muslims in their diversity was a sense of belonging and solidarity. A fascinating aspect of Mūshī Bin ʻImrān Kūhīn's statement is his awareness of the existence of Amazigh Jews and the dangers of the Berber Decree, which was passed in 1930 to apply customary law to Amazigh areas in Morocco, to both Jews and Muslims.[78]

In his book *Two Arabs, a Berber, and a Jew: Entangled Lives in Morocco*, American anthropologist Lawrence Rosen uses an experience he lived during the June 1967 War in Morocco to affirm "how entangled [Jews'] lives were with those of their Muslim neighbors."[79] Rosen lived in the city of Séfrou during the war and feared retaliation against the Jews after the defeat of the Arab armies. Yet, the catastrophe he thought would happen against the Jews of the city did not materialize. Instead, and against all his expectations, a Muslim tribal leader and his son showed up at Rosen's Jewish landlord's house offering the family protection in accordance with a pact he had inherited from his father. The Muslim chieftain's behavior is an act of community preservation that emanated from the sense of shared citizenship with the Jewish family. In the larger context of Arab-Israeli politics and war, the chieftain had a dilemma of choice between two allegiances: adherence to the larger Muslim/Arab umma or loyalty to a local Moroccan family of Jewish faith. The chief chose to protect the Jewish family. This deliberate choice differentiates this Jewish family in Séfrou—given its status as a member of the community of citizens—from its coreligionist who emigrated to Israel/Palestine. In its broader implications, this story seems to say that the Jews of Séfrou were part of a community of citizens who shared the same nationscape and underlying values of community. In contrast, Arab nationalism and the Islamic umma—though they may have a presence in the chieftain's life—were too distant from their lived reality where the Jewish family was more real, thus speaking to the type of shared citizenship that once existed throughout Morocco but is no longer. In the meantime, the same Muslim chieftain would most certainly be against occupation. These positions were not mutually exclusive, since lived citizenship brought him closer to the Moroccan Jews, whereas belonging to humanity at large led him to condemn colonialism. This very intricate balance has been at the heart of the development of mnemonic literature, which celebrates Moroccan Judaism without forgetting to support a just solution to the Palestinian question.

Bringing Emigration Home to Roost: Representing the Internal Causes of Jewish Emigration

Mnemonic literature depicts Jewish emigration and the end of Jewish-Muslim intimacy as resulting from internal political strife in Morocco. Morocco's history between the country's independence in 1956 and the passing of its second post-independence king, Hassan II, is now described as the Years of Lead. A period of political violence and repression, the Years of Lead entrenched and normalized the historiographical silences that the authors of mnemonic literature attempt to undermine. A very crucial contribution that mnemonic literature makes in this regard is linking the process of Jewish emigration and loss of the community citizenship to the political instability of these years.

The novel *Cintra* gestures to the mistakes made by the state during the political struggles of the 1960s, using one family as evidence. The novel underlines how the "struggle between those who employed the Protectorate structures in the 1960s and those who refused them" led to a number of tragedies that impoverished Morocco by derailing the democratic process, facilitating Jewish emigration, and forestalling the establishment of a citizenship-based nation-state.[80] The novel seems to say that had there been a united internal front against the dislocation of Moroccan Jews, global push factors would not have had the same impact.

Ḥārith al-nisyān is also set against the backdrop of a student uprising in Casablanca in March 1965. The setting of both works during the Years of Lead is indicative of the connection between the political situation inside Morocco and the ongoing emigration of Moroccan Jews. Even as the Jewish siblings José and Eléna leave Morocco, the sociopolitical situation in the country becomes more repressive. Moreover, the connection of Jewish emigration to these oppressive decades of post-independence Moroccan history allows novelists to be part of the wider discussion about the need to rewrite the history of this period.

Meanwhile, *Shāmma aw Shtrīt* creates a link between Khadīja's persecution by the authorities and her failure to keep the family together when Muṣṭafā disappears in the aftermath of Shāmma's and Immā's departure to Israel/Palestine. In fact, Khadīja, at the time, "avoided the police and hid from [them] because of [her] ideological convictions [during] that era."[81] These connections are explicitly stated in Khadīja's argument when she tries to convince Yūsuf to forgive his Jewish mother, Shāmma, for leaving Morocco without him: "politics, Mister Yūsuf, always creates victims. I was a victim of internal politics inside my country, and you, Shtrīt [Shāmma] and Fāṭima were victims of international politics."[82] Without, of course, denying the characters' agency to make different choices, the idea underlying this discourse of victimhood links the process that dislocated Moroccan Jews to the authoritarian state within Morocco itself. We are led to believe that without the state's persecution of Khadīja, she could have prevented the family's separation and spared it the traumatic disintegration represented in the novel.

Conclusion

This chapter has explored the myriad ways that Jews and Muslims built community and exercised their citizenship in Morocco, as represented in mnemonic literature. These literary renderings serve as both a statement about the past and a commentary about the socio-cultural and political impoverishment that followed Jewish emigration from Morocco. They are other-archives of a history whose crucial pieces are circulated in the oral stories of the people who lived, but whose consignment to writing still remains open.

This literary representation of the end of Jewish-Muslim intimacy happens at two interrelated levels. The first level depicts Jews and Muslims as a community, intermarrying, begetting children, supporting each other, and engaging in socially subversive actions that strengthen this sense of unity. The second level is the depiction of Moroccan authorities' passivity vis-à-vis Zionist networks that were active in the country and prodding Moroccan Jews to leave. In contrast to their tolerant attitude toward Zionists, Moroccan authorities dedicated their surveillance and policing to persecute leftist activists who, in addition to supporting a revolution against the monarchy, wanted Moroccan Jews to remain in their country. Indeed, the absence of Moroccan intelligence services and police apparatus from the novels triggers many questions about those authorities' complicity in the facilitation of emigration of the Jewish population, questions that Moroccan historiography has yet to dare to confront.[83]

While mnemonic literature reimagines a Jewish-Muslim Morocco that no longer exists, it also fictionalizes the local and global factors that led to its extinction. Mnemonic literature in this regard plays a historiographical role in elucidating how the different push factors coalesced to rob Morocco of its Jews and Moroccan society of the Jewish-Muslim community-building analyzed here. In depicting this bygone intimacy and the types of local citizenship that it enabled, mnemonic literature triggers re-interrogations of Jewish-Muslim Moroccan history and brings attention to its multilayered silences. However, mnemonic literature's deepest contribution to understanding Jewish emigration is its centering of the depictions of what was happening inside Morocco at the time when the events portrayed were unfolding, gesturing thus to other-archives' transnational dimensions.

Attention to both internal and external factors that resulted in Jewish emigration from Morocco has another equivalent in the story of the army soldiers disappeared to the secret prison of Tazmamart. A story that has had both local and global ramifications, Tazmamart has become the epicenter of Morocco's other-archives of enforced disappearance and arbitrary detention. The following chapter delves into the politics of constituting other-archives of political imprisonment in the local and the global contexts.

4
Making Tazmamart a Transnational Other-Archive

Tazmamart prison has never existed in Morocco. "This alleged jail only exists in the imagination of the enemies of our democracy," unabashedly declared a member of the Moroccan parliament.[1] Nevertheless, and despite persistent denial of its existence for eighteen years, twenty-eight survivors of this secret prison, which had been in operation since 1973, magically reappeared in 1991. Now that the tides of political and public opinion have turned, Moroccan officials have found refuge in silence, in the hope that this embarrassing symbol of their authoritarianism would just recede from collective memory. They were mistaken, because amnesia proved to be elusive even thirty years after the fact. The serialization of Tazmamart survivor Mohamed Raïss's prison memoirs, *Min Skhirāt ilā Tazmamart, tadhkiratu dhahāb wa iyyāb ilā al-jaḥīm* (*From Skhirat to Tazmamart: A Roundtrip Ticket to Hell*) in the socialist daily newspaper *al-Ittiḥād al-Ishtirākī* (*The Socialist Union*) in 2000 was a watershed moment that kindled the Moroccan people's curiosity about their collective memory of political disappearance, state violence, and repression, and established this jail as an icon for a burgeoning of other-archives.[2] Against all expectations of forgetting, Tazmamart, by the sheer quantity of literary, filmic, and journalistic publications generated by the plight of its survivors, has shifted boundaries of authorship, and instituted novel ways of thinking about archives and recording histories of forcible disappearance in Morocco.[3]

This chapter demonstrates that the trajectory of Tazmamart's eponymous prison from a site utterly denied to a transnational literary phenomenon has produced three complementary and interconnected sets of other-archives in which the repressed victims of this jail continue to exercise their historiographical agency[4]—that is, an intentional effort to write history as a civic endeavor—to transform a story of denial into a symbol of collective writing projects for a collective memory of the Years of Lead. I conceptualize and categorize writings about Tazmamart into *scandalous, embodied,* and *fictionalized* other-archives. Each of these three sets of other-archives corresponds to a specific period in the history of the secret jail. While the scandalous other-archives' creation coincided with the official denial of Tazmamart's existence between 1973 and 1990, embodied other-archives boomed between 1999 and 2014, which witnessed the prolific publication of survivors' memoirs; finally, fictionalized other-archives correspond to the literary appropriation of both scandalous and embodied other-archives in both Moroccan and foreign languages and by both Moroccan and foreign authors. In this analysis, I demonstrate that all these other-archives converge in the ongoing fictionalization of the story of Tazmamart in the form of novels. This process endows lived experiences with a procreative force that, while recognizing individual experiences, collectivizes and reglobalizes Morocco's history of enforced disappearance.

The first of three analytical prongs I develop in this chapter shows how, against all odds, a group of Paris-based activists such as Christine Daure-Serfaty, François Della Sudda, Gilles Perrault, and members of *La Ligue des droits de l'homme* (Human Rights League) and *Les Comités de lutte contre la repression au Maroc* (Committees Battling against Repression in Morocco [CBRM]) created a scandalous other-archive of political disappearance in Morocco.[5] By scandalous, I mean that this other-archive was first and foremost intended to cause a scandal that would shame the Moroccan state and push it to end its denial of the existence of the Tazmamart enforced disappearance camp. In fact, scandalous other-archives evolved gradually from whistleblower activist pamphlets to book form, thus becoming the first seed for the later burgeoning output of survivor testimonies. The second prong offers a theorization of embodied other-archives. Unlike the scandalous other-archive, which was mediated through secret and circuitous channels, the embodied other-archive is rooted in survivors' firsthand accounts of their survival of enforced disappearance.[6] The last prong of the chapter is an analysis of fictionalized other-archives: novels that draw on both scandalous and embodied other-archives, and which refigure the significance of politically motivated disappearance for Moroccan history. The novelistic works that constitute these growing loci of unsilenced histories—Tahar Ben Jelloun's *Cette aveuglante absence de lumière* (*This Blinding Absence of Light*), Belkassem Belouchi's *Rapt de voix* (*Voice Theft*), Youssef Fadel's *Ṭāʾir azraq nādir yuḥalliqu maʿī* (*A Rare Blue Bird Flies with Me*), and Radwa Ashour's *Farag* (*Blue Lorries*)—have opened up other-archives to controversy, appropriation issues, translation, circulation, and transnational connections between local and global violations of human rights.[7]

Two Coups d'état, One *Mouroir*: The Birth of Tazmamart

Tazmamart was the catastrophic result of two failed coups d'état against King Hassan II's regime, on July 10, 1971, and August 16, 1972. The first attempt was spearheaded by General Mohamed Medbouh, the director of the Royal Military Cabinet, and Colonel M'hamed Ababou, the director of the Ahermoumou Military Academy. The putschists attacked the royal palace in the resort town of Skhirat, where the king was celebrating his forty-second birthday in the presence of both Moroccan and foreign dignitaries. Colonel Ababou used his powerful position within the army to carry out this deadly putsch, into which he dragged over a thousand cadets of the Academy and their instructors.[8] Although unaware of Ababou's designs, the cadets and their instructors were tried for complicity in the attempt.[9] Almost four decades later, journalist Zakya Daoud would write that the 1971 coup was "a hecatomb of diplomats, ministers, musicians, and average people: some two hundred people would be killed and more than two hundred wounded for this *grotesque and bloody party*."[10] More complicated in nature, the second putsch, which involved downing King Hassan II's plane as he returned from a private visit to France and Spain, was a daring operation to eliminate him and his entourage. In addition to implicating members of the air force and General Mohamed Oufkir, then Minister of Defense and Hassan II's confidant, later documentation revealed that this second coup was merely the tip of an iceberg of concerted cooperation between the army and prominent civilian opposition members to take power from the king.[11]

The king survived both attempts at deposing him. The horrific punishment meted out to those who participated in these coups was designed to match the gravity of their failed regicide. Officers, cadets, and soldiers were tried in a military court, which, according to Article 4 of the 1956 Code of Military Justice, is "competent to try individuals accused of an offence against the external security of the state, as well as military personnel suspected of any offence in the penal code or of specifically military offences."[12] Despite the existence of this extraordinary court, "four generals, five colonels and one captain" were extralegally executed immediately after the coup in 1971.[13] In Daure-Serfaty's opinion, the summary execution of these officers was a decapitation of the Moroccan army.[14] Nevertheless, General Oufkir, who was in cahoots with the putschists, leveraged the court to yield unexpectedly lenient sentences for those implicated in the 1971 coup. For example, of the 1,154 soldiers who were tried, the court acquitted 1,008 cadets, delivered one death sentence, which the court of appeals commuted to life in prison, and sentenced "thirty-three [to] prison terms between three years and life in prison."[15] Unlike the leniency shown in the first trial, the trial of the 220 pilots, mechanics, and officers implicated in 1972 coup was an example of judicial cruelty. Although still presided over by the same civilian judge, the composition of the court was altered to include Colonel Ahmed Dlimi and Colonel Boubker Skiredj, who were aboard the royal Boeing when it was attacked.[16] Both colonels would have been killed had the attack succeeded, but the judge never heeded the conflict of interest posed by their membership in the court. Moreover, King Hassan II's dissatisfaction with the ruling in the cases involving the first coup pushed the judges to toughen their verdicts this time around. They delivered eleven death sentences and increased the amount of jail time each sentence incurred, ranging from three to twenty-five years.[17] These court decisions would have remained merely a matter of vengeful justice once the trials and appeals were over had not the Moroccan gendarmery carried out *Operation Florence* on August 7, 1973. This secret operation involved kidnapping and relocating to a then-unknown location sixty-two military prisoners whose sentence was three years or longer.[18] The dislocation of the convicted soldiers from their legal prison under the supervision of the Ministry of Justice to the secret jail in Tazmamart marked a shift in their existence from legally protected subjects to becoming forcibly disappeared outside the purview of the law.

Making Tazmamart Believable: Scandalous Other-Archives

On August 12, 1973, only five days after the soldiers' relocation, their families found out that they were no longer being held in the Kenitra High Security Prison.[19] Unfortunately for them, this was only the beginning of an eighteen-year battle to secure the release of the survivors. The perplexing question has always been how the state was able to keep the fifty-eight soldiers who ended up in Tazmamart forcibly disappeared for almost two decades. It is neither the state's ability to keep secrets nor the diligence of public servants that helped Tazmamart to endure. In fact, Tazmamart's covert existence was maintained and protracted by the failure of different opposition groups within its political ecosystem to engage in intersectional solidarity with the disappeared soldiers—groups such as the then-vocal Frontist prisoners, also known as Marxist-Leninists; leftist political parties; and the Moroccan media.[20] In this regard, Daure-Serfaty, a famous French human rights activist who became the champion of the rights of Tazmamart prisoners, calls attention to leftist political parties' unsympathetic attitudes toward the disappeared putschists, who they insisted were part of the Makhzan-(state)-system.[21] Daure-Serfaty stresses that when she regained the right to return to Morocco in 1986, after being banned for a decade, she discovered that even the revolutionary Marxist-Leninist political prisoners, who were sentenced to very long jail terms in their famous trial in 1977, knew little, if anything, about the fate of the disappeared soldiers.[22] Tazmamart survivor Ahmed Marzouki, who authored the prize-winning memoir *Tazmamart: Cellule 10* (*Tazmamart: Cell Number 10*), amplifies Daure-Serfaty's claim when he accuses the Moroccan left of being partly responsible, by its complicit silence, for the longevity of the disappearance camp.[23]

The aphasia that prevailed across the political spectrum in Morocco served the state's desire to protect its "public secret."[24] Anthropologist Michael Taussig defines a public secret as "that which is generally known, but cannot be articulated."[25] A secret is public when it is known by people but they continue to pretend that they have no knowledge of it, and this knowledge of what cannot be admitted fosters even more silence.[26] Tazmamart was a classic case of a public secret of enforced disappearance, which involved "illegal abduction by the police, military and paramilitary squads, detention in secret centers, torture, usually death and improper burial, and denial by the authorities."[27] Daure-Serfaty remembers how a "moment of silence" always followed each time she mentioned the name Tazmamart to people in Morocco.[28] This silence conveyed to Daure-Serfaty that her "interlocutors knew, and it is precisely this knowledge that created silence, retreat, refusal, and prevarication."[29] The open secret, then, was nothing but a confirmation that the Makhzan had secret dungeons, where people were held in dehumanizing conditions, but those who were in a position to know were silenced by what they knew. Knowledge in this case is a deterrent rather than a motivation to action. Aphasia about public secrets, however, is not a uniquely Moroccan condition. Scholars of Latin America have also underscored how silence about political disappearance has been induced by the prohibition of its public discussion.[30] The uniqueness of the Moroccan case lies specifically in the fact that complicit silence about Tazmamart extended to French intellectuals, journalists, academics, and even politicians, who, unlike Moroccans inside the country, had nothing to fear.[31]

Family members' accounts of their tribulations during the disappearance of their relatives are unified in stating that Moroccan officials, including opposition party leaders, shuddered at the mere mention of Tazmamart, since the latter was directly associated with the king.[32] Aïda Hachad, the wife of Tazmamart survivor Salah Hachad, for instance, lists the powerful Moroccan politicians and members of the security apparatus who, although in a position to know about the existence of Tazmamart, denied any knowledge about the whereabouts of her husband, before concluding "if these men could not help me, that meant that nobody could."[33] While it is only natural for generals to deny their inconvenient actions, it is especially baffling that Moroccan politicians willfully ignored constitutional mechanisms the law afforded them and that would have enabled them to speak out about violations of human dignity. This unsympathetic political attitude on the part of the Moroccan political stakeholders found its way into Amnesty International's 1981 report, which claims that its representatives "had not stated that these individuals [Tazmamart prisoners] were prisoners of conscience" when its delegates met with Moroccan officials to find out about their whereabouts.[34]

Fear and silence in Morocco sustained an international disbelief that such a barbaric form of punishment was still conceivable after the Holocaust.[35] Disbelief prolonged silence and played out in favor of the Moroccan state's enforced disappearance project.[36] As a result, families had to endure the burden of losing their relatives and the even more onerous task of proving, against Hassan II's regime's injunctions to disown their missing male family members, that the Moroccan state not only knew their location but also was fully responsible for their fate:[37] an unthinkable double-burden. Working in tandem with the prisoners and human rights activists in France, some families served as a nexus between their disappeared relatives and the outside world, where people still could not believe that several dozen military convicts could just vanish from a high-security prison without a trace.

Making Tazmamart believable would not have been possible without the contributions of the disappeared prisoners. In particular, while still imprisoned, they managed to convince several guards to smuggle out letters they had written, in which they recorded in graphic detail the appalling conditions of their detention.[38] The first of these letters made it to France in 1980.[39] Their raw messages about horrific conditions—such as tiny cells, lack of light, poor food, cold, vermin, and absence of any medical care—reached whistleblowers and activists who worked to debunk the Moroccan state's denials of the secret jail's existence. Among these groups, CBRM, which was created in 1972 in Paris to work against repression in Morocco, stood out as a major player in the endeavor to end political disappearance in Morocco and Tazmamart specifically. Not only did CBRM consistently advocate for the release of Tazmamart prisoners, but it also made sure that they were not forgotten, by commemorating the annual anniversary of their disappearance from Kenitra prison. The prisoners' redacted letters played an important role in this work of commemoration and memory.[40] Thanks to CBRM's sustained commitment, Tazmamart's center of gravity shifted to Paris, where most activism against political imprisonment in Morocco was taking place in these early years.

Many factors positioned Paris to be the center from which Tazmamart was constituted into a scandalous other-archive. Because of their colonial history, Morocco and France had developed linguistic, human, and cultural ties that facilitated the collection and dissemination of information about Tazmamart.[41] Paris also hosted a highly politicized Moroccan student body, as well as an active Moroccan political and trade union community whose members were at the forefront of human rights battles against Hassan II's authoritarianism.[42] Moreover, Christine Daure-Serfaty, who would dedicate two decades of her life to human rights activism on behalf of Moroccan political prisoners, lived in France and used her extended connections in the media and human rights circles in Paris not only to prove the existence of Tazmamart, but also to coordinate pressure on the Moroccan state to release the prisoners from it in 1991.[43] In 1980, the brother of one of the inmates held in Tazmamart arrived unannounced at Daure-Serfaty's apartment and gave her a bunch of letters smuggled from the secret jail.[44] She then disseminated them among human rights activists, and they even found their way to Amnesty International's 1982 report. This report contained an update about the prison and announced that although fifteen of the fifty-eight prisoners had already served their sentences, they had never been released from the secret location to which they had been transferred.[45]

In the capable hands of Daure-Serfaty and CBRM human rights activists, the prisoners' letters became fodder for a scandalous other-archive that exposed King Hassan II's secret dungeons. The letters provided exactly the kind of information journalists and human rights activists needed to embarrass a state and debunk the idyllic image Morocco enjoyed in Europe through its touristic facade. Among the many human rights and intellectual figures who condemned such violations in Morocco, Gilles Perrault, a famous journalist and activist, made a radical step by agreeing to collaborate with Daure-Serfaty to denounce the Moroccan state. When Perrault's *Notre ami le roi* was published in 1990, the chapter dedicated to Tazmamart divulged the primitive conditions in which the "living-dead" were kept captive.[46] The book recycled the terrifying details of the detention conditions which the prisoners had consigned to bits of cigarette wrappers, handkerchiefs, and match boxes, which families conveyed in turn to human rights activists in France: they were held in tiny cells designed to mete out a slow death, with the bare minimum of food and no possibility of seeing the sun or breathing fresh air.[47] These details were too concrete and too brutal to simply be ignored. Based on these pieces of information, Perrault charged, in a most condemning passage, that "Buchenwald, Mauthausen, Sachenhausen, and other camps *Nacht und Nebel* had not lasted as long [as Tazmamart]" before adding that "the most atrocious place on earth" is only "one hour away from Madrid, [and] two hours from Paris."[48] In an ingenious move, Perrault targeted Moroccan tourism, which was the regime's most coveted industry and the source of much-needed hard currency, reminding readers that Tazmamart was not far from a touristic road that was familiar to many French visitors. An international operation that Amnesty International had launched at the time of its report in 1982, almost a decade before the publication of *Notre ami*, also informed tourists that the disappeared soldiers were held in "horrible conditions" in Tazmamart.[49] With its sensational and scandal-focused narrative, *Notre ami* gave voice to the cacophony of horror inside Tazmamart. Through the coordinated efforts of human rights activists, this reverberation made its way to Paris, London, and New York before coming home to roost in 1991.[50]

Notre ami was an evidentiary bomb that transformed a local "public secret" of human rights abuse into a global, scandalous revelation. Its narrative force and substantiated claims about political detention in Morocco in general, as well as its revelations about Tazmamart in particular, achieved the desired shock and outrage among the rank and file of the Moroccan regime. Perrault and his backers sought to prove that what the Moroccan authorities denied existed, and he used scandal, shame, and undiplomatic language to do so. According to Edwy Plenel, the Gallimard agent who recruited Perrault to write the book, *Notre ami* "shook the foundations of the regime, sowing panic among courtiers and followers."[51] The vehement response to its publication by the Moroccan authorities was a testament to its success in embarrassing the monarchy by documenting and then disseminating Tazmamart's brutal story. In his book *Le Maroc et Hassan II* (*Morocco and Hassan II*), historian Abdallah Laroui reflects on *Notre ami*'s widespread impact, noting that the stature of "the prestigious Gallimard earned the book evening news coverage on the main television stations."[52] To forestall the damaging revelations of Perrault's book, Hassan II sent emissaries, including Laroui, to the French political class to warn them against the denigration campaign emanating from their country.[53] Additionally, in a move that was reminiscent of Moroccan nationalists' maneuvers to pressure the Protectorate rule, authorities urged Moroccans to send hundreds of telegrams to the French Prime Minister Michel Rocard to protest the publication of the book.[54] Ultimately, Abderrahaman Nouda—a former leader of the *Ilā al-Amām* secret organization and a former political detainee—attributes Morocco's political openness in the late 1990s to the effects of *Notre ami*'s publication.[55]

Notre ami's genesis in itself, however, is a case study in the deliberate creation of a scandalous other-archive. The genealogy of *Notre ami* demonstrates how this archive is the result of a contrived endeavor to transform absence into presence, disappearance into reappearance, and denial into admission. These operations allow survivors and victims of state violence to enter into the public space and exercise their historiographical agency to write silenced histories of political detention and state authoritarianism. In *Tazmamart: Une prison de la mort au Maroc*, the book she dedicated to historicizing the struggle against Tazmamart, Daure-Serfaty recounts how she and her colleagues spent ten years working to move Tazmamart from the realm of rumor to that of an unimpeachable truth. For Daure-Serfaty, "convincing all those who cared about human rights [. . .] that the story of the soldiers of Tazmamart was true and that everything should be done to secure their release" was a stupendous task.[56] The French/European public's reluctance to believe that such a form of punishment could still exist in the latter half of the twentieth century required a plan of action that focused on the prisoners' experiences in enforced disappearance. Daure-Serfaty underlines that the only way to achieve this goal was "to tirelessly inform [about] and narrate the disregard of verdicts and the scary detention conditions."[57] Once the collaborators reached the conviction that an explosive book was necessary to end human rights violations, the harder task was finding a writer "who had the talent to transform the secretly accumulated knowledge by those who were defending human rights in Morocco into a mesmerizing book."[58] Reflecting on the significance of narrating Tazmamart in book form, Daure-Serfaty writes:

> Before this [the project to furnish information for Gilles Perrault to write the book], we had information but were unable to make it heard. I was sure now that the information I would be able to glean would be useful, would be heard. I would have loved to know everything and anything, to bring everything back to France to make it exist in this book; inside, in the prison visiting room, I asked everyone about their story, their memory of the prison.[59]

Notre ami was born out of this desire to optimize the use of information about Tazmamart. Perrault, it is true, wrote the *brûlot* (scathing report); but it was his arch-accomplice, Daure-Serfaty, who collected all the supporting evidence during trips to Morocco. She had resumed these crucial investigative trips in 1986 after marrying Abraham Serfaty, a Marxist-Leninist revolutionary who had been serving a life sentence in prison since 1977.[60]

The struggle against disbelief opened Daure-Serfaty's eyes to the fact that information is worthless if it is not translated into action. This reveals how other-archives are a force not only for revelation or cauterization but also, importantly, for mobilization. *Notre ami*'s publication achieved the goal to which several human rights groups had been committed for ten years—freeing the prisoners. Its publication at a time when human rights and universal jurisdiction were becoming all too normal certainly contributed to its efficiency. As this example shows, scandalous other-archives have the capacity to rally people and debunk complicitous behavior. Moreover, scandalous other-archives have the potential to trigger empathy and compel people to act. Edwy Plenel underlines *Notre ami*'s effect even among supporters of the Moroccan state in France when he writes that it "opened a breach in the wall of silence, which, by continuing its cowardice and complacency, protected an indefensible regime in France."[61] Human Rights Watch called the book a "savage biography of the king."[62] The book became a powerful media phenomenon: "all television channels, radio stations invited Gilles Perrault [to speak about the book]: a spark and the fire extended to the entire meadow. [. . .] It was magical."[63] Tazmamart had become a household word globally; and, most importantly, it had come home to haunt its perpetrators in the Moroccan crown. Former freedom fighter MP Mohamed Bensaid Aït Idder made history when he directly addressed the minister of justice about Tazmamart and its prisoners.[64] When Aït Idder's question to the minister was reported the next day in *Anoual*, the newspaper of his *Organisation de l'action démocratique populaire* (Organization of Popular Democratic Action [OPDA]) party, it was the first time since the soldiers' initial disappearance—seventeen and a half years prior—that the word "Tazmamart" had been published or publicly pronounced in Morocco.[65] A huge taboo had been overcome: Tazmamart was named. A few months after Aït Idder's brave question, twenty-eight survivors of Tazmamart were released, and their firsthand accounts of enforced disappearance would set the stage for embodied other-archives.

The scandalous other-archives activated around Tazmamart were the result of a whistleblower strategy that involved documenting and exposing the state's violations of human dignity. The different actors who participated in this whistleblowing endeavor—prisoners, their families, and human rights activists—succeeded in proving that Tazmamart was not a figment of Morocco's enemies' imagination, but rather a real human tragedy—one that cost the lives of thirty-two prisoners, including a certain Miloudi Seddik and a soldier from sub-Saharan Africa, and of which survivors would later recount the truth in chilling details. The multiplicity of actors, from prison guards to human rights activists, highlights a distinctive characteristic of scandalous other-archives: collaboration. Scandalous other-archives are in fact constructed collaboratively, and this collective nature makes the histories they tell rich in terms of strategies and geographic reach.

Unlike what would happen starting from 2000, activism in the scandalous other-archive required a systematic redaction of names and sources. For instance, the authors of the smuggled letters are never named, which made it impossible for the Moroccan authorities to identify them. The scandalous other-archives contain, as a result, mostly anonymous stories. Interestingly, however, the dead and agonizing soldiers in Tazmamart were named and the descriptions of their ordeals were depicted in detail in the scandalous other-archives that are scattered all over the world.[66] The un/naming of prisoners divides scandalous other-archives into two categories: a complete and intact other-archive, which was unavailable to readers but was available to activists and family members, and an incomplete other-archive, which was circulated and quoted widely, but was censored by activists to protect its sources. The public information published between 1982 and 1991 may not have all been entirely accurate because of the very circuitous process human rights whistleblowers put in place to protect their sources. The chain was structured in the following way: prisoners convinced some guards to smuggle letters to their families, and the families shared this secret information with sympathetic local human rights activists or fellow family members who lived abroad. They, in turn, conveyed the information to human rights organizations. Between the completeness of the first and the incompleteness of the second, the scholar of state violence in Morocco is bequeathed the fulfilling task of cross-examining scandalous other-archives with embodied other-archives in order to restore the wholeness of the stories. Moreover, voices in scandalous other-archives are mediated. The actors involved in the whistleblowing enterprise translated, paraphrased, contextualized, and conveyed the prisoners' suffering to the outside world.[67] While these activist strategies complicate authorship and testimony, anonymity foregrounds atrocity as a generalized condition in Tazmamart. It does not matter that there was no nominal list of detainees with specific conditions. What mattered was that fifty-eight citizens had been disappeared, and they were potential candidates for extermination.

Finally, scandalous other-archives in the case of Tazmamart have resulted in a paradoxical situation in which the globalization of the prison's narrative during the 1990s also localized human rights issues in Morocco at the very same time. The dizzying number of journalistic articles, interviews, protests, sit-ins, pamphlets, and speeches generated in the context of this struggle for human rights brought enforced disappearance and the violation of human dignity back home as an internal issue. As a result of the scandalous reception of his regime's violations, King Hassan II established the Advisory Council on Human Rights, released political prisoners in 1994, issued a general amnesty for the exiled, acknowledged Amazigh language and culture, and started conversations with political parties to reform the constitution.[68] These measures, which were unimaginable before 1990, made respect for human rights a cornerstone of political discourse in Morocco. In the shift, or process, that ultimately moved the scandalous other-archive of the 1990s into a fictionalized other-archive in the present, the embodied other-archive formed a crucial intermediary that rekindled literary rediscovery of Tazmamart and ultimately allowed its reglobalization in a context in which memories and histories of human rights violations functioned as drivers for visions of democratization and the rule of law.

Embodied Other-Archives of Tazmamart

Although twenty-eight survivors of Tazmamart were released in September 1991, another eight years of silence had to pass before the death of King Hassan II in 1999 allowed them to finally speak out. Their stories were instrumental to the then-ongoing efforts to resolve the burdensome legacy of the deceased king's reign. The shocking details of Tazmamart mesmerized millions of Moroccan readers when the daily newspaper *al-Ittiḥād al-Ishtirākī* [*The Socialist Union*] serialized the Arabic translation of Raïss's memoirs *Min Skhirāt ilā Tazmamart* in 2000. Translated from the original French, *Min Skhirāt ilā Tazmamart* initiated the existence of embodied other-archives in which survivors provide testimonies—first-person accounts of lived experiences of survival, resistance, and confrontation with the consequences of Tazmamart for both prisoners and their families. Raïss's testimonial book paved the way for the publication of several additional memoirs, which together constitute this local embodied other-archive. These narratives of imprisonment and survival include Ahmed Marzouki's *Tazmamart*; Abdehak Serhane's edited book *Kabazal: Les Emmurés de Tazmamart* (*Kazabal: The Prisoners of Tazmamart*); Ahmed and Kalima El Ouafi's *Opération Boraq F5: 16 août 1972, l'attaque du Boeing royal* (*Operation Boraq F15: August 16, 1972, The Attack against the Royal Boeing*); Aziz BineBine's *Tazmamort: Dix-huit ans dans le bagne de Hassan II* (*Tazmadeath: Eighteen Years in Hassan II's Jail*); as well as Driss T. Chberreq's *Le Train fou: Mémoires d'un rescapé de Tazmamart, 10 juillet 1971 au 29 octobre 1991* (*The Mad Train: Memoirs of a Survivor of Tazmamart, July 10, 1971 to October 29, 1991*). Rabea Bennouna, ex-wife of survivor Captain Abdellatif Belkbir, published her own autobiographical memoir entitled *Tazmamart côté femme: Témoignage* (*Tazmamart from a Woman's Perspective: A Testimony*) in which she narrates her and her family's struggle with disappearance from her position as a woman and a mother outside the prison walls.[69]

Embodied other-archives are witness accounts of survivors' lived experiences of hitherto-silenced state violence. They are not, however, mere testimonies or depositories of information about enforced disappearance. In fact, embodied other-archives are sites in which survivors do more than just chronicle their plight—they are survivors' conduits into history as agents who survived the ordeal of state violence and now use their agency to bear witness, in order to transform Moroccan society's assumptions about its recent past. Bearing witness (*shahāda*) is from the Arabic verb *shahida*, which *Lisān al-ʿarab* defines as "to be present," and *shahāda*, which means "certain account."[70] The notion of *shahāda* in Islamic jurisprudence encompasses both truth and certainty, which endows *al-shāhid al-ʿayyān* (ocular/eyewitness) with both the power and the legitimacy of truth-telling.[71] Anthropologist Susan Slyomovics affirms that *shahāda*, with its double meaning of both testifying and witnessing, "narrates personal witness and puts it in a situation-specific register."[72] Unlike Shoshana Felman's assertion that "to bear witness is to *bear the solitude* of responsibility, and to *bear the responsibility*, precisely, of that solitude,"[73] *shahāda* in the Moroccan context is equivalent to being a member of a community of both witnesses and martyrs. Survivors/witnesses are not alone since both the *shuhūd* (witnesses) and *shuhadāʾ* (martyrs) bear witness together through the voices of those who survived. Even those who were unable to survive Tazmamart are witnesses to its atrocity through their ghostly presence as *shahīd*, which means both "martyr" and "witness," in their companions' testimonies.[74] Moreover, historical accuracy and the desire to avoid libeling innocent people further strengthen *shahāda*'s communal nature in Tazmamart's embodied other-archives. For example, survivor Marzouki dispels any implications of solitude in his testimony when underlining his happiness each time his "comrades confirm[ed] to [him] that what [he] wrote was the core of truth."[75] Embodied other-archives may carry individual authors' names, but they are, in fact, loci of co-witnessing in which both the living and the dead make statements about state violence. The survivors bear witness directly, but the dead do so through their dilapidated physical state and words mediated by survivors.

It is ironic that the disappeared body is also the site for embodied other-archives. The survivor's body symbolizes the failure of enforced disappearance to erase it from existence and, in the meantime, holds the indelible traces of the painful experience deposited in it. Hence, the battered, abused, and semi-dead body is the locus in which are sedimented two decades of stories of suffering, injustice, and abuse of authority that reshape the historical narrative about the state. Embodied other-archives therefore show that even the decrepit, paralyzed, wounded, exhausted, and withered corpse-like survivors carry within their bodies a radical history that defies ignorance or silence. Consequently, the body of the survivor is in and of itself a referential text, the source where the experience of a national trauma is inscribed, and in which a wealth of experiences that have historical significance reside before their exteriorization in the form of other-archives. Before becoming a book, the object of DNA testing,[76] or a dossier in the Equity and Reconciliation Commission (ERC) process, embodied other-archives were first and foremost a palimpsest of wounds, some healed and some still open, which torturers, unjust justices, and jailers have forever consigned to the formerly detained body.

Embodied other-archives rehabilitate both the bodies and the names of those who were excised from the historical record. Survivors of Tazmamart understood that naming their companions in suffering in the stories they tell about their ordeal would entrench them in history and entrust their suffering to future historical reconstruction. For instance, BineBine, one of only three survivors of the deadly Hangar 2 (*al-ʿanbar al-thānī*), documents how his cellmates died, what caused their sadness, and the types of people they were. Through the stories he tells about his now-deceased cellmates, BineBine's testimony recovers the life story of Mohamed Abdessadki, known as Monolo, who had lived in Algeria and fought valiantly in the Spanish civil war. Likewise, readers meet El Yakidi and "listen" to his lighthearted jokes. Moreover, BineBine's *Tazmamort* readers witness the process that cost Captain Ben Dourou his beautiful teeth and Bahbah his health. *Tazmamort* restores the dream of prisoner Boujmâa Azendour to save his younger sister from poverty by providing her with an education.[77] As a result of being written into the larger story of Tazmamart, these deceased cellmates will continue to serve as a source for history, thanks to other-archives' ability to revive them and endow them with sensorial presentness.

Depositing their narrated pain in embodied other-archives is fundamental for the rehumanization of Tazmamart victims as agents of history. Instead of pain being disempowering, both punishment and the suffering that results from it are an impetus for a radically alternate history. History-as-usual has, indeed, no place in embodied other-archives, which situate suffering at the core of the historical experiences of post-colonial Moroccan society. The focus on pain in embodied other-archives opens up space for a transformative historical narrative. By providing realistic images of their colleagues' suffering, survivors nip silence in the bud and create the conditions of possibility for the history that will acknowledge their existence. For instance, Marzouki compares Mohammed El Ghalou's suffering to that of the rest of the inmates: "Yes, we all have suffered from countless illnesses and tasted endless forms of humiliation. As a result, all of us were lowered to the abysses where only trash and dirt are thrown. Consequently, we were, in the eyes of our torturers, the basest of God's creatures. However, despite all of this, we would be wrong and we could commit a calumny if we alleged that we tasted even half of what Job of Tazmamart, Mohamed El Ghalou, experienced."[78] El Ghalou's suffering was such that when the guards allowed Marzouki and his cellmate, Captain Ghelloul, to assist him, "a piece of his shabby body came off with his wet shirt and a part of his bones was uncovered."[79] No horror film could match Marzouki's description of El Ghalou as a "deformed skeleton, wrapped in a sack of perforated, torn skin."[80] Job's pain is unsurpassable, for it is a mythical and ahistorical pain, but the pain Marzouki is describing was designed to exterminate prisoners in total disregard of their humanity. The perforated sack was El Ghalou's body, eaten away by the eschars. The survivor is aware that recovering their dead colleagues' stories is manifold as a way to "commemorate them and salute their resistance and show to all Moroccans what their brothers in religion, humanity, and homeland endured" in order to evoke the deceased in similar situations.[81] This comparison serves as a reminder, but most importantly as a substrate for "denunciation in order to prevent atrocity from happening again."[82]

Resistance and the historicization of the prisoners' survival are pivotal to the constitution of embodied other-archives. In fact, prisoners' resistance to secret jail conditions enables the possibility of a historical narrative that radically reconceives the significance of survival and the prisoners' contributions to their own liberation. The realization that Tazmamart was nothing but a *mouroir*—a place where people were sent to die in horrible conditions—pushed the disappeared soldiers to devise creative ways to outlive the inhumane treatment and to battle amnesia. From organizing their lives around prayer, language-learning, storytelling, imaginary tours of Paris, revisiting cinematographic films they saw during the halcyon days of freedom, renarrating stories from their favorite novels, and inviting each other to imaginary banquets, to finding ways to communicate with the outside world, Tazmamart survivors turned their embodied other-archives into a space for the exercise of their agency, to vanquish silences that prolonged the state violence they endured for eighteen years. Resistance in embodied other-archives is not only defiance, but also a securing of the means to succeed in the struggle to overcome disappearance, such as procuring radios, candles, pens, paper, olive oil, headache medicine, vitamins, and many other basic goods that their jailers prohibited. By describing the various strategies that allowed them to acquire these contraband items, the disappeared prisoners reveal that the mere procurement was a victory over the disappearance system that tried to wipe them out of existence. Indeed, pencils and paper were the only weapons available to the disappeared prisoners for communicating with human rights activists. Pencils and paper were therefore instrumental in constituting prisoner experiences as a scandalous other-archive, to return to my earlier argument, whose explosive effects still continue to loom large over the memory of state violence in Morocco.

Perpetrators' portraits are co-constitutive of embodied other-archives. Because what took place in Tazmamart is no longer in doubt,[83] survivors' depictions of perpetrators register the truth of political violence. Slyomovics has rightly underlined how the cultural production that I am calling embodied other-archives "calls out aloud and clearly the names of torturers and perpetrators."[84] Several considerations compel some of the former prisoners to use initials to conceal the identities of their torturers, but most Tazmamart survivors use their full names in their testimonies. Even more important than the names alone are the stories that survivors tell about each perpetrator, which allows us to conceptualize them into two categories based on whether they act locally or nationally. Local perpetrators were in charge of operating the disappearance center and discharging its daily duties.[85] This category of perpetrators includes the prison director, guard supervisors, and guards, who perfunctorily did the work to exterminate the prisoners.[86] Local-level perpetrators shared illiteracy, poverty, and a blind respect for orders. Except for three good guards, this category of jailers showed nothing but cruelty, callousness, and greed throughout the time they were in charge of the prisoners. Most importantly, however, these guards' names are now consigned to other-archives forever. National-level perpetrators are distinguished from local-level perpetrators by their only occasional visits to the prison camp as well as the nebulous nature of their work, which allows them to remain more anonymous.[87] Although most of their names are unknown, embodied other-archives contain their physical descriptions, ranks in the military hierarchy, and the security branch to which they belonged. Additionally, survivors describe the role played by medical doctors, psychiatrists, psychologists, dentists, ophthalmologists, nurses, and other professionals, who patched them up after their release from Tazmamart.[88]

Despite their historiographical significance, embodied other-archives would not be complete without those of the prisoners' relatives. Family members, especially women and children, attest to the devastating effects surveillance and discrimination had on them. For instance, disappeared soldiers' family members' embodied other-archives recount how their exclusion transformed them into social pariahs. A deliberately coordinated social, administrative, and judicial apparatus oppressed the families and further invisibilized the prisoners. In this regard, Bennouna's third-person narrative, *Tazmamart côté femme*, uncovers the institutions that undergirded this economy of invisibilization through her daily tribulations with both authority and society.[89] *Tazmamart côté femme* lays bare the interpenetration of the justice, security, and administrative systems, and their meticulous cooperation to crush targeted families. Moreover, Bennouna exposes a merciless, opportunistic society where longtime friends, neighbors, and colleagues turn against the individual in crisis by recounting how Rabea and her family became outcasts overnight from the bourgeois milieu in which they were formerly fully embraced.[90] Through her penetrating view into her Fassi society, Bennouna catalogues the different ways in which authoritarianism was endorsed by a society in which individuals and groups whose opinions or positions did not align with those of the regime were severely sanctioned.

At work in the family members' embodied other-archives is the imbrication of surveillance and Islamic jurisprudence to strip them of their rights. Women specifically reveal how repression used religion to prevent them from regaining any form of normalcy in their lives. After multiple attempts to obtain a passport, Bennouna realized that she "would have never thought that she would be a concern of a politico-religious battle between the different interpreters of Islamic rites."[91] Bennouna records how both religion and policing worked as ideal tools for her subjugation and served to strip her of her constitutional rights. Only later does Bennouna understand that: "the heart of her problem with authorities is not in the disappearance of her husband, but in his presence. As long as she is married to him, all the doors to her citizenship rights will remain closed to her."[92] Aïda Hachad, Salah Hachad's wife, adopts the same line of thinking in her comment on the confiscation of her passport in 1972. Hachad declares that she "had lost [her] first right, which will take a struggle of twenty-five years before recovering this document."[93] Elaborating on the significance of being deprived of her passport, Hachad philosophizes that "a passport is symbolically synonymous with liberty, a synonym of a possible outside where speech could set free and where the tongue could be untied. I know that I would never be an autonomous citizen because all the regime wanted was to turn all of us into servile subjects, deprived of freedom."[94] In the mind of power holders, families were an extension of the disappeared prisoners, which had, in their turn, to be prevented from the possibility of carrying their cause abroad. Marriage was a solid source of legitimacy to insist on knowing the whereabouts of their spouses, and passports would have made it possible for women to contact human rights organizations outside Morocco. State agents worked to deprive them of both.

Against the background of surveillance and intimidation, women's embodied other-archives register their ability to thwart the overwhelming pressure state agents exerted on them to sever their ties with their disappeared relatives. Neither dedicating an officer to permanently surveil Aïda nor summoning her to police stations for interrogations could persuade her to file for divorce or abdicate her relationship with her husband. Contrary to the anticipated outcome, police harassment became an impetus for her to obstinately struggle to secure her husband's release.[95] Women's resistance was not necessarily raucous, because even an ordinary act, such as wearing makeup, could be weaponized to deprive torturers and jailers of any pleasure that might emanate from them seeing that a disappeared person's wife was "sad, discouraged, and defeated."[96] Instead of slipping into depression, despite having "breathed, eaten, and dreamt of Tazmamart" for eighteen years, Aïda prevailed over the state surveillance machine, which failed to discover the underground network she put in place to funnel money and medication to Tazmamart.[97] Her wealth and determination contributed to saving the majority of lives in Hangar 1 (*al-'anbar al-awwal*), where her husband was held. In recognition of Aïda's work on behalf of the prisoners, ERC commissioners M'barek Bouderka and Ahmed Chouki Benyoub wrote that "Dr. Aïda Hachad's role will remain pivotal in leaking the first letters that were smuggled from Tazmamart to the international public opinion as she fought with all her energy to know her husband's and his colleagues' fate."[98] This conclusion was informed by Bouderka and Benyoub's insider knowledge of the secrets of the Moroccan state through their prominent roles within the ERC. Exemplifying the types of resistant strategies women deployed to protect themselves and their disappeared relatives, Aïda Hachad's embodied experience speaks for experiences of generations of Moroccan women who confronted state violence, but whose histories have yet to be written or recovered.

The proliferation of embodied other-archives between 1999 and 2006, which corresponded with the death of Hassan II in 1999 and the end of the work of the ERC in 2006, reflects how history was becoming the focus of transitional justice endeavors. Established on January 7, 2004, the ERC's mission included "assessment, inquiry, investigation, arbitration and formulating proposals concerning the grave violations of human rights" that were committed between Morocco's independence in 1956 and the passing of Hassan II in 1999.[99] For many victims of the Years of Lead, the ERC was a moment for financial reparation, rehabilitation, catharsis, and redress. However, history and the historiographical afterlife of their experiences of state violence were very present in their publications. History writing remained the ultimate horizon of embodied other-archives whose authors had a better access to the public sphere, and their voices were sought after by the media to shed more light on the past. The centrality of history—as awareness of the need to record and reconstruct past events—showed that embodied other-archives address two types of history: one academic and the other metaphysical. While academic history is a scholarly discipline that is invited to ponder the significance of this Moroccan past, metaphysical history is mostly concerned with the notions of *jazāʾ* (retribution/reward) in the absence of retributive justice. Either way, using their regained historiographical agency, Tazmamart survivors have placed their bodies and the palimpsestic legacies state violence inscribed on them at the core of Moroccan history.

Fictionalizing Tazmamart: Literary Fascination and Global Circulation

The process whereby Tazmamart came to be the object of scandalous and embodied other-archives has since morphed into an unending literary fascination that transcends the borders of Morocco. Of all the enforced disappearance experiences recorded during Morocco's Years of Lead, Tazmamart has informed a most extraordinary literary output. The public's incredulity vis-à-vis the existence of such a site in the first place, as Daure-Serfaty eloquently articulated, has been the lifeblood of fictionalized other-archives, which, in turn, have served as a basis for innovative fictionalizations.[100] Fictionalized other-archives refer to literary appropriation and reimagination of both scandalous and embodied other-archives. Writing into fiction stories and events that are already widely known endows them with a potent commemorative and historiographical force that both collectivizes and universalizes this local experience of enforced disappearance. Unlike sociologist Avery Gordon's assertation that "the exercise of state power through disappearance involves controlling the imagination," Moroccan anthropologist Abdellah Hammoudi attributes Tazmamart's literary popularity to the capacity of secrecy to mobilize literature—an explanation that is also confirmed by Abdallah Laroui's affirmation that "secrecy nourishes the most fanciful rumors."[101] Secrecy, rumor, and gossip about enforced disappearance, although they made the existence of Tazmamart hard to believe through the end of the 1980s, have also coalesced to enable an impressive fictionalized other-archive.

Inspired by Aziz BineBine's eighteen-year disappearance to Tazmamart, Tahar Ben Jelloun's novel *Cette aveuglante absence de lumière* was the earliest foray into a fictionalized other-archive of Tazmamart.[102] Salim, the protagonist and first-person narrator of the novel, recounts his extraordinary effort to stay physically and mentally sound in the dungeon in which he is held. Implicated in a coup against the king, Salim is transferred to a secret jail, where he spends eighteen years suffering inhuman punishment in a tiny cell "arranged [. . .] so that the body would experience all imaginable torments, endure them ever so slowly, and remain alive to undergo further agony."[103] Salim's descriptions of Tazmamart leave no doubt in the reader's mind that it is a necro-site—a place of death—where everything is designed to maximize pain, but also to kill slowly:

> The tomb was a cell just under ten feet long and half as wide. Most of all, it was low, only about five feet high. I could not stand up. There was a hole for pissing and crapping. A hole less than four inches in diameter. The hole was a part of our bodies. We had to forget our existence fast, stop smelling the shit and urine, stop smelling anything at all. We couldn't very well hold our noses, no, we had to keep them open without smelling a single thing.[104]

Salim's graphic depiction of the torment he endures is matched only by his resourcefulness to transcend the constraints of his jail cell, including accepting a split between his body and mind:

> Our bodies were rotting limb by limb. The only thing I possessed was my mind, my reason. I abandoned my arms and legs to our tormentors, hoping they would not manage to claim my spirit, my freedom, my breath of fresh air, my gleam of light in the darkness [. . .] I learned to renounce my body. The body is what is visible. They saw it, they could touch it, cut it with a red-hot blade, they could torture it, starve it, expose it to scorpions, to biting cold, but I strove to keep my mind out of reach.[105]

The renunciation of the body in favor of the mind indicates memory's crucial importance as a platform for history:

> Even if the soldiers manage to erase all trace of the dungeon, they will never erase from our memories what we endured there. Ah, my memory, my friend, my treasure, my passion! We must hang on. We must not fail. I know—weariness, and so many troubles. Ah, my memory, my child who will bear these words across to the other side

> of life, beyond the visible! So go ahead: demolish, lie, camouflage, dance on men's ashes, you will grow dizzy and then there will be . . . nothingness.[106]

The state could erase the traces of the prison or even the place from the topography of the region, but embodied memory would be there to bear witness to the atrocities the prisoners endured.

An immediate success, *Cette aveuglante* was awarded the 2004 *International IMPAC Dublin Literary Award*, whose recipient is determined based on recommendations from hundreds of libraries all over the world.[107] *Cette aveuglante* has also been translated into English, Chinese, and Arabic. However, Ben Jelloun's failure to be part of the struggle for the liberation of Tazmamart detainees during the period when the scandalous archives were being created led to a literary accountability scandal of its own, and this overshadowed the novel's groundbreaking nature. The association representing Tazmamart survivors published a strong condemnation of the novel.[108] Literary critics, journalists, and civil society members also denounced the novelist. Fundamentally, Ben Jelloun's failure to say anything about Tazmamart, as a recipient of the very prestigious *Goncourt* prize in 1987, was the survivors' only reproach against him. For example, Marzouki initially told a French news program that Ben Jelloun "had absolutely done nothing [for us]. So, that is what we have against him. Now, he has published a book about Tazmamart that will certainly make him a lot of money."[109] A few months later, however, the same Marzouki gave a statement to the Swiss daily newspaper *La Croix* in which he expressed a more sympathetic position: "Now I tell myself that Tahar's fame and great talent will help spread knowledge of the horrors of Tazmamart among a large readership. He will also help to prevent such barbarity from being possible ever [again]."[110] Some of Ben Jelloun's critiques were also tied to the Moroccan state, which, for obvious reasons, saw the reglobalization of Tazmamart ten years after the scandalous publication of *Notre ami* as a threat. When he was asked whether the monarchy was involved in the campaign against him, Ben Jelloun answered that "it is obvious that my book was not going to be liked at a moment when Morocco was remaking its image."[111]

Cette aveuglante's publication backfired for the most part because of Ben Jelloun's disagreements with survivor Aziz BineBine—the Tazmamart survivor who allowed him to fictionalize his story. Yet, it would be simplistic to merely focus on the scandal without examining its multiple dimensions, which speak to the intricacies of fictionalizing topics that have a bearing on ongoing memory and history. Rather, the scandal can be approached as a productive way to understand the complex process whereby fictionalized other-archives are created. As recounted to Claudia Esposito, Aziz BineBine's brother, novelist Mahi BineBine, urged Aziz to recount his story to Ben Jelloun.[112] Aziz agreed to collaborate with Ben Jelloun only if his name would be left out of the novelist's story and he would not be required to interact with the media.[113] Ben Jelloun agreed to Aziz's conditions. In Mahi's account, however, Ben Jelloun breached this agreement. Additionally, Mahi explains Ben Jelloun's need for a survivor to underwrite his novel by his awareness that "he didn't lift a finger for twenty years to help the living-dead in Tazmamart."[114] Mahi BineBine also admits that their letter, *Notre ami l'écrivain* (Our friend the novelist), which was modeled after the title of Perrault's *Notre ami le roi,* furnished the journalists who had accounts to settle with Ben Jelloun the ammunition they needed to discredit him.[115] Interestingly, however, Aziz the survivor is relegated to oblivion in the literary battle between his famous brother, Mahi, and the even more famous novelist, Ben Jelloun. The survivor's voice was occluded by two louder voices that claimed to speak on his behalf, but that only eclipsed him even further. This situation raises fundamental questions about the ethics of testimony and the appropriation of the survivor's voice.

Ben Jelloun's prescience regarding Tazmamart's richness and viability as a literary topic with deep historiographical and memorial implications escaped the attention of his detractors.[116] In response to reproaches of literary opportunism, Ben Jelloun retorted that "we don't forgo [writing about] an exceptional topic."[117] Therefore, it appears to me that the scandalous aspect of the BineBine–Ben Jelloun falling-out can be viewed from a more generative and less scandal-prone lens, that is, by focusing on the tension between fiction and testimony in crucial moments of histories of suffering. Before any of his Moroccan peers, Ben Jelloun understood that Tazmamart's afterlife would continue in fictionalized other-archives; yet, understanding the future significance of the story of the prison and putting this foreknowledge into action was, unfortunately, untimely, since it coincided with the publication of survivors' embodied other-archives. Unlike what has been advanced in several journalistic articles and hasty literary readings, the scandal was not so much the result of his theft of Aziz's story as one of timing. Compounded by a generalized lack of understanding of fiction's powerful ability to channel memory and history, the contemporaneous publications of *Cette aveuglante,* Raïss's *Min Skhirāt ilā Tazmamart,* and Marzouki's *Tazamamart: Al-zinzāna raqm 10* created a false feeling of competition between these naturally complementary other-archives. This mired the masterful novel *Cette aveuglante* in an unprecedented literary scandal. A closer examination of the facts reveals that competition was not justified for the simple reason that embodied other-archives are fundamental to the existence of fictionalized other-archives.[118] The two are coessential, rather than contradictory. The survivors' embodied other-archives will continue to be the background of and the source for intimate details about survivors' lived experiences; but fiction, in this case *Cette aveuglante*, opens up space for reshaping and refashioning their experiences in order to speak for a collective history of state repression. Additionally, fictionalized other-archives integrate stories of individual survivors of Tazmamart into circuits that facilitate their delocalization. By disrupting any anticipated compatibility between the survivor, the experience, and the tales reconstructed in fiction, individual experiences of Tazmamart are incorporated into a global semantics of memory. In this regard, *Cette aveuglante*, thanks to its hyperscandalous effects, initiated a transformative debate that pushed the boundaries of assumptions about ownership of Morocco's recent memory and political history.[119] This episode brought up the distinction between lived experience, which remains inherently unique and individual, and its fictionalization, which transforms the individual experience into public property—so long as the literary outcomes serve to archive and historicize violations of human rights.

This historical and archival commitment is obvious in *Cette aveuglante*. It is the only novel that attributes to prisoners a metaconsciousness of their own role in securing their release from Tazmamart. Set in the mid-1980s, which witnessed mobilization for the liberation of Tazmamart prisoners, the last third of *Cette aveuglante* depicts the prisoners' responses to the news of the struggle for their liberation. According to Salim, the guard M'Fadel offers Wakrine, a prisoner from his Amazigh region, a chance to send a letter to his illiterate wife, ultimately changing the course of the disappeared soldiers' fates. Salim then describes the process whereby this letter arrives in Paris, to be revealed to the human rights activist community: "M'Fadel took the piece of paper to Wakrine's wife without saying anything to her. Because she did not know how to read, she showed the letter to the mother of a pharmacist whose brother was also disappeared. In this way, the little brother of number 18, Omar, who was studying in France, was alerted."[120] M'Fadel "received medicine from the pharmacist, especially painkillers and anti-inflammatories, accompanied by a large sum of money,"[121] which he would bring to the prison at the end of his annual vacation. Contact with the outside world is depicted as not being limited to sending and receiving letters. Both corruptible and sympathetic guards (messengers) brought medicine and significant amounts of money, which empowered the prisoners even more to transcend the walls of their secret prison.

The impact of the scandalous other-archive is further represented in *Cette aveuglante* through the character of Christine, which refers to Christine Daure-Serfaty, who, as I have shown above, was a staunch defender of Tazmamart detainees. The novel describes Christine as being "an exceptional woman, an activist for human rights, a resistant, and a pasionaria, who dedicated years of her life to revealing the jail in which we were detained and struggled for our liberation."[122] Upon receiving Wakrine's letter, prisoner number 18's brother Omar takes it to Christine, who leaks it to the press. In Salim's terms, Christine "moved heaven and earth to inform the world of our imprisonment."[123] However, Christine's intervention also creates problems for the prisoners. As soon as M'Fadel hears about the contents of the letter he smuggled in the daily news, his attitude toward the prisoners changes; their mutual trust is shaken. Yet Salim does not regret the outcome: he learns later that "Christine had contacted Amnesty International and very influential journalists," placing the fate of the disappeared prisoners in the hands of "international [public] opinion."[124] In fact, since Aziz BineBine, the real witness, did not live these events from outside the jail walls, it is safe to surmise that Ben Jelloun drew on Daure-Serfaty's *Tazmamart.*

Like Daure-Serfaty, Christine plays a pivotal role in rallying support for the prisoners and their families through human rights networks in France. In addition to alerting the media and international organizations, Christine's activism involves convincing public figures, who enjoy high moral integrity, to make public statements that denounce the prison and force Hassan II to release the soldiers whose existence he denies. For example, Salim fantasizes about what human rights activists are doing in France to secure their liberation. He muses that "our distress signals must have been picked up by someone somewhere—maybe the foreign press was talking about us, maybe influential political figures were pressuring the authorities in Rabat, maybe intellectuals had mobilized to obtain our freedom . . ."[125] While representing the suffering of the disappeared soldiers in Tazmamart, *Cette aveuglante* highlights the human rights structures and individual agencies that made possible the acknowledgment of Tazmamart and forced the Moroccan state to release the survivors. Given this pioneering fusion of embodied and fictionalized other-archives, and the questions attendant on both, *Cette aveuglante* could not but be what it was: a harbinger of literature as a locus for histories of enforced disappearance. It was a new exercise in writing that neither the victims nor journalists and intellectuals were ready to embrace, because it marked a shift in testimonial temporality. It accelerated the process, at a pace that triggered all parties' defense mechanisms.

Fictionalized other-archives' ability to procreate and transform can be seen in *Rapt de voix.* This elaborate meta-novel by Belkassem Belouchi, a heart surgeon and novelist who writes in French, reimagines *Cette aveuglante*'s genealogy and fictionalizes its writing process. If anything, it demonstrates fictionalized other-archives' meiotic capability to grow and multiply infinitely and indefinitely. *Rapt de voix* delves into the mental and emotional toll that giving and receiving testimony takes on both the survivor and the seeker of testimony. Combining biography, psychoanalysis, literary analysis, and even gossip with investigative fiction, *Rapt de voix* depicts Jad (Ben Jelloun) as he attempts to convince Aziz (BineBine) to authorize him to novelize Aziz's disappearance story. Throughout negotiations between Jad, Aziz, and the latter's brother (a reference to Mahi BineBine), the novel depicts a greedy and manipulative litterateur who, feeling short of inspiration, finds in Aziz's story a lifeline for his dying literary career. The unbridgeable contrast between Jad, who stops at nothing to advance his career, and the survivor, Aziz, who has many things to consider, foregrounds the ethical risks that are embedded in fictionalizing lived experiences. Mahi tells Jad:

> I, for sure, talked to him about it [the book], but before he makes a decision he wants some clarity. You know that his existence has been shaped forever; all his life is set by a succession of rites and principles like a clock. I also believe that he wants the authorization of his former jail mates. They stand in solidarity with each other. Although free, their actions continue to be surveilled. Their phones are wiretapped. They [authorities] refuse to issue their passports. Their contact, especially with foreign journalists, is prohibited. One of them was even kidnapped and intimidated. Do you think that they trust anyone with all this in mind? Furthermore, they will not forgive the silence of politicians and intellectuals during their eighteen years of disappearance.[126]

Apart from any scandal-prone reading of this imagined dialogue between Mahi and Jad, the narrative demonstrates the complexity of the process involved in fictionalizing an experience in which both stakeholders and protagonists are still alive. Unlike Jad, who has the latitude to write whatever he wants, Aziz must consider the possibility of the state's revenge, loss of his community of former cellmates, and overcoming suspicion vis-à-vis an intellectual who did not contribute to releasing him from disappearance.

Rapt de voix is not a facile rejection of *Cette aveuglante*; rather, I consider it a challenging and realistic journey into the stakes involved in fictionalization itself. Unlike Valerie Orlando's reading that focused on Ben Jelloun's opportunism,[127] I contend that *Rapt de voix* is actually about a far deeper issue—the ethics of memory and history that are grounded in experiences of human suffering. The dialogical confrontation between the survivor, who expects the litterateur to speak on behalf of the victims, and the novelist, who admits to having failed to live up to the survivor's expectations, offers a space for channeling their core disagreements with regard to issues of memory and history. Aziz confronts Jad: "As a man of letters, you had many possibilities to carry the information into French intellectual circles,"[128] but, as we know by now, Jad did not rise to the occasion. Per Aziz's expectations, Jad would have been more useful if he had written about the plight of the prisoners when "the voice of conscience [. . .] could still redress some wrongs."[129] In fact, Aziz expects that the novelist would have become a scandalous other-archives creator, which explains his inability to comprehend Jad's belated interest in his story. Whereas Jad sees a transformative literary topic with humanist ramifications, Aziz sees a legitimate need for rehabilitation after surviving two decades of enforced disappearance.

Undergirded by the disturbing question of who has the legitimacy to write about past events that have collective consequences, *Rapt de voix* portrays the complicated psychological processes and discursive negotiations between the witness and the litterateur, as well as the disagreement that emerges between activists' instrumentalist expectations and the unlimited literary potential of other-archives. Jad reveals fictionalized other-archives' humanist dimensions when he responds to Aziz's question about why he wants to turn Tazmamart into a novel:

> Because this story means a lot to me, and it is a great challenge for me to write it. I also want to write it in order to tell the entire world about Tazmamart, to say everything that some men endured in it, to pay respect to the memory of the deceased, in order to show that human dignity was violated, so that there will be no other Tazmamart. You know more than I that every significant event naturally triggers a writing back. I am not interested in the political aspect of Tazmamart—I am interested in its ethics. What relates to ethics is much graver than the political aspect. This tragedy requires a universal dimension. Limiting it to Moroccan borders only is, in my opinion, very reductive. Tazmamart is a crime against humanity.[130]

Jad understands that Tazmamart is part of a larger human story of suffering and is fully aware that his project is dangerous. He also understands that he "runs the risk of finding [himself] confronted by other battles" that would ensue from the publication of his novel.[131] Jad's aggressive approach to obtain a survivor's testimony is a literary subterfuge that facilitates a deeper and more complicated reflection on the demanding labor and jarring process required by both giving and receiving testimony—a process throughout which both the giver and the recipient may oftentimes incur deep personal damage even as they move both literature and historical knowledge forward.

Unlike Ben Jelloun's *Cette aveuglante*, which is based on BineBine's true story, Fadel's *Ṭā'ir azraq nādir yuḥalliqu ma'ī* acknowledges no connection between the novel and any particular Tazmamart survivor's lived experience.[132] *Ṭā'ir azraq* tells the story of Aziz, a military pilot, who, following his wedding night, participates in a coup d'état against the king and is forcibly disappeared.[133] Although he hails from a broken family, Aziz had defied his social circumstances at a young age and became a military pilot whose passion for flying is only troubled by his inability to land a plane. His supervisor suspends him, joking that "One day, Aziz, you'll fly off and you won't come back."[134] To work through his sadness, Aziz finds refuge in the Stork Bar in the poor city of Azrou, where he and Madame Janeau, the old French owner of the bar, spend their time drinking alcohol and speaking French. This is how he meets and chooses to marry Zina. A poor, orphaned girl, Zina lives with her sister, Khatima, who, in addition to working at the Stork Bar, is exploited as a prostitute by a vicious pimp. Zina's happiness with Aziz is short-lived because of his enforced disappearance immediately after their wedding night. As it turns out, his supervisor uses his passion for flying to implicate him in a coup that involves gunning down the king's plane by army jetfighters. Their wedding night will be the last time Zina sees Aziz for the next twenty-six years.

Immediately after the coup, the authorities stop at nothing to abuse Zina mentally and physically. For example, soon after Aziz's imprisonment, a security agent, who takes possession of Aziz's car and other belongings, introduces himself to Zina as her disappeared husband's trustworthy friend. Because he showed her some kindness, a vulnerable Zina trusts him immediately: "He calmed me down and gave me a glass of tea. He then asked for my marriage certificate to be sure we were really married, me and Aziz. I handed him the certificate. I blushed as I waited for him to read it. Then calmly he tore it up into little pieces and put the small bits in his pocket, saying, with the same calmness, "The son of a bitch who's in your belly doesn't have a father anymore."[135] This scene shows that nothing is what it seems when one struggles against enforced disappearance. The gentleman who serves Zina tea turns into a monster as soon as he puts his hands on her marriage certificate. Tearing up the certificate is a symbolic representation of enforced disappearance's severance of filiation between Aziz, Zina, and their baby. As I have previously argued, destroying the prisoners' connections to family and the outside world was part and parcel of their disappearance.

Having lost both Aziz and their unborn child, Zina ekes out a living working as a server for her sister, Khatima, who inherits the Stork Bar after the passing of Madame Janeau. One day, however, a go-between leaves a furtive message that Aziz is still alive. The novel ends with Aziz's reappearance, nine years after Zina's last attempt to find his whereabouts, in the southeastern castle where he has been hidden. Interestingly, when Aziz returns, he finds that Zina has a nine-year-old daughter whom she has named Aziz in total defiance of social norms that discourage girls from having boys' names and vice-versa. The novel does not explain whether Zina has given birth herself or adopted little Aziz, but it does not stigmatize her for it either.

Ṭāʾir azraq is the pinnacle of a fictionalized recomposition of the stories that had already been recorded in both scandalous and embodied other-archives. Unlike Ben Jelloun's *Cette aveuglante,* which drew on one individual's verbal testimony about Tazmamart, *Ṭāʾir azraq* is a fusion of many enforced disappearance stories. The genealogies of the events recomposed in *Ṭāʾir azraq* can be traced back to *Min Skhirat ilā Tazmamart, Tazmamart: Cellule 10, Kabazal, Opération Boraq F5,* and *Tazmamart côté femme,* as well as Mohammed Nadrani's *La Capitale des roses* (*The Capital of Roses*), Mohammed Errahoui's *Mouroirs: Chronique d'une disparition forcée* (*Necroplaces: The Chronicle of an Enforced Disappearance*), and Daure-Serfaty's *Tazmamart.*[136] Drawing on these memoirs, Fadel constructs an original fictionalized other-archive in which testimonies of both civilians and soldiers are patched together to form a single story about one detention center in southeast Morocco. Thanks to this original choice, *Ṭāʾir azraq* is a testimonial crucible that gives a collective voice to a history recounted from the point of view of several survivors of state violence.

Part of the recomposition of this history takes place through the work of reshuffling imprisonment locations. Instead of having the novel unfold in Tazmamart directly, the story is set in a castle, which is described as "an old casbah of Pasha Glaoui [*sic*], or some other pasha, with a number of wings, like a small city."[137] In referencing Pasha El Glaoui's casbahs in southeast Morocco, the novel merges Tazmamart with Adgz, where the Banou Hachem group were held for eight years. This group comprised five students (Banou Hachem, Mohammed Errahoui, Lahrizi Moulay, Driss Abdenasser, Kounsi Abderrahman) who were kidnapped in 1977 and held without trial in several secret jails in the Ouarzazate area until their release in 1985. The Banou Hachem group's carceral experience is of particular interest because they were held with Sahrawi prisoners, including women and children, in the touristic castle of Agdz.[138] Whether the secret prison in *Ṭāʾir azraq* is called Agdz, Tagounite, Skoura, or Kelâat M'Gouna matters less compared with the collective dimension that the novel gives to these experiences of imprisonment. By introducing the fungibility of disappearance locations, Fadel proceeds like a historian who works to compose a coherent narrative about a dizzying hodgepodge of archival materials.

Ṭā'ir azraq marks a fundamental shift in Moroccan fictionalized other-archives, too. In the novel, Tazmamart serves as both a background and a backbone for a narrative that transcends survivors' individual experiences. Deploying Tazmamart's far-reaching, scandalous, and testimonial impact, Fadel is able to revisit the sites that testify to the sufferings of different social, political, and ethnic strata of Moroccan citizens in secret jails in southeast Morocco. This process, whereby different stories are put in dialogue with each other, only confirms fictionalized other-archives' collectivization of enforced disappearance as a structural and societal issue in Morocco during the Years of Lead. Fadel has underlined this aspect of the novel in interviews, recognizing that *Ṭā'ir azraq* is not a documentary work but rather a work of "a collective memory for an entire generation."[139] Reflecting on the process of writing the novel, Fadel underlines that the main question he faced was "how could one create a truly new work from [memoirs and testimonies of the survivors]?"[140] In answering this question, Fadel wrote a novel that has broken new ground in elevating accounts of lived experiences into an overarching narrative, encompassing diverse tales of state violence during the repressive Years of Lead. Tazmamart is therefore resignified to be about the nation—not about individual prisoners—which is even more damning to the state's masterminds of disappearance.

Ṭā'ir azraq is, indeed, Fadel's rewriting of the history of enforced disappearance in Morocco through Aziz, who stands for all victims and survivors of the Moroccan forcible disappearance system.[141] Every bit of detail about the character refers to a specific experience that has already been registered through embodied other-archives. For instance, Aziz describes how he goes against his uncle's will and enrolls in primary school.[142] He also reveals that he has a sister, whom the same uncle married off to a much older man in order to receive her dowry.[143] These elements from *Ṭā'ir azraq* refer to the story of Boujmâa Azendour, an actual prisoner whose story is discussed in BineBine's *Tazmamort*.[144] In another example, while in disappearance Aziz raises a bird named Faraj—a clear reference to the well-known pigeon that survivor Marzouki found and adopted in his cell six months before his release from jail, the story of which also inspired Radwa Ashour's novel *Farag*. Hinda, the dog that saves Aziz from death when two jail guards bury him alive, was made famous by Raïss and Marzouki and became the subject of Abdelhak Serhane's novella *La Chienne de Tazmamart* (*The Bitch of Tazmamart*). Unlike the realistic and self-referential Aziz around whom *Cette aveuglante* is constructed, *Ṭā'ir azraq*'s Aziz has American ancestry and uses a gold ring to bribe a guard to take a message to Zina. The American reference alludes to Tazmamart survivor M'bark Touil. Touil was married to an American citizen, Nancy Touil, who lobbied American officials to force the Moroccan state to treat him preferentially in detention. The gold ring scene is evocative of survivor Bouchaib Skiba's success in smuggling a ring into the prison despite the invasive search the gendarmery undertook before relocating the prisoners. Skiba would later trade his gold ring for a radio, allowing the prisoners in his block to know what was taking place in the outside world.[145] The parallel continues when Aziz initially attempts to bribe the guard, and the guard "tosses the ring into the basin and retreats, fleeing toward the door," reminiscent of the guard's first reaction to Skiba's offer in real life.[146] As a result, the Aziz of *Ṭā'ir azraq* is not one person—he is multiple people. His composite character reveals fictionalized other-archives' unlimited potential to transform scandalous and embodied other-archives into a generative history.

The power of Tazmamart in fictionalized other-archives has taken its story east, where Egyptian novelist Radwa Ashour published a successful novel entitled *Farag*. First published in 2008, *Farag* was met with immediate commercial success, leading to a second edition in 2009, followed by a Qatar Foundation–commissioned English translation in 2014 under the title *Blue Lorries*.[147] *Farag* is an intergenerational prison novel that weaves the struggles of three generations of Egyptian citizens into transnational stories of oppression in Africa and the Arabic-speaking world. Narrated by Nadā 'Abd al-Qādir, the daughter of a French mother and an Egyptian father, the novel covers a crucial period in Egyptian, Arab, and world history. *Farag* follows Nadā's desire to write a novel depicting political imprisonment under Gamal Abdel Nasser and Anwar al-Sadat, apartheid in South Africa, occupation in Palestine, and neocolonialism in Iraq. Interwoven with references to Tazmamart prison camp, the novel derives its title, *Farag*, which means "happy ending" and "happy denouement," from Marzouki's pigeon in Tazmamart.[148] Similar to the bird's foreshadowing of the end of enforced disappearance in Marzouki's memoir, *Farag* foretells a joyful conclusion to the repressive and neocolonialist situation in Egypt and the rest of the Arab world. Published only three years before the genesis of the Arab Uprisings in 2011, *Farag* endows Tazmamart with a predictive function by representing the end of five decades of intergenerational and collective oppression in Egypt.

Unlike *Cette aveuglante*, which explicitly refers to human rights activism in France, and *Ṭā'ir azraq*, which reimagines the Years of Lead through the allegorical character of Aziz, *Farag*'s Tazmamart connects a wide array of struggles in the Arab world and developing countries. *Farag*'s narrator is a female former political prisoner who is obsessed with the idea of writing a transnational book about political imprisonment. Nadā lays out her vision of the book to her former best friend, a communist named Ḥāzim:

> I tell Ḥāzim a lot about my desire to write a book about [political] imprisonment. I talk to him about every new book I acquire. I was assiduous about buying any books that are available about this topic. That's why I have a fairly rich library. It contains memoirs of political detainees in the Maḥāriq prison in al-Wāḥāt, the War Prison, the prisons of al-Qal'a, Ṭurra, Ūrdī Abu Zu'bul, al-Isti'nāf and al-Qanāṭir in Cairo, the Ḥadra prison in Alexandria, and the 'Izb prison in al-Fayyūm. I later added new books on similar experiences from al-Khiyyām prison in south Lebanon and Israeli prisons as well as Tazmamart prison camp in Morocco and the Robin Island prison in South Africa.[149]

The many prisons that Nadā plans to bring together in her book indicate the prevalence of political imprisonment and insinuate that there are connections between these global phenomena. Thus, Tazmamart is not just part of a widespread practice of political disappearance, but it is also placed in a comparative context with other notorious enforced disappearance sites from the Global South. Apart from 'Abd al-Raḥmān Munīf's masterpieces, *Sharq al-mutawassiṭ* (*East of the Mediterranean*) and *al-Ān hunā: Aw sharq al-mutawassiṭ marratan ukhrā* (*Here and Now: East of the Mediterranean Again*), which unfold in an unknown Arab country, *Farag* is the only novel to place Tazmamart side by side with other ill-reputed prisons such as Robin Island in apartheid South Africa, al-Qal'a prison in Nasser and Sadat's Egypt, and al-Khiyyām, an infamous prison in South Lebanon under Israeli occupation.[150] Transnational connections between these prisons also hark back to the importance of intersectional solidarities for releasing prisoners. For instance, Daure-Serfaty describes her happiness at seeing the photo of leftist prisoner Abraham Serfaty screened during the 1989 Bastille Day celebrations in Paris. The event marked the first time "a Moroccan was mingled with the prisoners of the world, those of the East, Latin America, and South Africa."[151] In this way, Ashour's novel integrates local violations of human rights into a more universal semiotics of violence. In the author's own words, "there is a real desire for national and human liberation," which the novel enables.[152]

The reception that each of these fictionalized other-archives received could not have been more different from one another. *Cette aveuglante* was published at a time when survivors of the Moroccan state's brutality were advocating for a transitional justice commission that would rehabilitate them.

By 1999, transitional justice commissions had become a common practice in endeavors to resolve legacies of dictatorship and gross violations of human rights in different parts of the world. Argentina, Chile, and South Africa, among others, had successfully used such commissions to combine truth-seeking with reconciliation, reparations, and pathways to justice beyond the retributive systems under indictment.[153] In Morocco, victims of the Years of Lead were fighting for institutional redress of their suffering. They deployed their embodied other-archives of torture and enforced disappearance to force the state to restore their rights and apologize for the wrongs it had done to them. Written, oral, and even journalistic testimonies—interviews with survivors or their descendants—were treated as pathways toward a transitional justice system that would create bulwarks against the repetition of state abuses. The "wrong" timing of *Cette aveuglante*'s publication incentivized both the survivors and the state to metaphorically assassinate the novel, albeit for antithetical reasons. On the one hand, international pressure was still crucial in the effort to make the Moroccan state amenable to a compromise with its victims, and *Cette aveuglante* had all the qualities that could have accelerated that endeavor. Ben Jelloun's fame, literary prestige, positive reception in reputable literary reviews, translation potential, and circulation in the French language globalized Tazmamart's story outside Morocco, compelling journalists, who were notoriously close to state circles, to denounce *Cette aveuglante*.[154] On the other hand, however, survivors focused on proving the authenticity of their suffering—requisite to officially proving victimhood and enabling transitional justice—did not initially perceive how *Cette aveuglante*'s global reach and impact could be beneficial to their cause. Scandal was inevitable in this situation. However, twenty years after its publication, *Cette aveuglante* has outlived many of those individual embodied other-archives, which are mostly out of print, and continues to renew relevance in a world where human rights violations are on the rise. This specific national context in which *Cette aveuglante* was published does not apply to *Ṭā'ir azraq* and applies even less to *Farag*. The crux of the negotiations about transitional justice and reparations had already passed by the time these latter novels were published. Also, Fadel was a political prisoner who served time for a play he wrote about the war in Western Sahara.[155] Ashour was not a Moroccan citizen, and her space to maneuver was even greater. Unhampered by survivors' feelings of competition and aided by a more complex understanding of literature, these fictionalizations adeptly articulated the transnational, interconnected, and intersectional lineaments of their sociopolitical era.

Tazmamart has also inspired poetic works in Arabic, English, and Tamazight, among others. Amazigh poet, Muḥammad Uḍmīn, published a poetry collection in Tamazight entitled *Urfān* (Hot Pebbles, 2004) in which he dedicated a poem to the prison camp. Uḍmīn's "Tazmmamart" [sic], written in Latin alphabet instead of the Arabic or Tifinagh script, focuses on the multiple layers of darkness encountered in Tazmamart:

Laḥ ak tafukt You are sunless
Laḥ ak ayyūr You are moonless
Laḥ ak asufu n itrān You have no stellar light

Ghin agha k jlan wadan d izaliwn There where your nights and days are lost
Mmerksen ak yiern d issgguwasn Months with days are confused
Max a tazmammart alligh gim illas uzal? O, Tazmamart, why are your days so dark?[156]

Like Uḍmīn, American poet Julith Jedamus has included a poem about Tazmamart in *The Swerve*, her 2012 poetry collection. Entitled "Two Ghazals for Aziz," this poem evokes the Arab tradition of love poetry to depict Aziz BineBine's survival in Tazmamart. A family friend of BineBine's, Jedamus had met Aziz and learned about his story from his book. Similarly to Uḍmīn, Jedamus renders the darkness of Tazmamart. Jedamus's "Two Ghazals" depicts the same vicious circle of lack of light and eternal darkness:

Night everlasting, night unfallen:
You drew it round you, a river swollen.[157]

As these two poetic examples reveal, Tazmamart has become a multigenre and multilingual other-archive that one can encounter anywhere and in any form. All one needs to do is pay attention to the word Tazmamart.

Unlike *Cette aveuglante*, *Ṭā'ir azraq* and *Farag* occupy an aporetic position between globalizing and decentering Tazmamart. Both works demonstrate fictionalized other-archives' ability to decenter human rights literature—which, as a standard practice, has been the province of authors who reside in Europe and America and use foreign languages to tackle issues (and definitions) of human rights violations in their countries of origin. *Ṭā'ir azraq*'s and *Farag*'s publication in Arabic decenters a story that first and foremost became public and believable because of human rights activism in Paris. In the meantime, translation has recentered this decentering effort as a result of the translation of *Farag* into English and *Ṭā'ir azraq* into English, French, and Italian.[158] This position is further consecrated by the awarding of the 2014 *Jā'izat al-Maghrib li-al-Kitāb* (Morocco's Book Award) to *Ṭā'ir azraq* only a few months after it was shortlisted for the same year's International Prize for Arabic Fiction. *Farag* and *Ṭā'ir azraq*'s decentering aspirations have in fact further integrated Tazmamart's fictionalized other-archives into global literary networks, which is a fitting achievement, given this secret jail's very transnational history. In addition to the fifty-eight soldiers (including Captain M'bark Touil who was married to an American citizen) detained there for nearly two decades, Tazmamart held three Franco-Tunisian citizens (brothers Ali, Bayazid, and Midhat Bourequat, whose transfer to Tazmamart in 1981 still remains a mystery because they were never accused of a crime) as well as a dozen sub-Saharan African citizens whose names and identities are still unknown.[159] The prison's history cannot be written without tapping into the different archives that are scattered in Morocco, France, the United States, and the United Kingdom, among others, thus making its fictionalized re-globalizations all the more meaningful for its afterlife.

Tazmamart's global reach does not, however, negate its continuous transformation within Morocco itself. The site of the former prison was bulldozed and vacated by the army, and the locale is now transformed into the headquarters for an association for local development as part of the ERC's recommended community reparations. The ERC's failed attempt to extract DNA from the dead bodies prevented it from relocating them and forced Tazmamart to also be a cemetery for the dead soldiers.[160] This fact alone weds this village's destiny with that of political imprisonment and violations of human rights in Morocco. Both the failed DNA identification and the everlasting burial of the bodies in the village emphasize the perpetual archival importance of this place. Although both the victims' families and the state would have preferred to relocate the bodies, it seems as though, ironically, the locale is jealously clinging to its own memory, which has been associated with the macabre death of these soldiers for the last four decades. Only by continuing to serve as a collective burial ground for the dead could Tazmamart keep its role as a site for pilgrimage and human rights caravans.

Conclusion

Since Tazmamart's inception in 1973, three types of other-archives evolved in different periods of Moroccan history to constitute Tazmamart into an other-archive. Combining analysis of human rights activists' mobilization to expose the existence of this secret jail with an examination of survivors' testimonies and their fictionalization, I have demonstrated that each type of other-archive builds on its predecessor to culminate in fictionalized other-archives. The three types of other-archives, which I have theorized as *scandalous*, *embodied*, and *fictionalized*, evolved in historical contexts for which archiving served different purposes. The creation of the scandalous other-archives helped establish the truth about enforced disappearance and forced the Moroccan state to release its survivors, whereas embodied other-archives were central for transitional justice, the further establishment of truth, and reconciliation of the violations that took place in Tazmamart. Finally, literary professionals who produced fictionalized other-archives have drawn upon both embodied and scandalous other-archives to reshape stories of survival into literary works that radically resignify Morocco's contentious political history.

I therefore contend that fictionalized other-archives have afforded their authors more freedom from formalities of convention and shape. Given the novelists' latitude to choose and depict their topics, they have distilled Tazmamart stories into collectivized histories of enforced disappearance that transcend the borders of Morocco. Unlike both scandalous and embodied other-archives, which approach the experience of Tazmamart from the prism of authenticity, truth, and accuracy, fictionalized other-archives are best described as enabling a process of gametogenesis—a constant process of procreative multiplication, which transfers the genetic traits of the original firsthand accounts into stories that resignify a collective experience of state violence. In the accomplished hands of fiction writers, Tazmamart has become a melting pot of histories and a network of interconnected plots. As a fictionalized other-archive, Tazmamart connects, reimagines, collapses, and repurposes the original other-archives to address a history-in-becoming—the history of a mutilated nation that is constantly rising from the spectral stories of the dead.

In tandem with the existence and phenomenal consumption of other-archives of enforced disappearance and arbitrary detention, along with the organization of various commemorative practices, which elicited unprecedented media and societal attention, Moroccan historiography was forced to witness its own transformation. The next chapter examines Moroccan academic historians' responses to the proliferation of other-archives and analyzes the myriad ways in which Moroccan historiography was pushed to stay abreast of societal and cultural debates about the legacy of the Years of Lead.

5
Other-Archives Transform Moroccan Historiography

The existence of other-archives in Moroccan public space has triggered a historiographical fervor among several stakeholders in Moroccan history.[1] An American historian of Morocco, Susan Gilson Miller, has caught the effects of this historical effervescence in writing that, through the publication of "memoirs, reviews, and news analyses that provide a counterpoint to 'official' accounts that glorify the monarchy," the Moroccan press has "disseminated information that contests the restrictive pro-makhzenian discourse that has monopolized the field [of history] since independence."[2] As Gilson Miller underlines, it is not only the historical material that has become profuse. The historical discourse itself has been transformed by the abundance of other-archives after King Hassan II's death in 1999 and the establishment of *hay'at al-inṣāf wa-al-muṣālaḥa* (Equity and Reconciliation Commission [ERC]) in 2004, which King Mohammed VI tasked with the daunting mission of reconciling Moroccans with their recent past.[3] The plenitude of history-oriented cultural production, which I have conceptualized as other-archives, has put Moroccan academic historians, cultural producers, and the state at the center of endeavors to write or rewrite Morocco's "immediate history."[4] The three-pronged analysis I offer in this chapter first discusses Moroccan academic historians' use of the concept of *tārīkh al-zaman al-rāhin* (history of the present) to both open up their discipline to new methodologies and engage in unprecedented discussions of Morocco's post-colonial history. Second, I analyze how the historiographical fervor between 1999 and 2006 played out in a collaboration between historian M'barek Zaki and novelist Ahmed Beroho, who chart a new path for a dialogical history of the state of exception in Morocco between 1965 and 1970. Zaki and Beroho's publications form only one example of the innovative approaches that cultural production triggered inside the discipline of history. Finally, I examine the state's stakes in the creation of the *Institut Royal pour la Recherche sur l'Histoire du Maroc* (The Royal Institute for Research on Moroccan History, RIRHM). I consider RIRHM, alongside the state's repurposing of human rights and migration institutions to take on the mission of writing a history in line with King Mohammed VI's "new concept of authority," which has been put in place to distinguish his reign from his father's in an effort to rebrand post-1999 Morocco as a democracy.[5]

Historiographical Negotiations of Memory and History Amid a Disciplinary Crisis

Participating in the ERC exposed both the limitations of Moroccan historiography vis-à-vis other-archives and the societal thirst for knowledge of Morocco's immediate political history. Upon its establishment by King Mohammed VI in 2004, partly in response to demands from Moroccan civil society to investigate political crimes committed between 1956 and 1999 and reconcile Moroccans with their past, the ERC invited several academic historians to be part of this historic process. Although the only historian appointed to the ERC as a commissioner was Brahim Boutaleb, a retired professor of history and former dean of the School of the Humanities and Social Sciences at Mohammed V University in Rabat, other historians led research teams and lived both the historical fervor and the memory frenzy from within the ranks of this commission whose task laid at the intersection of politics, history, and memory.[6] Considering their participation in the ERC as part of their social responsibility, several historians presented papers at the itinerant conferences the ERC organized on themes such as "prison writings: prison literature as a historical source" in Rabat on May 20, 2004; "state violence" in Marrakesh on June 12–14, 2004; "the notion of truth" in Tangiers on September 17–18, 2004; and finally "prosecutions and judicial trial of political nature between 1956 and 1999" in Casablanca on February 18–19, 2005, which mainly focused on legal issues.[7] As the titles of these historians' presentations indicate, these papers discussed questions of truth, post-independence writings, prison literature, incarceration and history, and state violence. Such issues brought Moroccan historians as a professional body face-to-face with the challenge of negotiating the place of their academic discipline, at a period when Moroccan society was voraciously consuming a significant quantity of cultural production about the country's recent political past through print media, blogs, protests, and the memory-focused publications of a fast-changing publication industry[8]—or, put another way, through other-archives.

Benjamin Stora has perceptively summarized the force of what I describe as other-archives in observing that because of "the ceaseless and dizzying proliferation of images, speeches, [and] words, states progressively lose 'control' over personal destinies. Aspirations to more rights and individual liberties have implications for the writing of a history that is detached from the state's needs."[9] In this sense, other-archives are sites for liberation and citizenship. Other-archives' creators use their agency to assert their freedom and civic rights by re-envisioning history, pushing against taboos, censorship, and self-censorship.[10] In fact, other-archives creators, in this particular period, are whistleblowers, but a brave brand of whistleblowers who do not cherish anonymity because their very understanding of citizenship hinges upon reclaiming history. It is certainly this desire to rewrite history as an exercise of citizenship that presents further challenges to historiography and demands that it transcend its traditional, self-imposed boundaries, or the "pro-makhzanian discourse" that obstructed the development of Moroccan historiography for decades.[11]

The phenomenal societal interest in history elicited by other-archives forced Moroccan historians to study the *histoire du temps présent* (*tārīkh al-zaman al-rāhin*/the history of the present), which has served since 2003 as a conceptual framework for reflection on the challenges of writing the history of a past that is not fully dead. Attributed to François Bédarida, the founding director of the *Institut d'Histoire du Temps Présent* (Institute of the History of the Present, IHP) at the *Centre National de la Recherche Scientifique* (National Center for Scientific Research, NCSR) in France in 1978, the history of the present, as Henry Rousso defines it, is distinguished by the interest it takes "in its *own* present, in a context where the past is not over and gone, where the subject of one's narrative is 'still there'."[12] Because it allows historians to examine histories whose protagonists are still alive, the history of the present has offered Moroccan historians a conceptual tool to probe methodological questions related to the writing of a history immersed in trauma, testimony, and memory, but one that still extends into the current day. One of the goals of the history of the present is to foster debates and counter-debates between historians and surviving historical actors in order to tease out the historical truth from a past whose events are still fresh in people's memories.[13] Faced with the new reality, which has made irrelevant their longstanding argument that historians need temporal distance from their topic of study in order to be objective in their reconstruction of the past, Moroccan academic historians organized a series of conferences between 1998 and 2007 in order to debate the appropriate methodologies for the navigation of a history that is still unfolding in other-archives circulating in society.[14] The primarily methodological nature of these discussions of the history of the present reveals a will to formulate new approaches to history-rewriting practices. These approaches would allow academic historians to reclaim their historical turf, which has gradually been occupied by popularized other-archives which the historians have yet to fully accept as participants in the rewriting of Morocco's recent political history.[15]

Such attention to the history of the present was a response to the divide Moroccan academic historians discovered between historiographical practice and the actual state of history in society, due to their participation in the ERC process. For instance, Mohammed V University historian Jilali El Adnani asserts that Moroccan historians need to learn from other social sciences in order to keep up with the changes taking place in the historical field in the context of ERC's investigations.[16] Mohammed Houbaida, a historian based at Ibn Tofail University in Kenitra, has also criticized the focus of Moroccan historians on monographs, which, in turn, are "prisoners of [archival] texts," and have no dialogue with other social sciences.[17] Despite these critical reflections from individual figures in the field of Moroccan history, the discipline itself could not instantaneously shed the flaws inherent to its nationalist foundation under colonialism.[18] Driven by the need to nationalize the discipline, establish a rudimentary national archive, and decolonize the writing of history, Moroccan academic historians in the early years of independence created a rigorous social-scientific field grounded in nationalist pride,[19] which some historians now blame for their discipline's alleged resistance to change. Interestingly, one of the prominent founders of the contemporary Moroccan school of history was none other than Germain Ayache, a Moroccan Jew and nationalist member of the Moroccan Communist Party, whose character we encountered in Hassan Aourid's novel *Cintra*, discussed in Chapter 3.[20] Ayache had strong positivistic persuasions and was a staunch believer in acquiring objective knowledge of the past through *al-arshīf al-mazkhzanī/al-wathā'iq al-makhzaniyya* (Makhzenian state manuscripts/documents).[21] Because he trained generations of graduate and undergraduate history students, Ayache's ideas about the sacredness of document-based history contributed to fossilizing the discipline, and only belatedly did many of his former students discuss how his legacy played a role in the difficulties their discipline faced in adapting its methodologies to the requirements of a quickly changing sociopolitical and cultural context.[22] Ayache's tradition of sanctifying official documents as the most valid source for history writing became an obstacle to the future evolution of Moroccan historiography, as other historians, like Mohammed Kenbib, Jamaâ Baïda, and Abderrahmane El Moudene, later acknowledged—particularly when faced with emerging historiographical practices, at the center of which were the exuberant post-1999 other-archives.[23]

The problems of this nationalist archive-based history were compounded by censorship and self-censorship under King Hassan II, which forced the majority of academic historians to study the pre-Protectorate period (before 1912) or else risk personal repercussions.[24] Both the existence of an abundant cache of archives about the pre-1912 years and the relatively innocuous nature of working on this period fostered Moroccan historians' focus on the study of the "dead past." This had the perverse effect of robbing many of them of the capacity to engage in both the theory and practice of new historical trends taking shape globally, such as oral history, history from below, history of the present, and trauma-informed history.[25] As a result, the only dissertation written and defended in Morocco about party politics after the independence was Ḥafiḍa Bilmuqaddim's "Ḥizb al-istiqlāl wa tadbīr al-intiqāl bayna al-insijām wa-al-taṣaddu', dujanbir 1955—yanāyr 1963" ("The Istiqlāl Party and the Management of Transition between Coherence and Division from December 1955–January 1963").[26] Bilmuqaddim's work was joined by very few dissertations written by Moroccans studying in France, like Maâti Monjib's "La Monarchie marocaine et la lutte pour le pouvoir: Hassan II face à l'opposition nationale, de l'indépendance à l'état d'exception" ("The Moroccan Monarchy and the Struggle for Power: Hassan II and National Opposition from Independence to the State of Exception") and Mostafa Bouaziz's "Aux origines de la Koutla démocratique" ("About the Origins of the Democratic Kuthla"),[27] which he wrote and defended at the Parisian École des Hautes Etudes en Sciences Sociales. The prevailing understanding of history as the study of a long-gone past had dire implications on job prospects for freshly minted historians. For example, Monjib was almost passed over for a position at Moulay Ismael University in Meknes because his would-be colleagues considered him more a political scientist than a historian.[28] Thus, Moroccan historiography produced inside the country between 1956 and 1999 remained silent on the political history of the Protectorate (1912–1955) and post-independence period (post-1956) until media coverage and journalistic investment in revealing more details about the Years of Lead.[29] Media coverage of rampant state violence and political repression between 1956 and 1999 led to the unprecedented circulation of prison testimonials, an other-archival subgenre, and pushed academic historians to take greater initiative as history became central to public debates in the wake of Hassan II's death in 1999.[30]

Gilson Miller has rightly captured the dire consequences of this historiography oriented toward the dead past, writing that "in the absence of a genuinely critical contemporary historiography, newspapers and magazines have been the vehicle of choice for rewriting recent political history."[31] Indeed, other-archives seeped into Moroccan people's collective memory through practices of serialization of prison memoirs, autobiographies, biographies, and interviews with dozens if not hundreds of the protagonists who shaped this political history. When the daily newspaper *al-Ittiḥād al-Ishtirākī* serialized Mohammed Raïss's memoirs *Min Skhirāt ilā Tazmamart*, the paper broke all records for newspaper sales in modern Morocco.[32] Countless Moroccan readers followed Raïss's memoirs about his eighteen-year disappearance to this notorious prison camp on a daily basis for over two months.[33] Ahmed Marzouki, Raïss's cellmate, also published a memoir; *Tazmamart: Cellule 10* sold over 25,000 copies a few weeks after its release in 2001 and close to 100,000 copies by 2017,[34] excluding the pirated copies available as PDFs online. This is a historic achievement for a book in a highly limited market, where a very successful book sells 3,000 copies on average. Additionally, *La Chambre noire ou Derb Moulay Cherif* (*The Black Chamber or Derb Moulay Cherif*), Jaouad Mdidech's prison memoir, sold over 8,000 copies and was made into a very successful film by director Hassan Benjelloun.[35] The international attention that the ERC garnered also sparked the interest of the transnational al-Jazeera Channel in testimonial prison literature. *Shāhid 'alā al-'aṣr* (*Witness of an Era*), one of the channel's most viewed programs, invited Ahmed Marzouki and Salah Hachad, two survivors of Tazmamart, for a multipart series to bear witness to their experiences in this prison of death.[36] In addition to publications by former victims of the state, platforms dedicated solely to history grew quickly, including the monthly history magazine *Zamane*, as well as Tarik Editions' memory series. Other-archives' incursions into the historiograhical field elicited a reaction from Mohammed Kenbib, who argued that, as a result of their profusion, "all the spotlights [are directed] fundamentally [. . .] toward History" to illuminate the contested post-independence past.[37]

Moroccan historians' initial reaction to the proliferation of other-archives was an outright dismissal and rejection of their historiographical value.[38] As early as 2003, a collection of articles published in *La Recherche Historique*, the official journal sponsored by the professional association of Moroccan historians (*Association Marocaine pour la Recherche Historique*), formulated a distinction between history and memory.[39] As a response to the way other-archives were transforming societal perceptions about the past in the public arena, the prominent historians who participated in this publication sought to draw a line between their academic work—as real and scientific history—and other-archives, specifically memoirs, testimonial prison literature, and journalistic investigations of past events. These historians still assigned other-archives to the realm of untrustworthy memory, even as they also credited them with the new dynamism in Moroccan historiography.[40]

Although *La Recherche Historique*'s 2003 articles now read more like defensive reactions from a field in crisis than a scholarly attempt to counter the other-archival activity shifting the boundaries of their discipline, this issue was only the beginning of a series of academic conferences and publications that strove to develop the distinction between other-archives and history. This distinction would subject other-archives to the epistemological power of history, by which I mean considering other-archives as an assortment of *stories* that are not history and which the historian should examine critically in order to construct a narrative in compliance with the requirements of the discipline. This endeavor was all the more important for academic historians because other-archives were filling the historiographical void left by academic historians' disinterest in the history of the present. This phenomenon is noticeable in the way bookstores classify memoirs and prison literature, which recount experiences of political disappearance and detention, under the category of history, as well as in cultural institutions' use of the word *tārīkh* (history) to introduce readings about the past that are not construed by trained historians.[41] The proceedings of one such conference were published under the title *Du Protectorat à l'indépendance: Problématique du temps présent* (*From the Protectorate to Independence: The Issue of the History of the Present*). The scholars who took part in this conference, organized at Morocco's prestigious public Mohammed V University based in Rabat, from November 10 to 12, 2005, formulated insightful theoretical responses to the demands of historicizing events that still have a bearing on the present time as well as on historians themselves. The papers presented suggested that Moroccan historians realized a categorical rejection of other-archives would only isolate their discipline from societal interest in the recent past.[42] This pragmatic need to be part of the general mood in the country—which was accepting of other-archives—marked a shift from the positions published in the 2003 *La Recherche Historique* issue. This shift is reflected in Mohammed V University–based historian Abdelahad Sebti's call for the use of writings by journalists, former victims, novelists, and even torturers in history writing, despite their lack of historiographical legitimacy in the eyes of academic historians.[43] Another sign of this fast-growing pragmatism was Sebti's call for "intellectual audacity" as a way to resolve the concerns over the lack of temporal distance and objectivity in other-archives, which had previously prevented his colleagues from studying the post-Protectorate past.[44]

Historian Mohammed Kenbib, a colleague of Sebti's in the same department at Mohammed V University, clearly describes this change in Moroccan historians' attitude vis-à-vis other-archives, stating that the "profusion of opinions, commentaries on radio and television, documentaries, newspaper articles, weekly 'dossiers,' memoirs, life writings and other writings" compelled academic historians to provide a historical perspective.[45] In fact, the subtext of Kenbib's statement is also a warning that academic historians could no longer ignore the changes taking place around them and that citizen-historians—creators of other-archives and amateur historians—would fill any void left by academic historians in the study of Morocco's immediate past. This is a fact that Gilson Miller also noticed, highlighting the notion that writings about the Years of Lead "fill the void between official dogma and suppressed memory."[46]

Other academic historians engaged in a more practical implementation of the history of the present to confront history and memory. *Al-Maghrib wa-al-zaman al-rāhin: Muʿṭayāt wa-muqārabāt* (*Morocco and History of the Present: Data and Approaches*), a conference organized by the RIRHM, convened in Rabat on July 14, 2007, and brought together the most prominent Moroccan academic historians to stage a confrontation between historiography, memory, testimony, and current events through the lens of the French concept of *histoire du temps présent*. In order to tease out historical truth from witnessing, the practitioners of this branch of history require that consideration must be given to the "weight of the traumatic event, confronting the witness, analysis of collective memory and the political uses of the past."[47] Using this unique format, RIRHM gathered historians interested in the study of the period in question alongside historical actors who had firsthand experience with the events under study, particularly the period of resistance to colonialism. By having academic historians present research papers in the presence of protagonists in the events analyzed, the organizers hoped to stage a debate between the protagonists' memories and the historical study of academic historians, to construct cross-checked historical knowledge about the past. However, the history of the present in its French version proved to be a failure in the Moroccan context, where self-censorship and fear of history had been internalized by the actors.

After the conference, the organizers admitted their failure to achieve the "anticipated goals behind the organization of this conference," attributing it to the "absence of the actors" and the reluctance of witnesses, especially political figures, to participate in the debates.[48] As a result, the conference was predominantly analytical rather than testimonial as the organizers had hoped.[49] Yet, examining the list of witnesses and historical actors invited to this event demonstrates that it was an elitist endeavor that probably overlooked the imbrication of these witnesses' interests with those of the state and its canonized versions of political history. Had former state victims, such as the prisoners of Tazmamart, Marxist-Leninist detainees, or Amazigh activists, been invited instead of nationalist leaders, historians would not have had a shortage of testimonies. Unsurprisingly—and as has been the case with every other conference dedicated to the study of post-1956 Moroccan history within an academic setting—the victims and survivors of state violence during this period were absented from the history of the present,[50] with Moroccan women victims of state violence being the biggest absence from this event. Hence, this conference proved Moroccan historians' understandings of the history of the present were oblivious to the "weight of the traumatic event[s]" that made this historical effervescence possible in the first place.[51]

Despite the organizers' avowal of having failed to achieve their objectives, a crucial confrontation did happen between historians and actors in one instance: when the participants discussed Moroccan Jews. Mohammed Hatimi, a historian of Moroccan Judaism, presented a paper in which he cautiously assessed the state of Moroccan Jewish historiography and discussed Jewish-Muslim cohabitation and the long-term impact of education on Jewish-Muslim relations.[52] Responding to Hatimi's presentation, Simon Lévy, a Moroccan Jewish professor of Spanish at Mohammed V University and a former member of the Moroccan Communist Party, urged historians to get rid of "the beautiful rhetoric that we have been using for the last thirty-one years" in order to see the danger that threatened Moroccan Judaism.[53] Lévy challenged historians to examine whether only Muslims had nationalist sentiments and, if so, to explain the love Jewish emigrants had sustained for Morocco despite decades of distance and separation from their country of origin. Referring to generalized assumptions that Jews were *khawana* (traitors of Moroccan nationalism) because they did not participate in sufficient numbers in the struggle for independence, Lévy reminded his interlocutors that they were wrong because "the biggest traitors were Muslim."[54] Drawing on his own experience, or embodied other-archive, Lévy used his presence among historians and nationalist leaders to dispel notions of alleged treachery on the part of Moroccan Jews, such as that of Jews' nonparticipation in nationalist action and of their disengagement from Morocco and incorporation into the colonial system. Lévy finished his powerful response by emphasizing that Jews, like Muslims under the Protectorate, traded with the French and simultaneously fought against them.[55] However, Lévy's critical remarks reached their pinnacle when he mentioned King Mohammed V and Allāl al-Fāsī. Lévy questioned the truism that King Mohammed V protected Jews from Vichy laws, which Nazi France had put in place to persecute Jews, and denounced the calls addressed to Jews by al-Fāsī, the founder of the Istiqlāl party, "to convert to Islam" in the period between 1961 and 1962,[56] a measure that led to spreading anti-Jewish sentiment.

Lévy's provocative comments elicited heated and sometimes confrontational responses from academic historians. For instance, Aïn Chok University historian Abdemajid Kaddouri focused his response on the fact that Lévy's testimony confirmed the necessity of distinguishing between memory and history, thus returning to the conservative, pro-Makhzanian approach that had reigned over Moroccan historiography for fifty years. According to Kaddouri, historians do not write history based on their individual subjectivity, but rather drawing on archives and documents. He continued that "memoirs are not history because memoirs narrate [stories] from a subjective point of view. For example, when Lévy just talked, he spoke from his perspective, but a professional historian cannot treat issues in the way we saw in [Lévy's] intervention, which means that in the historian's approach we can't give the answers we want in the way we want."[57] Historian 'Umar Affā expressed his clear disagreement with Hatimi's use of the word *tasāmuḥ* (tolerance) and urged his fellow historians to think in terms of Jews and Muslims being "partners in one homeland, and that the homeland is for all."[58] Affā also disagreed with Lévy regarding the persecution of Jews under the Almohad Dynasty.

Throughout these conversations, it becomes clear that Moroccan historians lack a homegrown conceptual tool for the study of other-archives and their incorporation into endeavors to write, or rather to rewrite, Morocco's recent political history. As previously stated, the combination of political repression and manuscript-based historical inquiry foreclosed academic historians' ability to stay abreast of developments in memory and trauma theory.[59] Even more critical, however, is French historian Daniel Rivet's observation in his review of the RIRHM's *Histoire du Maroc: Réactualisation et synthèse* (*Moroccan History: Reactualization and Synthesis*) that "at a time when the history of gender, body, minorities, margins, and the interstitial flourish, and as we move from one seminar to the next from *world history* to *microhistory*," the book's readership will "notice the minoring of women, *hatarin* (descendants of black slaves), Jews, and Berbers (*imazighen*)."[60] In this incisive comment, Rivet raises multiple issues about the minoritization of specific groups in Moroccan history of the present and connects that minoritization to global shifts in historical thinking. In so doing, he foregrounds how the historians who participated in this project missed an opportunity to place groups and, as I argue, other-archives at the heart of history. This is not shocking, however, since these limitations emanate from the unavailability of training in critical theory and gender studies during these historians' formative years. The historians involved in conversations about the history of the present do not seem to have succeeded at generating the analytical tools needed for the interdisciplinary study of the type of cultural production that gave birth to other-archives.[61] For example, multiple published papers and book chapters refer cursorily to testimonial prison literature without engaging in close reading of the works mentioned.[62] Even the cogent and well-researched papers presented by historians during the ERC's early conferences were not grounded in any theoretical approaches that would have attended to the traumatic and memory-related aspects of history. However, these very audacious attempts at making historical readings of subversive literature have since been replaced by scholarly conversations that are further removed from close engagement with testimonial prison literature and have become ever more focused on methodology. This shift, which took place at some point in 2005, has been a setback in historiographical engagement with other-archives' historical potential and has marked the rise to prominence of Mohammed V historians in these historiographical debates.[63] Although there is no evidence of any political involvement directing this process, the centrality of Mohammed V University and the funding partnerships that were available to its history department have been among the main bureaucratic reasons that most historians from other universities were left out of the conversation.

Clearly, Moroccan historians are not a homogeneous group, nor do they speak in unison. Nevertheless, throughout their methodological debates about the history of the present, there has been a relatively collective, gaping absence of engagement with the ethical dimensions of writing histories that involve trauma, suffering, and loss, such as is found in other-archives. Neither trauma nor "ethics" appear in any of the essays included in the various conference proceedings edited by Kenbib and Kably.[64] Despite the obvious ethical charge of histories involving violations of human dignity and human rights, the academic historians who partook in these conversations did not broach questions of ethics and trauma in their discussions, which in turn casts serious doubt on their very use of history of the present. It requires asking whether they put in place institutional and epistemological measures to embark on such a multilayered endeavor. These questions are all the more important because it was the emergence of stories from the victims of state violence that made Moroccan historians' discussions possible in the first place. When the topics of historiographical inquiry include torture, political disappearance, and violation of human dignity, the historian has an ethical duty to convey historical truth from a victim's point of view while also adhering to norms of historical accuracy and scientific integrity. Interpreting propositions by historians Dominic LaCapra and Saul Friedlander, art historian Alison Landsberg asserts that both scholars "suggest that for certain kinds of history—history of mass trauma in particular—the conventions of written academic history and its investment in objectivity not only are inadequate to the task but actually work against the production of historical knowledge."[65] Granted, despite the foundational work of philosopher of history Abdallah Laroui (who has remained silent on the questions attendant to the history of the present), Moroccan historians do not, to my knowledge, count among their ranks a LaCapra—whose work on trauma and history could inform the kind of scholarship Moroccan historians have been attempting to do—or Hayden White, whose germinal contribution helps bridge the gap between history and other narrative genres not grounded in facts.[66] Debating the history of the present requires the historian to take an ethical position, and studying other-archives demands that historians adopt an ethics of reading that surpasses any limited understanding of history as a mere reconstruction of the dead past from official or other traditional archives.

The question that emerges, then, concerns how the history-of-the-present framework gained appeal, becoming a sort of panacea, amid the challenges of rewriting Moroccan history during the early 2000s.[67] There are several reasons that explain why "history of the present" became a buzzword between 2000 and 2010. First, most senior Moroccan historians were trained in France, which makes the French version of this concept readily accessible and translatable into Arabic as *tārīkh al-zaman al-rāhin*. Relatedly, some of the historians involved in the early days of the ERC process were human rights activists who participated in Parisian political circles, which must have made them familiar with the concept's generative potential for the rewriting of Morocco's recent political history.[68] Second, the ERC recommended the creation of the *Centre de Recherche sur le Temps Présent* (Center for the History of the Present, CHP) at Mohammed V University, thus conferring an official status on the concept and its uses in the Moroccan context. Third, the European Union funded the implementation of many of the projects the ERC recommended to remedy the effects of the Years of Lead,[69] including the establishment of the CHP and other academic programs on human rights and contemporary history. This further undergirded the adoption and dissemination of the phrase "history of the present."[70] The EU's financial support of the ERC also demonstrates the influence of international aid related to human rights violations and their impact on local history writing.[71] Last, but not least, debates concerning the concept of history of the present itself and the attendant methodological questions allowed academic historians to safely remain in a purely theoretical realm. Academic historians' uncertainty about whether King Mohammed VI's reign would be democratic or repressive must have favored methodological discussions rather than history rewriting.

The focus on methodology thus left the actual writing of history in the hands of foreign historians. Apart from Brahim Boutaleb's long chapter entitled "Al-jidāl al-siyyāsī fī-al-maghrib 1956–1999" ("The Political Polemic in Morocco, 1956–1999"), an undocumented historical narrative of the period between 1956 and 1999, the actual critical rewriting of the country's recent history has been a Euro-American endeavor.[72] The long-term effects of political repression, censorship, and inaccessibility of archives made the state "the prime mover that dominates historical narrative" and imposed a division of labor between Moroccan historians, who mainly worked on pre-1912 history, and their foreign colleagues, who ventured into post-1956 history.[73] It is French historians Pierre Vermeren and Daniel Rivet, as well as American historian Susan Gilson Miller, who have penned most of the up-to-date, comprehensive histories of contemporary Morocco.[74] These historians recognize and incorporate the conflictual and all-too-recent post-independence era in their histories. Their work combines theoretical awareness of the fact that memory "can be treated as any other historical source by using methods of comparison, fact-checking, and common sense" with the practice of history writing, thus gaining an edge over their Moroccan colleagues.[75] To explain this perceived dissonance between Moroccan historians' investment in theoretical discussions at conferences and their reluctance to execute a practical rewriting of history, historian Mohammed Houbaida employs the concept of a "psychological barrier," which might be a residue of the fear of the prevalent censorship that has prevented Moroccan historians from writing newer versions of their country's history.[76] Another plausible explanation for this reluctance to write the history of the present is the conviction that it is still in flux, which is a daunting task for historians trained in the Moroccan tradition. Taking this into consideration, it is certain that theorizing how to write recent history is not as risky as the act of writing history itself: authorship comes with both risks and responsibilities that most Moroccan academic historians prefer not to face. Nevertheless, leaving comprehensive history writing in the hands of these world-class foreign historians is not the only challenge that conceptualizing the history of the present faces in Morocco.

In fact, generalized societal consumption of other-archives in the four corners of the country was not matched by the geography of historiographical debates, the lion's share of which were hosted at Mohammed V University, and, to a lesser degree, Hassan II University's Aïn Chok School of Humanities and Social Sciences in Casablanca. The oldest modern university in independent Morocco, headquartered in the Moroccan capital of Rabat, Mohammed V University's history department signed partnerships that allowed it to receive the funding for and to organize conferences about the history of the present. Some facets of the concentration of these discussions at Mohammed V University include the university's partnership with the *Conseil National des Droits de l'Homme* (the National Council for Human Rights, NCHR) to start new programs, such as a Master's degree in the History of the Present and a Master's in Human Rights, and to create the CHP.[77] Furthermore, while the ERC-recommended creation and preservation of regional museums and sites of memory have stalled, *Les Archives du Maroc*, whose founding director has been a historian at Mohammed V University for a long time, are now temporarily housed at the former headquarters of the National Library adjacent to the university's campus. As a result, even as Moroccan historians were debating the history of the present, the unbalanced spatial distribution of national resources was reproduced through Mohammed V University's monopoly of this new branch of history, at least during the period between 2000 and 2006. This, in turn, suggests these debates have not really captured the depth of the transformation Moroccan society has undergone thanks to its contact with other-archives since 1999, which the ERC has rightly underlined in its final report. Comparing Moroccan history between 1956 and after 1999, the ERC stated that "whereas the history that was written in the past was the history of the center, nowadays, the margins and the periphery are coming to the fore with their own histories and these margins have become a partner in the rewriting of this history."[78]

Dialoguing History: Blurring the Boundaries between History and Literature

Lest one assume that all Moroccan historians think alike or approach the writing of history in the same way, it is important to underline the diversity of approaches within the discipline. The predominance of Mohammed V University–based scholars has overshadowed or even excluded a very unique experience—a combination of history and literature—that developed concurrently with their discussions of the history of the present. This experimental approach, which brought together a historian and a novelist, focused on rewriting Morocco's political history during the state of exception, the de facto suspension of civil institutions, between 1965 and 1970. This period was a turning point in Moroccan history. In March 1965, protestors were repressed in Casablanca, and just a few months later, in October, longtime opposition leader Mahdi Ben Barka was assassinated in Paris. Drawing on the main events of this period, M'barek Zaki, an academic historian at the Office of the High Commissioner for Former Resistance Fighters and Members of the Liberation Army, and Ahmed Beroho, a novelist, journalist, and former diplomat, started a unique collaboration that brought this political history into an innovative dialogue. Zaki is the author of an important, albeit understudied book, *Résistance et armée de libération: Portée politique, liquidation, 1953–1958* (*Resistance and Liberation Army: Political Significance, Liquidation, 1953–1958*), in which he dispels myths about the country's independence movement.[79] Swimming against the current of historiographical trends in the 1980s, which relegated the story of the liberation army to oblivion, Zaki audaciously revealed the silenced role of the Moroccan monarchy in disbanding the resistance army in the south of Morocco. Zaki's provocative work is barely cited by his academic colleagues, however. Even during the 2007 discussion of *al-dhākira wa-al-muqāwama* (memory and resistance), which was most relevant to his research, Zaki was not present or mentioned in the proceedings.[80] Beroho is a prolific novelist with a discernible penchant for both historical and controversial topics in his novelistic output. Some of his publications include *Le Lion du Rif: Abdelkrim* (*The Lion of Rif: Abdelkrim*), *Les Mystères de Tanger* (*The Mysteries of Tangiers*), and *Histoire de Tanger* (*History of Tangiers*),[81] which are all grounded in the history of northern Morocco. As is well known, the Rif suffered tremendously from state repression of the revolt of 1958 and its increasing association with the memory of Abdelkarim, who defeated the Spanish in the battle of Anoual in 1921.

Zaki and Beroho's collaboration was part of a larger collaborative atmosphere between journalists, literary figures, and victims of state violence in the early 2000s. Ultimately, these collaborations led to novel prefaces, joint authorship, and translation practices that Morocco had never before witnessed. For instance, 'Abd al-Ḥamīd Jmāhrī, a journalist and literary critic, translated and serialized Ṛaïss's memoir *De Skhirat à Tazmamart* in *al-Ittiḥād al-Ishtirākī*, the daily newspaper. Ignace Dale, a French journalist, revised and prefaced in French the original manuscript of Marzouki's *Tazmamart: Cellule 10*. Abdelhak Serhane, a famous Francophone novelist, co-authored Salah and Aïda Hachad's memoir *Kabazal*, while François Trotet, a French litterateur co-wrote Ahmed and Kalima El Ouafi's testimony entitled *Opération Boraq F5*.

The zeitgeist of the period between 1999 and 2006 spurred Zaki's collaboration with Beroho as co-authors of *Hassan II ou Confessions d'outre-tombe: Tragicomédie* (*Hassan II or Confessions from beyond the Grave: Tragicomedy*), which historicized one of the most dramatic episodes in post-1956 Morocco.[82] One year after the publication of Beroho's "historical-novel-tragicomedy" under the title *Hassan II ou Confessions d'outre-tombe: Tragicomédie*, Zaki published the original historical text that Beroho fictionalized.[83] Zaki's historical book is entitled *Un Roi et deux républicains: Dialogues de l'au-delà: Hassan II, Ben Barka, Oufkir et les autres* (*One King and Two Republicans: Dialogues of the Hereafter: Hassan II, Ben Barka, Oufkkir, and Others*).[84] Written in the form of dialogues between King Hassan II, Mahdi Ben Barka, General Oufkir, and other deceased political actors, the book stages conversations between them to reassess their positions on internal politics when they were alive and politically active. Zaki drew on documentary archives to provide the historical substratum for the story, whereas Beroho turned the archival material into a novel. *Hassan II ou Confessions* is, therefore, just one among many historical-literary responses elicited by the groundbreaking effect of the production of other-archives on historical writing in Morocco. Influenced by the successful treatment of the recent Moroccan past in other-archives, the historian and the novelist combined their expertise to produce a work that abided by historical conventions regarding evidence and critical research without constraining their stylistic and authorial innovation to the strict exigencies of academic history writing. The result is a history created in dialogue with itself, whose style and language were both tailored to appeal to a wide readership.

Based on a creative reimagining of historical documentation from the time of the original events, *Un Roi et deux républicains*—strategically placed in the appendix of *Hassan II ou Confessions*—retells the tumultuous history of independent Morocco. This well-researched novel retraces the trajectories as well as the enmities of its characters of formerly powerful political figures. The novel depicts General Oufkir, former minister of defense and confidant of the king; Mahdi Ben Barka, a nationalist figure with republican proclivities; Mawlāy al-Haṣan, king of Morocco from 1961 to 1999; as well as Allāl al-Fāsī, one of the founders of the Istiqlāl party, among others. The story told in *Un Roi et deux républicains* starts with Mawlāy al-Ḥasan convening several meetings between himself, Oufkir, and Ben Barka to "review the events that left their profound imprint on the historical march of independent Morocco in order to define everyone's responsibility and hear each other's explanation and justification of these events."[85] However, al-Ḥasan, being dead, is stripped of his authority and earthly titles and is thus placed on equal footing with the rest of the characters. This fact empowers his interlocutors to indulge in an honest dialogue—without fear—that better historicizes the disastrous impact of their actions on Morocco's future. The characters' reimagined dialogues delve into the usually taboo zones of Morocco's past and provide multiple perspectives on the disagreements of these characters over several issues, including the future of the monarchy in post-independence Morocco and the assassination of resistance leader 'Abbās al-Misa'dī in 1957. The characters also discuss Ben Barka's controversial, pro-Algerian position during the Sand War, a conflict that pitted Morocco against Algeria in 1963. Finally, this history-in-the-form-of-dialogue portrays these historical actors as they reflect on their lives from their positions in the hereafter, which makes a significant difference in the way they see the world.

The juxtaposition of *Hassan II ou Confessions* and *Un Roi et deux républicains* demonstrates the breadth of stylistic and methodological innovation that other-archives could offer academic historians. Zaki's historiographical audacity and Beroho's literary skill revived Mawlāy al-Ḥasan, Oufkir, and Ben Barka to account for their past actions in their own (albeit reimagined) voices. Moreover, *Hassan II ou Confessions*' popular style simplifies history and makes its taboo topics all the more accessible to the average French-speaking Moroccan. Of course, the fact that the book was published in French raises a host of issues about the limitations of publishing a text in a foreign language in an overtly Arabized country, but circulation, in this context, is not as important as approach. *Hassan II ou Confessions* critically departed from usual approaches to history writing, to wed literary imagination with the unearthing of a silenced past.

Writing history as dialogue and theatricalizing the protagonists' impactful past is an important aspect of Zaki's collaboration with Beroho, in the Brechtian tradition. Theater and performance scholar Robert Gordon has underlined that "Brecht 'literarised' the performance by openly displaying the technical and dramaturgical mechanism of the play's construction."[86] In fact, Zaki and Beroho's tragicomedy is a Brechtian stage where history is accessed through dialogue, with historical actors whose voices address an eager readership. Portraying the historical actors' emotions, providing insights into intimate dialogues, and accessing fleeting moments inside the historical events witnessed by the protagonists all contribute to this theatricalized history. In the hands of Zaki and Beroho, history is reintegrated into the social sphere in the form of anecdotes, humor, gossip, and a new writing practice that is unlikely to be adopted by Moroccan academic historians—either in Morocco or abroad—in the near future. Reflective of the multiple exclusions within historiography, Zaki does not seem to have been part of any of the academic conferences or edited volumes discussed earlier, and his writings remain marginalized despite breaking new ground in historical thinking.

The State Rewrites Its Own Past

Concomitantly with the developments in academic history and literary-historical collaborations, the Moroccan state was also working to reclaim its erstwhile domination of history production, especially with the establishment of the RIRHM in 2006. The existence of other-archives in Moroccan historiographical practice has demonopolized the history of the present, but also incentivized the Moroccan state to recentralize itself as both a maker and writer of history.[87] Aided by their renewed legitimacy after the stellar international success of the ERC, public servants used the very implementation of the ERC's recommendations to openly tighten the state's supervision of historiographic practice. Indeed, the official state position is that the past and its uses are too significant and too sensitive to be left entirely to academic historians and other-archives' creators. A history from which the repression, excesses, and crimes committed by the state cannot be expunged is too dangerous for the future legitimacy and present standing of the monarchy and the entire Makhzen-state system. In fact, Moroccan history has always been the history of the monarchy, and the new institutional setup that the state put in place after 2006 is merely a reflection of this understanding of such a strategic discipline.

Creating New and Repurposing Existing Infrastructures for Historiographical Research

Leery of the immediate and long-term consequences of allowing historians and historical actors total autonomy, state officials have used official channels to write negotiated, but also dissenting, versions of its past violations. Their action stems from a belated realization that the state's scorched-earth policy regarding evidence during the Years of Lead had backfired by instead enabling other-archives' creators to speak for both the victims and the now-silent perpetrators.[88] The state response in this regard has been to further institutionalize both history and archives. Such efforts toward institutionalization seem to have been driven by a desire to contain the civic-responsibility-driven endeavors to rewrite the past through the prolific production of other-archives, which actually brings the state closer to the conservative positions of Moroccan historians in 2003 and those of some aforementioned historians discussed in the section on the history of the present. In the context of an unprecedented social interest in the state's recent violence, Moroccan officials have conceived, created, repurposed, and funded various institutions that have been rewriting Morocco's contested history.

In addition to creating RIRHM, whose work and mission I discuss in ample detail later in this chapter, the state mobilized its human rights institutions to rewrite Moroccan contemporary history. For example, both the NCHR (created in 1991 and renamed 2011) and the *Conseil de la Communauté Marocaine à l'Etranger* (The Council of the Moroccan Community Living Abroad, CMCLA, created in 2007 and renamed in 2011),[89] have slowly taken on historiographical roles in the form of co-sponsorship of history-themed conferences and publications. Although laypeople may find it strange that a human rights council and an immigration institution would partake in writing history, specialists in Moroccan affairs, who understand history as a battleground for democratic and civic change in post-1999 Morocco, do not. In fact, by mobilizing these institutions to rewrite its past, the state positions itself as a defender of democracy, human rights, and citizenship, thus co-opting the demands of its opposition to consider knowledge of the country's plural histories as a human right. Although the state co-opts its opponents' discourse regarding history to serve its own agendas, this interdependence of human rights and history speaks to the success of activists and producers of other-archives in placing history at the core of the political transition toward reconciliation and democracy. For the state, however, rewriting history through a human rights lens is crucial for marketing its image as a law- and human-rights-abiding polity.

The international conference entitled "Migration, Identity and Modernity in the Maghreb," which convened in the coastal city of Essaouira from March 17 to 21, 2010, illustrates how human rights and migration institutions have added history writing to their initial mission. Co-sponsored by the CCHR and the CMCLA, and organized under the auspices of André Azoulay, the only Jewish advisor to the king, the conference's broad title obscures the fact that it was focused on the emigration of North African Jews. The conference proceedings were edited in three copious volumes entitled *La Bienvenue et l'adieu: Migrants juifs et musulmans au Maghreb (XVe–XXe siècle)* (*Arrival and Departure: Jewish and Muslim Migrants in the Maghreb [15th–20th century]*).[90] In the introduction, the editors pay their respects to the President of the Essaouira Mogador Association (Azoulay), the CCHR's leadership (Driss El Yazami and Ahmed Herzenni), and the CMCLA for supporting the conference.[91] Organized at a time when Moroccan society and other-archive producers had become more openly interested in Morocco's Jewish heritage through films, mnemonic literature, and ethnographies on Morocco's Jewish past from within Morocco, the CCHR and CMCLA's co-sponsorship of this conference, their conspicuous contribution to the publication, and the wide dissemination of the proceedings demonstrate a convergence of the research agenda with the state's political needs. Incorporating the conference within the ERC's broader work, the then-president of the CCHR evoked the ERC's recommendation about "the necessity of restoring the country's memory and re-reading national history" to justify the importance of the conference.[92] In fact, the NCHR undertook an even broader initiative by publishing *Histoire du Maroc indépendant: Biographies politiques*, now withdrawn for unexplained reasons.[93] Consistent with its newly acquired roles related to the setting of the official history agenda, the CMCLA co-sponsored the Moroccan Association for Historical Research's conference "al-'unf fī tārīkh al-maghrib" (Violence in Moroccan History), which convened from November 14 to 16, 2013. Published under the title *al-'Unf fī tārīkh al-maghrib: Ashghāl al-ayyām al-waṭaniyya al-ḥādiyya wa-al-'ishrīn li-al-jam'iyya al-maghribiyya li-al-baḥth al-tārīkhī* (*Violence in Moroccan History: The Proceedings of the 21st National Days of the Moroccan Association for Historical Research*), the proceedings carry the CMCLA's logo on the first page alongside that of both the organizing association and the publisher.[94] The sixteen chapters included in the book are clearly oriented toward the dead past, with no chapters on violence in independent Morocco, and this begs pressing questions about the margin of freedom available to scholars in these types of collaborations. What is sure, however, is that state-funded immigration and human rights organizations are now partners in historical research and production in a rapidly transforming historiographical landscape.

This rush toward the institutionalization of history writing poses several questions about the need to repurpose human rights and immigration institutions instead of allocating their copious funding to history departments at different Moroccan universities where existing departments already have staff and thousands of undergraduate and graduate students from among whom the next generation of historians will rise. One answer to this issue, however, can be found in the fact that state-run institutions create research cultures as well as set norms about what can and cannot be said, which is likely a motivating factor for the state to extend the reach of its institutionalization of history writing outside of academic departments. Furthermore, high commissions and specialized entities have historically served to expand the state's cooptation of specifically skilled elites who may otherwise refuse to integrate into the system.[95] By agreeing to be part of such arrangements, the individuals concerned usually accept the unspoken rule of staying silent when their beliefs diverge from official directives. Therefore, by considering these questions within the context of the Moroccan state's well-tested practice of using *ad hoc* commissions to navigate inconvenient questions, we gain some insight as to why state-funded institutions outside academic departments would be asked to write the history of the present in Morocco—a history in which state agents have committed systematic violations of human rights.

The creation of an institutional structure does not mean that the state dictates what is to be written by that structure. Nevertheless, a historian's awareness of his or her privileged position within a highly selective institution may foster self-censorship. The fact that the state hires employees and funds researchers' salaries and benefits influences the scholarship that is produced. The efficiency of official institutions in setting the parameters for discussions can be seen in the noticeable difference between the quality of conference papers presented during the early months of the ERC's work and the proceedings of the different conferences organized afterward. This observation does not necessarily mean that all academic historians who work on projects underwritten by state institutions have been coopted. Rather, I wish to highlight the fact that the establishment of new institutions for the investigation and rewriting of Moroccan history is not an entirely positive development. Consequently, institutions dedicated to history outside the university can be a blessing, if endowed with autonomous and strong leadership—or a curse, if the state officials turn them into bureaucratic infrastructures for extoling their own achievements.

The Royal Institute for Research on the History of Morocco (RIRHM)

The culmination of the official effort to recuperate the historiographical field, which, in Gilson Miller's expertly rendered words, has been witnessing the birth of a "re-centered narrative characterized by diversity and inclusiveness," culminated in the establishment of the RIRHM in 2006.[96] The royal decree founding the RIRHM defined the institution as: "a national establishment of scientific research, in charge of sponsoring research in Moroccan history and promoting knowledge of Morocco's immediate and distant past(s) so as to anchor Moroccan identity and strengthen collective memory by being receptive to the different actors involved in [the creation of Moroccan] identity and character throughout [the different] eras."[97] The establishment of the RIRHM implemented the ERC's recommendation that an institute be created to "conduct documentation, research, and publication concerning the historical events relating to the gross human rights violations of the past, development of human rights and democratic reform issues."[98] Within the same recommendation, the ERC also prescribed that "all national archives should be preserved, and their regulation should be coordinated between the different departments involved. A law should also be enacted to regulate the archives' conditions of preservation, hours at which they are open to the public, the conditions for consulting them, and the sanctions for defacing them," before adding an important recommendation regarding the gradual revision of history curricula.[99] However, there is a substantial gap between the ERC recommendations and the official decree establishing the RIRHM. While the founding decree underlined the necessity of writing a plural Moroccan history that would be reflective of the different actors and stakeholders in the nation's identity and personality,[100] it remained silent on the importance of history for the advancement of human rights and citizenship, as the ERC had recommended.

In addition to its academic mission, the RIRHM is tasked with the production of books for educational purposes and the dissemination of Moroccan history in foreign languages, and, indeed, several of the institutes' publications have already been translated into French, English, and Spanish.[101] By combining scholarship and education, the RIRHM aims to create a collective ethos based on a newly rediscovered, shared history.[102] Nevertheless, if the intention of creating such an institution was, as its founding royal decree says, to contribute to the knowledge of the Moroccan past, one wonders about the reasons RIRHM has been placed under the supervision of the Ministry of Religious Endowments and Islamic Affairs, which is not known for the production of historiographical research. In a discussion between myself and historian Mohammed Kenbib, he indicated that the minister's training as a historian likely played a major role in this decision.[103] Aḥmad Tawfīq, a famous social historian who has held his position as Minister of Religious Endowments and Islamic Affairs since 2002, enjoys the trust of the monarchy, and his status must have been decisive in the decision to place RIRHM under the purview of his ministry.[104]

To achieve its academic and pedagogical mission, RIRHM hires both retired and still-active faculty to edit special volumes and publications. For instance, Abderrahmane El Moudden, a well-respected Princeton-trained specialist of Ottoman history, co-edited the book *al-Maghrib wa-al-zaman al-rāhin*—the institute's main contribution to the theorization of the history of the present in Morocco. The RIRHM's list of publications so far includes the results of the debates that took place between 2006, the year of its establishment, and 2014, when there was a remarkable deceleration in its work. In addition to *Histoire du Maroc: Réactualisation et synthèse* (*History of Morocco: Synthesis and Reactualization*), which has been translated into French, English, and Spanish, the RIRHM's websites displays the following titles: *Chronologie de l'histoire du Maroc* (*A Chronology of Moroccan History*); *al-Dhākira wa-al-muqāwama al-maghribiyya fīmā bayna sanatay 1946 wa*

1961 (*Memory and Moroccan Resistance between 1946 and 1961*); *Shamāl al-maghrib ibbāna fatra al-ḥimāya wa bidāyat 'ahd al-istiqlāl* (*The North of Morocco during the Protectorate and the Beginning of Independence*); *Muḥammad al-Khāmis min sulṭān ilā malik* (*Mohammed V from Dignified Sultan to King*); *Wāḥāt al-tukhūm wa ḥudūd al-maghrib al-sharqiyya (1800–1903)* (*Moroccan Confines, Oases and Eastern Borders in British Archives [1800–1903]*); and *Oasis orientales et espace frontalier entre l'Algérie occupée et le Maroc* (*Eastern Oases and Border Space between Occupied Algeria and Morocco*).[105] Although these works show an openness toward marginalized regions of the country, such as the eastern and northern parts, the themes are state-centered—verging on nationalistic—at times and have hagiographic overtones at others. As a result, the state of Morocco, its borders, the liberation movement, and the Sultans all seem to eclipse the people and their histories. RIRHM has so far excluded the narratives of the victims of the state from its publications. This barred the road for the inclusion of other-archives in academic histories, thus protracting the perceived opposition between academic history and other-archives as a whole.

The RIRHM's landmark achievement is the publication of *Histoire du Maroc*. This megaproject took six years to materialize and features contributions from fifty-one prominent academic historians covering all time periods of Moroccan history. In addition to its innovations in integrating the pre-Islamic period and creating a new periodization of Moroccan history, *Histoire du Maroc*'s authors dedicate the tenth chapter to contemporary Morocco.[106] Entitled "Independent Morocco," this chapter reviews the major events that marked the power struggle between the monarchy and the opposition, as well as the Years of Lead and their impact on human rights and cultural activity in the country. From Amazigh language to immigration and Jewish emigration to feminism, hitherto marginalized aspects of the Moroccan past have been brought into a collective Moroccan history book, which indicates that the taboos surrounding these topics have weakened. Yet *Histoire du Maroc* glosses over important details about the negotiations between the monarchy, the United States, and American Jewish organizations, namely the American Jewish Joint Distribution Committee and Hebrew Immigrant Aid Society, to facilitate Jewish emigration from Morocco. Nor is there any effort to tie the facilitation of Jewish emigration to authoritarianism and the difficult life prospects under King Hassan II's regime. Even the book's treatment of prison testimonial literature, which recovers individual and collective experiences of former political prisoners in different disappearance jails like Tazmamart, Agdz, and Derb Moulay Cherif, was selective and cursory, thus omitting its importance for this significant project. The Amazigh movement and its struggle for a culturally and linguistically pluralistic Morocco also received short shrift from the authors of the *magnum opus*, and the topics of race and racism have not fared any better.[107]

Most scholarly responses to the publication of *Histoire du Maroc* extolled its pioneering nature. In an extensive review, Daniel Nordman, an NCSR-based historian, concluded that *Histoire du Maroc* is "a work that is useful, often convincing, pedagogic, and accessible to different sorts of readers, because it is neither excessively skeptical, nor offensive, nor intransigent, nor polemic. Difficult to reduce to one or even several historical currents, it is a scholarly work, written with a balanced, reasonable mindset, in line with accepted rules and usages. It is underpinned by historical knowledge that is up-to-date, multiple, and without preconceived boundaries, and is equally attentive to studies which—after circumspect, critical examination—still deserve recognition."[108] Nordman goes on to emphasize that *Histoire du Maroc* is "at once experimental and pragmatic."[109] However, such praise for the publication of this important work has not dissipated all scholarly ambivalence in its reception. For instance, Abdellah Hammoudi, the Princeton-based Moroccan anthropologist, critiqued the weakness of the book's coverage of the post-independence period, whereas other scholars, like Rivet, found no justification for its overly cautious analysis of the contemporary period.[110] Rivet has written that "the last chapter will without doubt appear scanty and cautious in the point of view of historians who work in a scientific sphere that has neither borders nor territorial belonging of the sort that researchers in the social sciences have."[111] This cautiousness might be attributed to the tension between academic historians and the Ministry of Religious Endowments and Islamic Affairs, which supervises the institute.[112] Historian Mostafa Bouaziz wonders, in a review, if the noticeable tension felt when the book was presented publicly between Aḥmad Tawfīq, the Minister of Religious Endowments and Islamic Affairs, and Mohammed Kably, RIRHM's director, was due to some of the innovations contained in the book, or if they were due to political issues.[113] Regardless, as Bouaziz has noted, this work is proof that Moroccan historians are demanding more innovation in history writing.[114]

The publication of *Histoire du Maroc* seems to operate on the pretense that the book's genesis was the result of a natural historical development. Instead of foregrounding the role of Moroccan society's elevated historical awareness in the production of this momentous work, the editors have produced an excellent academic book that ignores the very circumstances of its birth. A direct result of this oversight is that both the introduction and conclusion of *Histoire du Maroc* fail to recognize the conjuncture that warranted not only the historiographical enterprise that culminated in the publication of the book, but also the RIRHM's very creation. Had the authors acknowledged the indispensable contribution of those oppressed and silenced by the post-independence state, they would have committed historians to an ethical responsibility to devise new methods of addressing historical human rights issues. However, by failing to contextualize the publication within the dynamics of other-archives' rewriting of the Moroccan past and the ERC's recognition of the need to revisit that past, the authors of *Histoire du Maroc* missed the chance to historicize the very socio-cultural and political dynamics that facilitated its existence in the first place. As a result, while writing the history of Morocco, *Histoire du Maroc* forgets to write both the history of its own genesis and that of the context in which it became a necessity.

More than a decade later, in the summer of 2021, this deliberate amnesia continues to inform Moroccan academic historians' disengagement from the writing of the history of the Years of Lead. The disinterest in the history of the present has been exacerbated by the fact that the national momentum that was garnered by the massive publication and discussion of other-archives in the public arena seems to have passed, and the state no longer has any incentive to encourage the resolution of outstanding issues in its authoritarian past. Morocco has been witnessing a tightening of national security's grip on society since 2014. The attack on the independent press, as evidenced by the jailing of several journalists, as well as the climate of repression, which many have rhetorically likened to the Years of Lead, has restricted academic freedom and pushed intellectuals of all persuasions to find refuge in self-censorship. In its most recent report in July 2021, the Euro-Mediterranean Human Rights Monitor writes that Moroccan authorities are trying to "muzzle the mouths of its critics by surveilling, arresting, imprisoning, and bringing them to unjust trials based on what appears to be readymade accusations."[115] The months-long ordeal of historian Maâti Monjib between December 2020 and March 2021 was a clear message that critical historical truth and freedom of opinion are still dangerous endeavors in Morocco.[116] Most importantly for the RIRMH, however, is dropping the word "research" from its name, which is now the Institut Royal de l'Histoire du Maroc (Royal Institute for Moroccan History) and its annexation to the Académie du Royaume du Maroc (Academy of the Kingdom of Morocco [AKM]). The aforementioned Mohammed Kenbib, an experienced historian who also worked as a cultural advisor for the Moroccan embassy in Paris (1997–2001), has been since June 2021 this institution's director. While the RIRMH was previously under the supervision of historian Aḥmad Tawfiq, the Minister of Endowment and Islamic Affairs, its current subsumption under the AKM brings it, according to the AKM's decree, under the king's direct patronage.[117] Although only time can tell the extent to which these changes will affect the RIRMH's already slow-paced production of historical knowledge, one thing is sure: The Moroccan state has turned the page on the short-lived liberal period that opened in the early 2000s and has allowed the trenchant historiographical discussions that are recorded and analyzed in this chapter.

Conclusion

The existence of other-archives has energized Moroccan historiography and pushed its boundaries more than ever before. While the repressive climate that reigns over the country has drastically curtailed what can be said and written, other-archives, particularly works pertinent to political repression and Jewish migration, continue to exist in various forms in an aggressively policed public sphere. Moreover, as during the Years of Lead, other-archives are mainly informing academic studies while continuing to spread knowledge about Morocco's post-independence past through unconventional channels that continue to challenge both historiography and historians.

Conclusion

Moroccan Other-Archives has provided an analysis of the rich ways Moroccan cultural producers have written and rewritten histories of exclusion and silencing in a context where traditional archives were either nonexistent or inaccessible between 1956 and 2020. Adopting a dialogical approach that examines Moroccan cultural production through the lens of cutting-edge theoretical scholarship on archives, memory, and loss, this work has addressed the ways in which Morocco's post-colonial history has been reclaimed and written by Moroccan cultural producers despite the lack of an official archive until 2011. In engaging the question of how this archival void could inform histories of loss, the book has delineated the emergence of other-archives as a cultural response to both the lack of official archives and the self-censorship and silence common among Moroccan historians of the time.

The period between 1994 and 2020 saw a proliferation of other-archives. The political transformations that took place in Morocco and across the world have created a fertile terrain for a wider societal mobilization aimed at transforming politics and re-envisioning the state through the recovered voices of Moroccan constituencies whose stories were left out of the official history of the nation. In subverting narratives of cohesion woven through notions of the "symbiotic" cultural, ethnic, and linguistic mosaic of Moroccan society,[1] cultural producers have called for a new *culture of citizenship*, which radically revises the historical status quo to shed light on the communities, histories, languages, and stories that have been repressed since independence in 1956. Even the Equity and Reconciliation Commission's (ERC) final report embraces the idea that open access to the past is a fundamental step toward a new form of citizenship that makes a radical break with the silence of the post-colonial past.[2]

A comparative investigation of the emergence of Imazighen, Jews, and political imprisonment as questions of mnemonic and historiographical importance, *Moroccan Other-Archives* opens up other-archives' creative potential beyond the ERC's approach, which stressed the temporary and cathartic nature of cultural production about political detention, a very restrictive notion of archives. Because of the ERC's narrow definition, scholarship has largely neglected both loss and comparative analysis as critical tools that could be used to study this period.[3] In foregrounding loss as a primary driver of Imazighens' locational citizenship, Jewish-themed mnemonic literature, and testimonial prison literature, the book has pushed back against the ERC's assumptions that the impact of authoritarianism was limited in both space and time. Moreover, the book has constructed a much-needed theoretical framework for the comparative study of a cultural memory—memory manifested in the form of artifacts, inscriptions, embodied experiences, sounds, or visual material—that has been flourishing in Morocco since 1999. Rather than framing loss as prohibitive and disabling, I conceive of it as the epicenter of cultural production about the Years of Lead. Thus, loss is framed as a catalyst for cultural producers to regain their historiographical agency by restoring, inscribing, and endowing a silenced past with staying power.

The examination of Amazigh historiographical agency infused in Tifinagh reveals how deeply the Amazigh language has transformed Morocco's visual identity. It also tells parallel histories of loss and oppression of Amazigh identity after fifty years of erasure from the public sphere. The performance of *Tankra Tamazight* (*al-nahḍa al-amāzīghīyya*/the Amazigh Renaissance) as an other-archive includes a transformation of musical, literary, and discursive traditions that remap Morocco through a reimagined cartography of Tamazgha, as well as an iconography that has changed the looks of urban spaces in Morocco since 2011.[4] The Moroccan Amazigh Cultural Movement's invention and reinvention of Amazigh traditions against the background of state repression and silencing of Amazigh identity between 1956 and 2001 yielded transformative results that re-Amazighized the Moroccan public sphere through the widespread use of Tifinagh.

Identifying and analyzing mnemonic literature about Jews authored by Muslim novelists will allow scholars to examine how these novelists remember Jews in a growing novelistic output in Arabic and French. Occupying an epistemological space between Jewish Studies and Arabic/Amazigh Studies, mnemonic literature challenges typical disciplinary boundaries. Written by Muslim novelists and instrumental in the intergenerational transference of memories, mnemonic literature reimagines Morocco with its Jewish population, complicating the ordinary, linear approach to the study of Moroccan literature. Almost all studies have focused on literature written by Jews who have left the country,[5] thus overlooking a mnemonic literary subgenre in which Muslims recover an imagined life with their former Jewish co-citizens. As a result of its unique lens, *Moroccan Other-Archives*' theorization of this subfield of Moroccan literature has two transformative consequences. (1) It shows that Moroccan Jews have become an object of loss in cultural memory, an observation which enriches the superb ethnographic work on Jews conducted in Morocco. (2) It illustrates that literary studies, and cultural memory specifically, can illuminate future ethnographic and historical work on Jews. Indeed, scholars have already conducted groundbreaking ethnographies, interpreted films, and even unearthed legal forum shopping practices, but as of yet, none have investigated the literary, inscribed cultural memory created by Muslim writers about Jews and its significance for Moroccan history.[6] Mnemonic literature places Moroccan Jews within a Moroccan temporality and reimagines their emigration, return, and struggle within the endogenous needs of Moroccan society, thereby departing from scholarship that has overlooked the study of Jews within the context of Morocco's authoritarianism.

In advancing the argument that Moroccan testimonial prison literature—situated at the intersection of witness accounts, fictionalized experiences, and nonacademic history—constitutes an other-archive, *Moroccan Other-Archives* reconstructs the story of Tazmamart and its transformation into three different types of other-archives across three different temporalities in Moroccan and world history. In connecting the transformation of Tazmamart into a globalizable, fictionalized other-archive—that is, a collection of multigenre literary works that appropriate narratives of embodied experience and testimony—to the rise of human rights activists in Paris who sought to secure the disappeared prisoners' release, the book gives more temporal and contextual depth to the processes that made Tazmamart the nexus of the traumas and losses of the Years of Lead. The oscillation among European human rights organizations between believing and disbelieving the existence of Tazmamart, while it put a damper on the moral outrage necessary for human rights activism in the early years, also allowed this prison to acquire a very productive afterlife. Across continents, cities, films (including documentaries), literature, and fine art, Tazmamart has been archived in unprecedented ways that have added layers of complexity to its story. Beyond the fact that human rights activists pressured the Moroccan state to release the prisoners in Tazmamart, their centering of conceptual "disappearance" on one location created an archival and literary template for a transnational engagement with this human rights violation.

If the deployment of historiographical agency to rewrite the nation's violent past is central to this book's argument, the challenges of exercising that agency are no less important a contribution to scholarship. The success of Amazigh locational citizenship through Tifinagh, the proliferation of mnemonic literature, and the wide dissemination of testimonial prison literature effectuated a significant change in Moroccan historiographical discourse. Arguably, it was the introduction of other-archives to social and cultural memory that incited Moroccan historians to reconnect with their social function and reembrace their role in ongoing societal debates. Academic historians of all walks of life have worked to reenergize their discipline and keep pace with a new historical reality. These historians also found themselves asking crucial questions about the relevance of their discipline and the place that it should occupy in a society that has risked confounding other-archives with academic history.[7] These discussions yielded an important body of publications in which Moroccan and foreign historians sought to rethink methods, reexamine research questions, complicate periodizations, and even explore nontraditional sources as a way to reconstruct a past that is not entirely divorced from the stakes of the present. The ensuing historiographical fervor resulted in the production of instrumental works on the subject. This book is the most comprehensive English-language work thus far to engage with this body of literature in a dialogical, multilingual, and interdisciplinary way.

Rewriting the nation is a long process. The societal interest in learning about Morocco's recent history, aided by the proliferation of independent media outlets and publication houses, has revolutionized post-1956 history writing.[8] These new publication platforms, which emerged at the same time as the ritualization of commemorative practices,[9] have provided a channel conducive to the circulation of other-archives in society. Wider circulation has allowed these works to make the past a constant presence in the lifeworld of Moroccan families. As a consequence of the publication and widespread consumption of other-archives in the public sphere, Moroccan-ness and Moroccan approaches to contemporary history can be discussed in terms of before and after other-archives. Even the spatial divide between center and periphery is no longer as trenchant as it used to be in terms of access to history. Populations in villages and semi-urban areas have the same access to these materials as inhabitants of metropolitan centers. The Rif, Jerada, and Zagora are just a few examples of places where youth draw on this history to confront the state, with a clear sense of their status as citizens who both reappropriate and make history.

In terms of archival, historiographical, and educational reform, the ERC's recommendations played a role in theorizing the crucial project of redefining the Moroccan nation through the rewriting of history.[10] Weaving together a number of cultural, legal, and political reforms, including the creation of the Royal Institute for Amazigh Culture, the ERC credits these contributions with Moroccan "citizens' awareness about the importance of their participation in public, national and local affairs."[11] The ERC places history at the heart of the transitional justice process in arguing that Morocco, in contrast to similar countries, "chose reconciliatory justice over an accusatory justice, and *historical truth over judicial truth*," thus prioritizing knowledge of the past over litigation that addresses the wrongs done to the victims by bringing legal action against the perpetrators.[12] Nevertheless, knowledge of the past has not been disseminated in a systematic and methodical way. Except for the recent and overly celebrated decision to include one lesson about Moroccan Jews in sixth-grade history curriculum, Moroccan history books from primary through high school are still silent on the Years of Lead.[13] There is an entrenched divide between the ERC's forward-looking recommendations regarding history and archives and the actual pedagogical practice, which is still operating in cautious, pre-1999 ways.

This book's findings about the historiographical functions of literature have crucial implications for how the Moroccan past is studied. The justified caution observed among academic historians is counterbalanced by the vividness of society's engagement with literature about the Years of Lead. By placing other-archives at the confluence of historiographical theory, historiographical agency, and cultural production, this work will hopefully enable scholars working on recent Moroccan or contemporary Arab history to draw on this conceptual framework to further explore the ways cultural productions rewrite nations traumatized by civil war, sectarian kidnappings, repression of minorities, racism and racialization, and organized violence. In conducting this research, I hope to have charted one of the many possible paths for the examination of historiographical questions related to post-1956 Morocco.

Moroccan Other-Archives also charts a path that will hopefully inspire further interdisciplinary scholarship. Using other-archives to write histories for which there are no conventional archives requires an approach that draws on different fields, including narratology, memory studies, historiography, literary studies, cinema studies, geography, rural studies, and legal studies, among others. Ahmed Chouki Benyoub, a lawyer and former ERC commissioner as well as a member of the CCHR, has captured this interdisciplinary requirement in inviting "laboratories of research on the history of the present, political science, [and] sociology of the violations [of human rights]" to engage in a collaborative writing of Morocco's contemporary history, using what I have theorized as other-archives.[14] The collaboration of these complementary fields is all the more urgent given the fact that the laws governing archives in Morocco have made it almost impossible to access archival sources about post-colonial history in our lifetime. Although the Archives du Maroc were put in place in 2011 to implement the ERC's recommendation pertinent to archives, Article 17 of the Law 69.99 stipulates that a period of one hundred years has to pass before archives containing private health and employment information can be accessed.[15] The same law sets the limitation at sixty years for archives concerning defense, foreign affairs, and personal information.[16] As a result, all of the ERC's official documents will remain inaccessible to historians for the foreseeable future. This, in fact, goes against the ERC's own initial recommendation, which suggested making its archives public.[17] The critical question, then, is whether Moroccans can afford to wait until these obviously narrowly defined archives are made available, or whether historians should collaborate with their colleagues in other disciplines to exploit the abundant other-archives.

The spatial dimension of historical silences in Morocco also warrants an interdisciplinary approach. The reemergence of long-forgotten toponymies, now utilized to tell stories of disappearance and forgetfulness, redirects attention to formerly forbidden places. Places that used to be taboo to even mention in conversation, like the Tazmamart and Agdz secret prisons, have now emerged as crucial loci for the history of the Moroccan nation. The global advocacy on behalf of Moroccan human rights in conversation with experiences of transitional justice worldwide fostered the climate in which other-archives creators were able to occupy center stage, shifting the boundaries of history to-be-written from the margins to the center. The continuity of spatial disparities despite the community reparations program and calls for geographical justice across the different regions of the country beg for a collaboration between agronomists, constitutional law specialists, geographers, rural anthropologists, and specialists in rural development to tease out historical knowledge from other-archives and assess the losses that state violence wrought upon Moroccan society.

These findings also shed light on the myriad ways in which cultural production feeds socio-cultural and political dissidence in Morocco today. These formerly unwritten histories have taken a prominent, concrete place in the daily struggles against socioeconomic exclusion and marginalization. Hitherto forgotten histories are being recovered in Moroccan people's protests against corruption, renewed authoritarianism, and economic inequalities. Manifesting in the uses of Riffian hero and freedom fighter Muhammad Ben Abd al-Karim al-Khattabi's portrait and the unfurling of his Rif Republic's flag in protests throughout Morocco, as well as in sentences such as *'awdat sanawāt al-raṣāṣ* (the return of the Years of Lead), the history of human rights violations is being used to bolster the public defense against the state's desire to recuperate spaces it relinquished as a result of the processes analyzed throughout this book. Moreover, these histories have empowered Moroccan women to make bolder demands in terms of communal land ownership and equity in inheritance, and they have fueled the emergence of a new class of women activists from marginal Morocco, making feminism a space in which the impact of the dissemination of this past is palpable.[18]

An important line of inquiry that can be pursued through the lens offered in this book is the investigation of a growing social discourse around the idea that many good things vanished with the emigration of the Jews. This investigation, which could be conducted mainly in villages in southeast Morocco, would most likely reveal deeper connections between melancholia and histories of loss in these locations and shed light on a lingering past whose unsutured wounds are still in need of closure. Many older villagers are willing to share their experiences with Jews with anyone who is willing to listen,[19] offering us the possibility to probe the persistence of this belief despite the shifting political winds in Israel/Palestine. *Houses of Life*, a state-driven effort to restore Jewish cemeteries in Morocco, is another project that can shed light on how the restoration and walling in of Jewish sites of memory preserves them but also isolates the meaningfulness of these formerly shared spaces from local populations. Finally, examining the imbrication of memory and tourism with the profusion of YouTube channels and social media outlets that give a transnational existence to Jewish sites in the Moroccan hinterlands reveals the potential of a digital Jewish-Muslim other-archive that is accessible all over the world.[20]

Without any advance notice, on December 9, 2020, the president of the United States announced the resumption of Morocco's relations with Israel in exchange for the recognition of Morocco's sovereignty over the disputed Western Sahara. Before this surprising decision, annexing Western Sahara and decolonizing Palestine were both considered sacred causes in Morocco.[21] Although the unanimity over these issues, particularly Western Sahara, seemed coerced, the Moroccan position had been an entrenched one. The bickering between pro-normalization and anti-normalization camps aside, restrictions—including a curfew the state imposed supposedly to combat COVID-19—prevented protests and shifted the conversation to social media networks. The weeks after December 9, 2020, saw Moroccans engaging with their Jewish history more than they had in the fifty years prior. Some probably heard about the *Misgueret*, the secret Israeli operation to smuggle Moroccan Jews out of the country, for the first time.[22] Newspaper articles confirmed rumors about Israeli participation in Ben Barka's assassination in Paris, and translated Israeli sources confirmed allegations that Moroccan officials received fifty million dollars for allowing Jews to emigrate.[23] This information was always available in foreign sources,[24] but its republication in the online press, such as on the widely read Arabic website *Lakome2*, brings this history back home to roost.[25] It remains to be seen how this top-down decision to resume relations with Israel will deter or incentivize the growth of mnemonic literature in the future. The one thing that is sure, however, is the fact that linking the resumption of Morocco-Israel diplomatic relations to the situation in Western Sahara has made Moroccan Jews and their connections to Morocco a household issue since the announcement.

Citizenship and Moroccan-ness have been recurrent agenda items of the heated debate spurred by Morocco's normalization of its relations with Israel. Interestingly, the citizenship of Moroccan Jews living in Israel/Palestine has been put forward as an essential reason for Morocco's decision to establish official ties with Israel. The use of citizenship in this context helps us to think beyond legal citizenship and explore how Moroccan Jews have returned as "guest" citizens. One is a guest citizen in a place where one has the legal status of a citizen, but neither political nor social rights. Fifty years ago, before emigration, the meaning of Jewish citizenship was entirely different from what it is today. In the past there was potential for Moroccan Jews to be a political and civic force, but their emigration and cultural and linguistic transformation have eliminated this potential. As recently as 2011, in fact, guest citizenship has been defended by Andre Azoulay, Mohammed VI's Jewish advisor. Azoulay urged people to leave Jews alone and not drag them into political discussions. Guest citizenship seems like a status that the Moroccan state would like to see generalized in the country. For the state, a guest citizen is the ideal citizen, and by focusing on development and alternative ways of participating in public affairs, Moroccans are thought of as first and foremost guest citizens, lacking agency and authority to participate in the government.

The study of histories of blackness and slavery in literature could also benefit from the analytical and theoretical conclusions of this book. A historically understudied topic, blackness has been enmeshed in histories of slavery, domestic servitude, and lopsided social relations that have extensions to land ownership, marriage, and even spatial configuration of villages in southeast Morocco.[26] Moroccan society has moved, in a matter of two decades, from being racially oblivious to having a deep racial awareness due to the increasing presence of sub-Saharan African immigrants in the country.[27] Moroccan cultural production has captured this historical moment, which requires every Moroccan to contend with their own racial position within their community. Artists, filmmakers, and novelists have engaged with the topic of blackness in very creative ways. A number of established and first-time authors have publications in which they represent Moroccan society's histories of blackness. Tahar Ben Jelloun's *Le Marriage de plaisir* revisits identity questions faced by Moroccans whose mothers were brought as Dadas—second wives—by Fassi merchants from sub-Saharan Africa in the twentieth century.[28] In her novel, *Dada l'Yakout*, Nouzha Fassi Fihri takes on the kidnapping and enslavement of a brown Moroccan girl.[29] Mubarak Rabi, a famous novelist who had already written about the Senegalese soldiers in the French colonial army, published *Gharb al-mutawassiṭ*, which tackles the tribulations of sub-Saharan immigrants in Morocco.[30] Finally, Ismail Ghazali's *Thalāthat ayyām fī Casablanca* delves into the nightlife in Casablanca and depicts, among other things, the life of sub-Saharan African musicians eking out a living in the city.[31] Moroccan cultural producers are at the forefront of historicization and archivization of a topic that still resides among the taboos of their recent history.

Unlike the ERC's approach, which treated reconciliation and truth-finding processes as temporary projects, other-archives serve as a space to think beyond both ephemerality and catharsis. Retrospectively, the ERC's approach to transitional justice has proven to be both limited and voguish, with very few concrete effects on the ground, based on the assumption that the disbursement of generous checks to victims and the staging of cathartic public hearings might explain the past away. Awareness of the ERC's limitations, which sixteen years later are being exposed daily, has proven time and again the importance of historiographical justice as the ultimate form of redress for the wrongs that the state committed in the past.[32] Rather than limit the traumatic effects of state crimes only to the direct victims and their next of kin, as is the case with the ERC's approach, a deep reading of other-archives necessarily leads to the conclusion that the larger political, civic, constitutional, and ethical issues that they pose were not entirely addressed in the ERC's work. The year 2022 marks the sixteenth anniversary of the publication of the ERC's final report, but forcible disappearance centers have not yet become museums, the use of excessive force to disband protests is still common practice, and self-censorship has increased in the academic field. As a result, one can assert, in fact, that the production of other-archives is the real representation of transitional justice, as they carry the voices and the political and cultural atmosphere of their time into a future history.

The state's rush to declare cases of its own violence closed necessarily leads to the conclusion that there is a deliberate incomprehension of the work of memory. Pretensions to having completely resolved the legacies of a complicated past cannot be anything but an act of self-deception, if not ignorance. There is no doubt that the ERC marked a transition between two reigns and two styles of authoritarianism. However, in order for the new reign to distinguish itself from its predecessor, memory and potential access to pluralistic histories of the nation were offered as a compromise that sought to achieve reconciliation as promised. This pipe dream was certainly supported, albeit reluctantly, by many former victims. It can be clearly seen in the attempts to steer societal energy away from memory and history *in society* toward development projects.[33] Despite the clear official position that the story of the Years of Lead has been read and reread to exhaustion, the continued cultural production that grapples with this past is the clearest indication that the ERC's actual work did not bring closure—rather, it was the start of a long process in which both history and memory will occupy the public space through other-archives. Moreover, cultural production undermines the simplistic assumption that, once the victims and their heirs have been paid off, the work of memory comes to an end. Instead, other-archives show that the process of paying off victims is only the start of the nation's longer path toward redefinition and democratization.

While Morocco, both locally and transnationally, is the focus of this book, the conclusions drawn in this work can inform studies of cultural production in similar situations in the Maghreb and the Middle East. War-torn and politically unstable, the populations of these two regions have yet to work through their traumas, and cultural production has a major role to play in healing, remembering, and refiguring their ongoing losses. A significant research project would further the questions addressed in this work through the study of Maghrebi and Middle Eastern creative writers' and filmmakers' efforts to represent societal traumas unfolding in these regions, especially after the 2011 Arab Uprisings. As novelists, filmmakers, and other producers of knowledge chronicle, represent, and account for daily realities of war-torn nation-states, displaced communities, and marginalized constituencies, they create the conditions for a better understanding of trauma as a generative force for the rewriting of recent histories by establishing other-archives that aid future generations in understanding their own past.

I moved to the United States in 2009 after a long career as a teacher in the High Atlas Mountains. I left the country, but the history to which I was a witness never left me. Walking by former prisons in the southeast in Agdz, Qalâat M'Gouna, and Tamadakht confronted me with a deep dissonance between myself and the people around me. The gap between what I learned from foreign sources and what the people around me ignored or chose not to talk about was instrumental to the long-term maturation of *Moroccan Other-Archives*. I might have escaped the brutality of the Years of Lead, but there are times when I find myself struggling with the fears and silences that living in an authoritarian setting instilled in me. Writing this book has been an act of reckoning with the Years of Lead, of closing the conceptual gap in our understanding of history and citizenship—the gap between what we are allowed and supposed to know, and what we should know and how we should strive to know it.

As I conclude *Moroccan Other-Archives*, Moncef Slaoui, the Morocco-born chief scientist in Operation Warp Speed, which was put in place to develop a vaccine for COVID-19, talked about his former activism in the Moroccan left and declared to *USA Today*: "Because my family was influential, I didn't end up in jail forever or disappear."[34] A few months before Slaoui's declaration, Aziz BineBine's memoir of his ordeal in Tazmamart was translated into English as *Tazmamart: 18 Years in Morocco's Secret Prison*, and Maël Renouard published *L'Historiographe du royaume* (*The Historiographer of the Kingdom*),[35] a novel that reimagines the trajectory of a historian appointed by the king to the strategic position of historian of the monarchy. For a few weeks, the Years of Lead captured both local and global media attention, triggering seminal questions about Moroccan history and its rewriting. This renewed resurgence of historiographical questions was reassuring because, if anything, it further confirms the necessity of the conceptual framework as well as the intervention that I have offered in *Moroccan Other-Archives* to reframing the study of cultural production's engagement with the historical ramifications of trauma and memory of loss in the Maghreb, the Middle East, and beyond.

Acknowledgments

Writing this book has certainly been an individual enterprise, but I owe many acknowledgments to the mentors, colleagues, and friends who supported me during the years it took to write it. I want to thank everyone for their invaluable encouragement. First and foremost, my gratitude goes to Professor Lital Levy for all the support and mentorship I have received from her since this book was a dissertation project in the Department of Comparative Literature at Princeton University. Professor Levy's input and trenchant questions were instrumental to the evolution of my project. I am equally grateful to professors Wendy Belcher, Nick Nesbitt, Abdellah Hammoudi, Roger Allen, and M'hamed Oualdi for their critical comments on the early drafts of this manuscript.

Professor Abdellah Hammoudi has been particularly generous with his unparalleled knowledge of both the field and the theory that I am working with in this book. I am honored to call Abdellah both a friend and a mentor who taught me how to pay attention to details while also keeping track of the broader picture as well as the temporal depth of my research. I will forever remember our discussions over Moroccan tea in his kitchen in Princeton.

Professors Lydie Moudileno and Tsitsi Jaji have earned my profuse thanks for teaching me about post-colonialism in Africa, the Caribbean, and beyond. Professors John Borneman and Barbie Zelzer initiated me to the field of memory studies, which has been foundational to the theoretical questions I undertake in the book.

Many colleagues and friends have read portions of this book at the different stages of its completion. My gratitude goes to Charlie Huntington, Muriel Carpenter, Max Dugan, Alison Hicks, Matthew Goldman, Alexander Elinson,

Jonathan Wyrtzen, Susan Gilson Miller, Benjamin Connor, Paul Silverstein, and Jonathan Smolin for agreeing to read the chapters that are relevant to their scholarly interests and areas of expertise.

At Williams College, I would like to thank my colleagues in Arabic Studies, professors Katarzyna Pieprzak, Gail Newman, Magnús Bernhardsson, Amal Eqeiq, and Lama Nassif, for their collegiality, intellectual and pedagogical engagement, and tireless efforts to make Arabic Studies a welcoming home for everyone. I also seize this opportunity to express my special gratitude to Professor Pieprzak for the exceptional mentorship she has shown me since I joined the department. Likewise, Professor Newman deserves my profuse thanks for the insightful suggestions she made on the final version of the introduction.

I am indebted to the Oakley Center for the Humanities and Social Sciences for affording me the opportunity to organize a manuscript review workshop to discuss an earlier stage of this book with top experts in the field. I was very privileged to spend an entire day reflecting on different aspects of the book with professors Aomar Boum, Susan Slyomovics, Abdellah Hammoudi, Jeffrey Israel, and Katarzyna Pieprzak, whose critical engagement with my work helped me to refine both my thoughts and the structure of the work. I cannot thank them enough for their generosity during and after the manuscript review workshop.

Patrick Mooney helped me streamline the introduction. My editor S.C. Kaplan has been incredibly responsive despite the COVID-19 pandemic, which was instrumental for me to stay on track, and her incisive comments and suggestions pushed me to improve the quality of the manuscript.

In 2017–18, I held a fellowship at The Princeton University Center for Human Values (UCHV). I hereby thank the UCHV as well as my fellow colleagues for creating a safe intellectual space where we shared our work in progress for an entire year. Kim Lane-Scheppele, the faculty mentor, went above and beyond to prepare us for our academic careers after graduation from Princeton University.

The two anonymous reviewers furnished extremely helpful suggestions, which I endeavored to implement in the most efficient way possible. I hereby thank them for their generosity and hope that I have met their expectations.

Thomas Lay, my editor at Fordham University Press, has been phenomenal in his support and responsiveness.

I have been blessed with several friends, mentors, and interlocutors who have been part of my journey in the last thirteen years. I specifically want to thank Billy Yalowitz, Michele Monserrati, Fernaz Perry, Ali Alalou, Miriam Lowi, Hassan Charai, Shana Minkin, Hisham Aidi, Zakia Salime, Hazami

Alsayed, Ibtisam Azem, Sinan Antoon, Majid Hannoum, Brahim Boussaid, Sibelan Forrester, Paraska Tolan-Szklnik, Sonja Hegasy, Maâti Monjib, Ibrahm Hariri, Fouad Abdelmoumni, Ben Twagira, Joe Small, Alice Small, Jill Jarvis, Francisco Eduardo Robles, Jim and Glenda Tansey, and Sourena Parham for their inspiration, friendship, and collegiality over the years. My special and heartfelt gratitude goes to Aman Attia, who taught me how to teach Arabic as a foreign language.

My sisters Fatima, Rabia, Fadma, Habiba, and Jamia, and brothers, Mohammed and Larbi, have taught me and continue to teach me the meaning of family and self-abnegation. My American family members, Joel Laser, Daniel Laser, Robin Adams, Bill Adams, and Robert and Courtney Adams are deserving of sincere thanks for being supportive in both happy and difficult times.

Last, but not least, I would like to thank my wife, Shaina Adams-El Guabli, for her support throughout the time it took me to write this book. My sons Ilyas and Naseem also deserve my thanks for agreeing, despite themselves, that I spend a lot of the time that I owed them for play on completing the manuscript. Words cannot convey how grateful I am to the three of them for the love and enthusiasm they bring to my life, most particularly amid the ravages of COVID-19 to our sense of normalcy.

Certain ideas in this book developed from published articles, which I reference in the appropriate sections. An earlier version of Chapter 1 was published under the title "(Re)Invention of Tradition, Subversive Memory, and Morocco's Re-Amazighization: From Erasure of Imazighen to the Performance of Tifinagh in Public Life," *Expressions Maghrébines* (2020): 143–68. The publication that served as a basis for Chapters 2 and 3 appeared under the title "Breaking Ranks with National Unanimity: Novelistic and Cinematic Returns of Jewish-Muslim Intimacy in Morocco," in *Generations of Dissent: Intellectuals, Cultural Production, and the State in the Middle East and North Africa*, ed. Alexa Firat and R. Shareah Taleghani (New York: Syracuse University Press, 2020), 159–87. I hereby extend my thanks to *Expressions Maghrébines* and Syracuse University Press for allowing me to reprint these articles. Sections from Chapter 5 have informed an article that is forthcoming in *History in Africa*.

Notes

Preface

1. Yacine Kateb and Amazigh Kateb, *Minuit passé de douze heures: Écrits journalistiques, 1947–1989* (Paris: Seuil, 1999), 171–73.

2. For a longer personal story, see Brahim El Guabli, "Les Voix et les voies du Maroc juif," in *Vues du Maroc juif: Formes, lieux, récits*, ed. Nadia Sabri (Casablana: Fennec, 2020), 107–11.

Introduction

1. Richard J. Cox, *No Innocent Deposits: Forming Archives by Rethinking Appraisal* (Lanham, MD: Scarecrow Press, 2004), 249–50.

2. Jacques Derrida, "Archive Fever: A Freudian Impression," trans. Eric Prenowitz, *Diacritics* 25 (Summer 1995): 10.

3. Both survivors and Moroccan media have used *sanawāt al-raṣāṣ* (Years of Lead), *sanawāt al-jamr wa-al-raṣāṣ* (years of ember and lead), and *les années noires/ al-sanawāt al-sawdā'* (black years) to reflect the length of the period as well as violence's constitutive role in the depictions of this time. Abraham Serfaty refers to the "black years" of repression in opposition to the "gray years" of political transition in post-1999 Morocco. See Abraham Serfaty, *Le Maroc, du noir au gris* (Paris: Editions Syllepse, 1998), 5–10; José Garçon, "Maroc: Retour sur les années noires. L'état et les victimes du régime prônent la réconciliation plutôt que la justice," *Libération*, March 21, 2000, http://www.liberation.fr/planete/2000/03/21/maroc-retour-sur-les-annees-noires-l-etat-et-les-victimes-du-regime-pronent-la-reconciliation-plutot_320643.

4. Abdellah Hammoudi, *Master and Disciple: The Cultural Foundations of Moroccan Authoritarianism* (Chicago: University of Chicago Press, 1997), 32.

5. Zakya Daoud, *Abdallah Ibrahim: L'histoire des rendez-vous manqués* (Casablanca: La Croisee des Chemins, 2019); Abdallah Laroui, *Le Maroc et Hassan II: Un témoignage* (Québec: Presses Inter Universitaires, 2005), 14.

6. Marguerite Rollinde, *Le Mouvement marocain des droits de l'homme: Entre consensus national et engagement citoyen* (Paris: Karthala; Saint-Denis, [France]: Institut Maghreb-Europe, 2002), 170; Human Rights Watch, "Morocco's Truth Commission Honoring Past Victims during an Uncertain Present," *Human Rights Watch* 17, no. 11 (2005): 28–29.

7. Fatna El Bouih, *Ḥadīth al-ʿatama* (Casablanca: Fennec, 2001), 21. All translations are my own unless otherwise indicated.

8. Amnesty International, "Recommendations of the Moroccan Consultative Council on Human Rights Relative to Prison Conditions, Medical Care of Prisoners and Investigation of Cases of Death in Detention," September 12, 1991, https://www.amnesty.org/download/Documents/196000/mde290261991en.pdf.

9. The CCHR became the National Council for Human Rights (NCHR) in 2011.

10. Mustapha Raissouni, "Taqdīm," in *Hay'at al-taḥkīm al-mustqilla li-taʿwīḍ ḍaḥāyā al-ikhtifā' al-qasrī wa-al-Iiʿtiqāl al-taʿassufī: al-labina al-ūlā fī masār al-ʿadāla al-intiqāliyya bi-al-maghrib* (Rabat: Manshūrāt al-Majlis al-Istishārī li-Ḥuqūq al-Insān, 2010), 9.

11. CCHR also recommended legal changes to the period known as *garde à vue*, during which the accused are held *incommunicado*, and which is notorious for the "ill-treatment and torture of detainees." (Amnesty International, "Recommendations of the Moroccan Consultative Council.")

12. "Maroc: L'amnistie royale pourrait décrisper la vie politique," *Le Monde*, July 23, 1994, https://www.lemonde.fr/archives/article/1994/07/23/maroc-l-amnistie-royale-pourrait-decrisper-la-vie-politique_3818417_1819218.html; Sami Lakmahri, "ʿAfwū 1994, al-ṣafḥ al-ʿaẓīm," *Zamane*, July 9, 2018.

13. "Maroc: L'amnistie royale."

14. Al-Majlis al-Istishārī li-Ḥuqūq al-Insān, *Hay'at al-taḥkīm al-mustqilla li-taʿwīḍ ḍaḥāyā al-ikhtifā' al-qasrī wa-al-iʿtiqāl al-taʿassufī: Al-labina al-ūlā fī masār al-ʿadāla al-intiqāliyya bi-al-maghrib* (Rabat: Manshūrāt al-Majlis al-Istishārī li-Ḥuqūq al-Insān, 2009), 16.

15. John Borneman, *Political Crimes and the Memory of Loss* (Indianapolis: Indiana University Press, 2011), 3.

16. Al-Majlis al-Istishārī li-Ḥuqūq al-Insān, *Hay'at al-taḥkīm al-mustqilla li-taʿwīḍ*, 25. For a detailed account of the laborious process among the members of the CCHR in the weeks and months leading up the recommendation to establish the ERC, see M'barek Bouderka and Ahmed Chouki Benyoub, *Kadhālika kān: Mudhakkirāt min tajribat hay'at al-inṣāf wa-al-muṣālaḥa* (Casablanca: Dār al-Nashr al-Maghribiyya, 2017), 15–71. On following the South African model, see Brahim El Guabli, "The Absent Perpetrators: Morocco's Failed Accountability, Tazmamart Literature and the Survivors' Testimony for Their Jailers (1973–1991)," *Violence: An International Journal* 1, no. 1 (2020): 84, https://doi.org/10.1177/2633002420904672.

17. Elizabeth Jellin, *State Repression and the Labors of Memory* (Minneapolis: University of Minnesota Press, 2003), 107–33; Susana Draper, *Afterlives of Confinement: Spatial Transitions in Postdictatorship Latin America* (Pittsburgh: University of Pittsburgh Press, 2012); Ksenja Bilbija and Leigh A. Payne, eds., *Accounting for Violence: Marketing Memory in Latin America* (Durham: Duke University Press, 2011).

18. Susan Slyomovics, *The Performance of Human Rights in Morocco* (Philadelphia: The University of Pennsylvania Press, 2005), 12.

19. Pierre Hazan, "The Nature of Sanctions: The Case of Morocco's Equity and Reconciliation Commission," *International Review of the Red Cross*, vol. 90, no. 870 (2008): 404.

20. ERC, *Truth, Equity, and Reconciliation* (Rabat: Le Conseil Consultatif des Droits de l'Homme, 2010), 12.

21. ERC, *Truth, Equity, and Reconciliation*, 12.

22. This number decreased to 16,861 after discarding the files that did not meet the acceptance criteria, then increased to 18,457 under the supervision of the National Human Rights Council, which inherited the execution of the ERC's recommendations and completed its unfinished work. ERC, *Justice and Reconciliation Commission, Summary of the Final Report* (Rabat: Le Conseil Consultatif des Droits de l'Homme, 2009), 22; Le Conseil National des Droits de l'Homme, "La Réparation individuelle," *CNDH*, accessed February 19, 2018, http://www.cndh.org.ma/fr/conference-de-presse-de-presentation-du-suivi-de-la-mise-en-oeuvre-des-recommandations-de-lier/la-1.

23. Borneman, *Political Crimes*, 3.

24. International Center for Transitional Justice, "What is Transitional Justice," accessed August 10, 2020, https://www.ictj.org/about/transitional-justice.

25. Brahim El Guabli, "Moroccan Society's Educational and Cultural Losses during the Years of Lead (1956–1999)," *Journal of Global Initiatives: Policy, Pedagogy, Perspective* 14, no. 2 (2019): 143–44.

26. Leïla Kilani, *Nos lieux interdits* (France: INA, Socco Chico, 2008).

27. For a detailed description of the context and the film, see Olivier Barlet, *Contemporary African Cinema* (East Lansing: Michigan State University Press, 2016), 266.

28. The story of Shaykh al-ʿArab is recounted by Susan Slyomovics in her book chapter "New Moroccan Publics: Prisons, Cemeteries and Human Remains," in *Knowledge, Authority and Change in Islamic Societies*, ed. Allen James Fromherz and Nadav Samin (Leiden: Brill, 2021), 137–42, https://doi.org/10.1163/9789004443341_008.

29. Maurice Buttin, *Ben Barka, Hassan II, de Gaulle: Ce que je sais d'eux* (Paris: Karthala, 2010), 189.

30. Kilani, *Nos lieux interdits*, 48:29–49:18. Translation modified.

31. In Boum's novel analysis, Moroccan Jews recede into social memory the further we move away from the lived experience Jews and Muslims shared in Morocco. See Yigal Bin Nun, "La Quête d'un compromis pour l'évacuation des Juifs

du Maroc," *Pardes* 1 (2003): 95; Aomar Boum, *Memories of Absence, How Muslims Remember Jews in Morocco* (Stanford, CA: Stanford University Press, 2013), 1–9.

32. Lakmahri, "'Afwū 1994, al-ṣafḥ al-'aẓīm." Jews were never persecuted by the Moroccan regime *as a community*, but the dictatorial atmosphere that reigned over the country impacted all Moroccans, Jews included.

33. Driss El Yazami, "Transition politique, histoire et mémoire," *Confluences Méditerranée* 3 (2007): 33.

34. I am mainly thinking about the work of Laura Menin, "'Descending into Hell': Tazmamart, Civic Activism and the Politics of Memory in Contemporary Morocco," *Memory Studies* 12, no. 3 (2019): 307–21; Naïma Hachad, "Narrating Tazmamart: Visceral Contestations of Morocco's Transitional Justice and Democracy," *The Journal of North African Studies* 2, no. 1–2 (2018): 208–24; and Sonja Hegasy, "Transforming Memories: Media and Historiography in the Aftermath of the Moroccan Equity and Reconciliation Commission," in *The Social Life of Memory: Violence, Trauma, and Testimony in Lebanon and Morocco*, ed. Norman Saadi Nikro and Sonja Hegasy (New York: Palgrave Macmillan, 2017), 83–112. These scholars made significant contributions to our understanding of the Years of Lead, but they engaged with neither the intersectional aspects nor the larger ramifications of loss Moroccans endured during this period.

35. Daniel J. Schroeter, "The Changing Landscape of Muslim-Jewish Relations in the Modern Middle East and North Africa," in *Modernity, Minority, and the Public Sphere: Jews and Christians in the Middle East*, ed. S.R. Goldstein-Sabbah and H.L. Murre van Den Berg (Leiden: Brill, 2016), 57.

36. Oren Kosansky and Aomar Boum, "The 'Jewish Question' in Postcolonial Moroccan Cinema," *International Journal of Middle East Studies* 44, no. 3 (2012): 222.

37. Both Abdellah Hammoudi and Lahcen Brouksy complicated this question of citizenship in very illuminating ways in their respective work on Mimouna and Amazighity. Abdellah Hammoudi, "Le Don entre juifs et musulmans: Ou comment concilier les identités opposées," *Revue Internationale d'Anthropologie Culturelle & Sociale* (Hors-Série) (2016): 91–106; Lahcen Brouksy, *Les Berbères face à leur destin* (Rabat: Bouregreg, 2006), 282, 285, 293.

38. A fear of the emergence and consolidation of demands for a citizenship-based state that would have ended the *ra'iyya* status must have motivated the *makhzan*-state's multi-pronged disappearance policies: the persecution and forcible disappearance of political dissidents and negation of Amazigh linguistic and cultural rights went hand in hand with assisting Zionist Jewish agencies in facilitating the departure of their coreligionists from their ancestral homeland to Israel/Palestine, Canada, and other host countries.

39. This Gallicization was fostered by the school network of the *Alliance Israélite Universelle*. Mikhael M. Laskier conducted the most comprehensive study of the UIA's work in Morocco to date, *The Alliance Israélite Universelle and the Jewish Communities of Morocco: 1862–1962* (Albany: State University of New York Press, 1983).

40. Félix Nataf, *Juif maghrébin: Une vie au Maghreb (racontée à ma fille)* (Paris: Fayolle, 1978), 169–78.

41. *Le Juif de Tanger et le Maroc* and *Les Israélites marocains à l'heure du choix.* Although de Nesry was part of important conversations that took place in the 1950s in Morocco, apart from a concise biography—published by Mitchell Serels in *Encyclopedia of Jews in the Islamic World*—his work and its theoretical thrust remain unknown in Morocco and underexplored in academic studies. See Mitchell Serels, "Carlos de Nesry," in *Encyclopedia of Jews in the Islamic World*, ed. Norman A. Stillman (2010), http://referenceworks.brillonline.com/entries/encyclopedia-of-jews-in-the-islamic-world/nesry-carlos-de-SIM_0016700?s.num=0&s.f.s2_parent=s.f.book.encyclopedia-of-jews-in-the-islamic-world&s.q=Carlos+de+nesry. Carlos de Nesry, *Les Israélites marocains à l'heure du choix* (Tangiers: Éditions internationales, 1958), 42–45, 111.

42. Carlos de Nesry, *Le Juif de Tanger et le Maroc* (Tangiers: Editions Internationales, 1956), 120–34.

43. Due to socioeconomic measures that sought to immunize Morocco's independence against foreign (mainly French) intervention in its internal affairs and its major institutions that became symbols of Morocco's economic and political independence. However, this government was hated by both Zionists, who loathed its endeavor to keep Jews in the country, and by Crown Prince Hassan, who was threatened by the socialist socioeconomic model that contradicted his liberal convictions: Daoud, *Abdallah Ibrahim*, 60. On the passport restrictions, see Bin Nun, "La Quête d'un compromis"; id., "Les Causes politiques et sociales du départ des Juifs du Maroc 1956–1966," in *Migrations maghrébines comparées: Genre, ethnicité et religions (France-Québec: De 1945 à nos jours)*, ed. Yolande Cohen, Mireille Calle-Gruber, and Élodie Vignon (Paris: Riveneuve, 2014), 39–62.

44. In the words of Zakya Daoud, "tradition has again become a value that openly displays its willingness to fight against socializing ideas. Obscurantism is cultivated, a frozen and alienating language has been set as a model, psychology as well as sociology were banned, individualism was fought, apart from in the economic success, the right to reflection and contestation and public freedoms are not legal tender anymore." Maâti Monjib, *La Monarchie marocaine et la lutte pour le pouvoir: Hassan II face à l'opposition nationale, de l'indépendance à l'état d'exception* (Paris: L'Harmattan, 1992), 218.

45. Zakya Daoud, *Les Années Lamalif: 1958–1988. Trente ans de journalisme au Maroc* (Casablanca: Tarik Editions, 2007), 202; Hammoudi, *Master and Disciple*, 35.

46. Fadma Aït Mous and Driss Ksikes, *Le Métier d'intellectual: Dialogue avec quinze penseurs au Maroc* (Casablanca: En Toutes Lettres, 2014), 46–47.

47. See Rémy Leveau's book about the importance of Moroccan farmers (*fallaḥ*) for the monarchy: *Le Fellah marocain défenseur du trône* (Paris: Presses de la Fondation Nationale des Sciences Politiques, 1976).

48. Monjib, *La Monarchie marocaine*, 215–18. These French colonial-era figures played a major role in the abortion of the country's democratic aspirations. For instance, Mohammed Bahnini, an officer who served in the French army, was

appointed prime minister in the first government after the country's independence. This maneuver excluded the nationalist leaders who forced France to grant Morocco its independence. Another legacy from the colonial era was Mohamed Oufkir, who would later play a prominent role in the butcheries the army committed during the catastrophic Rif War (1958–1959) as well as in the repression of the events of March 23, 1965, in Casablanca, and his roles in other disappearance and torture centers up until his own assassination in the aftermath of the second coup d'état in 1972. For a detailed discussion of the significance of the inheritance and use of leaders who cooperated with colonialism, see Hammoudi, *Master and Disciple*, 26–31.

49. Lucette Valensi goes as far as to talk about the "sealing of an alliance between a people, a monarch and a religion" to describe this historical re-traditionalization: "Le Roi chronophage: La construction d'une conscience historique dans le Maroc postcolonial," in "Maghreb: récits, traces, oublis," special issue, *Cahiers d'Études Africaines* 30, no. 119 (1990): 293.

50. Saïd Ghallab, "Les Juifs vont en enfer," *Les Temps Modernes* 229 (1965): 2252. Decades before Jacques Dahan's memoir, *Regard d'un Juif marocain sur l'histoire contemporaine de son pays* (Paris: L'Harmattan, 1995), Ghallab's article makes connections between the electoral policies of *Le Front démocratique pour la défense des institutions constitutionelles* (the Democratic Front for the Defense of Constitutional Institutions [DFDCI]) and the facilitation of Jewish emigration from Morocco. However, political conditions were not yet ripe for academia to take up the lines of inquiry offered in these memoirs and journalistic articles.

51. See also Stephen O. Hughes, *Morocco under King Hassan* (Reading: Ithaca Press, 2001), 42–47.

52. Ghallab, "Les Juifs vont en enfer." These same allegations would be repeated by Simon Levy in Kathy Wazana's film *They Were Promised the Sea* and by Driss Miliani in his novel *Casanfa*. The narrator of *Casanfa* says, "Indeed, Jews have been sold in exchange for wheat, and the American wheat specifically in the lean, dry years." See Driss Miliani, *Casanfa* (Cairo: Dār al-ʿAyn li al-Nashr, 2016), 248, and Kathy Wazana, "They Were Promised the Sea" (2013), 15:22–15:52.

53. In fact, this fear of communism was noticed as early as 1960, when Muḥammad V criticized Abraham Serfaty's communist politics during a meeting with the leaders of the Jewish community in Casablanca. See Salomon Benbaruk, *Trois-quarts de siècle pêle-mêle* (Montreal: Les Imprimeurs du 21e Siècle, 1990), 49. Serfaty's past as a former prisoner because of his pro-independence position did not assuage the monarch's criticism.

54. Bin Nun, "La Quête d'un compromis," 89. Toledano was also the president of the pro-Zionist Jewish World Congress in Casablanca. This is an interesting case that shows the tricky reconciliation of Zionism with Moroccan nationalism among certain leftist Jews. Yaron Tsur, "Les Dirigeants du judaïsme marocain," in *Perception et réalités au Maroc: Relations judéo-musulmanes*, ed. Robert Assaraf and Michel Abitbol (Paris: Editions Stavit, 1997), 230–31.

55. Benbaruk, *Trois-quarts de siècle pêle-mêle*, 51.

56. But his conservative understanding of religion and politics seemed incapable of transcending the antinomy between communism and religious belief: Hassan told Easterman during a secret meeting that "we do not accept that young Jews are implicated in communist action. Communism is the biggest peril against us. How could a Jew be a communist or have affinity with Communism?," suggesting religiosity should take precedence over all else, even a claim to the rights of citizenship. See Bin Nun, "La Quête d'un compromis," 16.

57. Bin Nun, "La Quête d'un compromis," 17. Decades later, Serfaty would write that "for all the cops, including the ones at the top of the state, Marxism would not have penetrated Morocco, a Muslim country, and swayed a good number of youth if it had not been brought by the Jews' bewitching power": Serfaty, *Le Maroc*, 26.

58. Dahan, *Regard d'un Juif marocain*, 90.

59. Dahan, *Regard d'un Juif marocain*, 90.

60. Victor Malka, *La Mémoire brisée des juifs du Maroc* (Paris: Entente, 1978), 15–27. In addition to providing an excellent description of Jewish-Muslim aspirations in the period immediately after Morocco's independence, Malka expresses his disappointment at the termination of the promising initiatives that sought to build more community between Jews and Muslims. Michel Abitbol traces back this confinement of Jewish participation exclusively to social matters to the Protectorate's desire to depoliticize the Jews. See Michel Abitbol, "De la tradition à la modernité: Les juifs du Maroc," *Diasporas* 27 (2016): 19–30.

61. Susan Slyomovics, "Abraham Serfaty: Moroccan Jew and Conscious Pariah," *Hesperis-Tamuda* 51, no. 3 (2016): 113–38; Brahim El Guabli, "Reading for Theory in the Moroccan Marxist-Leninist Testimonial Literature," *African Identities* 18, no. 1–2 (2020), 13–15, DOI: 10.1080/14725843.2020.1773243.

62. Including the Istiqlāl, the National Union of Popular Forces (NUPF), and the Moroccan Communist Party, rebranded as Le Parti du Progrès et du Socialisme (The Party of Progress and Socialism). Mostafa Bouaziz, "Mouvements sociaux et mouvement national au Maroc," in *Emeutes et mouvements sociaux au Maghreb*, ed. Didier Le Saout and Marguerite Rollinde (Paris: Karthala, 1999), 71; Mohammed El Ayadi, "Les Mouvements de la jeunesse au Maroc," in *Émeutes et mouvements sociaux au Maghreb*, ed. Didier Le Saout and Marguerite Rollinde (Paris: Karthala, 1999), 210–14.

63. *Ilā al-Amām* was the result of the merger of the March 23 Organization, an offshoot of the Moroccan Communist Party, and *Linakhdum al-sha'b* (Let's Serve the People), an extreme-left group that seceded from the NUPF. Abraham Serfaty and Christine Daure-Serfaty, *La Mémoire de l'autre* (Paris: Au Vif Stock, 1993), 90.

64. Abdelfattah Fakihani, *Le Couloir: Bribes de vérité sur les années de plomb* (Casablanca: Tarik Editions, 2005), 86.

65. While it was not the sole driving force behind the multilingual cultural dynamism of the 1960s, as was later alleged, *Souffles/Anfās* did spur a cultural, then political, movement that left an indelible imprint on Moroccan development in these realms. Many journals, "such as *Al-Muḥarrir*, and cultural journals *Lamalif*

(1966–1988), *Aqlām* (1964–1982), *al-Thaqāfa al-Jadīda* (1974–1984), *al-Zaman al-Maghribī* (1980–1984), *al-Jusūr* (1981–1984), and *al-Badīl* (1981–1984) were banned or pushed to bankruptcy through frequent seizures" (El Guabli, "Moroccan Society's Educational and Cultural Losses," 152.

66. Mahdi Ben Barka, *Al-ikhtiyyār al-thawrī fī al-maghrib* (Rabat: Dafātir Wijhat Naẓar, 2011), 10–11.

67. Maurice Buttin, Ben Barka's family's lawyer for over forty years, has written a very detailed book about Ben Barka's disappearance and the legal and political quagmire in which it has been enmeshed since his kidnapping in 1965. See Buttin, *Ben Barka, Hassan II, De Gaulle.*

68. Kably, *Histoire du Maroc*, 58–70.

69. Ben Barka, *al-Ikhtiyār al-thawrī*, 35.

70. ʿAbd al-Qādir al-Shāwī, *Bāb tāza* (Rabat: Manshūrāt al-Mawja, 1994).

71. ʿAbd al-Qādir al-Shāwī, *al-Sāḥa al-sharafiyya* (Casablanca: Dār al-Fanak, 2006).

72. al-Shāwī, *al-Sāḥa al-sharafiyya*, 51.

73. Abdelhak Serhane, *Kabazal: Les emmurés de Tazmamart, mémoires de Salah et Aïda Hachad* (Casablanca: Tarik Éditions, 2004).

74. Sue McKemmish and Michael Piggott, "Recordkeeping, Reconciliation and Political Reality" (*Australia Society of Archivists [ASA] 2002 Annual Conference*, Sydney, Australia, August 13–17, 2002), 9.

75. Jacques Derrida, *Archive Fever: A Freudian Impression*, trans. Eric Prenowitz (Chicago: University of Chicago Press, 1996), 2.

76. Michel Foucault, *The Archaeology of Knowledge* (New York: Pantheon Books, 1972), 129.

77. Jonathan Boulter writes, "the archive is doubly inflected by loss: it is a response to loss, to trauma [. . .] and it anticipates, perhaps creates, the conditions for future loss": *Melancholy and the Archive: Trauma, History and Memory in the Contemporary Novel* (New York: Bloomsbury Publishing, 2011), 7.

78. Pierre Nora has already noted that, no matter how much a society or people archives or memorizes, there will always be something outside the purview of their archiving or memorizing capacity—a part left to oblivion and loss: "Archive as much as you like: something will always be left out." Pierre Nora and Lawrence D. Kritzman, *Realms of Memory: Conflicts and Divisions*, trans. Arthur Goldhammer, 3 vols. (New York: Columbia University Press, 1996), I:9.

79. Eric Ketelaar, "Archival Temples, Archival Prisons: Modes of Power and Protection," *Archival Science* 2, no. 3–4 (2002): 237.

80. Aleida Assmann, "Canon and Archive," in *Cultural Memory Studies: An International and Interdisciplinary Handbook*, ed. Astrid Erll, Ansgar Nünning, and Sara B. Young (Berlin: De Gruyter, 2008), 103.

81. Assmann's important distinction between "political archives and historical archives" has demonstrated that surrounding archives with secrecy is in fact a power mechanism. Assmann's distinction between political archives, which are still

functional for the exercise of power, and historical archives, concerned with long-dead events that have no relevance to the present, which should be consultable by all makes sense theoretically. However, power-holders still tend to shield archives, both political and historical, from those not deemed qualified to consult them. Assmann, "Canon and Archive," 103.

82. Ann Laura Stoler, "Colonial Archives and the Arts of Governance," *Archival Science* 2, no. 1–2 (2002): 89; George Yudice, "Testimonio and Postmodernism," *Latin American Perspectives* 18, no. 3 (1991): 15–31; McKemmish and Piggott, "Recordkeeping, Reconciliation"; Ciaran B. Trace, "On or Off the Record? Notions of Value in the Archive," in *Currents of Archival Thinking*, ed. Terry Eastwood and Heather MacNeil (Santa Barbara, CA: Libraries Unlimited, 2010), 58–62. See also Livia Maria Iacovino, "Archives as Arsenals of Accountability," in *Currents of Archival Thinking*, ed. Terry Eastwood and Heather MacNeil (Santa Barbara, CA: Libraries Unlimited, 2010), 187–88.

83. Michel Rolph Trouillot, *Silencing the Past: Power and the Production of History* (Boston: Beacon Press Books, 1995), 24.

84. Trouillot, *Silencing the Past*, 48.

85. As one Moroccan historian interviewed by *Zamane* expressed, historiographical self-censorship—which is tantamount to silence—in these contexts "starts from the moment when the topic of study is chosen," adding new layers of silence to the ones that are already in the archives. Jamaâ Baida, in "Historiens vs journalistes," *Zamane*, July 11, 2012, accessed May 12, 2017, https://zamane.ma/fr/blog/2020/05/22/historiens-vs-journalistes/.

86. Michel Foucault, *La Vie des hommes infâmes* (Paris: Les Cahiers du Chemin 29, 1977), 12–13.

87. Maurice Papon's recent accusation that Jean-Luc Einaudi defamed him after Einaudi highlighted Papon's role in the October 17, 1961, events in Paris placed archives at the very heart of the political upheavals: a trial intended to silence Einaudi ended up calling two archivists to the stand who defended Einaudi's innocence by providing the court with notes from archival material that would still be classified for another thirty years. Moments like these, when archives go against their ingrained silences, abound, but they are not the norm. Chloé Leprince, "Une Lanceuse d'alerte au placard: L'archiviste qui avait raconté le massacre du 17 octobre 1961," *Franceculture*, November 16, 2018, https://www.franceculture.fr/histoire/une-lanceuse-dalerte-au-placard-larchiviste-qui-avait-raconte-le-massacre-du-17-octobre-1961.

88. Despite the extremely rich literature on archives, canonical works seem to agree on this Western conceptualization of an archive as something that already exists, which does not take into account the archival void and its implications, as in the case of the Moroccan Years of Lead. Derrida, *Archive Fever*; Carolyn Steedman, *Dust: The Archive and Cultural History* (New Brunswick: Rutgers University Press, 2002); Ann Laura Stoler, *Along the Archival Grain: Epistemic Anxieties and Colonial Common Sense* (Princeton: Princeton University Press, 2009); Carolyn Hamilton,

Verne Harris, Michèle Pickover, et al., eds., *Refiguring the Archive* (Dordrecht: Kluwer Academic Publishers, 2002); Boulter, *Melancholy and the Archive.*

89. Ketelaar, "Archival Temples, Archival Prisons," 225.

90. Assmann, "Canon and Archive," 103.

91. Driss El Yazami, interview by Grand Angle Reportage 2M, 2M (CD 10, minute 47–48), distributed by the National Council for Human Rights in the kit entitled "Programme de réparation communautaire au Maroc," n.d. El Yazami also underlined the fact that the ERC had noticed an actively systematic *un*-archiving between 1965 and the 1990s: the destruction of medical records, hospital admission ledgers, and cemetery registers of the dead, as well as the use of pseudonyms in order to hide the identities of victims of torture when they were taken to hospitals, which made their future identification and the reconstruction of their stories based on official archives impossible. The opposite has also happened: for fear of repression and long jail sentences, activists used to destroy all tracts and documents that could potentially be used against them in a court of law. Apartheid South Africa has also witnessed this phenomenon in response to the state's repressive policies. See Sarah Nuttall, "Literature and the Archive: The Biography of Texts," in *Refiguring the Archive*, ed. Carolyn Hamilton Verne Harris, Michèle Pickover, et al. (Dordrecht, Netherlands: Kluwer Academic Publishers, 2002), 290–91.

92. Ketelaar, "Archival Temples, Archival Prisons," 222.

93. As a result, three generations of post-independence Moroccan historians dedicated their research to the pre-Protectorate period to avoid the consequences of examining taboo histories: Mohammed Houbaida, "al-Tārīkh al-ijmtimāʿī wa-al-iqtiṣādī fī al-maghrib min al-mūnūghrāfiyya ilā al-tarkīb," in *50 sana min al-baḥt al-tārīkhī fī al-maghrib*, ed. Abderrahame El Moudden (Rabat: Rabat Net Maroc, 2003), 11–23.

94. For example, the state's policy vis-à-vis Amazigh language and culture effectively "invisibilized" Amazigh culture, which, while never officially outlawed, remained a historical taboo from independence to the establishment of the *Institut Royal de la Culture Amazighe* (Royal Institute for Amazigh Culture [RIAC]) in 2001. Likewise, the archives of the negotiations and operations that led to the emigration and de facto disappearance of Moroccan Jews from Morocco do not seem to exist. Israeli scholars have used their state archives to write on negotiations between Moroccan officials and Israeli state envoys, but there is no evidence that such an archive ever existed in Morocco. Moroccan political actors are also known to be averse to writing their memoirs or donating their private archives to organizations that would make them available to researchers. See Bin Nun's articles "Les Causes politiques et sociales" and "La Quête d'un compromis," which discuss Zionist archives as well as the Israeli National Archives of the Israeli Ministry of Foreign Affairs.

95. Asmaa Fahli, "Les Archives de l'IER, une responsabilité pour demain," accessed June 10, 2019, https://www.ccdh.org.ma/fr/bulletin-d-information/les-archives-de-lier-une-responsabilite-pour-demain.

96. Fahli, "Les Archives de l'IER."

97. ERC, *Establishing Truth and Responsibility Regarding Human Right Violations* (Rabat: Le Conseil Consultatif des Droits de l'Homme, 2009), 23.

98. Slyomovics, "The Moroccan Equity and Reconciliation Commission: The Promises of a Human Rights Archive," *The Arab Studies Journal* 24, no. 1 (2006): 11–12.

99. Achille Mbembe, "The Power of the Archive and Its Limits," in *Refiguring the Archive*, ed. Carolyn Hamilton, Verne Harris, Jane Taylor, et al. (Cape Town: David Philip, 2002), 19.

100. Michel de Certeau, *The Writing of History*, trans. Tom Conley (New York: Columbia University Press, 1988), 75.

101. What is striking in Slyomovics's discussion of Moroccan human rights archives is the exhortation "to dream the file before writing the special exemption to see it": access remains elusive, and the archive itself, which is rooted in the premise that collective suffering has the potential to avoid the repetition of violence, has the contradictory effect of further immersing these stories in silence and loss (Slyomovics, "The Moroccan Equity and Reconciliation Commission," 37).

102. Slyomovics, "The Moroccan Equity and Reconciliation Commission," 2.

103. Most important in Miller's analysis is the fact that these new forms of archive "fill the void between official dogma and suppressed memory." Susan Gilson Miller, *A History of Modern Morocco* (Cambridge: Cambridge University Press, 2013), 219.

104. Miller, *A History of Modern Morocco*, 218.

105. It should be noted here that I am not including hagiographies, legers, and Sūfī literature, and other forms of documentation that Moroccan historians have been using to write the pre-twentieth-century history. These archival documents, whether owned by the state, families, or religious lodges, still address a dead past that is not linked to the present situation of Moroccan post-colonial history.

106. Written in the absence of emigrated Moroccan Jews, this subgenre of Moroccan literature draws on memory to document this void, which has yet to be called what it is: disappearance.

107. The richness and multidimensional nature of the diverse cultural production that I conceptualize as other-archives is such that Ahmed Chouki Benyoub, a former ERC commissioner and current Ministerial Delegate in Human Rights, has called for the interdisciplinary cooperation of researchers in political science, sociology of political violence, history of the present, and literature to rewrite the contemporary political history of Morocco. (Ahmed Chouki Benyoub, interview by *Mashārf*, March 16, 2017, accessed March 22, 2017, initially available in https://www.youtube.com/watch?v=HLXTLmNp07I.) (The video has since been deleted from YouTube, but the author owns a copy of the episode.)

108. Likewise, the decomposing corpses of soldiers taken to the secret military prison in Tazmamart and the tortured bodies of young students in the notorious prison centers in Derb Moulay Cherif, Courbis, and PF3 elicited a wealth of sentiments that can serve as a source for Morocco's emotional histories.

109. Mohammed El Ayadi, "Commentaire," in *Mémoire et histoire* (Rabat: Les Cahiers Bleus, 2006), 17–25.

110. Abderrahmane El Moudden, "'Awda ilā mas'alat al-arshīf al-makhzanī," in *Germain Ayache al-mu'arrikh wa-al-munāḍil*, ed. Abderrahmane El Moudden and Abdelaziz Belfaida (Rabat: Nabat Net, 2015), 41.

111. Mohamed El Ayadi, "Al-Madrasa al-tārīkhiyya al-maghribiyya al-ḥadītha: Al-ishkāliyyāt wa-al-mafāhīm," *Mandumah*, accessed July 10, 2021, http://search.mandumah.com/Record/594930/Details, 266.

112. El Moudden, "'Awda ilā mas'alat al-arshīf al-makhzanī"; Jamaâ Baïda, "Historiographie marocaine: De l'histoire contemporaine à l'histoire du temps présent," in *Du Protectorat à l'indépendance: Problématique du temps présent*, ed. Mohammed Kenbib (Rabat: Publication of the Faculty of Literatures and Human Sciences, 2006), 16. The publication of Monjib's *La Monarchie marocaine* has strained his relationship with the state since the early 1990s. He has been the object of legal proceedings based on accusations that everyone knows are mostly—or at least partially—motivated by his audacious historiographical work.

113. "Professor Maâti Monjib," in *al-Maghrib wa-al-zaman al-rāhin*, ed. Mohammed Kably and Abderrahmane El Moudden (Rabat: Manshūrāt al-Ma'had al-Malakī li-al-Baḥth fī Tārīkh al-Maghrib, 2013), 131; Mohammed Kenbib, ed., *Du Protectorat à l'indépendance: Problématique du temps présent* (Rabat: Publication of the Faculty of Literatures and Human Sciences, 2006), 8.

114. Kenbib, *Du Protectorat à l'indépendance*; Mohamed Kably and Abderrahmane El Moudden, eds., *al-Maghrib wa-al-zaman al-rāhin* (Rabat: Manshūrāt al-Ma'had al-Malakī li-al-Baḥth fī Tārīkh al-Maghrib, 2013).

115. Discussions of methodology have been a sign of uneasiness with the profusion of what I have theorized as other-archives as well as a tool for processing issues related to the objectivity of these sources and the lack of temporal distance between the historian and the events that are still fresh in the minds of historical actors, meaning that they are too close to memory.

116. These historians are likely unaware of Antoinette Burton's critique: "Questioning the verifiability of the evidence produced in sites of memory like oral histories, letters, autobiographies, and testimonies throws doubt on the narratives drawn from them *as history*, leaving women's (and others') accounts of their own experience—most often found in 'unreliable' sources—in the realm of memory and clearing the way for an apparently superior, because disinterested, 'History.'" Antoinette Burton, *Dwelling in the Archive: Women Writing House, Home, and History in Late Colonial India* (New York: Oxford University Press, 2003), 23.

117. Benyoub, interview by *Mashārif.* My translation of Ahmed Chouki Benyoub's interview aired as part of the TV show *Mashārif.*

118. Literary scholar Abdessamad Belkbir has also articulated the precursory function of literature in emphasizing that "writing was not only a result, it was indeed a cause [of political change]. The fact that prison and detention literature

predated the much-lauded political transition is proof." Ittiḥād kuttāb al-Maghrib, *Al-dhākira wal-ibdā': A'māl nadwa* (Rabat: Manshūrāt Ittiḥād Kuttāb al-Maghrib, 2010), 7. Jacques Rancière, *The Politics of Aesthetics* (New York: Continuum, 2004), 36–37; Alison Landsberg, *Prosthetic Memory: The Transformation of American Remembrance in the Age of Mass Culture* (New York: Columbia University Press, 2004), 12.

119. Benyoub, interview by *Mashārif.*

120. Sigmund Freud, "Mourning and Melancholia," in *The Standard Edition of the Complete Psychological Works of Sigmund Freud*, ed. James Strachey and Anna Freud (London: The Hogarth Press and The Institute of Psycho-Analysis, 1917), XIV:243–244.

121. Judith Butler, *Precarious Life: The Power of Mourning and Violence* (London/New York: Verso, 2004), 22; David L. Eng and David Kazanjian, eds., *Loss: The Politics of Mourning* (Berkeley and Los Angeles: University of California Press, 2003), 3–4; Rosalind Shaw, "Afterword: Violence and the Generation of Memory," in *Remembering Violence: Anthropological Perspectives on Intergenerational Transmission*, ed. Nicolas Argenti and Katharina Schramm (New York: Berghahn Books, 2010), 255; Meera Atkinson, *The Poetics of Transgenerational Traumas* (New York: Bloomsbury Academic, 2017). Shaw in particular has critiqued the Western pathologization of trauma and highlighted how it ignores the ways in which societies come to terms with traumatic experiences. See Shaw, "Afterword," 253–55, 257.

122. Atkinson, *The Poetics of Transgenerational Traumas*, 190.

123. Atkinson, *The Poetics of Transgenerational Traumas*, 189–90, 194.

124. Testimonial prison literature has inscribed into the record Azendour, El Yakidi, Manolo, Haïfi, El Fagouri, and others who lost their lives in Tazmamart in the painful story of the nation and transformed them into agents of history whose voices reach us from beyond the grave, and the human rights efforts to locate their whereabouts and secure their release has transformed Tazmamart into a global story that spans Africa, Europe, and America. Tazmamart's other-archives have become an object of translation, filmmaking, literary collaborations, reappropriation, and local and global commentary. The media campaign that accompanied the publication of the translation of Tazmamart survivor Aziz BineBine's memoirs in London in June 2020 is evidence of the persistence of memory in this center of Moroccan national trauma. Aziz BineBine, *Tazmamart: 18 Years in Morocco's Secret Prison*, trans. Lulu Norman (London: Haus Publishing, 2020).

125. Boum, *Memories of Absence*; Trevisan Semi and Sekkat Hatimi, *Mémoire et représentations des Juifs au Maroc: Les voisins absents de Meknès* (Paris: Publisud, 2011).

126. Peter Burke, "History of Events and the Revival of Narrative," in *New Perspectives on Historical Writing*, ed. Peter Burke, 2nd ed. (State College: Penn State University Press, 1991), 239. Quotation from Jacob Climo and Maria G. Cattell, *Social Memory and History: Anthropological Perspectives* (New York: Altamira Press, 2002), 24.

127. Renate Lachmann, "Cultural Memory and the Role of Literature," *European Review* 12, no. 2 (2004): 173.

128. Mnemonic literature also implicates both local and global structures in the processes that led to the emigration of Moroccan Jews from 1948 to 1967, portraying both Jews and Muslims navigating transformations beyond their control in their reality, resulting in their eventual separation and fragmentation: the state's lack of archives of Jewish emigration is more an indictment of the state's negligence and ambivalence than a failure to stress its responsibility in letting Jews go. Structural oppression can also be gleaned from MACM members' works about Morocco's long path to recognizing Amazigh identity from 1967 to 2001. Mohamed Mestaoui and Ali Sidqi Azaykou's Amazigh poetry responds to contemporary events and registers the poets' sense of oppression in an Amazigh country where Imazighen were made to feel invisible. Mohamed Mestaoui, *Smmūs idlisn n tmdiāzīn* (Rabat: IDGL, 2010); Ali Sidqi Azaykou, *Timitār: Majmū'a shi'riyya amāzīghiyya* (Rabaṭ: 'Ukāẓ, 1988).

129. Despite their widespread dissemination and use in society, other-archives have been censored by the Archives du Maroc, the institution put in place in 2011 to help remedy the effects of the Years of Lead on Moroccan history. During a research visit to the Archives du Maroc in the summer of 2016, I asked the director whether magazines, memoirs, literature, interviews, and artistic expressions about the Years of Lead were considered an archive and whether they would be included in the holdings of the institution. The director, an academic historian by profession, recommended that I reach out to the National Council for Human Rights because those types of documents did not constitute an archive. This archival practice represents a stark contradiction to the kind of history that other-archives' producers seek to document. Since most of the memoirs and written sources about the Years of Lead were made available by the authors themselves, excluding them from the Archives du Maroc's holdings fosters amnesia; though a few works are still available in the market, most writings about political detention are out of print today. The National Library in Rabat is no better: though it owns some of the richest holdings that students and scholars can readily access, the only ten testimonial prison literature titles in its catalog are impossible to find on the shelves, whether due to deliberate withholding or attrition, leaving significant materials out of readers' reach.

130. Jim Sharpe, "History from Below," in *New Perspectives on Historical Writing*, ed. Peter Burke (State College: Penn State University Press, 1991), 33–37.

131. Sharpe, "History from Below," 33–37.

132. Sharpe, "History from Below," 37; see also Paul Connerton, *How Societies Remember* (Cambridge: Cambridge University Press, 1988), 16–21.

133. Paul Thompson, *The Voice of the Past: Oral History* (Oxford: Oxford University Press, 2000), 1–2.

134. Royaume du Maroc, *Bulletin officiel*, no. 5484 (December 21, 2006), 2177–78, http://www.habous.gov.ma/fr/files/insitut_bo.pdf.

135. In the introduction to her classic work *The Return of Martin Guerre*, historian

Natalie Zemon Davis admitted that "what I offer you here is in part my invention, but held tightly in check by the voices of the past." Natalie Zemon Davis, *The Return of Martin Guerre* (Cambridge, MA: Harvard University Press, 1984), 5.

136. Heather Murray, a Canadian literary scholar, writes that microhistory has merits in that it is "a method suited to the writing of history on the margins, where documentation may be scant. It assumes that the lives and activities of the subaltern classes need not be told in the aggregate, but can be seen (at least some of them) in the particular; and that these features can emerge even through dominant documentation. Microhistorians see this particular focus—the individual, event, or text—as a uniquely situated nodal point of social, political, economic, and ideational forces. In this way, and perhaps most radically, microhistory undermines the model of historical 'centres' and 'margins' in the first place." See Heather Murray, "Literary History as Microhistory," in *Home-Work: Postcolonialism, Pedagogy, and Canadian Literature*, ed. Cynthia Sugars (Ottawa: University of Ottawa Press, 2004), 411.

137. Benedict Anderson, *Imagined Communities: Reflections on the Origin and Spread of Nationalism* (London: Verso, 1983).

138. Miller, *A History of Modern Morocco*, 219.

139. Yasemin Nuhoğlu Soysal and Hanna Schissler emphasize the use of education in the fields of history, geography, and language in turning subjects into citizens. While Nuhoğlu Soysal's and Schissler's argument may accurately describe situations in a democratic context, these academic fields can also be officially deployed to further deepen allegiance to the monarchy and thus sustain people's subjecthood. Consequently, the alternative histories and geographies of the nation that are found in other-archives resist the state's arrogation of the channels through which citizenship could be gained. See Yasemin Nuhoğlu Soysal and Hanna Schissler, eds., *The Nation, Europe, and the World* (New York: Berghahn Books, 2005), 2.

140. ERC, *The Components of Reform and Reconciliation* (Rabat: Le Conseil Consultatif des Droits de l'Homme, 2009), 68.

141. State repression during the Years of Lead did not spare the field of education, since its aim to "end [. . .] the individual and the citizen" targeted critical thinking, creativity, and free initiative, deeply impacting the entire society. ERC, *The Components of Reform*, 67 (the English wording is modified).

142. While the former hastens to change curricula in order to preserve the state's legitimacy, the latter emphasizes the necessity of entrenching and enshrining a human rights culture "in all streams of national culture by means of research, organizing conferences, supervising training courses and publishing *academic* journals." ERC, *The Components of Reform*, 87.

143. ERC, *The Components of Reform*, IV:21, 51.

144. The supreme law of the land finally acknowledged the identities that had been suppressed for fifty years. *Morocco's Constitution of 2011*, trans. Jefir J. Ruchti, *Constitution Project*, last modified February 4, 2020, §Preamble, https://www.constituteproject.org/constitution/Morocco_2011.pdf?lang=en.

145. ERC, *The Components of Reform*, 53.

146. ERC, *The Components of Reform*, 52–53.

147. ERC, *The Components of Reform*, 54–55 (English wording modified).

148. ERC, *The Components of Reform*, 57. The reemergence of long-forgotten toponymies, utilized now to tell stories of disappearance and forgetfulness, is a clear sign that the marginalized have used their historiographical agency to occupy the center of historical narrative production and shifting the discourse to history and memory as bedrocks for the effective exercise of citizenship, which is first and foremost the ability to define and rewrite what it means to be Moroccan today.

149. "The constitution, rule of law, and civic responsibility are main features" of the civic conception of identity and history. The deployment of historical knowledge to legitimize the order in place and delegitimize its opponents came at the expense of civic history erased in favor of a subject-ruler conception of the past. See Karina Korostelina, "History Education and Social Identity," *Identity* 8, no. 1 (2008): 39–40. As Paul E. Lovejoy has argued of slavery, denial of past transgressions undermines a population's full access to citizenship, which relies on an awareness of inconvenient truths about the past and an embrace of the corollary changes in attitudes and "social relationships" this knowledge requires. Paul E. Lovejoy, "Introduction: Slavery, Memory, Citizenship," in *Slavery, Memory, Citizenship*, ed. Paul E. Lovejoy and Vanessa S. Oliveira (Trenton: Africa World Press, 2016), XIX.

150. State-affiliated human rights and immigration institutions seem to be tasked with the mission to address the questions related to the taboo memory and history of Moroccan Jews. Specifically, The National Council for Human Rights and the Council of Moroccans Living Abroad have been active in organizing conferences that involve discussing Morocco's recent past, particularly integrating the Jewish dimension into these discussions. There is probably an endeavor to consider the return of Moroccan Jews in history and memory a human rights rather than an exercise of citizenship issue. Proceedings of the conference organized in Essaouira in 2010, Frédéric Abécassis, Karima Dirèche, and Rita Aouad, eds., *La Bienvenue et l'adieu: Migrants juifs et musulmans au Maghreb (XVᵉ–XXᵉ siècle)* (Paris: Karthala, 2012).

151. Abdelmajid Kaddouri, Abdelkader Gangai, and Kacem Marghata, *'Abd Allāh Al-'Arawī: Al-Ḥadātha wa-as'ilat al-tārīkh* (Casablanca: Manshūrāt Kullīyat al-Ādāb wa-al-'Ulūm al-Insāniyya Bin-Msīk, 2007), 185.

152. Abdelkébir Khatibi, *Le Scribe et son ombre* (Paris: Éditions de la Différence, 2008), 35–37.

153. Abdelkébir Khatibi and Jacques Hassoun, *Le même livre* (Paris: Éditions de l'Éclat, 1985), 103.

154. Khatibi and Hassoun, *Le même livre*, 106–07.

155. El Guabli, Brahim. "Textual Traces: Khatibi and His Jews." *PMLA/ Publications of the Modern Language Association of America* 137, no. 2 (2022): 347–54, doi:10.1632/S0030812922000165.

1. (Re)Invented Tradition and the Performance of Amazigh Other-Archives in Public Life

1. Mohamed Kably, ed., *Histoire du Maroc: Réactualisation et synthèse* (Rabat: Publications de l'Institut Royal pour la Recherche sur l'Histoire du Maroc, 2012), 730.

2. Al-Jam'iyya al-Maghribiyya li-al-Baḥth wa-al-Tabādul al-Thaqāfī, *Ayyu mustaqbal li-al-amāzīghiyya bi-al-maghrib* (Rabat: Manshūrāt al-Jam'iyya al-Maghribiyya li-al-Baḥth wa-al-Tabādul al-Thaqāfī, 2009), 7. Gilles Lafuente, "Dossier marocain sur le dahir berbère de 1930," *Revue de l'Occident Musulman et de la Méditerranée* 38, no. 2 (1984): 83–116, https://doi.org/10.3406/remmm.1984.2047.

3. Patricia M. Lorcin, *Imperial Identities: Stereotyping, Prejudice and Race in Colonial Algeria* (London: I.B. Tauris Publishers, 1995), 2–3.

4. Marguerite Rollinde, "Le Mouvement amazighe au Maroc: Défense d'une identité culturelle, revendication du droit des minorités ou alternative politique?" in "Mouvements sociaux, mouvements associatifs," special issue, *Insaniyat /* إنسانيات 8 (1999): 63–70, https://doi.org/10.4000/insaniyat.8325, para. 1; Mustapha El Qadéry, "Les Berbères entre le mythe colonial et la négation nationale: Le cas du Maroc," *Revue d'Histoire Moderne et Contemporaine* 45, no. 2 (1998): 425–50.

5. Lahcen Brouksy, *Les Berbères face à leur destin* (Rabat: Bouregreg, 2006), 255–63.

6. Brahim Akhiyyat, *al-Nahḍa al-amāzīghiyya kamā 'ishtu mīlādaha wa taṭawwurahā* (Rabat: Manshūrāt al-Jam'iyya al-Maghribiyya li-al-Baḥth wa-al-Tabādul al-Thaqāfī, 2012), 34.

7. This human rights focus is informed by the legal background of its founder, lawyer Hassan Id Belkacem.

8. See Organisation Tamaynut, "Le statut de Tamaynut," TAMAYNUT.org, accessed September 20, 2020, https://wayback.archive-it.org/org-304/20090619212549/http://tamaynut.org/article.php3?id_article=16; Brouksy, *Les Berbères*, 287.

9. For example, the Amazigh collective called *Tansīqiyyāt Amāzīghiyya* has over 370 associations under its banner. See "Mi'āt al-jam'iyyāt al-amāzīghiyya tastaghīthu bi-al-malik muḥammad al-sādis al-ḥāmī al-tārīkhī li-al-amāzīghiyya lughatan wa taqāfatan wa hawīyyatan," *Maghreb Alaan*, September 8, 2016, https://www.maghrebalaan.com/archives/25315.

10. Akhiyyat, *al-Nahḍa al-amazīghiyya*, 383.

11. This connection is also important to underline here given the fact that some Amazigh activists look at Hebrew as a model for the revival and prosperity of Amazigh language and culture.

12. Mohamed Chtatou, "The Amazigh Cultural Renaissance," The Washington Institute, January 18, 2019, para. 7, https://www.washingtoninstitute.org/fikraforum/view/the-amazigh-cultural-renaissance. Many members, including historian Ali

Sidqi Azaykou, lawyer Hassan Id Belkacem, and physician Ouissaden, were involved in politics.

13. Many of what became MACM's arguments about language, culture, and identity were articulated by Mahjoubi Ahardane, the founder of the DAP, in an interview with the magazine *Jeune Afrique* on December 20, 1964. See Claude Palazzoli, *Le Maroc politique: De l'indépendance à 1973* (Paris: Sindbad, 1973), 180–81, and Chtatou, "The Amazigh Cultural Renaissance," para. 7.

14. Kaci Recelma, "Dissolution du Parti démocrate amazigh marocain: La communauté berbère condamne," Afrik.com, April 22, 2008, https://www.afrik.com/dissolution-du-parti-democrate-amazigh-marocain-la-communaute-berbere-condamne.

15. Mahjoubi Aherdane, the co-founder of the *Mouvement Populaire* with Abdelkarim El Khatib, would appear on TV during the electoral campaigns and address Moroccans in the Amazigh language. For generations of Moroccan youth, this populist movement created in 1957 was the only political party that used the occasion of elections to speak to Imazighen in their language on national TV.

16. The Moroccan state is known for its long history of imploding serious political parties from within and establishing new parties before elections. From the establishment of *Le Front pour la défense des institutions constitutionnelles* (The Front for the Defense of Constitutional Institutions) in 1963 to the establishment of *Le Parti authenticité et modernité* (Authenticity and Modernity Party) in 2008, state strategies to control the partisan field have not changed. Powerful advisors to the king intervene to shape the partisan map, which both limits the parties' margin of maneuver and weakens their ability to exercise their constitutional prerogatives.

17. On marginalization, see Bruce Maddy-Weitzman, *The Berber Identity Movement and the Challenge to North African States* (Austin: University of Texas Press, 2011); on gendered spaces, see Cynthia Becker, *Amazigh Arts in Morocco: Women Shaping Berber Identity* (Austin: University of Texas Press, 2006), and Katherine Hoffman *We Share Walls: Language, Land, and Gender in Berber Morocco* (Massachusetts: John Wiley & Sons, 2008); on racial dynamics, Paul Silverstein and David Crawford, "Amazigh Activism and the Moroccan State," *Middle East Report*, no. 233 (2004): 44–48, https://doi.org/10.2307/1559451.

18. Ahmed Boukous, *Masār al-lugha al-amāzīghiyya, al-rihānāt wa-al-istrātījiyyāt* (Rabat: Manshūrāt al-Ma'had al-Malakī li-al-Thaqāfa al-Amāzīghiyya, 2013); id., "Revitalisation de l'amazighe enjeux et stratégies," *Langage et Société*, no. 143 (2013): 9–26; Mahfoud Asmhri, ed., "al-Ta'addud al-lughawī bishamāl ifrīqiya 'abra al-tārīkh," *Asinag* 11 (2016): 7–86.

19. Maddy-Weitzman, however, does gesture to some issues of identity and history writing practices in "Berber/Amazigh Memory Work," in *The Maghreb in the New Century: Identity, Religion, and Politics*, ed. Bruce Maddy Weitzman and Daniel Zisenwine (Gainsville: University Press of Florida, 2007), 50–71.

20. Akhiyyat, *Al-Nahda al-amāzīghiyya*, 316.

21. Al-Jarīda al-Rasimiyya, "Ẓahīr sharīf raqm 1.01.299 ṣādir fī 29 min rajab al-khayr 1422 (17 octūbr 2001) yaqḍī bi-iḥdāth al-ma'had al-malakī li-al-thaqāfa al-amāzīghiyya," October 1, 2001, art. 8, at 3677–80.

22. Al-Jarīda al-Rasimiyya, "Ẓahīr sharīf raqm 1.01.299," Preamble.

23. RIAC, "Texte du Dahir portant création de l'Institut Royal de la Culture Amazighe," Institut Royal de la Culture Amazighe [2001], Preamble§2, http://www.ircam.ma/?q=fr/node/4668.

24. Although some activists, like Mohammed Boudhan, reject the recognition of Morocco as having multiple identities because they see it primarily as an Amazigh land, advocating a plural identity was a productive way to convince Arab nationalists that the recognition of Amazigh identity and cultural rights did not aim to exclude Arabness and Islam. See Mohammed Boudhan, *Fī al-hawiyya al-amāzīghiyya li-al-al-maghrib* (Morocco: Manshūrāt Tawiza, 2013), 20.

25. See Jām'iyyat al-Jāmi'a al-Ṣayfīyya bi-Agādīr, A'māl al-dawra al-ūlā li-al-Jāmi'iyya al-Ṣayfīyya bi-Agādīr : al-thaqāfa al-sha'biyya, al-waḥda fī al-tanawwu' (Mohammadia: Maṭba'at Faḍāla, 1982).

26. Al-Jarīda al-Rasimiyya, "Ẓahīr sharīf raqm 1.01.299," Article 2.

27. Younes Alami et al., "Que veulent les Berbères," *Le Journal Hedomadaire*, October 30–November 4, 2004, 26.

28. Although I highlight MACM's achievements through Tifinagh's functions in the public space, I do recognize that many Amazigh activists complain about setbacks and constraints that are imposed on Tamazight in Morocco (Amina Ben Cheikh, "Ṣarkha lābudda minhā," *Amadal Amazigh*, 222/Māy 2969/2019, https://www.amadalamazigh.press.ma/archivesPDF/220.pdf?_ga=2.164516863.15562416.1662861015-961590116.1662861015).

29. Silverstein and Crawford, "Amazigh Activism and the Moroccan State," 46; Dris Soulaimani, "Writing and Rewriting Amazigh/Berber Identity: Orthographies and Language Ideologies," *Writing Systems Research* 8, no. 1 (2016): 5, https://doi.org/10.1080/17586801.2015.1023176. Hélène Claudot-Hawad has mentioned—although without any detail—the fact that North African Amazigh activists adopted Tuareg Tifinagh in order to "reberberize" their region ("Les Tifinagh comme écriture du détournement," *Études et documents berbères*, no. 23 [2008]: 11). I build on Claudot-Hawad's suggestion to analyze how MACM re-Amazighized the public sphere in Morocco through the use of Tifinagh.

30. This line of argument, which underlined Amazigh activism, was articulated by Brahim Akhiyyat: "throughout history, Tamazight is the mother tongue of all citizens of North Africa. It is the national language of its people, which is a historical, social, and civilizational reality that we wait for no one to acknowledge" (Brahim Akhiyyaṭ, *al-Amāzīghiyya: Hūwwiyyātuna al-waṭaniyya* [Rabat: Manshūrāt al Jam'īyya al Maghribiyya li-al-Baḥth wa-al-Tabādul al-Thaqāfī, 2007], 118).

31. Mohammed Boudhan, "Badala makhzanat al-amāzīghiyya, yajibu al-'amal 'ala tamzīgh al-makhzan," *Hespress*, May 24, 2018, https://www.hespress.com/writers/392677.html.

32. Boudhan, "Badala makhzanat al-amāzīghiyya."

33. Brahim Akhiyyat in *al-Jam'iyya al-Maghribiyya, Ayyu mustaqbal li-al-amāzīghiyya*, 76.

34. Eric Hobsbawm and Terence Ranger, "Introduction," in *The Invention of Tradition*, ed. Eric Hobsbawm and Terence Ranger (1983; repr. New York: Cambridge University Press, 2012), 1.

35. Hobsbawm and Ranger, "Introduction," 1–2.

36. Hobsbawm and Ranger, "Introduction," 4.

37. Lucette Valensi, "Le Roi chronophage: La construction d'une conscience historique dans le Maroc postcolonial," *Cahiers d'Études Africaines*, no. 119 (1990): 279–98.

38. Ali Sidqi Azaykou, "Tārikh al-maghrib bayna mā huwwa 'alayh wa mā yanbaghī an yakūna 'alyh," *Majallat al-Kalima*, no. 1 (1971), 18.

39. Yael Zerubavel, *Recovered Roots: Collective Memory and the Making of Israeli National Tradition* (Chicago: University of Chicago Press, 1995), 7.

40. Zerubavel, *Recovered Roots*, 8.

41. Ali Sidqi Azaykou, *Namādhij min asmā' al-a'lām al-jughrāfiyya wa-al-bashariyya al-maghribiyya* (Rabat: Manshūrāt al-Ma'had al-Malakī li-al-Thaqāfa al-Amāzīghiyya, 2004); Mohammed Chafik, *Lamḥa min thalāta wa thalāthīn qarnan min tārīkh al-amāzīghiyyīn* (Rabat: Dār al-Kalām li-al-Tawzī' wa-al-Nashr, 1989); Claudot-Hawad, "Les Tifinagh"; "AMAZIGH—Origine du drapeau amazigh," posted by Taddart nneɣ, August 30, 2018, YouTube video, https://www.youtube.com/watch?v=Wt1GGFQTIOg.

42. Gabriel Camps, *Les Berbères, mémoires et identité* (Casablanca: Éditions Le Fennec, 2007), 272–75; Hélène Claudot-Hawad, *Les Touaregs: Portraits en fragments* (Aix-en-Provence: EDISUD, 1993); Chafik, *Lamḥa min thalāta wa thalāthīn*, 65–67; Malika Hachid, *Les Premiers berbères entre méditerranée, Tassili et Nil* (Alger: Ina-Yas Editions, 2001), 173–83; Joseph Sternberg, "The Origin of the Libyan Alphabets Revisited," *Scientific Cultures* 1, no. 2 (2015): 8, 11.

43. Karima Dirèche, "La Vulgate historique berbère en Algérie: Savoirs, usages et projections," in *Les Revendications amazighes dans la tourmente des "printemps arabes": Trajectoires historiques et évolutions récentes des mouvements identitaires en Afrique du Nord*, ed. Mohand Tilmatine and Thierry Desrues (Rabat: Centre Jacques-Berque, 2017), para. 2–7; Chafik, *Lamḥa min thalāta wa thalāthīn*; Azaykou, *Namādhij min asmā'*; Akhiyyat, *al-Nahda al-amāzīghīyya*, 398.

44. Chafik, *Lamḥa min thalāta wa thalāthīn*, 79–86. In fact, it was not just the historical figures who were commemorated. Brahim Akhiyyat dedicated an entire book to the dead "men of Amazigh action" in the twentieth century, including novelist Mohammed Khaïr-Eddine, singer/poet Mohammed Demsiri, and historian Ali Siqdi Azaykou, among others (Brahim Akhiyyat, *Rijālāt al-'amal al-amāzīghī* [Rabat: Manshūrāt al-Jam'iyya al-Maghribiyya li-al-Baḥth wa-al-Tabādul al-Thaqāfī, 2004]).

45. Mohand Tilmatine, "Du Berbère à l'amazighe: De l'object au sujet

historique," in *AlAndalus Maghreb* 14 (2007): 242; Sidqi Azaykou, "Tārikh al-maghrib bayna mā huwwa 'alayh wa mā yanbaghī an yakūna 'alyhi," 17; Chafik, *Lamḥa min thalāt wa thalāthīn*, 82–86.

46. Tilmatine, "Du Berbère à l'amazighe," 241.

47. Akhiyyat, *al-Nahda al-amazīghiyya*, 75–87.

48. AMREC, *Min ajli tarsīm abajadiyyat Tifinagh li-tadrīs al-amāzīghiyya: Taḥālīl wa wath'āiq wa 'ārā'* (Rabat: Manshūrāt al-Jam'iyya al-Maghribiyya li-al-Baḥth wa-al-Tabādul al-Thaqāfī, 2002), 5–6; Akhiyyat, *al-Nahda al-amāzīghiyya*, 51.

49. Akhiyyat, *al-Nahda al-amazīghiyya*, 50–51.

50. See Brahim El Guabli, "Where is Amazigh Studies?," *The Journal of North African Studies*, 1-8; Brahim El Guabli, "Tankra Tamazight: The Revival of Amazigh Indigeneity in Literature and Art," Jadaliyya, November 1, 2021, https://www.jadaliyya.com/Details/43440.

51. Tirra, or The Alliance of Writers in Amazigh Language, has published over four hundred books. In January 2020, it held its tenth annual gathering of Amazigh writers. For more details, see the association's website: *Tirra, Alliance des Écrivains en Amazighe*, http://tirra.net/web/.

52. Brahim El Guabli, "Literature and Indigeneity: Amazigh Activists' Construction of an Emerging Literary Field," *Los Angeles Review of Books*, forthcoming.

53. Claudot-Hawad, "Les Tifinagh," 3–4.

54. George L. Campbell and Christopher Moseley, *The Routledge Handbook of Scripts and Alphabets* (New York: Routledge, 2012), 59.

55. Mohand Aarav Bessaoud, *Histoire de l'Académie Berbère* (Alger: L'Artisan, 2000), 91.

56. Bessaoud, *Histoire de l'Académie*, 91.

57. Bessaoud, *Histoire de l'Académie*, 91.

58. Soulaimani, "Writing and Rewriting Amazigh/Berber Identity," 4.

59. Akhiyyat, *al-Nahda al-amazīghiyya*, 78–87.

60. Akhiyyat, *al-Nahda al-amazīghiyya*, 86.

61. Despite its powerful presence and popularity, the impact this band had on the creation of an Amazigh consciousness in Morocco has not been addressed in any scholarly work. Newspapers are the main source of information on its impact. For more information on the context of its emergence, see M'bark Chbani, "Musique amazighe: Izenzaren de retour après une longue absence," *Libération*, May 12, 2012, https://www.libe.ma/Musique-amazighe-Izenzaren-de-retour-apres-une-longue-absence_a27289.html

62. El Guabli, "Literature and Indigeneity," *Los Angeles Review of Books*, forthcoming

63. Taddart nneɣ, "AMAZIGH—Origine du drapeau amazigh."

64. Taddart nneɣ, "AMAZIGH—Origine du drapeau amazigh."

65. The Board of CMA, "Amazigh Flag Day," Amazighworld.org, August 28, 2019, http://www.amazighworld.org/eng/history/index_show.php?id=179

66. Tilmatine, "Du Berbère à l'amazighe," 238.

67. Abderrahim Yuba Amdjar, "Al-thulātī al-amāzīghī 'akāl,' 'afgān,' 'awāl,' awwal shi'ār li-al-insāniyya . . . !," Amazighworld.org, December 15, 2016.

68. André Levy, *Return to Casablanca: Jews, Muslims, and an Israeli Anthropologist* (Chicago: Chicago University Press, 2015), 148.

69. Levy, *Return to Casablanca*, 152–72.

70. For more analysis of this idea of autochthony, see Abdellah Hammoudi, "Le Don entre juifs et musulmans: Ou comment concilier les identités opposées," *Revue Internationale d'Anthropologie Culturelle & Sociale* Hors-Série [Special Issue] (2016): 91–106.

71. Mohammed Boudhan, "Aherdan aḥad ākhir al-rijāl al-aḥrār," *Al-Hiwār al-Mutamaddin* 6769, December 23, 2020, https://www.ahewar.org/debat/show.art.asp?aid=703297.

72. Benedict Anderson, *Imagined Communities: Reflections on the Origin and Spread of Nationalism* (New York: Verso, 1991); Boudhan, "Aherdan."

73. Brahim El Guabli, "My Amazighitude: On the Indigenous Identity of North Africa, themarkaz.or, June 6, 2022, https://themarkaz.org/my-amazighitude-on-the-indigenous-identity-of-north-africa/

74. See Paul Silverstein, "The Pitfalls of Transnational Consciousness: Amazigh Activism as a Scalar Dilemma," *The Journal of North African Studies* 18, no. 5 (2013): 768–78.

75. Silverstein and Crawford, "Amazigh Activism," 48.

76. His literary work includes two poetry collections: *Timitār: Majmū'a shi'riyya amāzīghiyya* (Rabat: 'Ukāẓ, 1988) and *Izmuln: Majmū'a shi'riyya amāzīghiyya* (Casablanca: Maṭba'at al-Najāḥ al-Jadīda, 1995).

77. Ali Sidqi Azaykou, "Fī sabīl mafhūm ḥaqīqī lithqāfatina al-waṭaniyya," in *Ma'ārik fikriyya ḥawla al-amāzīghīyya*, ed. Markaz Tarik Ibn Ziad (Rabat: Markaz Tarik Ibn Ziad, 2002): 35–41.

78. Azaykou, "Fī sabīl mafhūm ḥaqīqī lithqāfatina al-waṭaniyya," 39.

79. Azaykou, "Fī sabīl mafhūm ḥaqīqī lithqāfatina al-waṭaniyya," 41.

80. Maddy-Weitzman, *The Berber Identity Movement*, 99.

81. Akhiyyat, *al-Nahda al-amāzīghiyya*, 137.

82. Akhiyyat, *al-Nahda al-amāzīghiyya*, 137.

83. Rollinde, "Le Mouvement amazighe au Maroc," para. 11.

84. "The Berbers Come Fighting Back," *The Economist*, February 13, 1999, 46.

85. Kably, *Histoire du Maroc*, 729–30.

86. El Houssaine Jouhadi El Baâmrani, *Tarjamat ma'ānī al-qur'ān al-karīm bi-al-lugha al-amāzīghiyya* (Casablanca: J.al-Ḥ. al-Bā'umrānī, 2003), n.p.

87. Ali Sidqi Azaykou, "al-Aṣāla wa-al-'umq fī al-'awda ilā al-thaqāfa al-sha'biyya," in *Ma'ārik fikriyya ḥawla al-amāzīghīyya*, ed. Markaz Tarik Ibn Ziad (Rabat: Markaz Tarik Ibn Ziad, 2002): 15.

88. Azaykou, "al-Aṣāla wa-al-'umq," 15; Muḥammad Arjdāl, "Amānār—wī-mūzār—wa bidāyat tadwīn al-shi'r al-amāzīghī," *Ahewar*, no. 2504 (2008).

89. Azaykou, "Tārikh al-maghrib," 16–18.
90. Azaykou, "Tārikh al-maghrib," 16.
91. Azaykou, "Tārikh al-maghrib," 16.
92. Azaykou, "Tārikh al-maghrib," 16.
93. Azaykou, "Tārikh al-maghrib," 16.
94. Azaykou, "Tārikh al-maghrib," 17.
95. Azaykou, "Tārikh al-maghrib," 17.
96. See Chapter 5 of this book for a lengthy discussion of this question.
97. Ali Sidqi Azaykou, "Min mashākil al-baḥt fī tārīkh al-maghrib," in *Ma'ārik fikriyya ḥawla al-amāzīghīyya*, ed. Markaz Tarik Ibn Ziad (Rabat: Markaz Tarik Ibn Ziad, 2002): 19–21.
98. Azaykou, "Min mashākil al-baḥt fī tārīkh al-maghrib," 20.
99. See the conversations in Abderrahmane El Moudden and Abdelaziz Belfaida, eds., *Germain Ayache, l'historien et le militant* (Rabat: Imprimerie Rabat Net, 2015)
100. Azaykou, "Min mashākil al-baḥt fī tārīkh al-maghrib," 20.
101. Azaykou, "Min mashākil al-baḥt fī tārīkh al-maghrib," 20–21.
102. Azaykou, "Min mashākil al-baḥt fī tārīkh al-maghrib," 21. He goes on to underline how knowledge of rural history is crucial for knowing the "human milieu" that will be the site of the desired development.
103. Ali Sidqi Azaykou, "al-Ta'wīl al-nasabī (al-jiniālūjī) hal yumkinu tajāwuzuhu?," *Majallat Kulliyat al-'Ādāb wa-al-'Ulūm al-Insāniyya al-Ribāṭ*, no. 15 (1989–90), 20.
104. Azaykou, "al-Ta'wīl al-nasabī (al-jiniālūjī) hal yumkinu tajāwuzuhu?," 9.
105. Azaykou, "al-Ta'wīl al-nasabī (al-jiniālūjī) hal yumkinu tajāwuzuhu?," 23.
106. Ali Sidqi Azaykou, *Tārikh al-maghrib aw al-ta'wīlāt al-mumkina* (Rabat: Markaz Ṭāriq Ibn Ziyyād, 2001); id., *Namādhij min asmā'*.
107. Ali Sidqi Azaykou, *Tārikh al-maghrib aw al-ta'wīlāt al-mumkina*; id., *Namādhij min asmā'*.
108. Mohammed Boudhan, "Ali Sidqi Azaykou: Dhālika al-mufakkir al-majhūl," September 11, 2020, http://www.amadalamazigh.press.ma/%D8%B9%D9%84%D9%8A-%D8%B5%D8%AF%D9%82%D9%8A-%D8%A3%D8%B2%D8%A7%D9%8A%D9%83%D9%88-%D8%B0%D9%84%D9%83-%D8%A7%D9%84%D9%85%D9%81%D9%83%D8%B1-%D8%A7%D9%84%D9%85%D8%AC%D9%87%D9%88%D9%84/.
109. Azaykou, *Tārikh al-maghrib aw al-ta'wīlāt al-mumkina*, 8.
110. AMREC, *30 Sanatan min al-'amal al-thaqāfī al-amāzīghī* (Rabat: Manshūrāt al-Jam'iyya al-Maghribiyya li-al-Baḥth wa-al-Tabādul al-Thaqāfī, 1997), 59.
111. AMREC, *30 Sanatan*, 59.
112. AMREC, *30 Sanatan*, 59.
113. AMREC, *30 Sanatan*, 59.
114. See *Jam'iyyat al-Jāmi'a al-Ṣayfiyya bi-Agadir, Tārīkh al-amāzīgh: Al-nadwa al-dawliyya ḥawla tārīkh al-amāzīgh, al-tārīkh al-mu'āṣir* (Rabat: Dār Ibī Raqrāq, 2002).

115. Jefri J. Ruchti, "Morocco's Constitution of 2011," Constituteproject, February 4, 2020, https://www.constituteproject.org/constitution/Morocco_2011.pdf, 4.

116. Ruchti, "Morocco's Constitution of 2011," 3.

117. Their names are Ali Hrach Errass, Ali Aken, Mbark Tauss, Ahmed Kiche, Said Jaafar, Omar Darouiche, and Omar Ochna. For more details about their case, see Amnesty International, "Further information on UA 187/94 (MDE 29/03/94, 12 May 1994)—Detention of possible prisoners of conscience/fear of unfair trial and new concern: Imprisonment of prisoners of conscience," May 31, 1994, https://www.amnesty.org/download/Documents/184000/mde290041994en.pdf.

118. Akhiyyat, *al-Nahda al-amāzīghiyya*, 218.

119. Maddy-Weitzman, *The Berber Identity Movement*, 120.

120. Wizārat al-Awqāf wal-Shu'ūn al-Islāmiyya, "Al-Khiṭāb al-malakī al-sāmī al-ladhī wajjahahu ṣāḥib al-jalāla al-malik al-ḥasan al-thānī ilā al-umma bi-munāsabat thawrat al-malik wal-sha'b," August–September 1994, http://www.habous.gov.ma/daouat-alhaq/item/7773.

121. Mohammed Chafik, "Le Manifeste berbère," *L'Aménagement linguistique dans le monde*, March 1, 2000, http://www.axl.cefan.ulaval.ca/afrique/berbere-manifeste-2000.htm.

122. Chafik, "Le Manifeste berbère."

123. Stéphanie Pouessel, "Écrire la langue berbère au royaume de Mohamed VI: Les enjeux politiques et identitaires du tifinagh au Maroc," *Revue des Mondes Musulmans et de la Méditerranée* 124 (2008): 221, https://doi.org/10.4000/remmm.6029; Akhiyyat, *al-Nahda al-amazīghiyya*, 209.

124. Agadir, "Maroc: Charte d'Agadir relative aux droits linguistiques et culturels," August 5, 1991, http://www.unesco.org/culture/fr/indigenous/Dvd/pj/IMAZIGHEN/AMAZC4_3.pdf.

125. Mohammed VI, "Khitāb ṣāhib al-jalāla al-malik muḥammad al-sādis naṣarahu al-lāh bi-munāsabat waḍ' al-ṭāba' al-sharīf 'alā al-ẓhīr al-muḥdith wa-al-munaẓẓim li-al-ma'had al-malakī li-al-thaqāfa al-amāzīghiyya," Institut Royal de la Culture Amazighe, October 17, 2001, http://www.ircam.ma/?q=ar/node/4662.

126. Mohammed VI, "Khitāb ṣāhib al-jalāla al-malik muḥammad al-sādis naṣarahu al-lāh bi-munāsabat waḍ' al-ṭāba' al-sharīf."

127. Mbark Boulguid, "Mulāḥaẓāt 'alā hāmish khiṭāb al-abajadiyya," in *Min ajli tarsīm abajadiyyat tifinagh li-tadrīs al-amāzīghiyya: Taḥālīl wa wathāiq wa ārā'*, ed. AMREC (Rabat: Manshūrāt al-Jam'iyya al-Maghribiyya li-al-Baḥth wa-al-Tabādul al-Thaqāfī, 2002), 85–90; Soulaimani, "Writing and Rewriting Amazigh/Berber Identity."

128. El Houcine Ouazzi, "Tifinagh: Al-abajadiyya al-aṣlaḥ li-kitābat al-amāzīghiyya," in *Min ajli tarsīm abajadiyyat Tifinagh li-tadrīs al-amāzīghiyya: Taḥālīl wa wathāiq wa ārā'*, ed. AMREC (Rabat: Manshūrāt al-Jam'iyya al-Maghribiyya li-al-Baḥth wa-al-Tabādul al-Thaqāfī, 2002), 35–45.

129. AMREC, *Min ajli tarsīm abajadiyyat*, 5–6.

130. AMREC, *Min ajli tarsīm abajadiyyat*, 6–7.

131. "Quffāz amāzīghī fīhi yadun faransīyya," *Al-Tajdīd*, October 25, 2002, https://www.maghress.com/attajdid/13673, and Alami et al., "Que veulent les Berbères," 20–27.

132. El Qadéry, "Les Berbères entre le mythe colonial et la négation nationale," 430.

133. Mohamed Chtatou, an Amazigh academic, has argued that AMREC and its overrepresentation in RIAC reflected the fact that it has since "the very beginning been used as the Amazigh arm of the Moroccan establishment to further its own vision of Amazigh culture: obsequious and subservient" (Chtatou, "The Amazigh Cultural Renaissance," para. 6). The "Meknes declaration" elicited a scathing response from a number of Amazigh associations that disagreed with its signatories' rejection of both Tifinagh and the Arabic script. See Muḥammad al-Rāwī's article, "Jam'iyyāt amāzīghiyya maghrībiyya tastankir al-da'wa li-'timād al-aḥurūf al-lātīniyya fī kitābat al-lugha al-amāzīghiyya," *Al-Sharq al-Awsat*, October 26, 2002, https://archive.aawsat.com/details.asp?article=132126&issueno=8733#.Xi2ZUC2ZNPM; 'Alī Ḥusnī, "'Bayān maknās wa 'umalā' al qawmiyya al-'arabiyya," *Tawiza*, December 2020, http://tawiza.eu5.org/Tawiza67/Asidd121002.htm.

134. For more details about these debates, see AMREC, *Min ajli tarsīm abajadiyyat.*

135. Ouazzi, "Tifinagh: al-Abajadiyya al-aṣlaḥ," 40.

136. Akhiyyat, *al-Nahda al-amāzīghīyya*, 350; Maddy-Weitzman, *The Berber Identity Movement*, 170.

137. Pouessel, "Écrire la langue berbère," 227; Mustapha El Khalfi, "al-Islāmīyyūn al-maghāriba wa-al-amāzīghiyya," in AMREC, *Ayyu mustaqbal li-al-amāzīghiyya bi-al-maghrib* (Rabat: Manshūrāt al-Jam'iyya al-Maghribiyya li-al-Baḥth wa-al-Tabādul al-Thaqāfī, 2009), 110–11; Soulaimani, "Writing and Rewriting Amazigh/Berber Identity," 6.

138. Akhiyyat, *al-Nahda al-amāzīghiyya*, 349.

139. Ali Housni "'Bayān maknās wa 'umalā' al-qawmiyya al-'arabiyya," *Tawiza*, December 2002, http://tawiza.byethost10.com/Tawiza68/Husni.htm; Boulguid, "Mulāḥaẓāt 'alā hāmish khiṭāb al-abajadiyya," 85–88.

140. Ahmad Assid, "Aḥmad Aṣīd ilā jarīdat al-'alam: Kayfa tamma tabannī ḥarf tifināgh?" *Amazigh World*, July 30, 2011, http://www.amazighworld.org/arabic/history/index_show.php?id=1993.

141. Ahmed Boukous, "Tadrīs al-amāzīghiyya . . . al-'awda ilā al-ṣifr," *Assabah*, February 6, 2018, https://assabah.ma/286574.html.

142. Andrés di Masso, "Micropolitics of Public Space: On the Contested Limits of Citizenship as a Locational Practice," *Journal of Social and Political Psychology* 3, no. 2 (2015): 63–83.

143. Di Masso, "Micropolitics of Public Space," 66.

144. Di Masso, "Micropolitics of Public Space," 66.

145. El Kably, *Histoire du Maroc*, 730.

146. Agadir, "Maroc: Charte d'Agadir."

147. Marién Sloboda et al., "The Policies on Public Signage in Minority Languages and Their Reception in Four Traditionally Bilingual European Locations," *Media and Communication* 63 (2012): 52.

148. Becker, *Amazigh Arts in Morocco*, 8.

149. al-Jarīda al-Rasimiyya, "Ẓahīr sharīf raqm 1.01.299 ṣādir fī 29 min rajab al-khayr 1422 (17 octūbr 2001)," Art. 3.

150. Dirèche, "La Vulgate historique berbère."

151. RIAC, *Dalīl manshūrāt al-ma'had al-malakī li-al-thaqāfa al-amāzīghiyya 2003–2016*, accessed December 11, 2018, http://www.ircam.ma/sites/default/files/publications/Guide%20des%20publications%20de%20l%27IRCAM_0.pdf.

152. RIAC, *Dalīl manshūrāt al-ma'had al-malakī li-al-thaqāfa al-amāzīghiyya 2003–2016*, [2].

153. Gray literature refers to a host of nonconventional sources and materials that are produced and circulated outside the commercial publication channels. V. Alberani, Paola de Castro Pietrangeli, and A.M. Mazza have underlined the fact that "librarians have been reluctant to acquire this material and add it to their catalogs" ("The Use of Grey Literature in Health Sciences: A Preliminary Survey," *Bulletin of the Medical Library Association* 78, no. 4 (1990): 358); Dirèche, "La Vulgate historique berbère," para. 6.

154. Mohammed Awzal and 'Umar Afā, *Baḥr al-dumū': Bi-al-lughatayn al-amāzīghiyya wa-al-'arabiyya* (Al-Dār al-Bayḍā': Maṭba'at al-Najāḥ al-Jadīda, 2009); Ibrāhīm I'zza, *Iskla n yiḍ* (Rabat: Marsam, 2016); Hassan Aourid, *Taghuyt n tīn hinān* (Rabat: Groupe, 2014); Mohammed Mestaoui, *Smmūs idlisn n tmdiāzīn* (Rabat: IDG, 2010); Sidqi Azaykou, *Tīmmītār*. While only *Baḥr al-dumū'* is available in English under the title *Ocean of Tears* (2009), the other titles can be translated respectively as: *Shadows of the Night, Tinhinan's Cry, Ponder and Learn, Five Books of Poetry*, and *Signs*.

155. Mohamed Agounad, "Tajribatī fi al-kitāba bi-al-amāzīghiyya," in *al-Adab al-amāzīghīy al-ḥadīth*, ed. Abdelali Talmansour (Agadir: Sous, 2016), 17.

156. Azaykou, *Tīmmītār*, 5.

157. Mestaoui, *Smmūs*, 271.

158. Ra'īs al-Ḥukūma, "Mashrū' qānūn tanẓīmī raqm 04.16 yata'allaqu bi-al-majlis al-waṭanī li-al-lughāt wal-al-thaqāfa al-maghribiyya," *Chambredesrepresentants*, September 30, 2016, https://www.chambredesrepresentants.ma/sites/default/files/loi/04.16.pdf.

159. Al-Jarīda al-Rasimiyya, "Ẓahīr sharīf raqm 1.01.299 ṣādir fī 29 min rajab al-khayr 1422 (17 octūbr 2001).

2. Emplaced Memories of Jewish-Muslim Morocco

1. I shared my conceptualization of "mnemonic literature" and the histories of loss in Moroccan literature with Professor Emily Gottreich, upon her request after a MESA panel, in November 2017.

2. Megan O'Grady, "Why Are We Living in a Golden Age for Historical Fiction?," *The New York Times*, July 5, 2019, https://www.nytimes.com/2019/05/07/t-magazine/historical-fiction-books.html.

3. O'Grady, "Why Are We Living."

4. Michael Frank, "In Morocco, Exploring Remnants of Jewish History," *The New York Times*, May 30, 2015. In an article from November 30, 2017, the website of the Israeli Foreign Affairs Ministry places the number of Jews still living in the country at only 3,000.

5. Mohamed Kably, ed., *Histoire du Maroc: Réactualisation et synthèse* (Rabat: Éditions de l'Institut Royal pour la Recherche sur l'Histoire du Maroc, 2011), 712.

6. Quoted in Kably, *Histoire du Maroc*, 712. All the translation from Arabic and French in this chapter are the author's unless otherwise noted.

7. Omar Mounir, *Nécrologie d'un siècle perdu: Essai sur le Maroc* (Casablanca: Marsam, 2003), 116.

8. Samir Ben-Layashi and Bruce Maddy-Weitzman, "Myth, History and Realpolitik: Morocco and Its Jewish Community," *Journal of Modern Jewish Studies* 9, no. 1 (2010): 101.

9. Simon Lévy, "Professor Simon Levy." In *al-Maghrib wa-al-zaman al-rāhin*, edited by Mohamed Kably and Abderrahmane El Moudden (Rabat: Manshūrāt al-Ma'had al-Malakī li-al-Baḥth fī Tārīkh al-Maghrib, 2013), 53.

10. Emily Benichou Gottreich and Daniel J. Schroeter, eds., *Jewish Culture and Society in North Africa* (Bloomington: Indiana University Press, 2011), 12.

11. Aomar Boum, *Memories of Absence: Moroccans Remember Jews* (Stanford, CA: Stanford University Press, 2013), 9, 131–32, 135–36.

12. El Hassane Aït Moh, *Le Captif de Mabrouka* (Paris: L'Harmattan, 2009); Mohamed Ezzeddine Tazi, *Anā al-mansī* (Casablanca: al-Markaz al-Thaqāfī al-'Arabī, 2015); Driss Miliani, *Casanfa* (al-Iskandarīyya: Dār al-'Ayn li-al-Nashr, 2016); Hassan Aourid, *Cintra* (Rabat: Tūsnā, 2016). In addition to these novels, Abdelkarim Jouaiti's *Zaghārīd al-mawt* (*Ululations of Death*) (al-Jazā'ir: Manshūrāt al-Ikhtilāf, 2015) and Ibrahim Hariri's *Shāmma aw Shtrīt* (*Shāmma or Shtrīt*) (Casablanca: Afrīqia al-Sharq, 2013) are part of this growing corpus. I discuss these two works in the next chapter.

13. However, this is not just specific to Morocco. James Goodman has written that "historians are not, by and large, interested in what most interests novelists: the sound of words, imagery, the shape of the story, voice. They approach fiction no differently than they approach history, discussing what the novelist got right and what he or she got wrong, the analytic ends but not the literary means, the content but not the form." Quoted in David Harlan, "Historical Fiction and Academic History," in *Manifestos for History*, ed. Sue Morgan, Keith Jenkins, Alun Munslow, and Keith Jenkins (London: Routledge, 2007), 110.

14. My co-edited book, *Refiguring Loss: Jews Remembered in Maghrebi and Middle Eastern Literature and Film* (forthcoming with Penn State University Press) is dedicated to these questions in the larger Maghreb and the Middle East.

15. These numbers are from Julie Chauder, "Au Maroc, les protecteurs

musulmans du patrimoine juif," *Le Figaro*, May 26, 2019, https://www.lefigaro.fr/international/au-maroc-les-protecteurs-musulmans-du-patrimoine-juif-20190526.

16. Boutaleb writes that "[t]his Jewish minority was significant, and played fundamental roles in Morocco's general history. However, historiography has not dedicated [to the Jewish minority] the scholarly works it deserves. Then, it got lost and scattered after emigrating from the country." See Abderrahmane El Moudden and Abdelaziz Belfaida, *Jirmān 'Ayyāsh al-mu'arrikh wa-al-munāḍil* (Rabat: Manshūrāt al-Jam'iyya al-Maghribiyya li-al-Baḥth al-Tārīkhī, 2015), 76.

17. *Al Bayane*, the daily newspaper of *ḥizb al-taqaddum wa-al-ishtirākhiyya* (the former Moroccan Communist Party), has taken up some of these questions. Entitled "Le Rôle des juifs amazighs dans l'édification de l'Etat marocain," the article calls on "serious historians to opt for objective research that will illuminate future generations on the contributions of a large portion of Amazigh Jews to the edification of the Moroccan state" (*Al Bayane*, July 27, 2020, http://albayane.press.ma/le-role-des-juifs-amazighs-dans-ledification-de-letat-marocain.html).

18. Pierre Nora, "Between Memory and History: Les lieux de mémoire," *Representations* 26, no. 1 (1989): 7.

19. Pierre Nora and Lawrence D. Kritzman, *Realms of Memory: Conflicts and Divisions* (New York: Columbia University Press, 1996), I:1.

20. Boum, *Memories of Absence.*

21. Astrid Erll and Ann Rigney, "Literature and the Production of Cultural Memory: Introduction," *European Journal of English Studies* 10, no. 2 (2006): 111–15.

22. Giovanni Levi, "On Microhistory," in *New Perspectives on Historical Writing*, ed. Peter Burke (Cambridge: Polity Press, 1991), 107; Carlo Ginzburg, "Microhistory: Two or Three Things That I Know about It," *Critical Inquiry* 20, no. 1 (1993): 25; Heather Murray, "Literary History as Microhistory," in *Home-Work: Postcolonialism, Pedagogy and Canadian Literature*, ed. Cynthia Sugars (Ontario: University of Ottawa Press, 2004), 415.

23. Levi, "On Microhistory," 105.

24. Edward S. Casey, *The Fate of Place: A Philosophical History* (Berkeley: University of California Press, 1998), XIII. See also Carlo Ginzburg and Carlo Poni, "The Name and the Game: Unequal Exchange and the Historiographic Marketplace," in *Microhistory and the Lost Peoples of Europe*, ed. Edward Muir (Baltimore, MD: Johns Hopkins University Press, 1991), 3.

25. Beverley Southgate, *History Meets Fiction* (New York: Routledge, 2009), 76. See also Ginzburg, "Microhistory," 24.

26. Binne De Haan and Konstantin Mierau, *Microhistory and the Picaresque Novel: A First Exploration into Commensurable Perspectives* (Newcastle upon Tyne: Cambridge Scholars Publishers, 2014), 10.

27. This conclusion does not ignore the work of historians such as Mohammed Kenbib, Mohammed Hatimi, and Jamaâ Baïda, who each work on a specific aspect of Moroccan Jewish history.

28. Mohammed Kenbib, ed., *Du Protectorat à l'indépendance: Problématique du temps présent* (Rabat: Publication of the Faculty of Literatures and Human Sciences, 2006), 8.

29. Southgate, *History Meets Fiction*, 37.

30. Southgate, *History Meets Fiction*, 50.

31. Antoinette Burton, *Dwelling in the Archive: Women Writing House, Home, and History in Late Colonial India* (Oxford: Oxford University Press, 2003), 12.

32. Burton, *Dwelling in the Archive*, 20–21.

33. Burton, *Dwelling in the Archive*, 27–28.

34. Cooperants were young French professionals who, because of their Marxist or communist convictions, chose to live abroad to help formerly colonized nations rebuild themselves. Independent Morocco needed French cooperants to fill the void left by the French colonizers who were repatriated back to France. Even though these cooperation programs were the result of bilateral agreements, a significant number of those who decided to relocate to Morocco were either communists or socialists. Christine Daure-Serfaty was one of the teachers whose contracts were terminated before she married Abraham Serfaty, the co-founder of the Moroccan Marxist-Leninist Movement. Daure-Serfaty was famous for revealing important information about political detention in Morocco (discussed in detail in Chapter 4). Thus, it is possible that French cooperants' contracts were ended because the state did not want any foreign witnesses to its repressive methods during the Years of Lead. See Zakya Daoud, *Maroc: Les années de plomb, 1958–1988, chroniques d'une résistance* (Houilles, France: Éditions Manucius, 2007), 175.

35. Richard describes the entanglement of his life with Kinston's: "For this astonishing encounter to take place between me and Kinston, France had to be present in Morocco, and my father had to be assigned to Ouarzazate as a *coopérant*. In the meantime, Jews also had to go to Israel so that the Barūkhs would sell their house to my father" (Aït Moh, *Le Captif de Mabrouka*, 146).

36. Aït Moh, *Le Captif de Mabrouka*, 134.

37. Jacques Hassoun, *Les Contrebandiers de la mémoire* (Toulouse: Éditions érès, 2011), 16.

38. Joëlle Bahloul, *La Maison de mémoire: Ethnologie d'une demeure judéo-arabe en Algérie (1937–1961)* (Paris: Métaillé, 1992), 28.

39. Aït Moh, *Le Captif de Mabrouka*, 146.

40. Aït Moh, *Le Captif de Mabrouka*, 147.

41. Despite the fact that cities like Tangiers did not have a Jewish quarter, other cities, such as Fez (1438), Marrakesh, and Meknes had mellahs at different times in their history. In "each of these locations, the impetus for relocating the Jews from the religiously mixed neighborhoods of the medina to a separate, walled quarter, and the mellah's subsequent integration into the life of the city had much to do with local circumstances and immediate exigencies and relatively little to do with defined Islamic precepts as such." Emily Gottreich, "Rethinking the 'Islamic City' from the Perspective of Jewish Space," *Jewish Social Studies* 11, no. 1 (Fall 2004): 7. See also

Mohammed Kenbib, "Études et recherches sur les Juifs du Maroc: Observations et réflexions générales," *Hespéris-Tamuda* 51, no. 2 (2016): 30.

42. Tazi, *Anā al-mansī*, 25.

43. Tazi, *Anā al-mansī*, 125.

44. Victor Malka, *La Mémoire brisée des Juifs du Maroc* (Paris: Editions Entente, 1978), 11–12.

45. Malka, *La Mémoire brisée*, 11–12.

46. William G. Hoskins, *The Making of the English Landscape* (London: Hodder and Stoughton, 1955), 14.

47. See Maoz Azaryahu's "The Politics of Commemorative Street Renaming: Berlin 1945–1948," *Journal of Historical Geography* 37, no. 4 (2011): 483–92, and id., "Street Names and Political Identity: The Case of East Berlin," *Journal of Contemporary History* 21, no. 4 (1986): 581–604.

48. Luanga A. Kasanga, "Odonymic Changes in Central Pretoria: Representation, Identity and Textual Construction of Place," *International Journal of the Sociology of Language* 234 (2015): 27–45.

49. Tazi, *Anā al-mansī*, 216.

50. Kably, *Histoire du Maroc*, 712.

51. Quoted in Chris Gosden and Jon G. Hather, eds., *The Prehistory of Food: Appetites for Change* (New York: Routledge, 2004), 230.

52. Gottreich has also written against the assumption that the mellah was a closed space. She specifically underlines the shared festivities and the various ways in which this place was frequented by Muslims and Jews. See Gottreich, "Rethinking the 'Islamic City'," 122; see also Simon Lévy, *Essais d'histoire* (Rabat: Centre Tarik Ibn Zyad, 2001), 38.

53. Tazi, *Anā al-mansī*, 92.

54. Tazi, *Anā al-mansī*, 56.

55. Chapter 3 uses the concepts of intimacy and citizenship as community-building to delve more into memories of intimacy and their significance in accounting for loss of Muslim-Jewish life in Morocco.

56. Miliani, *Casanfa*, 86.

57. Miliani, *Casanfa*, 88.

58. Miliani, *Casanfa*, 90.

59. Miliani, *Casanfa*, 95.

60. Michel Foucault, "Of Other Spaces: Utopias and Heterotopias," trans. Jay Miskowiec, originally published in *Architecture/Mouvement/Continuité* (October 1984), accessed October 22, 2017, http://web.mit.edu/allanmc/www/foucault1.pdf.

61. Tazi, *Anā al-mansī*, 96.

62. The bar is also very central to the storyline of Hassan Benjelloun's successful film, *Where Are You Going Moshé?* The film takes place in Boujaad, in central Morocco, right around the time when Moroccan Jews were leaving the country *en masse*. As Jews leave, Mustapha, the Muslim owner of the only bar in town, has

to fight to save his bar from political machinations of the city council, especially after the death of his French business partner. Because Moroccan law prohibits the opening of bars for Muslims, Mustapha engages in all sorts of tricks and stratagems to keep one Jew in town. The bar itself proves to be a space where Jewish-Muslim relations were initiated and solidified.

63. Miliani, *Casanfa*, 96.

64. Miliani, *Casanfa*, 247–48.

65. Saïd Ghallab, "Les Juifs vont en enfer," *Les Temps Modernes* 229 (June 1965): 2252.

66. Daoud, *Maroc: Les années de plomb*, 100; Abdallah Laroui, *Le Maroc et Hassan II: Un témoignage* (Cap-Rouge , Québec: Les Presses Inter Universitaires, 2010), 56.

67. Quoted in "They Were Promised the Sea Trailer," dir. Kathy Wazana, *Vimeo*, September 8, 2016, 01:25–01:44, https://vimeo.com/ondemand/theywerepromisedthesea/169703595. Translation from the trailer.

68. Miliani, *Casanfa*, 249.

69. Miliani, *Casanfa*, 249.

70. Aourid, *Cintra*, 170.

71. Aourid, *Cintra*, 15.

72. Aourid, *Cintra*, 15.

73. Aourid, *Cintra*, 71.

74. Aourid, *Cintra*, 141.

75. Aourid, *Cintra*, 142.

76. Aourid, *Cintra*, 23.

77. Tazi, *Anā al-mansī*, 134.

78. Tazi, *Anā al-mansī*, 142.

79. Carlos de Nesry, *Les Israélites marocains à l'heure du choix* (Tanger : Éditions Internationales, 1958).

80. Southgate, *History Meets Fiction*, 44.

81. Janet Donohoe, *Remembering Places: A Phenomenological Study of the Relationship between Memory and Place* (Lanham, MD: Lexington Books, 2014), xii.

82. Donohoe, *Remembering Places*, xiii.

83. Robert R. Archibald, *A Place to Remember: Using History to Build Community* (New York: Rowman Altamira, 1999), 16.

84. Archibald, *Place to Remember*, 12.

85. An important aspect of the works that I analyze is the connection made between political repression and Jewish emigration. Lital Levy already referred to this in a recent article through the example of ʿAbd al-Qādir Shāwi's *al-Sāḥa al-sharafiyya*. See Lital Levy, "The Arab Jew Debates: Media, Culture, Politics, History," *Journal of Levantine Studies* 7, no. 1 (2017): 187.

86. Miliani, *Casanfa*, 245.

87. Binmanṣūr says that "time had not come yet to reveal many things" (Aourid, *Cintra*, 217).

88. Edward Erwin, *The Freud Encyclopedia: Theory, Therapy, and Culture* (New York: Routledge, 2002), 4.

89. Aït Moh, *Le Captif de Mabrouka*, 146.

90. Aourid, *Cintra*, 257.

91. Several of the novels under study feature characters who are endowed with supernatural powers. For instance, Hannū in Abdelkarim Jouaiti's *Zaghārid al-mawt*, Sāmī in Kamal El Khamlichi's *Ḥārith al-nisyān*, and Ibn 'Amitha'īl Zāz in *Anā al-mansī* straddle two different worlds—the "real" and the mythical—which complicates this literature. Although I only focus on Ibn 'Amitha'īl Zāz in *Anā al-mansī* and al-Mūtshū in *Cintra* in this analysis, the conclusions drawn here also apply to the other novels.

92. Renate Lachmann, "Cultural Memory and the Role of Literature," *European Review* 12, no. 2 (2004): 173.

93. The character of Hannū in *Zaghārid al-mawt* is one hundred years old, which allows her to bear witness to the transformations that take place in the lives of Jews and Muslims in Beni-Mellah.

94. Tazi, *Anā al-mansī*, 15–16.

95. Tazi, *Anā al-mansī*, 16.

96. Tazi, *Anā al-mansī*, 15.

97. Ruth M. Van Dyke and Susan E. Alcock, eds., *Archaeologies of Memory* (Malden, MA: Blackwell, 2003), 3.

98. Tazi, *Anā al-mansī*, 224.

99. Aourid, *Cintra*, 83–84.

100. Aourid, *Cintra*, 89.

3. Jewish-Muslim Intimacy and the History of a Lost Citizenship

1. Kamal El Khamlichi, *Ḥārith al-nisyān* (Rabat: Kamal El Khamlichi, 2003).

2. For a detailed history of the UIA, see Michael M. Laskier, *The Alliance Israélite Universelle and the Jewish Communities of Morocco, 1862–1962* (Albany: SUNY series in Modern Jewish Literature and Culture, 1984).

3. See Carlos de Nesry's books: *Le Juif de Tanger et le Maroc* (Tanger: Éditions Internationales, 1956) and *Les Israélites marocains à l'heure du choix* (Tanger: Éditions Internationales, 1958).

4. Jamaâ Baïda, "The Emigration of Moroccan Jews, 1948–1956," in *Jewish Culture and Society in North Africa*, ed. Emily Benichou Gottreich and Daniel J. Schroeter (Bloomington: Indiana University Press, 2011), 322–33.

5. Baïda, "The Emigration of Moroccan Jews," 322–33.

6. Michael M. Laskier. "Jewish Emigration from Morocco to Israel: Government Policies and the Position of International Jewish Organizations, 1949–56," *Middle Eastern Studies* 25, no. 3 (1989): 323.

7. Abdelmajid Kaddouri, Abdelkader Gangai, and Kacem Marghata, *'Abd Allāh al-'Arawī: al-Ḥadātha wa-as'ilat al-tārīkh* (Casablanca: Manshūrāt Kullīyat al-Ādāb wa-al-'Ulūm al-Insāniyya Bin-Msīk, 2007), 184.

8. For more details, see Yigal Bin Nun's two articles, "La Quête d'un compromis pour l'évacuation des Juifs du Maroc," *Pardès* 1 (2003): 75–98, and "Les Causes politiques et sociales du départ des Juifs du Maroc, 1956–1966," in *Migrations maghrébines comparées: Genre, ethnicité, religions: France-Québec, de 1945 à nos jours*, ed. Mireille Calle-Gruber et al. (Paris: Riveneuve éditions, 2015), 39–62, as well as Robert Assaraf, *Mohammed V et les Juifs du Maroc à l'époque de Vichy* (Paris: Plon, 1999), 19. This does not ignore the fact that Moroccan historians have done some crucial work on Jews before the Protectorate. See Chapter 5 of this book for a detailed analysis of this issue.

9. See Ahmed El Madini, "al-yahūdī 'al-mansī' fī mir'āt al-riwāya al-maghribiyya," *Al-Ḥayāt*, January 25, 2016.

10. Synchronous intimacy, a concept I develop more later in the chapter, refers to the intimacy that happens as the two communities live in the same place and share the same temporality. Unlike the imagined or delayed intimacy that we find in novels, synchronous intimacy allowed Jews and Muslims to live with and appreciate each other as their lives unfold together in the same place.

11. Harry Blatterer, "Intimacy as Freedom: Friendship, Gender and Everyday Life," *Thesis Eleven* 132, no. 1 (2016): 63.

12. Blatterer, "Intimacy as Freedom," 63.

13. Lynn Jamieson, "Boundaries of Intimacy," in *Families in Society: Boundaries and Relationships*, ed. Linda McKie and Sarah Cunningham-Burley (Bristol: Policy Press, 2005), 190.

14. Harry T. Reis and Phillip Shaver, "Intimacy as an Interpersonal Process," *Handbook of Personal Relationships* 24, no. 3 (1988): 385.

15. Anthony Giddens, *The Transformation of Intimacy: Sexuality, Love and Eroticism in Modern Societies* (Cambridge: Polity Press, 1992), 3.

16. Reis and Shaver, "Intimacy as an Interpersonal Process," 384.

17. This statistic is based on my reading of the different numbers contained in Mohammed Kably's *Histoire du Maroc: Réactualisation et synthèse* (Rabat: Publications de l'Institut Royal pour la Recherche sur l'Histoire du Maroc, 2012), 710–12.

18. Aomar Boum, *Memories of Absence: How Muslims Remember Jews in Morocco* (Stanford, CA: Stanford University Press, 2013).

19. Reis and Shaver, "Intimacy as an Interpersonal Process," 367–75.

20. Joëlle Bahloul, *La Maison de mémoire: Ethnologie d'une demeure judéo-arabe en Algérie (1937–1961)* (Paris: Métaillé, 1992), 156.

21. The same argument underlies Boum's *Memories of Absence*.

22. Thomas H. Marshall, "Citizenship and Social Class," in *Inequality and Society*, ed. Jeff Manza and Michael Sauder (New York: W. W. Norton and Co., 2009), 149.

23. Richard Bellamy, *Citizenship: A Very Short Introduction* (Oxford: Oxford University Press, 2008), 13.

24. Paul B. Clarke, *Deep Citizenship* (Chicago: Pluto Press, 1996), 1.

25. Ibrahim Hariri, *Shāmma aw Shtrīt* (Casablanca: Afriqia al-Sharq, 2013), 7, 10.

26. Hariri, *Shāmma aw Shtrīt*, 7.

27. Hariri, *Shāmma aw Shtrīt*, 10.
28. Hariri, *Shāmma aw Shtrīt*, 45.
29. Hariri, *Shāmma aw Shtrīt*, 53.
30. Hariri, *Shāmma aw Shtrīt*, 78–79.
31. Hariri, *Shāmma aw Shtrīt*, 80.
32. Hariri, *Shāmma aw Shtrīt*, 80.
33. Hariri, *Shāmma aw Shtrīt*, 68.
34. Trevisan Semi and Sekkat Hatim point out the difficulty of finding people who were born in Jewish-Muslim households, especially those willing to be interviewed. Emanuela Trevisan Semi and Hanane Sekkat Hatimi, *Mémoire et représentations des Juifs au Maroc: Les voisins absents de Meknès* (Paris: Publisud, 2011), 197.
35. Hariri, *Shāmma aw Shtrīt*, 80.
36. For a description of the events of 1965 in the context of social movements in Morocco, see Mostafa Bouaziz, "Mouvements sociaux et mouvement national au Maroc: De la liaison organique à l'amorce du disengagement," in *Émeutes et mouvements sociaux au Maghreb: Perspective comparée*, ed. Didier Le Saout and Marguérite Rollinde (Paris: Karthala, 1999), 67–76.
37. El Khamlichi, *Ḥārith al-nisyān*, 26.
38. El Khamlichi, *Ḥārith al-nisyān*, 260; this translation of Kafka is from Philip Boehm, *Letters to Milena* (New York: Shocken, 1990), 217.
39. El Khamlichi, *Ḥārith al-nisyān*, 261.
40. Hariri, *Shāmma aw Shtrīt*, 126.
41. Hariri, *Shāmma aw Shtrīt*, 127. Although I am aware that this is a very simplistic binary that does not take into consideration the many shades of grey that exist in this situation, I am quoting it in this context to also show how a writer from today's Morocco has chosen to depict the conflict.
42. Boum, *Memories of Absence*; Semi and Hatimi, *Mémoire et représentations des Juifs*.
43. Semi and Hatimi, *Mémoire et représentations*, 22.
44. Abdelkébir Khatibi and Jacques Hassoun. *Le Même livre* (Paris: Éditions de l'Éclat, 1985), 106–07.
45. For a more robust discussion of these ideas, see Brahim El Guabli, "Textual Traces: Khatibi and His Jews," *PMLA/Publications of the Modern Language Association of America* 137, no. 2 (2022): 347–54, doi:10.1632/S0030812922000165.
46. Khatibi and Hassoun, *Le Même livre*, 108.
47. Abdelkarim Jouaiti, *Zaghārīd al-mawt* (Al-Jazā'ir: Manshūrāt al-Ikhtilāf, 2015), 125.
48. Abdellah Hammoudi, "Le Don entre juifs et musulmans: Ou comment concilier les identités opposées," *Revue Internationale d'Anthropologie Culturelle & Sociale* (Hors-Série) (2016): 91–106. Hammoudi bases his new reading of Mimouna on a text from the 1950s authored by Elias Harrus, a Moroccan Jew from the region of Demnat, and an older manuscript by an unknown nineteenth-century author discovered by the historian Aḥmad al-Tawfīq.

49. Hammoudi, "Le Don entre juifs et musulmans," 95.

50. Hammoudi, "Le Don entre juifs et musulmans," 101.

51. Hammoudi, "Le Don entre juifs et musulmans," 101.

52. Shimon Ballas, "Iyya," in *Keys to the Garden: New Israeli Writing*, ed. Ammiel Alcalay, trans. Susan Einbinder (San Francisco, CA: City Lights Books, 1996), 69–99.

53. Lital Levy, "Self and the City: Literary Representations of Jewish Baghdad," *Prooftexts* 26, no. 1 (2006): 187.

54. Joseph Lévy, "Témoignages d'un militant juif marocain," in *Juifs du Maroc: Identité et Dialogue* (Grenoble: Éditions la Pensée Sauvage, 1980), 281.

55. Daniel Rivet, *Le Maghreb à l'épreuve de la colonisation* (Paris: Hachette Littératures, 2003), 307.

56. Bahloul, *La Maison de mémoire*, 146.

57. Hariri, *Shāmma aw Shtrīt*, 120.

58. Hariri, *Shāmma aw Shtrīt*, 124.

59. Serfaty was the founder of the Moroccan Marxist-Leninist revolutionary movement in 1970. He was arrested in 1974, sentenced to life in prison for wanting to depose the monarchy, and spent seventeen years in jail before his deportation to France in 1991.

60. Abraham Serfaty and Mikhaël Elbaz, *L'Insoumis: Juifs, Marocains et rebelles* (Paris: Desclée de Brouwer, 2001), 87.

61. See Lévy's critical comments on Mohammed Hatimi's paper in Mohamed Kably and Abderrahmane El Moudden, eds., *Al-Maghrib wa-al-zaman al-rāhin* (Rabat: Manshūrāt al-Ma'had al-Malakī li-al-Baḥth fī Tārīkh al-Maghrib, 2013), 51–52.

62. Frantz Fanon, *A Dying Colonialism* (New York: Grove Books, 1956), 154–57.

63. See Chapter 2 for a detailed summary and additional discussion.

64. It is important to observe the absence of the avant-garde thinker Abraham Serfaty from the list of Jewish intellectuals to whom the novel is dedicated. Perhaps Serfaty was too confrontational with the palace to deserve a place in Aourid's dedication.

65. Hassan Aourid, *Cintra* (Rabat: Tūsnā, 2016), 5.

66. Aourid, *Cintra*, 5.

67. Simon Lévy, "Professor Simon Levy," in *al-Maghrib wa-al-zaman al-rāhin*, ed. Mohammed Kably and Abderrahmane El Moudden (Rabat: Manshūrāt al-Ma'had al-Malakī li-al-Baḥth fī Tārīkh al-Maghrib, 2013), 51.

68. Aourid, *Cintra*, 202.

69. See Chapter 5 for a longer discussion of Ayache's role in the Moroccan historiographical school.

70. Jouaiti, *Zaghārīd al-mawt*, 230.

71. Mohammad Ezzeddine Tazi, *Anā al-mansī* (Casablanca: Al-Markaz al-Thaqāfī al-'Arabī, 2015), 126.

72. Tazi, *Anā al-mansī*, 126.

73. Tazi, *Anā al-mansī*, 127.

74. Tazi, *Anā al-mansī*, 189.

75. Tazi, *Anā al-mansī*, 189.

76. The novel uses both Berber and Amazigh in this order.

77. Tazi, *Anā al-mansī*, 147.

78. The promulgation of this decree, known in Arabic as *al-ẓahīr al-barbarī*, was part of the French Berber Policy, but Imazighen (Amazigh people) had no say in its conception or implementation. Nevertheless, its existence served Arab-Islamic nationalism's plan to exclude Imazighen in the post-independence period. This historical aspect of this decree has since been challenged. See Muḥammad Munīb, *al-Ẓahīr al-barbarī akbar ukdhūba fī tārīkh al-maghrib al-muʿāṣir* (Rabat: Dār Abī Rāqrāq, 2002); Brahim El Guabli, "Where is Amazigh Studies?," *The Journal of North African Studies*, 1–8.

79. Lawrence Rosen, *Two Arabs, a Berber, and a Jew: Entangled Lives in Morocco* (Chicago: University of Chicago Press, 2015), 249.

80. Aourid, *Cintra*, 223.

81. Hariri, *Shāmma aw Shtrīt*, 103.

82. Hariri, *Shāmma aw Shtrīt*, 119.

83. See Driss Miliani, *Casanfa* (al-Iskandarīyya: Dār al-'Ayn li-al-Nashr, 2016).

4. Making Tazmamart a Transnational Other-Archive

1. MP Faiṣal al-Khaṭīb, quoted in Ahmed Marzouki, *Tazmamārt: Al-zinzānah raqm 10* (Casablanca: Editions Tarik, 2001), 222.

2. Mohammed Raïss, *Min al-Skhirāt ilā Tazmamārt tadhkiratu dhahāb wa iyyāb ilā al-jaḥīm* (Casablanca: Afriqia al-Sharq, 2001).

3. The rich cultural production about Tazmamart has generated an important methodological question for me regarding the appropriate approach to study these disparate materials, which include novels, memoirs, films, poetry, and newspaper articles. My attempt to resolve this methodological question has led me to adopt a deeply comparative approach that puts the different genres and media in which Tazmamart is other-archived in dialogue with each other. This trans-genre and trans-media approach reveals the depth and breadth of Tazmamart's other-archives as well as this prison's transnational impact. Instead of approaching the diversity of cultural production about Tazmamart as a handicap, I decided to tap into its potential as a multidimensional experience that can enable newer and complex ways of reading and theorizing enforced disappearance and their myriad archives.

In addition to countless TV shows, newspaper articles, and online stories about Tazmamart, this place has become famous for the memoirs and novels that recount the experiences of its survivors and their dead compatriots. Among the memoirs, I found: Ahmed Marzouki, *Tazmamart: Cellule 10* (Casablanca: Tarik Editions, 2001); Raïs, *Min al-Skhirāt ilā Tazmamārt*; Abdelhak Serhane, *Kabazal: Les emmurés de Tazmamart* (Casablanca: Tarik Editions, 2004); Ahmed and Kalima El Ouafi, *Opération Boraq F5: 16 Août 1972, l'attaque du Boeing royal* (Casablanca:

Tarik Editions, 2004); Driss T. Chberreq, *Le Train fou: Mémoires d'un rescapé de Tazmamart* (Rabat: al M'ārif al-Jadīda, 2014); id., *Le Suicide de Mimoun: Drame vécu au bagne de Tazmamart* (Rabat: Imprimerie al M'ārif al-Jadīda, 2015). Fictionalizations of Tazmamart to date include Tahar Ben Jelloun, *Cette aveuglante absence de lumière* (Paris: Seuil, 2001); Abdelhak Serhane, *La Chienne de Tazmamart* (Paris: Éditions Paris-Méditerranée, 2001); Belkassem Belouchi, *Rapt de voix* (Casablanca: Afrique Orient, 2004); Radwa Ashour, *Farag* (Cairo: Dār al-Shurūq, 2008); Youssef Fadel, *Ṭā'ir azraq nādir yuḥalliqu ma'ī* (Beirut: Dār al-Ādāb, 2013); for a detailed study of these works and more see: Brahim El Guabli, "Joint Authorship and Preface Writing Practices as Translation in post-'Years of Lead' Morocco," in *The Routledge Handbook of Translation and Activism*, ed. Rebecca Ruth Gould and Kayvan Tahmasebian (New York: Routledge, 2020), 237–57.

4. There is much to be said about the tumultuous relations between Morocco and France in the 1970s and the 1980s, and the ways the ebb and flow in their relations impacted their management of human rights dossiers. However, I prefer to focus on non-state actors and their creation of other-archives that were scandalous for both Morocco and France. French language is central to any serious debate about how the world found out about human rights violations in Morocco. By looking at how French, Arabic, and even English work across genres and time to sustain the memory of Tazmamart, I furnish a new approach that places Tazmamart in a complex web of connections locally, globally, and linguistically. This approach reveals the myriad possibilities of theorization of archives through the rich cultural production about Tazmamart.

5. See *Zamane* magazine's editorial "Ces Français amis du Maroc," *Zamane*, Sept. 4, 2019, https://zamane.ma/fr/ces-francais-amis-du-maroc/. Hayat Berrada-Bousta discusses the importance of these synergies for the release of prisoners and the improvement of human rights conditions in Morocco in Hayat Berrada-Bousta, "Soulèvements au Maroc et engagement des marocains en France," *Migrations Société* 143, no. 5 (2012): 139–54.

6. I use "survivors" in this context to refer to both prisoners and their family members. While prisoners experienced enforced disappearance inside prison, their families were also disappeared in society.

7. Tahar Ben Jelloun, *This Blinding Absence of Light*, trans. Linda Coverdale (New York: New Press, 2002); Youssef Fadel, *A Rare Blue Bird Flies with Me*, trans. Jonathan Smolin (Cairo: AUC Press, 2016); Radwa Ashour, *Blue Lorries*, trans. Barbara Romaine (Doha: Bloomsbury Qatar Foundation Publishing, 2014).

8. Although the cadets and their instructors continue to deny any prior knowledge of the coup of 1971, Raïs does mention that a French officer who was working in the military base at the time warned them—albeit jokingly—that they were going to carry out a coup d'état (*Min al-Skhirāt ilā Tazmamārt*, 17).

9. Aziz BineBine, for instance, realized his implication in the coup after the fact. He wrote that "I henceforth have a clear idea about the events: we participated in

an apparently failed coup d'état." Aziz BineBine, *Tazmamort: Dix-huit ans dans le bagne de Hassan II* (Paris: Denoël, 2009), 25.

10. Zakya Daoud, *Les Années Lamalif* (Casablanca: Tarik Editions, 2007), 220–21; italicized in the original.

11. In 2000, two independent weekly magazines *Le Journal* and *al-Ṣaḥīfa* published a letter proving the involvement of the National Union of Popular Forces' leadership in the 1972 coup d'état. Because the letter was published during what was called the "alternance government" under the helm of *al-Ittiḥād al-Ishtirākī li-al-quwwāt al-sha'biyya* (the Popular Union of Popular Forces), then–prime minister Abderrahame El Youssoufi ordered the magazines to be closed forever and their issues to be recalled from the kiosks. Tazmamart survivor Ahmed El Ouafi also reports his conversations with Amekrane about his connections with opposition members, such as Aït Kaddour, Dr. El Khattabi, and Fakih El Basri. See El Ouafi, *Opération Boraq*, 86–87.

12. Amnesty International, *Report of an Amnesty International Mission to the Kingdom of Morocco: 10–13 February 1981* (Nottingham: Amnesty International Publications, 1982), 11.

13. Driss El Yazami and Bernard Wallon, *Le Livre blanc sur les droits de l'homme au Maroc* (Paris: Études et Documentation Internationales, 1991), 43.

14. Christine Daure-Serfaty, *Letter from Morocco* (East Lansing: Michigan State University Press, 2003), 24.

15. El Yazami and Wallon, *Le Livre blanc*, 44.

16. Marzouki, *al-Zinzāna raqm 10*, 55. In Marzouki's analysis, the judge was not qualified to chair such a trial, which required a deep understanding of military discipline (Marzouki, *al-Zinzāna raqm 10*, 48). BineBine also blames the vindictiveness of the judge against someone in his family (probably his father) for his unjustified ten-year jail term (*Tazmamort*, 34).

17. El Yazami and Wallon, *Le Livre blanc*, 44.

18. The four prisoners who were kidnapped but not transferred to Tazmamart were Harrouch Akka, Captain Mohamed Chellat, Lieutenant-Colonel Mohamed Ababou, and Ahmed Mzirek. Their whereabouts remain unknown even today. See Amnesty International, "The 'Disappeared' in Morocco: Case Studies," April 1993, https://www.amnesty.org/download/Documents/188000/mde290041993en.pdf.

19. Rabéa Bennouna reports the words of the Kenitra prison guard: "The prisoners are not here anymore. They were taken to an unknown destination. We cannot give you any information [about their whereabouts]. Never come back here again. The [prison] director does not want to see anyone wandering around the prison gates. Please be understanding, because if you stay here, we will be punished for it. Go away!! May God help you!" Rabéa Bennouna, *Tazmamart côté femme: Témoignage* (Casablanca: Addar Al Alamia Lil Kitab, 2003), 48.

20. The *Frontistes* refers to members of *Ilā al-Amām*, the March 23 Movement, and *Li-nakhdum al-Sha'b* (Let's Serve the People) who sought to lay the foundation for the Moroccan proletariat's revolution. In their notorious trial in 1977, "almost

twenty-five centuries" of jail time were distributed among the Frontiste detainees just for daring to dream of a revolution in Morocco. See Aziz Mouride, *On affame bien les rats* (Casablanca: Tarik, 2000), 31.

21. While they are not the only books about this era, this section of the chapter draws extensively on Christine Daure-Serfaty's book *Tazmamart: Une prison de la mort au Maroc* (Paris: Editions Stock, 1992) (here 69, 128–29), and Abraham Serfaty and Christine Daure-Serfaty's *La Mémoire de l'autre* (Paris: Stock, 1992). Even though some Tazmamart narratives, like Hachad's and El Ouafi's, downplay her role in liberating them, others, mainly Raïs and Marzouki, foreground her instrumental role in their release. For instance, Marzouki entitles the final chapter of his memoirs "Le Retour de Christine Daure-Serfaty" ["The Return of Christine Daure-Serfaty"] (*Tazmamart: Cellule 10*, 371–76). In this chapter, Marzouki acknowledges that Daure-Serfaty edited and helped him publish his story about Faraj in *Les Temps Modernes* (as Hananou, "Une Histoire de Tazamamart," *Temps Modernes*, no. 565–66 [1993]: 13–27; *Tazmamart: Cellule 10*, 373).

22. Daure-Serfaty, *Tazmamart*, 105.

23. Translated by the author into Arabic as *Tazmamart: Al-zinzānah raqm 10*. Interview with Ahmed Marzouki, "Al-Marzūqī: Hādhihi lughatunā bi-tazmamart wa hakadhā tasabbaba yasārī bāriz fi ikhtiṭāfī, al-'Umq al-Maghribi," posted by "al-'Umq al-Maghribī," January 4, 2018, YouTube video, 11:25, https://www.youtube.com/watch?v=kgr9XProoPw, at 04:00–04:52. Daure-Serfaty has also underlined the trans-Mediterranean impact of Moroccan political parties' silence on their French partners. The French left dismissed the existence of Tazmamart because, as they responded to Daure-Serfaty, their Moroccan colleagues would have told them about it if it existed (Daure-Serfaty, *Tazmamart*, 128).

24. Michael T. Taussig, *Defacement, Public Secrecy, and the Labor of the Negative* (Stanford, CA: Stanford University Press, 1999), 6.

25. Taussig, *Defacement*, 6.

26. Almost all the testimonial works that I have read indicate that leaders of political parties, administrative officials, and army cadres were made aware of the existence of Tazmamart. This awareness was crippling because it made an open secret a tool of deterrence against any adventurous moves to overthrow the monarchy.

27. Avery Gordon, *Ghostly Matters: Haunting and the Sociological Imagination* (Minneapolis: University of Minnersota Press, 2008), 72.

28. Daure-Serfaty, *Tazmamart*, 127.

29. Daure-Serfaty, *Tazmamart*, 127.

30. See Lucila Edelman, Diana Kordon, and Darío Lagos, "Transmission of Trauma: The Argentine Case," in *International Handbook of Multigenerational Legacies of Trauma*, ed. Yael Danieli (Boston, MA: Springer, 1998), 448.

31. Daure-Serfaty, *Tazmamart*, 128–29.

32. See Bennouna's *Tazmamart côté femme* and Aïda Hachad's section in Serhane, *Kabazal*.

33. Serhane, *Kabazal*, 253.

34. Amnesty International, *Report*, 33.

35. Daure-Serfaty, *Tazmamart*, 73–74.

36. Daure-Serfaty, *Tazmamart*, 128.

37. Daure-Serfaty, *Tazmamart*, 97–99. One such example is Aziz BineBine's father. Mohamed BineBine was Hassan II's personal jester and, upon finding out that his son Aziz was involved in the coup d'état, he disowned him in front of the king. Marzouki and Aïda Hachad also report that some families refused to be part of the support network for family members detained in Tazmamart. For the anecdote about Mohamed BineBine disowning his son Aziz, see Daure-Serfaty, *Tazmamart*, 100.

38. See El Ouafi's and Hachad's memoirs for samples of these letters.

39. Daure-Serfaty, *Tazmamart*, 65.

40. For instance, the CBRM's January 1985 newsletter reminds its readers that "it has been eleven years since the soldiers of the Skhirat trial have been disappeared to the jail of Tazmamart or beyond in 1973." See François Della Sudda, "1985," *Bulletin 67*, December 1984–January 1985, 1.

41. An instance demonstrating the power of these ties to embarrass Hassan II's regime in France happened during Nass El Ghiwane's concert at the prestigious Olympia Theater in 1976. At the very start of this legendary band's concert, members of the audience started chanting in unison: "Where are they? Where are they? The kidnapped children of the people." See Nass El Ghiwane, "Soirée Nass El Ghiwane 1976," posted by "Fī dhākira [sic] al-maghribiya," February 23, 2016, YouTube video, 1:13:37, https://www.youtube.com/watch?v=7M3DO3vR23E [0:07–1:00]. In *Tazmamart*, Daure-Serfaty expounds on how information from Tazmamart circulated between Morocco and France. She explains that strangers would show up at her house to provide information about the soldiers. This information was crucial to her endeavor to spread knowledge about Tazmamart (74–76).

42. For information about Moroccan associations in France, see Berrada-Bousta, "Soulèvements au Maroc."

43. Marzouki, *al-Zinzānah raqm 10*, 321. Of course, this is an entire movement, but individuals, such as Daure-Serfaty and Della Sudda, who both were teachers in Morocco in the 1960s, occupied prominent positions in the defense of human rights in Morocco.

44. Daure-Serfaty, *Tazmamart*, 76.

45. In its 1982 report, Amnesty International revealed that it "has received disturbing information concerning the whereabouts, conditions and fate of a number of these prisoners. At least 58 appear to be held in a secret detention center in Tazmamert [*sic*], and are completely isolated from the outside world. They are permitted no contact and no correspondence with their families. The information indicates that the sanitary and medical conditions in the detention centre are totally inadequate." Amnesty International, *Report*, May 1982, 33.

46. Gilles Perrault, *Notre ami le roi* (Paris: Gallimard, 1990), 267–78.

47. Comités de Lutte Contre la Répression au Maroc, "Les Détenus militaires: Tazmamart le 5 août 1980," *Bulletin* 42 (April 1982), 1.

48. Perrault, *Notre ami le roi*, 277.

49. Amnesty International, "Le Maroc, vous connaissez?" *Comités de Lutte Contre la Répression au Maroc*, June 1982, 15.

50. While the circuits through which these writings were smuggled from the prison camp to families have been elucidated and written about by the survivors and their families in their memoirs, the ways in which the letters were smuggled abroad has not been revealed. Additionally, the sporadic nature of correspondence between the disappeared soldiers and their families impacted communication. Some of these letters remained without answer. However, the letters reached the French media as well as Amnesty International's offices, which allowed them to serve as a basis for pressure on the Moroccan government.

51. Edwy Plenel, "Christine Daure-Serfaty (1926–2014): Résistante et Juste, entre France et Maroc," *Europe Solidaire Sans Frontières*, May 27, 2014, http://www.europe-solidaire.org/spip.php?article32044.

52. Abdallah Laroui, *Le Maroc et Hassan II: Un témoignage* (Québec: Presses Inter Universitaires, 2005), 160. Laroui here refers to the fact that the evening news is widely watched in France, which allowed the voice of the Moroccan political detainees to potentially reach every French home.

53. Laroui, *Le Maroc*, 149.

54. Laroui, *Le Maroc*, 149.

55. Abderrahman Nouda, "Pourquoi Christine Daure Serfaty [*sic*] mérite la considération du peuple," *LivresChaud* (blog), June 2014, https://livreschauds.files.wordpress.com/2014/06/article-pourquoi-christine-daure-serfaty-mc3a9rite-la-considc3a9ration-du-peuple-marocain-par-a-nouda.pdf; Berrada-Bousta makes a similar argument within a larger context of mobilization for human rights in "Soulèvements au Maroc," 144–45.

56. Daure-Serfaty, *Tazmamart*, 106.

57. Daure-Serfaty, *Tazmamart*, 107.

58. Serfaty and Daure-Serfaty, *La Mémoire de l'autre*, 304.

59. Serfaty and Daure-Serfaty, *La Mémoire de l'autre*, 306.

60. The 1992 edition of *Notre ami le roi* lists Daure-Serfaty as a collaborator in the writing of the book, in belated recognition of her information-gathering efforts.

61. Plenel, "Christine Daure-Serfaty."

62. Human Rights Watch, *Human Rights Watch World Report 1992—Morocco and Western Sahara*, January 1, 1992, available at: https://www.refworld.org/docid/467fca5bc.html.

63. Serfaty and Daure-Serfaty, *La Mémoire de l'autre*, 313.

64. Serfaty and Daure-Serfaty, *La Mémoire de l'autre*, 315; Daure-Serfaty, *Tazmamart*, 141.

65. Serfaty and Daure-Serfaty, *La Mémoire de l'autre*, 315; Daure-Serfaty, *Tazmamart*, 141.

66. Daure-Serfaty, *Tazmamart*, 54–55, 124–25.

67. Daure-Serfaty gives us a glimpse into this journey in discussing how the last letter from Tazmamart was made available in French: "a family gave it to a friend who typed it in the typing machine in Arabic with a lot of difficulty because of the illegible scribbles. I received it in Paris, and a Moroccan friend in Belgium translated it [into French] in three days. I urgently gave it to all those I met" (Daure-Serfaty, *Tazmamart*, 143).

68. See Bouchra Sidi Hida, *Mouvements sociaux et logiques d'acteurs: Les ONG de développement face à la mondialisation et à l'Etat au Maroc; L'altermondialisme marocain* (Louvain: Université catholique de Louvain, 2007), 23.

69. See Brahim El Guabli, "Intergenerational Trauma in Tazmamart Testimonial Literature and Docu-Testimonies," *Middle East—Topics & Arguments* 11 (Fall 2018): 120–30.

70. Jamāl al-Dīn ibn Manẓūr, *Lisān al-'Arab* (Beirut: Dar El Fikr for Printing Publishing and Distribution, 2015), II:181–83.

71. Although requirements differ from case to case, the witness is usually required to have "maturity, reason, memory, speech, and visual and audible perception, good character or justice (*'adala*), authenticity, manhood, and Islam." See Tarek Badawy, "Towards a Contemporary View of Islamic Criminal Procedures: A Focus on the Testimony of Witnesses," *Arab Law Quarterly* 23, no. 3 (2009): 289.

72. Susan Slyomovics, "The Moroccan Equity and Reconciliation Commission: The Promises of a Human Rights Archive," *The Arab Studies Journal* 24, no. 1 (2016): 18.

73. Shoshana Felman and Dauri Lob, *Testimony: Crises of Witnessing in Literature, Psychoanalysis, and History* (New York: Routledge, 1992), 3.

74. Ibn Manẓūr, *Lisān al-'Arab*, II:181–83.

75. Ḥuzal 'Abd al-Raḥīm, *al-Kitāba wa-al-sijn: Ḥiwārāt wa-nuṣūṣ* (Casablanca: Afrīqiā al-Sharq, 2008), 44.

76. Susan Slyomovics, "New Moroccan Publics: Prisons, Cemeteries and Human Remains," in *Knowledge, Authority and Change in Islamic Societies*, ed. Allen James Fromherz and Nadav Samin (Leiden: Brill, 2021), 143–44.

77. BineBine, *Tazmamort*, 59–66, 84–86, 104–5, 162, 178, 203–4.

78. Marzouki, *al-Zinzāna raqm 10*, 153.

79. Marzouki, *al-Zinzāna raqm 10*, 161.

80. Marzouki, *al-Zinzāna raqm 10*, 161.

81. Marzouki, *al-Zinzāna raqm 10*, 172.

82. Marzouki, *al-Zinzāna raqm 10*, 172.

83. Susan Slyomovics, *The Performance of Human Rights in Morocco* (Philadelphia: The University of Pennsylvania Press, 2005), 63.

84. Slyomovics, *The Performance of Human Rights*, 18.

85. Brahim El Guabli, "The Absent Perpetrators: Morocco's Failed Accountability, Tazmamart Literature and the Survivors' Testimony for their Jailers (1973–1991)," *Violence: An International Journal* 1 (2020): 88–92.

86. Marzouki, *al-Zinzāna raqm 10*, 74–89.

87. El Guabli, "The Absent Perpetrators," 92–94.

88. El Guabli, "The Absent Perpetrators," 93–94.

89. El Guabli, "Intergenerational Trauma in Tazmamart," 124.

90. El Guabli, "Intergenerational Trauma in Tazmamart," 123.

91. Bennouna, *Tazmamart côté femme*, 89.

92. Bennouna, *Tazmamart côté femme*, 89.

93. Serhane, *Kabazal*, 202.

94. Serhane, *Kabazal*, 267.

95. Aïda describes how a familiar person was put in charge of her surveillance and how she navigated the circumstance of being surveilled: "the officer in charge of my surveillance was part of military intelligence. Some people talked to me about him when I was still living on the military base. I pretended that I noticed nothing abnormal and continued to live my life as normal as it could be" (Serhane, *Kabazal*, 221).

96. Serhane, *Kabazal*, 243.

97. Serhane, *Kabazal*, 268.

98. M'barek Bouderka and Ahmed Chouki Benyoub, *Kadhālika kān: Mudhakkirāt min tajribat hay'at al-inṣāf wa-al-muṣālaḥa* (Casablanca: Dār al-Nashr al-Maghribiyya, 2017), 132.

99. ERC, *Final Report: Truth, Equity and Reconciliation* (Rabat: The Advisory Council on Human Rights Publications, 2009), 12.

100. Daure-Serfaty, *Tazmamart*, 73–74.

101. Gordon, *Ghostly Matters*, 124. I had this discussion with Abdellah Hammoudi at his house in Princeton, NJ, in December 2017. Laroui, *Le Maroc*, 158.

102. For a detailed study of *Cette aveuglante*'s circulation, prizes, translations, and sales numbers, see Brahim El Guabli, "Cette aveuglante absence de lumière: The Politics of Novelizing Human Rights Violations in the Former Colonizer's Language," *Francosphères* 5, no. 1 (2016): 59–80.

103. Ben Jelloun, *This Blinding*, 3.

104. Ben Jelloun, *This Blinding*, 3.

105. Ben Jelloun, *This Blinding*, 103–04.

106. Ben Jelloun, *This Blinding*, 178.

107. El Guabli, "Cette aveuglante," 64.

108. Sālima al-Mūshī, "al-Tarīq ilā hunāk: Tazmamārt al-khurūj mina al-hāwiyya wa-al-junūn," *Alriyadh*, October 1, 2009, http://www.alriyadh.com/463139, para. 8.

109. Joseph Tual, "Polémique autour de livres sur Tazmamart," *Ina.fr*, January 17, 2001, accessed December 22, 2017, https://www.ina.fr/video/CAC01004329.

110. Julia Facatier, "La Question," *La Croix*, January 15, 2001, https://www.la-croix.com/Archives/2001-01-15/LA-QUESTION-_NP_-2001-01-15-125011.

111. "Edition—L'écrivain au centre de deux polémiques Ben Jelloun, Fatna et Tazmamart," *L'Orient-le-Jour*, September 13, 2000, https://www.lorientlejour.com/article/432536/Edition_-_Lecrivain_au_centre_de_deux_polemiques_Ben_Jelloun%252C_Fatna_et_Tazmamart.html.

112. Claudia Esposito, "'Ce Maroc qui nous fait mal': Entretien avec Mahi Binebine," *Contemporary French and Francophone Studies* 17, no. 3 (2013): 306.

113. Esposito, "Ce Maroc," 306.

114. Esposito, "Ce Maroc," 307.

115. Esposito, "Ce Maroc," 307–8.

116. This does not invalidate earlier novelistic and poetic works by 'Abd al-Qādir al-Shāwī and Abdellatif Laâbi. The difference, however, is that Ben Jelloun was not a prisoner, and his literary position had already been established by the time he undertook this project.

117. Florence Aubenas and José Garçon, "Ben Jelloun s'enferre dans Tazmamart," *Libération*, January 15, 2001, http://next.liberation.fr/culture/2001/01/15/ben-jelloun-s-enferre-dans-tazmamart_351003.

118. For a discussion of questions related to the competition of memories and the debates surrounding this question, see Michael Rothberg, *Multidirectional Memory: Remembering the Holocaust in the Age of Decolonization* (Stanford, CA: Stanford University Press, 2009), 1–29, and Jean-Michel Chaumont, *La Concurrence des victimes: Génocide, identité, reconnaissance* (Paris: Editions la Découverte, 1997).

119. *See* Brahim El Guabli, "Testimony and Journalism: Moroccan Prison Narratives," in *The Social Life of Memory: Violence, Trauma, and Testimony in Lebanon and Morocco*, ed. Norman Saadi Nikro and Sonja Hegasy (New York: Palgrave Macmillan, 2017), 113–44.

120. Ben Jelloun, *Cette aveuglante*, 170.

121. Ben Jelloun, *Cette aveuglante*, 170.

122. Ben Jelloun, *Cette aveuglante*, 170.

123. Ben Jelloun, *Cette aveuglante*, 170.

124. Ben Jelloun, *Cette aveuglante*, 171.

125. Ben Jelloun, *This Blinding*, 166.

126. Belouchi, *Rapt de voix*, 18.

127. Valérie Orlando, *Francophone Voices of the "New" Morocco in Film and Print: (Re)presenting a Society in Transition* (New York: Palgrave McMillan, 2009), 58.

128. Belouchi, *Rapt de voix*, 21.

129. Belouchi, *Rapt de voix*, 22.

130. Belouchi, *Rapt de voix*, 22–23.

131. Belouchi, *Rapt de voix*, 174.

132. Fadel, according to his translator Alexander Elinson, denies that his novel makes any reference to Aziz BineBine (Alexander Elinson, "Court Jesters and Black Mirrors: Translator Alex Elinson on Bringing Moroccan Literature into English," *Arablit*, January 24, 2018, accessed October 10, 2019, https://arablit.org/2018/01/24/court-jesters-and-black-mirrors-translator-alex-elinson-on-bringing-moroccan-literature-into-english/). However, any specialist who has read sufficient works about the Years of Lead and Tazmamart specifically would notice the different traces of previous publications in the novel. See Jonathan Smolin's "Foreword," in

Youssef Fadel, *A Rare Blue Bird Flies with Me*, trans. Jonathan Smolin (Cairo: AUC Press, 2016), xi.

133. For more details about the author, the novel, and its topic as it relates to other Tazmamart works, see Brahim El Guabli, "Youssef Fadel's Re-imagination(s)," *The Journal of North African Studies*, 23, no. 1–2 (2018): 282–91.

134. Fadel, *A Rare Blue Bird*, 66.

135. Fadel, *A Rare Blue Bird*, 143.

136. Mohammed Nadrani and Abderrahmane Kounsi, *La Capitale des roses* (Casablanca: Éditions Alayam, 2009); Mohammed Errahoui, *Mouroirs: Chronique d'une disparition forcée* (Rabat: Saad Warzazi Éditions, 2008).

137. Fadel, *A Rare Blue Bird*, 13.

138. Myriam Barbera, "Pire que des chiens," *Humanité*, January 11, 1992, https://www.humanite.fr/node/24906.

139. ʻĀlā' ʻUthmān, "Yūsuf Fāḍil: ʻṬā'ir azraq nadir yuḥalliqu maʻī tu'arrikhu li-jīl al-thamānīnāt fī al-maghrib'," *Youm 7*, March 16, 2014, https://www.youm7.com/story/2014/3/16/.

140. ʻUthmān, "Yūsuf Fāḍil."

141. In adopting this narrative reconstruction strategy, Fadel distinguishes his work from Ben Jelloun's single-narrator narrative as well as from Serhane's analyst/analysand approach in *La Chienne de Tazmamart.*

142. Fadel, *A Rare Blue Bird*, 155.

143. Fadel, *A Rare Blue Bird*, 157.

144. BineBine, *Tazmamort*, 178–89.

145. Brahim El Guabli, "The 'Hidden Transcript' of Resistance in Moroccan Tazmamart Prison Writings," *Arab Studies Journal* 22, no. 1 (2014): 194–95; see also Zakaria Rhani's important article, "The Inmate's Two Bodies: Survival and Metamorphosis in a Moroccan Secret Prison," *Revista Crítica de Ciências Sociais* 120 (2019): 183–208, https://doi.org/10.4000/rccs.9884. Rhani's article is based on Skiba's experience in Tazmamart.

146. Fadel, *A Rare Blue Bird*, 41; BineBine, *Tazmamort*, 156–57.

147. Ashour, *Blue Lorries.*

148. Before reproducing an updated version of Faraj's story in *Tazmamart*, Marzouki had published a first iteration of the story in the prestigious French literary magazine *Les Temps Modernes* in 1993. I note, however, that Marzouki used a pseudonym (Hananou) to publish the story. See Hananou, "Une Histoire de Tazmamart." The last chapter in Achour's novel provides a translation and a summary of Faraj's story as Marzouki tells it in *Tazmamart.*

149. Ashour, *Farag*, 34.

150. Abdulrahman Munif [ʻAbd al-Raḥmān Munīf], *Sharq al-mutawassiṭ: Riwāya* (Beirut: Dār al-Ṭalīʻah, 1975), and id., *Al-ān hunā, aw, sharq al-mutawassiṭ marra ukhrā* (Beirut: al-Mu'assasa al-ʻArabiyya li-al-Dirāsat wa-al-Nashr, 1991).

151. Serfaty and Daure-Serfaty, *La Mémoire de l'autre*, 303.

152. Bassil Abu Hamda [Bāsil Abū Ḥamda], "Raḍwā ʻĀshūr: al-Riwāyāt ka-al-

'afārīt taẓharu fī ayyi waqt," *Albayan*, July 1, 2012, https://www.albayan.ae/paths/art/2012-07-01-1.1679380.

153. El Guabli, "The Absent Perpetrators," 2, 8.

154. El Guabli, "Cette aveuglante," 59–80. The hatred of Ben Jelloun is alluded to by Mahi BineBine in his aforementioned interview with Esposito. Mahi told Esposito that after the publication of Aziz's letter in *Le Monde*, "all the journalists who were against him [Ben Jelloun] used this letter to attack him. This lasted for three months. I received phone calls from journalists everyday" (Esposito, "Ce Maroc," 308).

155. El Guabli, "Youssef Fadel's Re-imagination(s)," 282–91.

156. Muḥammad Uḍmīn, *Urfān* (Rabat: Réseau Amazigh pour la Citoyennté-Azêtta, 2005), 51.

157. Julith Jedamus, *The Swerve* (Manchester: Carcanet, 2012), 35.

158. The French translation done by Philippe Vigreux remained faithful to the novel's title in Arabic: *Un Oiseau bleu et rare vole avec moi* (*A Rare Blue Bird Flies with Me*) (Paris: Actes Sud, 2017), whereas the Italian version by Cristina Dozio was published under a somewhat altered title: *Ogni volta che prendo il volo* (*Whenever I Take a Flight*) (Rome: Brioschi, 2019).

159. Marzouki, *Tazmamart: Cellule 10*, 124–25. More information about them can be found in their memoirs: René Midhat Bourequat, *Mort Vivant* (Paris: Pygmalion, 2000), and Ali-Auguste Bourequat and François Thibaux, *Tazmamart: Dix-huit ans de solitude* (Paris: M. Lafont,1993).

160. Slyomovics, "New Moroccan Publics," 143–44; Bouderka and Benyoub, *Kadhālika kān*, 126–27.

5. Other-Archives Transform Moroccan Historiography

1. This historiographical effervescence led to the production of *Zamane* magazine in 2011. Published in both French and Arabic, the magazine has been one of the most successful media projects in post-2011 Morocco. In an insightful article on the importance of history in Morocco today, Susan Gilson Miller provides a perceptive diagnosis of the field (excluding literature's contribution to historiographical debates) and its challenges in the post-ERC period. See Susan Gilson Miller, "Why History Matters in Post-2011 Morocco," *Jadaliyya*, November 30, 2016, http://www.jadaliyya.com/pages/index/25584/why-history-matters-in-post-2011-morocco#_edn8.

2. Susan Gilson Miller, *A History of Modern Morocco* (Cambridge: Cambridge University Press, 2013), 119.

3. Hay'at al-Inṣāf wa-al-Muṣālaḥa, *al-Ḥaqīqa wa-al-inṣāf wa-al-muṣālaḥa* (Rabat: al-Majlis al-Istishārī li-Ḥuqūq al-Insān, 2006), 16–18.

4. For instance, see Abdellah Laroui's *Les Origines sociales et culturelles du nationalisme marocain, 1830–1912* (Paris: F. Maspero, 1977). Many concepts and terms have been used to describe historians' engagement with the recent past,

including "immediate history," "direct history," and "history of the present time," among others. For a detailed study of this terminology and its theoretical implications for historiography, see Jean Francois Soulet, *L'Histoire immédiate: Historiographie, sources et méthodes* (Paris: Armand Colin, 2009), and Henry Rousso, *The Latest Catastrophe* (Chicago: University of Chicago Press, 2016).

5. For a first occurrence of this phrase in the American press, see Craig R. Whitney, "Popular New King Has a Goal: A Modern Morocco," *The New York Times*, November 12, 1999, http://www.nytimes.com/1999/11/12/world/popular-new-king-has-a-goal-a-modern-morocco.html.

6. In their groundbreaking memoirs about their experience as members of the ERC, *Kadhālika kān: Mudhakkirāt min tajribat hay'at al-inṣāf wa-al-muṣālaḥa* (Casablanca: Dār al-Nashr al-Maghribiyya, 2017), M'barek Bouderka and Ahmed Chouki Benyoub write that Boutaleb's "scientific training, academic expertise, and political culture helped to illuminate perceptions about issues related to the historical context" (31).

7. Moussaoui Aajlaoui, Mohammed Hatimi, and Mostafa Bouaziz presented papers entitled, respectively, "Kitābāt al-i'tiqāl: Al-mafāhīm wa-al-ishkāliyyāt" ("Prison Writings: Concepts and Problematics"), "Adabiyyāt al-sujūn ka-maṣdar tārīkhī: Al-ishkāliyyāt wa-al-muqāraba" ("Prison Literature as a Historical Source: The Problematics and the Approach"), and "Adabiyyāt al-i'tiqāl wa-al-tawthīq al-tārīkhī" ("Prison Literature and Historical Documentation"); Abdelahad Sebti talked about "'Unf al-dawla: Taṣawwurāt wa-mumārasāt wa-munṭalaqāt" ("State Violence: Representations, Practices, and Starting Points"); and Mohammed Kenbib discussed "Al-ḥaqīqa al-tārīkhiyya bayna al-ḍawābiṭ al-'ilmiyya li-al-dawla wa-al-mujtama'" ("Historical Truth between Scientific Controls for State and Society"). Because of the legal nature of the topic of the Casablanca conference, the invited speakers were almost exclusively lawyers who were part of the trials.

8. For instance, Tarik Editions has an entire series dedicated to memoirs, in which some important testimonial prison writings, such as Rabéa Bennouna's *Tazmamart côté femme: Témoignage* (Casablanca: Addar Al Alamia Lil Kitab, 2003); Abdelhak Serhane's *Kabazal: Les emmurés de Tazmamart, mémoires de Salah et Aïda Hachad* (Casablanca: Tarik Editions, 2004); and Ahmed El Ouafi and Kalima El Ouafi's *Opération Boraq F5: 16 août 1972, l'attaque du Boeing royal* (Casablanca: Tarik Editions, 2004) were published; see Mohammed Kenbib, *Du Protectorat à l'indépendance: Problématique du temps présent* (Rabat: Publications de la Faculté des Lettres et des Sciences Humaines, 2006), 7.

9. Benjamin Stora, "Maroc, le traitement des histoires proches," *Esprit*, no. 266/267 (2000): 102.

10. As recently as December 28, 2020, Ali Lmrabet, a famous journalist who supposedly uses a pseudonym to write for *Zamane* magazine, published a story on Twitter about the late Abdellah Bensouda, the brother of Ahmed Bensouda. Ahmed was mostly known for being King Hassan II's advisor, but his brother had

been a nationalist figure as well as the first governor of Laayoune after Morocco's annexation of Western Sahara in 1975. Digging into Bensouda's past, Lmrabet unearthed hidden aspects of his personality. Needless to say, Lmrabet's post elicited criticism, but his response was that he was presented with "the opportunity to talk about a repressed topic that historians do not want to talk about" (Twitter, December 27). Censorship and self-censorship are still very much alive even in 2020.

11. Abdelahad Sebti, "Bayna al-tārīkh wa-al-dhākira al-jamā'iyya: Tashakkulāt wa-rihānāt," *La Recherche Historique*, no. 1 (2003): 33. In the same vein, Mohammed Kenbib wonders if "historians must take into consideration the concerns of their co-citizens and the significant political stakes of their time or should they, to the contrary, stick to strictly scientific questions that the past suggests to them? Do they have to incorporate present considerations and civic goals in their reflections or continue their silent efforts, which do not go beyond the classical academic framework?" Mohammed Kenbib, "Historiens, journalistes et essayistes," in *Temps présent et fonctions de l'historien*, ed. Mohammed Kenbib (Rabat: Publications de la Faculté des Lettres et des Sciences Humaines, 2009), 41. For the "pro-makhzanian discourse," see Gilson Miller, *A History of Modern Morocco*, 219.

12. Rousso, *The Latest Catastrophe*, 4; italics in the original. On Bédarida, see Pierre Vermeren, "Histoire récente, histoire immédiate: L'historiographie française et le cas du Maghreb," in *Temps présent et fonctions de l'historien*, ed. Mohammed Kenbib (Rabat: Publications de la Faculté des Lettres et des Sciences Humaines, 2009), 119–26. The need to resolve the legacies of World War II, colonialism, and other events of recent history motivated the creation of the Institut d'Histoire du Temps Présent in 1978. Inheriting the "Comité d'histoire de la Deuxième guerre mondiale" ("Committee on the History of the Second World War") which was put in place by General De Gaulle in 1951, Bédarida founded the IHP within the NCSR in 1978 and directed it until 1990.

13. L'Institut d'Histoire du Temps Présent, http://www.ihtp.cnrs.fr/content/linstitut-dhistoire-du-temps-present.

14. See Mohamed Kably, *Chronologie de l'histoire du Maroc* (Rabat: Éditions de l'Institut Royal pour la Recherche sur l'Histoire du Maroc, 2013); Mohamed Kably and Abderrahmane El Moudden, eds., *al-Maghrib wa-al-zaman al-rāhin* (Rabat: Manshūrāt al-Ma'had al-Malakī li-al-Baḥth fī Tārīkh al-Maghrib, 2013); and Mohamed Kably, *Histoire du Maroc: Réactualisation et synthèse* (Rabat: Éditions de l'Institut Royal pour la Recherche sur l'Histoire du Maroc, 2011). See also Kenbib, *Du Protectorat à l'indépendance*.

15. Sebti rejects the use of the word "history" to describe a former intelligence officer's memoir. Although Ahmed Boukhari drew on archives to write his memoirs, Sebti still classifies his work within the category of memory. See Abdelahad Sebti, *al-Tārīkh wa-al-dhākira: Awrāsh fī tārīkh al-maghrib* (Casablanca: al-Markaz al-Thaqāfī al-'Arabī, 2012), 212.

16. See Jilali El Adnani, "Réforme universitaire et production scientifique en

sciences humaines et sociales au Maroc (histoire et anthropologie)," *La Recherche Historique* 7–8 (2009–2010): 10.

17. Mohammed Houbaida, "al-Tārīkh al-iqtiṣādī wa-al-ijtimāʿī fi-al-maghrib, min al-mūnūghrāfia ilā al-tarkīb," *al-Baḥt al-Tārīkhī* 7–8 (2009–10): 16.

18. Stora, "Maroc, le traitement," 99; Jamaâ Baïda, "Historiographie marocaine: De l'histoire contemporaine à l'histoire du temps présent," in *Temps présent et fonctions de l'historien*, ed. Mohammed Kenbib (Rabat: Publications de la Faculté des Lettres et des Sciences Humaines, 2009), 14–16.

19. Houbaida, "Al-Tārīkh al-iqtiṣādī wa-al-ijtimāʿī fil-maghrib," 13.

20. Abdelahad Sebti, *Al-māḍī al-mutaʿaddid: Qirāʾāt wa muḥāwarāt tārīkhiyya* (Rabat: Dār Tubqāl li-al-Nashr, 2016), 23–26.

21. Mohammed Houbaida, *Buʾs al-tārīkh: Murājaʿāt wa-muqārabāt* (Rabat: Dār al-Amān, 2016), 11; Germain Ayache, "L'Utilisation et l'apport des archives historiques marocaines," *Hespéris Tamuda* 7 (1966): 82–85.

22. Kenbib, *Du Protectorat à l'indépendance*, 14, 22; Jamaâ Baïda, "Le Maroc au XXème siècle: Entre histoire et mémoire," *La Recherche Historique*, no. 1 (2003): 51–52. See also multiple contributions to the collective volume dedicated to the memory of Germain Ayache, Abderrahmane El Moudden, and Abdelaziz Belfaida, *Jirmān ʿAyyāsh al-muʾarrikh wa-al-munāḍil* (Rabat: Imprimerie Rabat Net, 2015), especially those by Abderrahmane El Moudden and Mohammed Kenbib.

23. Abderrahmane El Moudden, "ʿAwda ilā al-arshīf al-makhzanī," in *Jirmān ʿAyyāsh al-muʾarrikh wa-al-munāḍil*, ed. Abderrahmane El Moudden and Abdelaziz Belfaida (Rabat: Imprimerie Rabat Net, 2015), 41–48; Baïda, "Le Maroc," 52.

24. Kenbib, *Du Protectorat à l'indépendance*, 25–26; El Adnani, "Réforme universitaire et production scientifique," 9–10.

25. Sebti, *al-Tārīkh wa-al-dhākira*, 55–56.

26. Hafiḍa Bilmuqaddim's dissertation was later published as a book entitled *Ḥizb al-istiqlāl wa tadbīr al-intiqāl bayna al-insijām wa-al-taṣaddu', dujanbir 1955–yanāyr 1963* (Rabat: Manshūrāt Fikr, 2006).

27. Maâti Monjib's dissertation was later published as a book entitled *La Monarchie marocaine et la lutte pour le pouvoir: Hassan II face à l'opposition nationale, de l'indépendance à l'état d'exception* (Paris: L'Harmattan, 1992). Mostafa Bouaziz's dissertation was later published as a book entitled *Aux Origines de la Koutla démocratique* (Casablanca: Faculté des Lettres Ain-Chock, 1997).

28. "Professor Maâti Monjib," in *al-Maghrib wa-al-zaman al-rāhin*, ed. Mohammed Kably and Abderrahmane El Moudden (Rabat: Manshūrāt al-Maʿhad al-Malakī li-al-Baḥth fī Tārīkh al-Maghrib, 2013), 70.

29. Kenbib, *Du Protectorat à l'indépendance*, 23–24.

30. "Professor Maâti Monjib," 70. Political scientist Abdellah Ben Mlih has also written a dissertation that was published as *Structures politiques du Maroc colonial* (*Political Structures of Colonial Morocco*) (Paris: L'Harmattan, 1990), but the word "history" was added to its Arabic translation by Muḥammad al-Nājī under the title *al-Tārīkh al-siyyāsī li-al-maghrib ibbāna al-istiʿmār: al-binyāt al-siyyāsiyya*

(*Morocco's Political History during Colonization: Political Structures*) (Casablanca: Afrīqiyā al-Sharq, 2014). For a detailed study of the circulation of Tazmamart memory in social and cultural memory, see Brahim El Guabli, "Testimony and Journalism: Moroccan Prison Narratives," in *The Social Life of Memory: Violence, Trauma, and Testimony in Lebanon and Morocco*, ed. Norman Saadi Nikro and Sonja Hegasy (New York: Palgrave Macmillan, 2017), 113–44.

31. Gilson Miller, *A History of Modern Morocco*, 219.

32. Conseil National des Droits de l'Homme, *L'Enfermement, le partage: Lieux de mémoire* (Bilnet: Éditions Les Croisées des Chemins, 2015), http://cndh.ma/sites/default/files/cndh_-_lenfermement_le_partage_monte_-.pdf, 305.

33. Stephen Smith, "Des Vies de revenants," *Libération*, October 5, 2000, http://www.liberation.fr/planete/2000/10/05/des-vies-de-revenants_339598.

34. Ignace Dalle, "Le Salon du livre de Paris pris en otage par les autorités marocaines," *Orient XXI*, March 24, 2017, https://orientxxi.info/magazine/le-salon-du-livre-de-paris-pris-en-otage-par-les-autorites-marocaines,1760.

35. Jaouad Mdidech, *La Chambre noire ou Derb Moulay Cherif* (Casablanca: Eddif, 2002); Amin Rboub, "'Visages et paysages du cœur du Maroc': L'autre Maroc raconté par un reporter," *L'Economiste*, March 27, 2017, http://leconomiste.com/article/1010170-visages-et-paysages-du-coeur-du-maroc-l-autre-maroc-raconte-par-un-reporter.

36. These interviews took place in 2009, and the videos are available online. Al Jazeera Channel, "Shāhid 'alā al-'aṣr—Aḥmad al-Marzūqī," Episode no. 1, YouTube video, 50:36, February 24, 2009, https://www.youtube.com/watch?v=1-MhOJIZeNY; "Shāhid 'alā al-'aṣr—Salah Hachad," Episode no. 1, YouTube video, 50:10, May 5, 2009, https://www.youtube.com/watch?v=Uo_bTD7IGAo&list=FLQOE534ak5pSKpaE_JeU4_A&index=50.

37. Mohammed Kenbib, "À propos de l'histoire contemporaine du Maroc," *Perspectives Universitaires* 1 (2008): 106.

38. For a nuanced discussion of some of these issues, see Mustapha Lotfi, "al-Mudhakkirāt laysat tārīkhan," *Assabah*, January 14, 2014, https://assabah.ma/61624.html.

39. See individual papers in *La Recherche Historique*'s first issue (2003) for specific details.

40. Houbaida, *Bu's al-tārīkh*, 164–68; Mohammed Kenbib, "Ecriture et réécriture de l'histoire contemporaine du Maroc: Acquis, interrogations et perspectives," in *Du Protectorat à l'indépendance*, 20, 30.

41. During my visit to Rabat in June 2019, I observed that several bookstores shelved testimonial prison memoirs under the category of "history," which further supports the argument I have been making throughout this book.

42. Sebti is again an important exception in this regard. In addition to his call for a dialogue and engagement with other-archival production, he translated a chapter entitled "L'Unité intrinsèque de l'histoire" ("The Intrinsic Unity of History") from Kzysztof Pomian's important book *Sur l'histoire* (*On History*). Pomian engages

in this chapter with the question of history writing and the relationship between professional and lay historians. Unlike Pomian's rather general title, Sebti published Pomian's translated article under the title "History Writing between 'Amateurism' and 'Professionalism,'" which clearly entrenches the divisive binary between memory and history. See Sebti, *al-Tārīkh wa-al-dhākira*, 169–82.

43. Sebti, *al-Tārīkh wa-al-dhākira*, 212.

44. El Guabli, "Testimony and Journalism," 135; Sebti, *al-Tārīkh wa-al-dhākira*, 217.

45. Kenbib, *Du Protectorat à l'indépendance*, 20.

46. Gilson Miller, *A History of Modern Morocco*, 219.

47. Institut d'Histoire du Temps Présent, "Historique," IHP, accessed September 11, 2020, http://www.ihtp.cnrs.fr/spip.php?rubrique241&lang=fr.html.

48. Kably and El Moudden, *al-Maghrib wa-al-zaman al-rāhin*, 206.

49. Kably and El Moudden, *al-Maghrib wa-al-zaman al-rāhin*, 206.

50. Kably and El Moudden, *al-Maghrib wa-al-zaman al-rāhin*, 6.

51. IHTP, "Historique."

52. Mohammed Hatimi, "al-Jamāʿāt al-yahūdiyya al-maghribiyya khilāla marḥalat al-ḥimāya: Ḥaṣīlat al-abḥāth al-akādīmiyya," in *al-Maghrib wa-al-zaman al-rāhin*, ed. Mohammed Kably and Abderrahmane El Moudden (Rabat: Manshūrāt al-Maʿhad al-Malakī li-al-Baḥth fī Tārīkh al-Maghrib, 2013), 33–43.

53. Simon Lévy, "Professor Simon Lévy," in *al-Maghrib wa-al-zaman al-rāhin*, ed. Mohammed Kably and Abderrahmane El Moudden (Rabat: Manshūrāt al-Maʿhad al-Malakī li-al-Baḥth fī Tārīkh al-Maghrib, 2013), 50.

54. "Professor Simon Lévy," 51.

55. "Professor Simon Lévy," 51.

56. "Professor Simon Lévy," 52.

57. Abdelmajid Kaddouri, "Professor Abdelmajid Kaddouri," in *al-Maghrib wa-al-zaman al-rāhin*, ed. Mohammed Kably and Abderrahmane El Moudden (Rabat: Manshūrāt al-Maʿhad al-Malakī li-al-Baḥth fī Tārīkh al-Maghrib, 2013), 54.

58. Omar Affa, "Professor ʿUmar Affā," in *al-Maghrib wa-al-zaman al-rāhin*, ed. Mohammed Kably and Abderrahmane El Moudden (Rabat: Manshūrāt al-Maʿhad al-Malakī li-al-Baḥth fī Tārīkh al-Maghrib, 2013), 55.

59. Sebti, *al-Tārīkh wa-al-dhākira*, 198–99.

60. Daniel Rivet, "Pour une histoire du Maroc revisitée," *Revue Historique*, no. 670 (2014): 382; italics in the original. In this regard, Jonathan Wyrtzen's monograph *Making Morocco: Colonial Intervention and the Politics of Identity* (Ithaca, NY: Cornell University Press, 2015) provides a model for the kind of approaches and historical thinking that Rivet argues was missing from *Histoire du Maroc*.

61. Driss Maghraoui provides an insightful comment on the interweaving of history and memory in present-day Morocco in his paper "Histoire et mémoire: Quels enjeux politiques au Maroc," in *Temps présent et fonctions de l'historien*, ed. Mohammed Kenbib (Rabat: Publications de la Faculté des Lettres et des Sciences Humaines, 2009), 17–27.

62. This assertion does not negate the contents of those historical papers that engaged deeply with other-archival texts in the early months of the ERC's mission. While it is hard to provide a firmly grounded explanation as to why there has been less engagement with literature over time, it is still possible to conjecture that the predominance of methodological debates and the rise of less politically engaged historians from Mohammed V University have sidelined other, more engaged scholars. An interesting tendency has emerged from these debates for some Francophone historians to criticize their Arabist colleagues for a lack of creativity and innovation.

63. This is in comparison with Moussaoui Aajlaoui's and Mostafa Bouaziz's essays on prison literature and history presented at the ERC's 2004 conference in Rabat. Those essays, which offer hands-on, close readings of the literary materials, were a useful demonstration of what historians can gain from engaging with literary texts as historical sources.

64. Kenbib, *Du Protectorat at l'indépendance* and Mohammed Kenbib, ed., *Temps présent et fonctions de l'historien* (Rabat: Publications de la Faculté des Lettres et des Sciences Humaines, 2009); Kably, *Chronologie de l'histoire du Maroc* and *Histoire du Maroc*; Kably and El Moudden, *al-Maghrib wa-al-zaman al-rāhin.*

65. Alison Landsberg, *Engaging the Past: Mass Culture and the Production of Historical Knowledge* (New York: Columbia University Press, 2015), 9.

66. Hayden White and Robert Doran, eds., *The Fiction of Narrative: Essays on History, Literature, and Theory, 1957–2007* (Baltimore, MD: Johns Hopkins University Press, 2010), 284.

67. Sebti would build on Krzysztof Pomian's article, "L'Unité intrinsèque de l'histoire," in his *Sur l'histoire* (Paris: Gallimard, 1999) to introduce the concept of *al-tārīkh al-rāhin* (present-day history) in an article published under the title "Bayna al-tārīkh wa-al-dhākira al-jamā'iyya: Tashakkulāt wa-rihānāt," *La Recherche Historique* 1 (2003): 27–33. The same article is included in *al-Tārīkh wa-al-dhākira* (201–07).

68. Bouaziz was involved in the leftist circles when he was doing his PhD in Paris. Bouaziz was in charge of the archives of the branch of the Moroccan Marxist-Leninist Movement that became *Munaẓẓamat al-'amal al-dimuqrāṭī al-sha'bī* (the Organization of Popular Democratic Action).

69. In "Why History Matters," Gilson Miller mentions a European Commission grant of eight million euros to the CNDH, which the director of the institution, Driss El Yazami, used to promote the rewriting of history.

70. Kenbib, *Temps présent*, 9.

71. See Paige Arthur, "Sending the Wrong Message: International Assistance and the Decline of Civil Society Action on Transitional Justice in Morocco," in *Transitional Justice, International Assistance, and Civil Society: Missed Connections*, ed. Paige Arthur and Christalla Yakinthou (Cambridge: Cambridge University Press, 2018), 86–113, and Centre international pour la justice transitionnelle, "Maroc: La perspective de genre dans le processus de justice transitionnelle,"

September 2011, https://www.ictj.org/sites/default/files/ICTJ-%20Morocco-Gender-Transitional%20Justice-2011-French.pdf.

72. The chapter extends over forty pages without any bibliographical notes. The text is a rich history containing a personal, positive assessment of Hassan II's reign. See Brahim Boutaleb, *Tārīkh al-maghrib al-ḥadīth al-muʿāṣir* (Rabat: Manshūrāt Kulliyyat al-ʾĀdāb, 2014), 555–98. I exclude Laroui's *Le Maroc et Hassan II* from this evaluation. The book is an innovative rewriting of the entire period of Hassan II from the perspective of the historian as an actor, witness, or both.

73. Gilson Miller, *A History of Modern Morocco*, 218. Gilson Miller underscores the problem of access to archives by stressing that as a foreigner, she had access to archives that her Moroccan colleagues were denied. She regretfully writes, "I made the terrifying discovery that, as a foreigner, I had better access to the Moroccan historical patrimony than did Moroccans themselves" (Gilson Miller, "Why History Matters").

74. Pierre Vermeren, *Histoire du Maroc depuis l'indépendance* (Paris: La Découverte, 2006); Daniel Rivet, *Histoire du Maroc* (Paris: Fayard, 2012); Gilson Miller, *A History of Modern Morocco*.

75. Gilson Miller, *A History of Modern Morocco*, 5.

76. Houbaida, "al-Tārīkh al-iqtiṣādī wa-al-ijtimāʿī fil-maghrib," 20.

77. Conseil National des Droits de l'Homme (NCHR), "Convention entre le CNDH et l'Université Mohamed V," CNDH, accessed September 14, 2020, http://www.cndh.org.ma/fr/article/convention-entre-le-cndh-et-luniversite-mohamed-v-agdal-pour-la-creation-du-centre-de; NCHR, "Le CNDH et la Faculté de Droit de Rabat-Agdal signent une convention cadre," CNDH, accessed September 14, 2020, http://www.cndh.ma/fr/actualites/le-cndh-et-la-faculte-de-droit-de-rabat-agdal-signent-une-convention-cadre-relative-au.

78. ERC, *The Components of Reform and Reconciliation* (Rabat: The Advisory Council on Human Rights Publications, 2009), 57.

79. M'barek Zaki, *Résistance et Armée de libération: Portée politique, liquidation, 1953–1958* (Tangiers: E.T.E.I., 1987).

80. Mohammed Kably, *al-Dhākira wa-al-muqāwama al-maghribiyya fīmā bayna sanatay 1944 wa 1961* (Rabat: Manshūrāt al-Maʿhad al-Malakī li-al-Baḥt fī Tārīkh al-Maghrib, 2014).

81. Ahmed Beroho, *Abdelkrim: Le lion du Rif* (Tangiers: Corail, 2003); id., *Les Mystères de Tanger* (Tangiers: Corail, 2006); id., *Histoire de Tanger* (Tangiers: Corail, 2008).

82. M'barek Zaki and Ahmed Beroho, *Hassan II ou Confessions d'outre-tombe: Tragicomédie* (Tangiers: Corail, 2005).

83. This novel's reference to French historian François-René de Chateaubriand's *Mémoires d'Outre-Tombe* (Paris: Le Club Français du Livre, 1969) is all too clear.

84. M'bark Zaki, *Un Roi et deux républicains: Dialogues de l'au-delà: Hassan II, Ben Barka, Oufkir et les autres* (Rabat: Omega Communication Edition & Distribution, 2006).

85. Zaki, *Un Roi et deux républicains*, 14.

86. Robert Gordon, "Brecht, Interruptions and Epic Theatre," British Library. UK, September 7, 2017, https://www.bl.uk/20th-century-literature/articles/brecht-interruptions-and-epic-theatre.

87. Although the state is an inanimate object, I use the phrase "the state" as a subject to refer to the different public servants who work under the purview of the state to write history.

88. See Gilson Miller, "Why History Matters," for more details about the inner workings of archive-destruction in Morocco; Brahim El Guabli, "The Absent Perpetrators: Morocco's Failed Accountability, Tazmamart Literature and the Survivors' Testimony for their Jailers (1973–1991)," *Violence: An International Journal* 1 (2020): 80–101.

89. Gilson Miller, "Why History Matters."

90. Frédéric Abécassis, Karima Dirèche, and Rita Aouad, eds., *La Bienvenue et l'adieu: Migrants juifs et musulmans au Maghreb (XVe–XXe siècle)*, 3 vols. (Casablanca: Karthala, 2012).

91. Ahmed Herzenni, "Lettre de soutien du CCDH," in Abécassis, Dirèche, and Aouad, eds., *La Bienvenue et l'adieu*," I :7.

92. Herzenni, "Lettre de soutien du CCDH," I:7.

93. A source at Mohammed V University informed me during my research trip in June 2017 that some biographies were misappropriated from other sources.

94. Otmane Mansouri and Mohammed Yasir El Hilali, eds., *al-ʿUnf fī tārīkh al-maghrib: Ashghāl al-ayyām al-waṭaniyya al-ḥādiyya wa-al-ʿishrīn li-al-jamʿiyya al-maghribiyya li-al-baḥth al-tārīkhī* (Casablanca: Manshūrāt Multaqā al-Ṭṭuruq, 2015).

95. Gilson Miller, for instance, writes that "the regime's progressive stance on human rights has paid multiple political dividends, allowing it to co-opt and neutralize many of its former adversaries on the left" (*A History of Modern Morocco*, 223).

96. Gilson Miller, *A History of Modern Morocco*, 220.

97. Royaume du Maroc, *Bulletin officiel*, no. 5484 (December 21, 2006), 2177–78, http://www.habous.gov.ma/fr/files/insitut_bo.pdf.

98. ERC, *The Components of Reform*, 87.

99. ERC, *The Components of Reform*, 87.

100. The RIRHM's founding decree also defines the institute's tasks. In cooperation with other governmental departments, the RIRHM's mission includes, among other things, "develop[ing] and spread[ing] historical knowledge and spreading knowledge about Moroccan history both inside and outside the country"; "develop[ing] studies related to the history of the Kingdom of Morocco and consolidat[ing] archives and documentary holdings in this field"; and "publish[ing] texts and books on Moroccan history and its civilizational patrimony" (Royaume du Maroc, *Bulletin officiel*, 2177).

101. The deactivation of the RIRMH's website has led to the loss of the list of publications that used to be available for online consultation.

102. Royaume du Maroc, *Bulletin officiel*, 2177.

103. This conversation took place at the Jewish Museum in Berlin in October 2017.

104. For more information about the RIRHM and its director, see Ann Marie Wainscott, *Bureaucratizing Islam: Morocco and the War on Terror* (New York: Cambridge University Press, 2017), 117–19. In June 24, 2015, decree 1.15.71 annexed the RIRHM to al-Qarawiyyīn University in Fez, thus placing it under the guardianship of a university renowned for its specialization in religious sciences. The move is significant because it means that "historical security" is as important to the state as its "religious safety."

105. Mohammed Kably, ed., *Shamāl al-maghrib ibbāna fatrat al-ḥimāya wa bidāyat 'ahd al-istiqlāl* (Place: Manshūrāt al-Ma'had al-Malakī li-al-Baḥt fī Tārīkh al-Maghrib, 2014); Mohammed Larbi Messari, *Muḥammad al-Khāmis min sulṭān ilā malik* (Rabat: Manshūrāt al-Ma'had al-Malakī li-al-Baḥt fī Tārīkh al-Maghrib, 2013); Khālid Bin al-Ṣaghīr, *Wāḥāt al-tukhūm wa ḥudūd al-maghrib al-sharqiyya* (Rabat: Manshūrāt al-Ma'had al-Malakī li-al-Baḥt fī Tārīkh al-Maghrib, 2013); Jamaâ Baïda, *Oasis orientales et espace frontalier entre l'Algérie occupée et le Maroc* (Rabat: Manshūrāt al-Ma'had al-Malakī li-al-Baḥt fī Tārīkh al-Maghrib, 2013).

106. Mostafa Bouaziz, "Des petits grands pas," *Zamane*, January 29, 2013, http://zamane.ma/fr/des-petits-grands-pas/.

107. For race in Moroccan history, see Chouki El Hamel, *Black Morocco: A History of Slavery, Race, and Islam* (New York: Cambridge University Press, 2013).

108. Daniel Nordman, "Of Space and Time: On a History of Morocco," *Annales* (English ed.) 71, no. 4 (2016): 607.

109. Nordman, "Of Space and Time," 607.

110. Hammoudi, in discussion with the author, Princeton, NJ, March 2017. Rivet, "Pour une histoire du Maroc," 382.

111. Rivet, "Pour une histoire du Maroc," 382.

112. Bouaziz, "Des petits grands pas."

113. Bouaziz, "Des petits grands pas."

114. Bouaziz, "Des petits grands pas."

115. Euro-Mediterranean Human Rights Monitor, "al-Maghrib..khanq al-ra'yi al-'ākhar: Mulāḥaqat al-suluṭāt al-maghribīyya li-al-nushaṭā' wa-al-ḥuqūqiyyīn wa-al-ṣaḥafiyyīn," *Euro-Mediterranean Human Rights Monitor*, July 12, 2021, https://euromedmonitor.org/ar/article/4514/%D8%AE%D9%86%D9%82-%D8%A7%D9%84%D8%B1%D8%A3%D9%8A-%D8%A7%D9%84%D8%A2%D8%AE%D8%B1:%C2%A0%D9%85%D9%84%D8%A7%D8%AD%D9%82%D8%A9-%D8%A7%D9%84%D8%B3%D9%84%D8%B7%D8%A7%D8%AA-%D8%A7%D9%84%D9%85%D8%BA%D8%B1%D8%A8%D9%8A%D8%A9-%D9%84%D9%84%D9%86%D8%B4%D8%B7%D8%A7%D8%A1-%D9%88%D8%A7%D9%84%D8%AD%D9%82%D9%88%D9%82%D9%8A%D9%8A%D9%86-%D9%88%D8%A7%D9%84%D8%B5%D8%AD%D8%A7%D9%81%D9%8A%D9%8A%D9%86.

116. Majid Amnay, "Free Maati Monjib," *London Review of Books*, March 23, 2021, https://www.lrb.co.uk/blog/2021/march/free-maati-monjib.

117. Muhammad Bin al-Haṣan Bin Muhammad, "I'ādat tanẓīm acādimiyyat al-mamlaka al-maghribiyya," al-Jarīda al-Rasmiyya, February 9, 2021, http://www.sgg.gov.ma/Portals/1/BO/2021/BO_6959-bis_Ar.pdf?ver=2021-02-09-150856-173.

Conclusion

1. This idea of mosaic was first articulated in the works of physical anthropologist Carleton S. Coon, *Caravan: The Story of the Middle East* (New York: Holt, Rhinehart and Winston, 1964); see also Clifford Geertz, "'From the Native's Point of View': On the Nature of Anthropological Understanding," *Bulletin of the American Academy of Arts and Sciences* 28, no. 1 (1974): 26–45.

2. See the sections on education, history, and citizenship in ERC, *The Components of Reform and Reconciliation* (Rabat: The Advisory Council on Human Rights Publications, 2009).

3. There are two notable exceptions to this rule: Marguerite Rollinde, *Le Mouvement marocain des droits de l'homme: Entre consensus national et engagement citoyen* (Paris: Karthala; Saint-Denis, [France]: Institut Maghreb-Europe, 2002), and Susan Slyomovics, *The Performance of Human Rights in Morocco* (Philadelphia: The University of Pennsylvania Press, 2005). These two works are comparative in bringing together experiences of both leftist and Islamist prisoners.

4. Brahim el Guabli, "Tankra Tamazight: The Revival of Amazigh Indigeneity in Literature and Art," Jadaliyya, November 1, 2021, https://www.jadaliyya.com/Details/43440.

5. The most recent example is Ewa Tartakowsky's *Les Juifs et le Maghreb: Fonctions sociales d'une littérature d'exil* (Tours: Presses Universitaires François Rabelais, 2016).

6. Aomar Boum, *Memories of Absence: How Muslims Remember Jews in Morocco* (Stanford, CA: Stanford University Press, 2013); Emanuela Trevisan Semi and Hanane Sekkat Hatimi, *Mémoire et représentations des Juifs au Maroc: Les voisins absents de Meknès* (Paris: Publisud, 2011); Jessica M. Marglin, *Across Legal Lines: Jews and Muslims in Modern Morocco* (New Haven, CT: Yale University Press, 2016).

7. Mohammed Kenbib, ed., *Du Protectorat à l'indépendance: Problématique du temps présent* (Rabat: Publication of the Faculty of Literatures and Human Sciences, 2006), 20–21, 31–33.

8. In this regard, Tarik Editions' memory series has been instrumental to the publication of many memoirs in both Arabic and French. Some newspapers and magazines, such *Zamane*, *al-Aḥdāt al-Maghrbiyya*, *al-Ittiḥād al-Ishtirākī*, *Le Journal Hebdo*, and *al-Ṣaḥīfa* also played an important role in uncovering this repressed past. For a detailed study, see Brahim El Guabli, "Testimony and Journalism: Moroccan Prison Narratives," in *The Social Life of Memory*, ed. Saadi Nikro and Sonja Hegasy (New York: Palgrave Macmillan, 2017), 113–44.

9. Slyomovics, *The Performance of Human Rights.*

10. Equity and Reconciliation Commission (ERC), "Summary of the Final

Report," 2006, accessed February 23, 2018, http://www.ccdh.org.ma/sites/default/files/documents/rapport_final_mar_eng-3.pdf.

11. ERC, "Final Report," 29.

12. ERC, "Final Report," 29. Italics added.

13. It is noticeable that the American Sephardi Federation and the Conference of Presidents of Major American Jewish Organizations announced the news in a joint statement posted on Twitter on November 12, 2020, even before the decision was announced to Moroccans living in the country.

14. Ahmed Chouki Benyoub, interview by *Mashārf*, March 16, 2017 (the recording has since disappeared from YouTube, bt the author owns a copy).

15. "al-Qānūn 69.99 al-muta'alliq bi-al-arshīf," accessed June 15, 2021, https://www.archivesdumaroc.ma/ArchivesDuMaroc/media/ArchivesDuMaroc/Files/Textes-juridiques-AR.pdf?ext=.pdf&disposition=attachment.

16. "al-Qānūn 69.99 al-muta'alliq bi-al-arshīf."

17. Hay'at al-Inṣāf wa-al-Muṣālaḥa, *al-Taqrīr al-khitāmī: Muqawwimāt tawṭīd al-iṣlāḥ* (Rabat: Al-Majlis al-Istishārī li-Ḥuqūq al-Insān, 2006), 94.

18. Brahim El Guabli, "From Lalla Batoul to Oum Hamza: New Trends in Moroccan Women's Fight for Citizenship," in *Arab Women's Activism and Socio-Political Transformation*, ed. Sahar Khamis and Amel Mili (New York: Palgrave Macmillan, 2018), 219–40.

19. Aomar Boum's work in the region of Tata is an exemplary case in this regard.

20. By searching for Aït Baroukh, the saint located in my natal village, I found many online videos and resources about the village in a global network of Jewish memories that no one in the area knows about.

21. Brahim El Guabli, "Breaking Ranks with National Unanimity: Novelistic and Cinematic Returns of Jewish-Muslim Intimacy in Morocco," in *Generations of Dissent: Intellectuals, Cultural Production, and the State in the Middle East and North Africa*, ed. Alexa Firat and R. Shareah Taleghani (New York: Syracuse University Press, 2020), 159–87.

22. Ian Black and Benny Morris, *Israel's Secret Wars: A History of Israel's Intelligence Services* (New York: Grove Press, 1991), 176.

23. Yossi Melman, "Assassination, Bribes and Smuggling Jews: Inside the Israeli Mossad's Long Secret Alliance with Morocco," *Haaretz*, December 17, 2020, https://www.haaretz.com/israel-news/.premium.HIGHLIGHT-assassination-bribes-smuggling-jews-inside-mossad-s-secret-alliance-with-morocco-1.9372580.

24. See Agnès Bensimon, *Hassan II et les juifs: Histoire d'une émigration secrète: Essai* (Paris: Seuil, 1991).

25. The online news website *Lakome2* translated Yossi Melman's article into Arabic on Tuesday, December 22, 2020. *Lakome2*'s nuanced introduction to the article provides their readership with the gist of the ideas therein: "when Lakome2 translates from a Hebrew newspaper, that should not be inscribed within the context of the rush toward normalization that takes many aspects in Morocco, but an indicator of the value of a testimony that uncovers the hidden side of the

secret relationship between the state of Israel and Morocco and in which the two countries' intelligence services played a big role in crystalizing. This report from a Hebrew newspaper is an exemplum of 'a witness from her family testified.' It confirms what was circulated about the coordination of the intelligence services of the two countries in very sensitive dossiers, such as the kidnapping and assassination of the leftist leader Mehdi Ben Barka, the eavesdropping on the Arab summit that facilitated Israel's defeat of Nasser's Egypt in 1967, also known as the year of the 'setback,' and the smuggling of Jews of Moroccan origins who were sold for a total of 50 million dollars paid to Moroccan rulers as bribes." See "'Haaretz' ḥikāyat al-ta'āwūn al-sirrī al-ṭawīl bayna 'al-mūsād' wa-al-maghrib," *Lakome2*, December 22, 2020, https://lakome2.com/decryptage/211714/.

26. An important exception is Chouki El Hamel's *Black Morocco: A History of Slavery, Race, and Islam* (Cambridge: Cambridge University Press, 2013). See also Abdallah Hammoudi, "L'Évolution de l'habitat dans la vallée du Draa," *Revue de géographie du Maroc* 18 (1970): 33–45; Hsain Ilahiane, "The Social Mobility of the Haratine and the Re-Working of Bourdieu's Habitus on the Saharan Frontier, Morocco," *American Anthropologist* 103, no. 2 (2001): 380–94; Paul Silverstein, "Masquerade Politics: Race, Islam and the Scale of Amazigh Activism in Southeastern Morocco," *Nations and Nationalism* 17, no. 1 (2011): 65–84.

27. Brahim El Guabli, ""The Sub-Saharan African Turn in Moroccan Literature," *MERIP*, https://merip.org/2021/03/the-sub-saharan-african-turn-in-moroccan-literature/.

28. Tahar Ben Jelloun, *Le Marriage de plaisir* (Paris: Gallimard, 2016).

29. Nouzha Fassi Fihri, *Dada l'Yakout* (Casablanca: Le Fennec, 2009/2019).

30. Mubarak Rabi, *Gharb al-mutawassit* (Beirut: al-Mu'assasa al-'Arabīyya li-al-Dirāsāt wa-al-Nashr, 2018).

31. Ismail Ghazali, *Thalāthat ayyām fī Casablanca* (Milan: Almutawassit Books, 2019).

32. See Brahim El Guabli, "The Absent Perpetrators: Morocco's Failed Accountability, Tazmamart Literature and the Survivors' Testimony for their Jailers (1973–1991)," *Violence: An International Journal* 1, no. 1 (2020): 80–101.

33. The clearest expression of this line of thought can be found in King Mohammed VI's speech on the occasion of the presentation of the ERC's final report on January 6, 2006. Mohammed VI addressed the audience in these terms: "I chose to focus my speech on the future direction to complete the construction of an honorable citizenship by renewing the promise to implement the permanent work of human development and general mobilization of our youth's energies and giving a chance for all initiatives that can be generative of economic wealth or that are creative in all fields of science and art in Morocco and beyond." See Mohammed VI, "Naṣ khiṭāb jalālat al-malik bi-munāsabat intihā' muhimmat hay'at al-inṣāf wa-al-muṣālaḥa wa-taqdīm al-dirāsa ḥawla al-tanmiyya al-bashariyya bi-al-maghrib," *Maghress*, January 6, 2006, https://www.maghress.com/attajdid/22414.

34. Karen Weintraub, "Race to the Vaccine: Deliver a safe, effective COVID-19 vaccine in less than a year? Impossible. Meet Moncef Slaoui," Decermber 1, 2020, https://www.usatoday.com/in-depth/news/health/2020/12/01/operation-warp-speeds-moncef-slaoui-guided-covid-19-vaccine-creation/6375043002/.

35. Aziz BineBine, *Tazmamart: 18 Years in Morocco's Secret Prison*, trans. Lulu Norman (London: Haus Publishing, 2020); Maël Renouard, *L'Historiographe du royaume* (Paris: Grasset, 2020).

Bibliography

Aajloui, Moussaoui. "Kitābāt al-i'tiqāl: Al-mafāhīm wa-al-ishkāliyyāt." Paper presented at the *Nadwa kitābāt al-i'tiqāl al-siyyāsī*, Rabat, May 20, 2004.

'Abd al-Raḥīm, Ḥuzal. *Al-Kitābah wa-al-sijn: Ḥiwārāt wa-nuṣūṣ*. Al-Dār al-Bayḍā': Afrīqiā al-Sharq, 2008.

Abécassis, Frédéric, Karima Dirèche, and Rita Aouad, eds. *La Bienvenue et l'adieu: Migrants juifs et musulmans au Maghreb (XVᵉ–XXᵉ siècle)*. Paris: Karthala, 2012.

Abitbol, Michel. "De la tradition à la modernité: Les juifs du Maroc." *Diasporas* 27 (2016): 19–30.

Abu Hamda, Bassil [Bāsil Abū Ḥamda]. "Raḍwā 'Āshūr: Al-riwāyāt ka-al-'afārīt taharu fī ayyi waqt." *Albayan*, July 1, 2012, https://www.albayan.ae/paths/art/2012-07-01-1.1679380.

Affa, Omar ['Umar Affā]. "Professor 'Umar Affā." In *al-Maghrib wa-al-zaman al-rāhin*, edited by Mohammed Kably and Abderrahmane El Moudden, 55–56. Rabat: Manshūrāt al-Ma'had al-Malakī li-al-Baḥth fī Tārīkh al-Maghrib, 2013.

Agadir. "Maroc: Charte d'Agadir relative aux droits linguistiques et culturels." August 5, 1991, http://www.unesco.org/culture/fr/indigenous/Dvd/pj/IMAZIGHEN/AMAZC4_3.pdf.

Agounad, Mohamed. "Tajribatī fi al-kitāba bi-al-amāzīghiyya." In *al-Adab al-amāzīghī al-ḥadīth*, ed. Abdelali Talmansour, 15–20. Agadir: Sous, 2016.

Aït Moh, El Hassane. *Le Captif de Mabrouka*. Paris: L'Harmattan, 2009.

Aït Mous, Fadma, and Driss Ksikes. *Le Métier d'intellectuel: Dialogue avec quinze penseurs au Maroc*. Casablanca: En Toutes Lettres, 2014.

Akhiyyat, Brahim. *al-Amāzīghiyya: Hūwwiyyātuna al-waṭaniyya*. Rabat: Manshūrāt al Jam'iyya al Maghribiyya li-al-Baḥth wa-al-Tabādul al-Thaqāfī, 2007.

———. *al-Nahḍa al-amazīghiyya kamā 'ishtu mīlādaha wa taṭawwurahā*. Rabat: Manshūrāt al-Jam'iyya al-Maghribiyya li-al-Baḥth wa-al-Tabādul al-Thaqāfī, 2012.

——. *Rijālāt al-ʻamal al-amāzīghī*. Rabat: Manshūrāt al-Jamʻiyya al-Maghribiyya li-al-Baḥth wa-al-Tabādul al-Thaqāfī, 2004.

al-Ḥukūma, Ra'īs. "Mashrūʻ qānūn tanẓīmī raqm 04.16 yataʻallaqu bi-al-majlis al-waṭanī li-al-lughāt wa-al-thaqāfa al-maghribiyya." *Chambredesrepresentants*, September 30, 2016, https://www.chambredesrepresentants.ma/sites/default/files/loi/04.16.pdf.

al-Jamʻiyya al-Maghribiyya li-al-Baḥth wa-al-Tabādul al-Thaqāfī (AMREC). *30 Sanatan min al-ʻamal al-thaqāfī al-amāzīghī*. Rabat: Manshūrāt al-Jamʻiyya al-Maghribiyya li-al-Baḥth wa-al-Tabādul al-Thaqāfī, 1997.

——. *Ayyu mustaqbal li-al-amāzīghiyya bi-al-Maghrib*. Rabat: Manshūrāt al-Jamʻiyya al-Maghribiyya li-al-Baḥth wa-al-Tabādul al-Thaqāfī, 2009.

——. *Min ajli tarsīm abajadiyyat Tifinagh li-tadrīs al-amāzīghiyya: Taḥālīl wa wathā'iq wa 'ārā'*. Rabat: Manshūrāt al-Jamʻiyya al-Maghribiyya li-al-Baḥth wa-al-Tabādul al-Thaqāfī, 2002.

al-Majlis al-Istishārī li-Ḥuqūq al-Insān. *Hay'at al-taḥkīm al-mustqilla li-taʻwīḍ ḍaḥāyā al-ikhtifā' al-qasrī wa-al-iʻtiqāl al-taʻassufī: Al-labina al-ūlā fī masār al-ʻadāla al-intiqāliyya bi-al-maghrib*. Rabat: Manshūrāt al-Majlis al-Istishārī li-Ḥuqūq al-Insān, 2009.

"al-Marzūqī: Hādhihi lughatunā bi-tazmamart wa hakadhā tasabbaba yasārī bāriz fi ikhtiṭāfī, al-ʻUmq al-Maghribi." Posted by "al-'Umq al-Maghribī," January 4, 2018, YouTube video, 11:25, https://www.youtube.com/watch?v=kgr9XProoPw.

al-Mūshī, Sālima. "al-Tarīq ilā hunāk: Tazmamārt al-khurūj min al-hāwiyya wa-al-junūn." *Alriyadh*, October 1, 2009, http://www.alriyadh.com/463139.

al-Rasimiyya, al-Jarīda. "Ẓahīr sharīf raqm 1.01.299 ṣādir fī 29 min rajab al-khayr 1422 (17 octūbr 2001) yaqḍī bi-iḥdāth al-maʻhad al-malakī li-al-thaqāfa al-amāzīghiyya." October 1, 2001.

al-Rāwī, Muḥammad. "Jamʻiyyāt amāzīghiyya maghrībiyya tastankir al-daʻwa li-ʻtimād al-aḥruf al-lātīniyya fī kitābat al-lugha al-amāzīghiyya." *al-Sharq al-Awsat*, October 26, 2002, https://archive.aawsat.com/details.asp?article=132126&issueno=8733#.Xi2ZUC2ZNPM.

al-Shāwī, ʻAbd al-Qādir. *al-Sāḥa al-sharafiyya*. Casablanca: Dār al-Fanak, 2006.

——. *Bāb tāza*. Rabat: Manshūrāt al-Mawja, 1994.

Alami, Younes, et al. "Que veulent les Berbères." *Le Journal Hedomadaire*, October 30–November 4, 2004, 26.

Alberani, V., Paola De Castro Pietrangeli, and A.M. Mazza. "The Use of Grey Literature in Health Sciences: A Preliminary Survey." *Bulletin of the Medical Library Association* 78, no. 4 (1990): 358–63.

"AMAZIGH—Origine du drapeau amazigh." Posted by Taddart nneɣ, August 30, 2018, YouTube video, https://www.youtube.com/watch?v=Wt1GGFQTIOg.

Amnay, Majid. "Free Maati Monjib." *London Review of Books*, March 23, 2021, accessed April 10, 2021, https://www.lrb.co.uk/blog/2021/march/free-maati-monjib.

Amnesty International. "The 'Disappeared' in Morocco: Case Studies." April 1993, https://www.amnesty.org/download/Documents/188000/mde290041993en.pdf.

———. "Further information on UA 187/94 (MDE 29/03/94, 12 May 1994)—Detention of Possible Prisoners of Conscience/Fear of Unfair Trial and New Concern: Imprisonment of Prisoners of Conscience." May 31, 1994, https://www.amnesty.org/download/Documents/184000/mde290041994en.pdf.

———. "Le Maroc, vous connaissez?" *Comités de Lutte Contre la Répression au Maroc*, June 1982.

———. "Recommendations of the Moroccan Consultative Council on Human Rights Relative to Prison Conditions, Medical Care of Prisoners and Investigation of Cases of Death in Detention." September 12, 1991, https://www.amnesty.org/download/Documents/196000/mde290261991en.pdf.

———. *Report of an Amnesty International Mission to the Kingdom of Morocco: 10–13 February 1981*. Nottingham: Amnesty International Publications, 1982. https://www.amnesty.org/download/Documents/200000/mde290011982en.pdf.

Anderson, Benedict. *Imagined Communities: Reflections on the Origin and Spread of Nationalism*. New York: Verso, 1991.

Aourid, Hassan. *Cintra*. Rabat: Tūsnā, 2016.

———. *Taghuyt n tīn hinān*. Rabat: Groupe, 2014.

Archibald, Robert R. *A Place to Remember: Using History to Build Community*. New York: Rowman Altamira, 1999.

Arjdāl, Muḥammad. "Amanār—wī-mūzār—wa bidāyat tadwīn al-shi'r al-amazīghī." *Ahewar*, no. 2504 (2008).

Arthur, Paige. "Sending the Wrong Message: International Assistance and the Decline of Civil Society Action on Transitional Justice in Morocco." In *Transitional Justice, International Assistance, and Civil Society: Missed Connections*, edited by Paige Arthur and Christalla Yakinthou, 86–113. Cambridge: Cambridge University Press, 2018.

Ashour, Radwa. *Blue Lorries*. Translated by Barbara Romaine. Doha: Bloomsbury Qatar Foundation Publishing, 2014.

———. *Farag*. Cairo: Dār al-Shurūq, 2008.

Asmhri, Mahfoud, ed. "al-Ta'addud al-lughawī bi-shamāl ifrīqiyya 'abra al-tārīkh." *Asinag* 11 (2016): 7–86.

Assaraf, Robert. *Mohammed V et les Juifs du Maroc à l'époque de Vichy*. Paris: Plon, 1999.

Assid, Ahmed [Ahmad 'Aṣīd]. "Aḥmad 'Aṣīd ilā jarīdat al-'alam: Kayfa tamma tabannī ḥarf tifināgh?" *Amazigh World*, July 30, 2011, http://www.amazighworld.org/arabic/history/index_show.php?id=1993.

Assmann, Aleida. "Canon and Archive." In *Cultural Memory Studies: An International and Interdisciplinary Handbook*, edited by Astrid Erll, Ansgar Nünning, and Sara B. Young, 97–108. Berlin: De Gruyter, 2008.

Atkinson, Meera. *The Poetics of Transgenerational Traumas.* New York: Bloomsbury Academic, 2017.

Aubenas, Florence, and José Garçon. "Ben Jelloun s'enferre dans Tazmamart." *Libération,* January 15, 2001, http://next.liberation.fr/culture/2001/01/15/ben-jelloun-s-enferre-dans-tazmamart_351003.

Awzal, Mohammed, and 'Umar Affā. *Baḥr al-dumū': Bi-al-lughatayn al-amāzīghiiya wa-al-'arabiyya.* al-Dār al-Bayḍā': Maṭba'at al-Najāḥ al-Jadīda, 2009.

Ayache, Germain. "L'Utilisation et l'apport des archives historiques marocaines." *Hespéris-Tamuda* 7 (1966): 69–85.

Azaryahu, Maoz. "The Politics of Commemorative Street Renaming: Berlin 1945–1948." *Journal of Historical Geography* 37, no. 4 (2011): 483–92.

———. "Street Names and Political Identity: The Case of East Berlin." *Journal of Contemporary History* 21, no. 4 (1986): 581–604.

Badawy, Tarek. "Towards a Contemporary View of Islamic Criminal Procedures: A Focus on the Testimony of Witnesses." *Arab Law Quarterly* 23, no. 3 (2009): 269–305.

Bahloul, Joëlle. *La Maison de mémoire: Ethnologie d'une demeure judéo-arabe en Algérie (1937–1961).* Paris: Métaillé, 1992.

Baïda, Jamaâ. "The Emigration of Moroccan Jews, 1948–1956." In *Jewish Culture and Society in North Africa,* edited by Emily Benichou Gottreich and Daniel J. Schroeter, 322–33. Bloomington: Indiana University Press, 2011.

———. In "Historiens vs journalistes." *Zamane,* July 11, 2012, https://zamane.ma/fr/blog/2020/05/22/historiens-vs-journalistes/.

———. "Historiographie marocaine: De l'histoire contemporaine à l'histoire du temps présent." In *Du Protectorat à l'indépendance: Problématique du temps présent,* edited by Mohammed Kenbib, 13–18. Rabat: Publication of the Faculty of Literatures and Human Sciences, 2006.

———. "Le Maroc au XXème siècle: Entre histoire et mémoire." *La Recherche Historique* 1 (2003): 49–55.

———. *Oasis orientales et espace frontalier entre l'Algérie occupée et le Maroc.* Rabat: Manshūrāt al-Ma'had al-Malakī li-al-Baḥt fī Tārīkh al-Maghrib, 2013.

Ballas, Shimon. "Iyya." Translated by Susan Einbinder. In *Keys to the Garden: New Israeli Writing,* edited by Ammiel Alcalay, 69–99. San Francisco, CA: City Lights Books, 1996.

Barbera, Myriam. "Pire que des chiens." *Humanité,* January 11, 1992, https://www.humanite.fr/node/24906.

Barlet, Olivier. *Contemporary African Cinema.* East Lansing: Michigan State University Press, 2016.

Becker, Cynthia. *Amazigh Arts in Morocco: Women Shaping Berber Identity.* Austin: University of Texas Press, 2006.

Bellamy, Richard. *Citizenship: A Very Short Introduction.* Oxford: Oxford University Press, 2008.

Belouchi, Belkassem. *Rapt de voix.* Casablanca: Afrique Orient, 2004.

Ben Barka, Mahdi. *al-Ikhtiyyār al-thawrī fī al-maghrib*. Rabat: Dafātir Wijhat Naẓar, 2011.

Ben Cheikh, Amina. "Ṣarkha lābudda minhā," *Amadal Amazigh*, 222/Māy 2969/2019, https://www.amadalamazigh.press.ma/archivesPDF/220.pdf?_ga=2.164516863.15562416.1662861015-961590116.1662861015.

Ben Jelloun, Tahar. *Cette aveuglante absence de lumière*. Paris: Seuil, 2001.

———. *Le Mariage de plaisir*. Paris: Gallimard, 2016.

———. *This Blinding Absence of Light*. Translated by Linda Coverdale. New York: New Press, 2002.

Ben-Layashi, Samir, and Bruce Maddy-Weitzman. "Myth, History and Realpolitik: Morocco and Its Jewish Community." *Journal of Modern Jewish Studies* 9, no. 1 (2010): 89–106.

Ben Mlih, Abdellah. *al-Tārīkh al-siyyāsī li-al-maghrib ibbāna al-isti'mār: Al-binyāt al-siyyāsiyya*. Translated by Muḥammad al-Nājī. Casablanca: Afrīqiyā al-Sharq, 2014.

———. *Structures politiques du Maroc colonial*. Paris: L'Harmattan, 1990.

Benbaruk, Salomon. *Trois-quarts de siècle pêle-mêle*. Montreal: Les Imprimeurs du 21e Siècle, 1990.

Benichou Gottreich, Emily, and Daniel J. Schroeter, eds. *Jewish Culture and Society in North Africa*. Bloomington: Indiana University Press, 2011.

Bennouna, Rabéa. *Tazmamart côté femme: Témoignage*. Casablanca: Addar Al Alamia Lil Kitab, 2003.

Bensimon, Agnès. *Hassan II et les juifs: Histoire d'une émigration secrète: Essai*. Paris: Seuil, 1991.

"The Berbers Come Fighting Back." *The Economist*, February 13, 1999, 46.

Beroho, Ahmed. *Abdelkrim: Le lion du Rif*. Tangiers: Corail, 2003.

———. *Histoire de Tanger*. Tangiers: Corail, 2008.

———. *Les Mystères de Tanger*. Tangiers: Corail, 2006.

Berrada-Bousta, Hayat. "Soulèvements au Maroc et engagement des marocains en France." *Migrations Société* 143, no. 5 (2012): 139–54.

Bessaoud, Mohand Aarav. *Histoire de l'Académie Berbère*. Alger: L'Artisan, 2000.

Bilmuqaddim, Hafiḍa. *Ḥizb al-istiqlāl wa tadbīr al-intiqāl bayna al-insijām wa l-taṣaddu', dujanbir 1955–yanāyr 1963*. Rabat: Manshūrāt Fikr, 2006.

Bin al-Ṣaghīr, Khālid. *Wāḥāt al-tukhūm wa ḥudūd al-maghrib al-sharqiyya*. Rabat: Manshūrāt al-Ma'had al-Malakī li-al-Baḥt fī Tārīkh al-Maghrib, 2013.

Bin Nun, Yigal. "Les Causes politiques et sociales du départ des Juifs du Maroc, 1956–1966." In *Migrations maghrébines comparées: Genre, ethnicité et religions (France-Québec: De 1945 à nos jours)*, edited by Mireille Calle-Gruber et al., 39–62. Paris: Riveneuve, 2014.

———. "La Quête d'un compromis pour l'évacuation des Juifs du Maroc." *Pardès* 1 (2003): 75–98.

BineBine, Aziz. *Tazmamart: 18 Years in Morocco's Secret Prison*. Translated by Lulu Norman. London: Haus Publishing, 2020.

———. *Tazmamort: Dix-huit ans dans le bagne de Hassan II.* Paris: Denoël, 2009.

Black, Ian, and Benny Morris. *Israel's Secret Wars: A History of Israel's Intelligence Services.* New York: Grove Press, 1991.

Blatterer, Harry. "Intimacy as Freedom: Friendship, Gender and Everyday Life." *Thesis Eleven* 132, no. 1 (2016): 62–76.

Boehm, Philip. *Letters to Milena.* New York: Shocken, 1990.

Borneman, John. *Political Crimes and the Memory of Loss.* Indianapolis: Indiana University Press, 2011.

Bouaziz, Mostafa. "Adabiyyāt al-iʿtiqāl wa-al-tawthīq al-tārīkhī." Paper presented at *Nadwat kitābāt al-iʿtiqāl al-siyyāsī*, Rabat, May 20, 2004, 2–9.

———. "Mouvements sociaux et mouvement national au Maroc: De la liaison organique à l'amorce du disengagement." In *Émeutes et mouvements sociaux au Maghreb: Perspective comparée*, edited by Didier Le Saout and Marguérite Rollinde, 67–76. Paris: Karthala, 1999.

———. *Aux Origines de la Koutla démocratique.* Casablanca: Faculté des Lettres Ain-Chock, 1997.

———. "Des petits grands pas." *Zamane*, January 29, 2013, http://zamane.ma/fr/des-petits-grands-pas/.

Bouderka, M'barek, and Ahmed Chouki Benyoub. *Kadhālika kān: Mudhakkirāt min tajribat hay'at al-inṣāf wa-al-muṣālaḥa.* Casablanca: Dār al-Nashr al-Maghribiyya, 2017.

Boudhan, Mohammed. "Aherdan aḥad ākhir al-rijāl al-aḥrār." *al-Hiwār al-Mutamaddin* 6769, December 23, 2020, https://www.ahewar.org/debat/show.art.asp?aid=703297

———. "Ali Sidqi Azaykou: Dhālika al-mufakkir al-majhūl." *Amadal Amazigh*, September 11, 2020, http://www.amadalamazigh.press.ma/%D8%B9%D9%84%D9%8A-%D8%B5%D8%AF%D9%82%D9%8A-%D8%A3%D8%B2%D8%A7%D9%8A%D9%83%D9%88-%D8%B0%D9%84%D9%83-%D8%A7%D9%84%D9%85%D9%81%D9%83%D8%B1-%D8%A7%D9%84%D9%85%D8%AC%D9%87%D9%88%D9%84/

———. "Badala makhzanat al-amāzīghiyya, yajibu al-ʿamal ʿala tamzīgh al-makhzan." *Hespress*, May 24, 2018, https://www.hespress.com/writers/392677.html

———. *Fī al-hawiyya al-amāzīghiyya li-al-maghrib.* Morocco: Manshūrāt Tawiza, 2013.

Boukous, Ahmed. *Masār al-lugha al-amāzīghiyya, al-rihānāt wal-istrātījiyyāt.* Rabat: Manshūrāt al-Maʿhad al-Malakī li-al-Thaqāfa al-Amāzīghiyya, 2013.

———. "Revitalisation de l'amazighe enjeux et stratégies." *Langage et Société* 143 (2013): 9–26.

———. "Tadrīs al-amāzīghiyya . . . al-ʿawda ilā al-ṣifr." *Assabah*, February 6, 2018, https://assabah.ma/286574.html.

Boulguid, Mbark. "Mulāḥaẓāt ʿalā hāmish khiṭāb al-abajadiyya." In *Min ajli tarsīm abajadiyyat tifinagh li-tadrīs al-amāzīghyya: Taḥālīl wa wathā'iq wa ārā'*, edited

by AMREC, 77–91. Rabat: al-Jamʿiyya al-Maghribiyya li-al-Baḥth wa-al-Tabādul al-Thaqāfī, 2002.
Boulter, Jonathan. *Melancholy and the Archive: Trauma, History and Memory in the Contemporary Novel.* New York: Bloomsbury Publishing, 2011.
Boum, Aomar. *Memories of Absence: How Muslims Remember Jews in Morocco.* Stanford, CA: Stanford University Press, 2013.
Bourequat, Ali-Auguste, and François Thibaux. *Tazmamart: Dix-huit ans de solitude.* Paris: M. Lafont,1993.
Boutaleb, Brahim. *Tārīkh al-maghrib al-ḥadīth al-muʿāṣir.* Rabat: Manshūrāt Kulliyyat al-'Ādāb, 2014.
Brouksy, Lahcen. *Les Berbères face à leur destin.* Rabat: Bouregreg, 2006.
Burke, Peter. "History of Events and the Revival of Narrative." In *New Perspectives on Historical Writing,* edited by Peter Burke, 283–300. 2nd ed. State College: Penn State University Press, 1991.
Burton, Antoinette. *Dwelling in the Archive: Women Writing House, Home, and History in Late Colonial India.* Oxford: Oxford University Press, 2003.
Butler, Judith. *Precarious Life: The Power of Mourning and Violence.* London: Verso, 2004.
Buttin, Maurice. *Ben Barka, Hassan II, De Gaulle: Ce que je sais d'eux.* Paris: Karthala, 2010.
Campbell, George L., and Christopher Moseley. *The Routledge Handbook of Scripts and Alphabets.* New York: Routledge, 2012.
Camps, Gabriel. *Les Berbères, mémoires et identité.* Casablanca: Éditions Le Fennec, 2007.
Casey, Edward S. *The Fate of Place: A Philosophical History.* Berkeley: University of California Press, 1998.
Centre international pour la justice transitionnelle. "Maroc: La perspective de genre dans le processus de justice transitionnelle." ICTJ, September 2011, https://www.ictj.org/sites/default/files/ICTJ-%20Morocco-Gender-Transitional%20Justice-2011-French.pdf.
Chafik, Mohammed. *Lamḥa min thalāt wa thalāthīn qarnan min tārīkh al-amāzīghiyyīn.* Rabat: Dār al-Kalām li-al-Tawzīʿ wa-al-Nashr, 1989.
———. "Le Manifeste berbère." *L'Aménagement linguistique dans le monde,* March 1, 2000, http://www.axl.cefan.ulaval.ca/afrique/berbere-manifeste-2000.htm.
Chauder, Julie. "Au Maroc, les protecteurs musulmans du patrimoine juif." *Le Figaro,* May 26, 2019, https://www.lefigaro.fr/international/au-maroc-les-protecteurs-musulmans-du-patrimoine-juif-20190526.
Chaumont, Jean-Michel. *La Concurrence des victimes: Génocide, identité, reconnaissance.* Paris: Editions la Découverte, 1997.
Chbani, M'bark. "Musique amazighe: Izenzaren de retour après une longue absence." *Libération,* May 12, 2012, https://www.libe.ma/Musique-amazighe-Izenzaren-de-retour-apres-une-longue-absence_a27289.html.

Chberreq, Driss T. *Le Suicide de Mimoun: Drame vécu au bagne de Tazmamart.* Rabat: Imprimerie al-Ma'ārif al-Jadīda, 2015.

———. *Le Train fou: Mémoires d'un rescapé de Tazmamart.* Rabat: al-Ma'ārif al-Jadīda, 2014.

Chouki Benyoub, Ahmed. Interview by Mashārf, March 16, 2017, accessed March 22, 2017, initially available at https://www.youtube.com/watch?v=HLXTLmNp07I.

Chtatou, Mohamed. "The Amazigh Cultural Renaissance." *The Washington Institute,* January 18, 2019, para. 7, https://www.washingtoninstitute.org/fikraforum/view/the-amazigh-cultural-renaissance.

Clarke, Paul B. *Deep Citizenship.* Chicago, IL: Pluto Press, 1996.

Claudot-Hawad, Hélène. "Les Tifinagh comme écriture du détournement." *Études et documents berbères,* no. 23 (2008): 1–14.

———. *Les Touaregs: Portraits en fragments.* Aix-en-Provence: EDISUD, 1993.

Climo, Jacob, and Maria G. Cattell. *Social Memory and History: Anthropological Perspectives.* New York: Altamira Press, 2002.

Comités de Lutte Contre la Répression au Maroc. "Les Détenus militaires: Tazmamart le 5 août 1980." *Bulletin* 42 (April 1982): 1–5.

Connerton, Paul. *How Societies Remember.* Cambridge: Cambridge University Press, 1988.

Conseil National des Droits de l'Homme (CNDH). "Le CNDH et la Faculté de Droit de Rabat-Agdal signent une convention cadre." NCHR, accessed September 14, 2020, http://www.cndh.ma/fr/actualites/le-cndh-et-la-faculte-de-droit-de-rabat-agdal-signent-une-convention-cadre-relative-au.

———. "Convention entre le CNDH et l'Université Mohamed V." NCHR, accessed September 14, 2020, http://www.cndh.org.ma/fr/article/convention-entre-le-cndh-et-luniversite-mohamed-v-agdal-pour-la-creation-du-centre-de.

———. *L'Enfermement, le partage: Lieux de mémoire.* Bilnet: Éditions Les Croisées des Chemins, 2015. http://cndh.ma/sites/default/files/cndh_-_lenfermement_le_partage_monte_-.pdf.

———. "La Réparation individuelle." CNDH, accessed February 19, 2018, http://www.cndh.org.ma/fr/conference-de-presse-de-presentation-du-suivi-de-la-mise-en-oeuvre-des-recommandations-de-lier/la-1.

Coon, Carleton S. *Caravan: The Story of the Middle East.* New York: Holt, Rhinehart and Winston, 1964.

Cox, Richard J. *No Innocent Deposits: Forming Archives by Rethinking Appraisal.* Lanham, MD: Scarecrow Press, 2004.

Dahan, Jacques. *Regard d'un Juif marocain sur l'histoire contemporaine de son pays.* Paris: L'Harmattan, 1995.

Dalle, Ignace. "Le Salon du livre de Paris pris en otage par les autorités marocaines." *Orient XXI,* March 24, 2017, https://orientxxi.info/magazine/le-salon-du-livre-de-paris-pris-en-otage-par-les-autorites-marocaines,1760.

Daoud, Zakya. *Abdallah Ibrahim: L'histoire des rendez-vous manqués.* Casablanca: La Croisée des Chemins, 2019.

———. *Les Années Lamalif : 1958–1988. Trente ans de journalisme au Maroc.* Casablanca: Tarik Editions, 2007.

———. *Maroc: Les années de plomb, 1958–1988, chroniques d'une résistance.* Houilles, France: Éditions Manucius, 2007.

Daure-Serfaty, Christine. *Letter from Morocco.* East Lansing: Michigan State University Press, 2003.

———. *Tazmamart: Une prison de la mort au Maroc.* Paris: Editions Stock, 1992.

De Certeau, Michel. *The Writing of History.* Translated by Tom Conley. New York: Columbia University Press, 1988.

De Chateaubriand, François-René. *Mémoires d'outre-tombe.* Paris: Le Club Français du Livre, 1969.

De Haan, Binne, and Konstantin Mierau. *Microhistory and the Picaresque Novel: A First Exploration into Commensurable Perspectives.* Newcastle upon Tyne: Cambridge Scholars Publishers, 2014.

De Nesry, Carlos. *Les Israélites marocains à l'heure du choix.* Tangiers: Éditions Internationales, 1958.

———. *Le Juif de Tanger et le Maroc.* Tangiers: Éditions Internationales, 1956.

Della Sudda, François. "1985." *Bulletin* 67, December 1984–January 1985.

Derrida, Jacques. *Archive Fever: A Freudian Impression.* Translated by Eric Prenowitz. Chicago: University of Chicago Press, 1996.

———. "Archive Fever: A Freudian Impression." Translated by Eric Prenowitz. *Diacritics* 25 (Summer 1995): 9–63.

Di Masso, Andrés. "Micropolitics of Public Space: On the Contested Limits of Citizenship as a Locational Practice." *Journal of Social and Political Psychology* 3, no. 2 (2015): 63–83.

Dirèche, Karima. "La Vulgate historique berbère en Algérie: Savoirs, usages et projections." In *Les Revendications amazighes dans la tourmente des "printemps arabes": Trajectoires historiques et évolutions récentes des mouvements identitaires en Afrique du Nord,* edited by Mohand Tilmatine and Thierry Desrues, 67–89. Rabat: Centre Jacques-Berque, 2017.

Donohoe, Janet. *Remembering Places: A Phenomenological Study of the Relationship between Memory and Place.* Lanham, MD: Lexington Books, 2014.

Draper, Susana. *Afterlives of Confinement: Spatial Transitions in Postdictatorship Latin America.* Pittsburgh: University of Pittsburgh Press, 2012.

Edelman, Lucila, Diana Kordon, and Darío Lagos. "Transmission of Trauma: The Argentine Case." In *International Handbook of Multigenerational Legacies of Trauma,* edited by Yael Danieli, 447–63. Boston, MA: Springer, 1998.

"Edition—L'écrivain au centre de deux polémiques Ben Jelloun, Fatna et Tazmamart." *L'Orient-le-Jour,* September 13, 2000, https://www.lorientlejour.com/article/432536/Edition_-_Lecrivain_au_centre_de_deux_polemiques_Ben_Jelloun%252C_Fatna_et_Tazmamart.html.

El Adnani, Jilali. "Réforme universitaire et production scientifique en sciences humaines et sociales au Maroc (histoire et anthropologie)." *La Recherche Historique* 7–8 (2009–10): 5–15.

El Ayadi, Mohammed. "al-Madrasa al-tārīkhiyya al-maghribiyya al-ḥadītha: Al-ishkāliyyāt wa-al-mafāhīm." *Mandumah*, accessed July 10, 2021, http://search.mandumah.com/Record/594930/Details, 255–311.

———. "Commentaire." In *Mémoire et histoire*, 17–25. Rabat: Les Cahiers Bleus, 2006.

———. "Les Mouvements de la jeunesse au Maroc." In *Emeutes et mouvements sociaux au Maghreb*, edited by Didier Le Saout and Marguerite Rollinde, 201–30. Paris: Karthala, 1999.

El Bouih, Fatna. *Hadīth al-ʿatama*. Casablanca: Fennec, 2001.

El Ghiwane, Nass. "Soirée Nass El Ghiwane 1976." Posted by "Fī dhākira [sic] al-maghribiya," February 23, 2016, YouTube video, 1:13:37, https://www.youtube.com/watch?v=7M3DO3vR23E.

El Guabli, Brahim. "The Absent Perpetrators: Morocco's Failed Accountability, Tazmamart Literature and the Survivors' Testimony for their Jailers (1973–1991)." *Violence: An International Journal* 1 (2020): 80–101.

———. "Breaking Ranks with National Unanimity: Novelistic and Cinematic Returns of Jewish-Muslim Intimacy in Morocco." In *Generations of Dissent: Intellectuals, Cultural Production, and the State in the Middle East and North Africa*, edited by Alexa Firat and R. Shareah Taleghani, 159–87. New York: Syracuse University Press, 2020.

———. "*Cette aveuglante absence de lumière*: The Politics of Novelizing Human Rights Violations in the Former Colonizer's Language." *Francosphères* 5, no. 1 (2016): 59–80.

———. "From Lalla Batoul to Oum Hamza: New Trends in Moroccan Women's Fight for Citizenship." In *Arab Women's Activism and Socio-Political Transformation*, edited by Sahar Khamis and Amel Mili, 219–40. New York: Palgrave Macmillan, 2018.

———. "The 'Hidden Transcript' of Resistance in Moroccan Tazmamart Prison Writings." *The Arab Studies Journal* 22, no. 1 (2014): 170–207.

———. "Intergenerational Trauma in Tazmamart Testimonial Literature and Docu-Testimonies." *Middle East—Topics & Arguments* 11 (Fall 2018): 120–30.

———. "Joint Authorship and Preface Writing Practices as Translation in post-'Years of Lead' Morocco." In *The Routledge Handbook of Translation and Activism*, edited by Rebecca Ruth Gould and Kayvan Tahmasebian, 237–57. New York: Routledge, 2020.

———. "Literature and Indigeneity: Amazigh Activists' Construction of an Emerging Literary Field." *Los Angeles Review of Books*. https://lareviewofbooks.org/article/literature-and-indigeneity-amazigh-activists-construction-of-an-emerging-literary-field/.

———. "Moroccan Society's Educational and Cultural Losses during the Years of

Lead (1956–1999)." *Journal of Global Initiatives: Policy, Pedagogy, Perspective* 14, no. 2 (2019): 143–62.

———. "Reading for Theory in the Moroccan Marxist-Leninist Testimonial Literature." *African Identities* 18, no. 1–2 (2020): 145–61. DOI: 10.1080/14725843.2020.1773243.

———. "(Re)Invention of Tradition, Subversive Memory, and Morocco's Re-Amazighization: From Erasure of Imazighen to the Performance of Tifinagh in Public Life." *Expressions Maghrébines* (2020): 143–68.

———. "The Sub-Saharan African Turn in Moroccan Literature." *MERIP*, https://merip.org/2021/03/the-sub-saharan-african-turn-in-moroccan-literature/.

———. "Tankra Tamazight: The Revival of Amazigh Indigeneity in Literature and Art." Jadaliyya, November 1, 2021, https://www.jadaliyya.com/Details/43440.

———. "Testimony and Journalism: Moroccan Prison Narratives." In *The Social Life of Memory*, edited by Saadi Nikro and Sonja Hegasy, 113–44. New York: Palgrave Macmillan, 2017.

———."Textual Traces: Khatibi and His Jews." *PMLA/Publications of the Modern Language Association of America* 137, no. 2 (2022): 347–54. DOI:10.1632/S0030812922000165.

———. "Les Voix et les voies du Maroc juif." In *Vues du Maroc juif: Formes, lieux, récits*, edited by Nadia Sabri, 107–11. Casablana: Fennec, 2020.

———. "Where is Amazigh Studies?" *The Journal of North African Studies*, 1–8.

———. "Youssef Fadel's Re-imagination(s) of Moroccan Testimonial Literature: A Book Review Essay." *The Journal of North African Studies* 23, no. 1–2 (2017): 281–91.

El Guabli, Brahim, and Mostafa Hussein, eds. *Refiguring Loss: Jews Remembered in Maghrebi and Middle Eastern Literature and Film*. Penn State University Press, forthcoming.

El Hamel, Chouki. *Black Morocco: A History of Slavery, Race, and Islam*. New York: Cambridge University Press, 2013.

El Khalfi, Mustapha. "al-Islāmīyyūn al-maghāriba wa-al-amāzīghīyya." In *Al-Jam'iyya al-Maghribiyya li-al-Baḥth wa-al-Tabādul al-Thaqāfī, Ayyu Mustaqbal li-al-Amāzīghiyya bi-al-Maghrib*, edited by AMREC, 95–111. Rabat: Manshūrāt al-Jam'iyya al-Maghribiyya li-al-Baḥth wa-al-Tabādul al-Thaqāfī, 2009.

El Khamlichi, Kamal. *Ḥārith al-nisyān*. Rabat: Kamal El Khamlichi, 2003.

El Madini, Ahmed. "al-Yahūdī 'al-mansī' fī mir'āt al-riwāya al-maghribiyya." *Al-Ḥayāt*, January 25, 2016, http://www.alhayat.com/Articles/13613967/اليهودي—المنسي—في-مرآة-الرواية-المغربية.

El Moudden, Abderrahmane. "'Awda ilā mas'alat al-arshīf al-makhzanī." In *Jirmām 'Ayyāsh al-mu'arrikh wa-al-munāḍil*, edited by Abderrahmane El Moudden and Abdelaziz Belfaida, 41–48. Rabat: Nabat Net, 2015.

El Moudden, Abderrahmane, and Abdelaziz Belfaida. *Jirmān 'Ayyāsh al-mu'arrikh wa-al-munāḍil*. Rabat: Al-Jam'iyya al-Maghribiyya li-al-Baḥth al-Tārīkhī, 2015.

El Ouafi, Ahmed, and Kalima El Ouafi. *Opération Boraq F5: 16 Août 1972, l'attaque du Boeing royal*. Casablanca: Tarik Editions, 2004.

El Qadéry, Mustapha. "Les Berbères entre le mythe colonial et la négation nationale: Le cas du Maroc." *Revue d'Histoire Moderne et Contemporaine* 45, no. 2 (1998): 425–50.

El Yazami, Driss. Interview by Grand Angle Reportage 2M, 2M (CD 10, minute 47–48), distributed the National Council for Human Rights in the kit entitled "Programme de la réparation communautaire au Maroc," n.d.

———. "Transition politique, histoire et mémoire." *Confluences Méditerranée* 3 (2007): 25–34.

El Yazami, Driss, and Bernard Wallon. *Le Livre blanc sur les droits de l'homme au Maroc*. Paris: Études et Documentation Internationales, 1991.

Elinson, Alexander. "Court Jesters and Black Mirrors: Translator Alex Elinson on Bringing Moroccan Literature into English." *Arablit*, January 24, 2018, https://arablit.org/2018/01/24/court-jesters-and-black-mirrors-translator-alex-elinson-on-bringing-moroccan-literature-into-english/.

Eng, David L., and David Kazanjian, eds. *Loss: The Politics of Mourning*. Berkeley: University of California Press, 2003.

Equity and Reconciliation Commission. *The Components of Reform and Reconciliation*. Rabat: Le Conseil Consultatif des Droits de l'Homme, 2009.

———. *Establishing Truth and Responsibility Regarding Human Right Violations*. Rabat: Le Conseil Consultatif des Droits de l'Homme, 2009.

———. *Final Report: Truth, Equity and Reconciliation*. Rabat: The Advisory Council on Human Rights Publications, 2009.

———. *Justice and Reconciliation Commission, Summary of the Final Report*. Rabat: Le Conseil Consultatif des Droits de l'Homme, 2009.

———. *Truth, Equity, and Reconciliation*. Rabat: Le Conseil Consultatif des Droits de l'Homme, 2009.

Errahoui, Mohammed. *Mouroirs: Chronique d'une disparition forcée*. Rabat: Saad Warzazi Éditions, 2008.

Erll, Astrid, and Ann Rigney. "Literature and the Production of Cultural Memory: Introduction." *European Journal of English Studies* 10, no. 2 (2006): 111–15.

Erwin, Edward. *The Freud Encyclopedia: Theory, Therapy, and Culture*. New York: Routledge, 2002.

Esposito, Claudia. "'Ce Maroc qui nous fait mal': Entretien avec Mahi Binebine." *Contemporary French and Francophone Studies* 17, no. 3 (2013): 299–308.

Euro-Mediterranean Human Rights Monitor. "al-Maghrib..khanq al-ra'yi al-ākhar: Mulāḥaqat al-sulutāt al-maghribiyya li-al-nushaṭā' wa-al-ḥuqūqiyyīn wa-al-ṣaḥafiyyīn." *Euro-Mediterranean Human Rights Monitor*, July 12, 2021, accessed July 12, 2021, https://euromedmonitor.org/ar/article/4514/%D8%AE%D9%86%D9%82-%D8%A7%D9%84%D8%B1%D8%A3%D9%8A-%D8%A7%D9%84%D8%A2%D8%AE%D8%B1:%C2%A0%D9%85%D9%84%D8%A7%D8%AD%D9%82%D8%A9-%D8%A7%D9%84%D8%B3%D9%84%D8%B7%D8%A7%D8%AA

-%D8%A7%D9%84%D9%85%D8%BA%D8%B1%D8%A8%D9%8A%D8%A9-%D9%84%D9%84%D9%86%D8%B4%D8%B7%D8%A7%D8%A1-%D9%88%D8%A7%D9%84%D8%AD%D9%82%D9%88%D9%82%D9%8A%D9%8A%D9%86-%D9%88%D8%A7%D9%84%D8%B5%D8%AD%D8%A7%D9%81%D9%8A%D9%8A%D9%86.

Facatier, Julia. "La Question." *La Croix*, January 15, 2001, https://www.la-croix.com/Archives/2001-01-15/LA-QUESTION-_NP_-2001-01-15-125011.

Fadel, Youssef. *Ogni volta che prendo il volo*. Translated by Cristina Dozio. Rome: Brioschi, 2019.

———. *Un Oiseau bleu et rare vole avec moi*. Translated by Philippe Vigreux. Paris: Actes Sud, 2017.

———. *A Rare Blue Bird Flies with Me*. Translated by Jonathan Smolin. Cairo: AUC Press, 2016.

———. *Ṭā'ir azraq nādir yuḥalliqu ma'ī*. Beirut: Dār al-Ādāb, 2013.

Fahli, Asmaa. "Les Archives de l'IER, une responsabilité pour demain." CNDH, accessed June 10, 2019, https://www.ccdh.org.ma/fr/bulletin-d-information/les-archives-de-lier-une-responsabilite-pour-demain.

Fakihani, Abdelfattah. *Le Couloir: Bribes de vérité sur les années de plomb*. Casablanca: Tarik Éditions, 2005.

Fanon, Frantz. *A Dying Colonialism*. New York: Grove Books, 1956.

Fassi Fihri, Nouzha. *Dada l'Yakout*. Casablanca: Le Fennec, 2019.

Felman, Shoshana, and Dauri Lob. *Testimony: Crises of Witnessing in Literature, Psychoanalysis, and History*. New York: Routledge, 1992.

Foucault, Michel. *The Archaeology of Knowledge*. Translated by A. M. Sheridan Smith. New York: Pantheon Books, 1972.

———. "Of Other Spaces: Utopias and Heterotopias." Translated by Jay Miskowiec. Originally published in *Architecture/Mouvement/Continuité* (October 1984), accessed October 22, 2017, http://web.mit.edu/allanmc/www/foucault1.pdf.

———. "La vie des hommes infâmes." *Les Cahiers du Chemin* 29 (1977): 16–17.

"Ces Français amis du Maroc." *Zamane*, September 4, 2019, https://zamane.ma/fr/ces-francais-amis-du-maroc/.

Frank, Michael. "In Morocco, Exploring Remnants of Jewish History." *The New York Times*, May 30, 2015.

Freud, Sigmund. "Mourning and Melancholia." In *The Standard Edition of the Complete Psychological Works of Sigmund Freud*, edited by James Strachey and Anna Freud, XIV:243–58. London: The Hogarth Press and The Institute of Psycho-Analysis, 1917.

Garçon, José. "Maroc: Retour sur les années noires; L'état et les victimes du régime prônent la réconciliation plutôt que la justice." *Libération*, March 21, 2000, http://www.liberation.fr/planete/2000/03/21/maroc-retour-sur-les-annees-noires-l-etat-et-les-victimes-du-regime-pronent-la-reconciliation-plutot_320643.

Geertz, Clifford. "'From the Native's Point of View': On the Nature of

Anthropological Understanding." *Bulletin of the American Academy of Arts and Sciences* 28, no. 1 (1974): 26–45.

Ghallab, Saïd. "Les Juifs vont en enfer." *Les Temps Modernes* 229 (June 1965): 2247–55.

Ghazali, Ismail. *Thalāthat ayyām fī Casablanca*. Milan: Almutawassit Books, 2019.

Giddens, Anthony. *The Transformation of Intimacy: Sexuality, Love and Eroticism in Modern Societies*. Cambridge: Polity Press, 1992.

Gilson Miller, Susan. *A History of Modern Morocco*. Cambridge: Cambridge University Press, 2013.

———. "Why History Matters in Post-2011 Morocco." Jadaliyya, November 30, 2016, http://www.jadaliyya.com/pages/index/25584/why-history-matters-in-post-2011-morocco#_edn8.

Ginzburg, Carlo, and Carlo Poni. "The Name and the Game: Unequal Exchange and the Historiographic Marketplace." In *Microhistory and the Lost Peoples of Europe*, edited by Edward Muir, 1–10. Baltimore, MD: Johns Hopkins University Press, 1991.

Ginzburg, Carlo, John Tedeschi, and Anne C. Tedeschi. "Microhistory: Two or Three Things that I Know about It." *Critical Inquiry* 20, no. 1 (1993): 10–35.

Gordon, Avery. *Ghostly Matters: Haunting and the Sociological Imagination*. Minneapolis: University of Minnesota Press, 2008.

Gordon, Robert. "Brecht, Interruptions and Epic Theatre." BritishLibrary.uk, September 7, 2017, https://www.bl.uk/20th-century-literature/articles/brecht-interruptions-and-epic-theatre.

Gosden, Chris, and Jon G. Hather, eds. *The Prehistory of Food: Appetites for Change*. New York: Routledge, 2004.

Gottreich, Emily. "Rethinking the 'Islamic City' from the Perspective of Jewish Space." *Jewish Social Studies* 11, no. 1 (Fall 2004): 118–46.

"'Haaretz' ḥikāyat al-ta'āwūn al-sirrī al-ṭawīl bayna 'al-mūsād' wa-al-maghrib." *Lakome2*, December 22, 2020, https://lakome2.com/decryptage/211714/.

Hachad, Naïma. "Narrating Tazmamart: Visceral Contestations of Morocco's Transitional Justice and Democracy." *The Journal of North African Studies* 2, no. 1–2 (2018): 208–24.

Hachid, Malika. *Les premiers berbères entre méditerranée, Tassili et Nil*. Algiers: Ina-Yas Editions, 2001.

Hamilton, Carolyn, et al., eds. *Refiguring the Archive*. Dordrecht: Kluwer Academic Publishers, 2002.

Hammoudi, Abdellah. "Le Don entre juifs et musulmans: Ou comment concilier les identités opposées." *Revue Internationale d'Anthropologie Culturelle & Sociale*, Special issue (2016): 91–106.

———. "L'Évolution de l'habitat dans la vallée du Draa." *Revue de géographie du Maroc* 18 (1970): 33–45.

———. *Master and Disciple: The Cultural Foundations of Moroccan Authoritarianism*. Chicago: University of Chicago Press, 1997.

Hananou. "Une Histoire de Tazmamart." *Temps Modernes*, no. 565–66 (1993): 13–27.
Hariri, Ibrahim. *Shāmma aw Shtrīt*. Casablanca: Afrīqia al-Sharq, 2013.
Harlan, David. "Historical Fiction and Academic History." In *Manifestos for History*, edited by Sue Morgan et al., 108–30. London: Routledge, 2007.
Hassoun, Jacques. *Les Contrebandiers de la mémoire*. Toulouse: Éditions érès, 2011.
Hatimi, Mohammed [Muḥammad al-Ḥatimī]. "Adabiyyāt al-sujūn ka-maṣdar tārīkhī: Al-ishkāliyyāt wa-al-muqāraba." Paper presented at *Nadwat kitābāt al-i'tiqāl al-siyāsī*, Rabat, May 20, 2004.
———. "Al-jamā'āt al-yahūdiyya al-maghribiyya khilāla marḥalat al-ḥimāya: Haṣīlat al-abḥāth al-akādīmiyya." In *al-Maghrib wa-al-zaman al-rāhin*, edited by Mohammed Kably and Abderrahmane El Moudden, 33–43. Rabat: Manshūrāt al-Ma'had al-Malakī li-al-Baḥth fī Tārīkh al-Maghrib, 2013.
Hazan, Pierre. "The Nature of Sanctions: The Case of Morocco's Equity and Reconciliation Commission." *International Review of the Red Cross* 90, no. 870 (2008): 399–407.
Hay'at al-Inṣāf wa-al-Muṣālaḥa. *al-Ḥaqīqa wa-al-inṣāf wa-al-muṣālaḥa*. Rabat: al-Majlis al-Istishārī li-Ḥuqūq al-Insān, 2006.
———. *al-Taqrīr al-khitāmī: Muqawwimāt tawṭīd al-iṣlāḥ*. Rabat: al-Majlis al-Istishārī li-Ḥuqūq al-Insān, 2006.
Hegasy, Sonja. "Transforming Memories: Media and Historiography in the Aftermath of the Moroccan Equity and Reconciliation Commission." In *The Social Life of Memory: Violence, Trauma, and Testimony in Lebanon and Morocco*, edited by Norman Saadi Nikro and Sonja Hegasy, 83–112. New York: Palgrave Macmillan, 2017.
Herzenni, Ahmed. "Lettre de soutien du CCDH." In *La Bienvenue et l'adieu: Migrants juifs et musulmans au Maghreb (XVe–XXe siècle)*, edited by Frédéric Abécassis, Karima Dirèche, and Rita Aouad, I:1. Paris: Karthala, 2012.
Hobsbawm, Eric, and Terence Ranger. "Introduction." In *The Invention of Tradition*, edited by Eric Hobsbawm and Terence Ranger, 1–14. 1983; repr. New York: Cambridge University Press, 2012.
Hoffman, Katherine. *We Share Walls: Language, Land, and Gender in Berber Morocco*. Malden, MA: John Wiley & Sons, 2008.
Hoskins, William G. *The Making of the English Landscape*. London: Hodder and Stoughton, 1955.
Houbaida Mohammed. "al-Tārīkh al-ijtimā'ī wa-al-iqtiṣādī fī-al-maghrib min al-munughrāfīyya ilā al-tarkīb." In *50 sana min al-baḥt al-tārīkhī fī al-maghrib*, edited by Abderrahame El Mouddene, 11–23. Rabat: Rabat Net Maroc, 2003.
———. *Bu's al-tārīkh: Murāja'āt wa-muqārabāt*. Rabat: Dār al-Amān, 2016.
Housni, Ali. "'Bayān maknās' wa-'umalā' al qawmiyya al-'arabiyya." *Tawiza*, November 2002, http://tawiza.eu5.org/Tawiza67/Asidd121002.htm.
Hughes, Stephen O. *Morocco under King Hassan*. Reading: Ithaca Press, 2001.
Human Rights Watch. *Human Rights Watch World Report 1992—Morocco and*

Western Sahara. January 1, 1992, available at: https://www.refworld.org/docid/467fca5bc.html.
———. "Morocco's Truth Commission Honoring Past Victims during an Uncertain Present." *Human Rights Watch* 17, no. 11 (2005): 1–49.
Iacovino, Livia Maria. "Archives as Arsenals of Accountability." In *Currents of Archival Thinking*, edited by Terry Eastwood and Heather MacNeil, 181–212. Santa Barbara, CA: Libraries Unlimited, 2010.
Ibn Manẓūr, Jamāl al-Dīn. *Lisān al-'Arab*. Beirut: Dar El Fikr for Printing Publishing and Distribution, 2015.
Ilahiane, Hsain. "The Social Mobility of the Haratine and the Re-Working of Bourdieu's Habitus on the Saharan Frontier, Morocco." *American Anthropologist* 103, no. 2 (2001): 380–94.
Institut d'Histoire du Temps Présent. http://www.ihtp.cnrs.fr/content/linstitut-dhistoire-du-temps-present.
Institut Royal de la Culture Amazighe. *Dalīl manshūrāt al-ma'had al-malakī li-al-thaqāfa al-amazīghīyya 2003–2016*. RIAC, accessed December 11, 2018, http://www.ircam.ma/sites/default/files/publications/Guide%20des%20publications%20de%20l%27IRCAM_0.pdf.
———. "Texte du Dahir portant création de l'Institut Royal de la Culture Amazighe." RIAC [2001], Preamble§2, http://www.ircam.ma/?q=fr/node/4668.
Institut Royal pour la Recherche sur l'Histoire du Maroc (RIRHM). "Publications." RIRHM, accessed September 15, 2020, http://www.irrhm.org/LangFr.aspx?r=17.
International Center for Transitional Justice. "What is Transitional Justice." Accessed August 10, 2020, https://www.ictj.org/about/transitional-justice.
I'zza, Ibrāhīm. *Iskla n yiḍ*. Rabat: Marsam, 2016.
Ittiḥād Kuttāb al-Maghrib. *al-Dhākira wa-al-ibdā': A'māl nadwa*. Rabat: Manshūrāt Ittiḥād Kuttāb al-Maghrib, 2010.
Jām'iyyat al-Jāmi'a al-Ṣayfiyya bi-Agādīr. *A'māl al-dawra al-ūlā li-al-jāmi'iyya al-ṣayfiyya bi-agādīr : Al-thaqāfa al-sha'biyya, al-waḥda fī al-tanawwu'*. Mohammadia: Maṭba'at Faḍāla, 1982.
———. *Tārīkh al-amāzīgh: Al-nadwa al-dawliyya ḥawla tārīkh al-amāzīgh, al-tārīkh al-mu'āṣir*. Rabat: Dār Abī Raqrāq, 2002.
Jamieson, Lynn. "Boundaries of Intimacy." In *Families in Society: Boundaries and Relationships*, edited by Linda McKie and Sarah Cunningham-Burley, 189–206. Bristol: Policy Press, 2005.
Jedamus, Julith. *The Swerve*. Manchester: Carcanet, 2012.
Jellin, Elizabeth. *State Repression and the Labors of Memory*. Minneapolis: University of Minnesota Press, 2003.
Jouaiti, Abdelkarim. *Zaghārīd al-mawt*. al-Jazā'ir: Manshūrāt al-Ikhtilāf, 2015.
Jouhadi El Baâmrani, El Houssaine. *Tarjamat ma'ānī al-qur'ān al-karīm bi-al-lugha al-amāzīghiyya*. Casablanca : J.al-Ḥ. al-Bā'umrānī, 2003.
Justice and Reconciliation Commission. "Summary of the Final Report." 2006,

http://www.ccdh.org.ma/sites/default/files/documents/rapport_final_mar_eng-3.pdf.

Kably, Mohamed, ed. *Chronologie de l'histoire du Maroc*. Rabat: Éditions de l'Institut Royal pour la Recherche sur l'Histoire du Maroc, 2013.

———. *al-Dhākira wa-al-muqāwama al-maghribiyya fīmā bayna sanatay 1944 wa 1961*. Rabat: Manshūrāt al-Ma'had al-Malakī li-al-Baḥt fī Tārīkh al-Maghrib, 2014.

———. *Histoire du Maroc: Réactualisation et synthèse*. Rabat: Publications de l'Institut Royal pour la Recherche sur l'Histoire du Maroc, 2012.

———. *Shamāl al-maghrib ibbāna fatra al-ḥimāya wa bidāyat 'ahd al-istiqlāl*. Rabat: Manshūrāt al-Ma'had al-Malakī li-al-Baḥt fī Tārīkh al-Maghrib, 2014.

Kably, Mohamed, and Abderrahmane El Moudden, eds. *al-Maghrib wa-al-zaman al-rāhin*. Rabat: Manshūrāt al-Ma'had al-Malakī li-al-Baḥth fī Tārīkh al-Maghrib, 2013.

Kaddouri, Abdelmajid. "Professor Abdelmajid Kaddouri." In *al-Maghrib wa-al-zaman al-rāhin*, edited by Mohammed Kably and Abderrahmane El Moudden, 54–55. Rabat: Manshūrāt al-Ma'had al-Malakī li-al-Baḥth fī Tārīkh al-Maghrib, 2013.

Kaddouri, Abdelmajid, and Abdelkader Gangai, and Kacem Marghata, eds. *'Abd Allāh al-'Arawī: Al-ḥadātha wa-as'ilat al-tārīkh*. Casablanca: Manshūrāt Kullīyat al-Ādāb wa-al-'Ulūm al-Insāniyya bi-Namsīk, 2007.

Kasanga, Luanga A. "Odonymic Changes in Central Pretoria: Representation, Identity and Textual Construction of Place." *International Journal of the Sociology of Language* 234 (2015): 27–45.

Kateb, Yacine, and Amazigh Kateb. *Minuit passé de douze heures: Écrits journalistiques, 1947–1989*. Paris: Seuil, 1999.

Kenbib, Mohammed [Muḥammad Kanbīb]. "Études et recherches sur les Juifs du Maroc: Observations et réflexions générales." *Hespéris-Tamuda* 51, no. 2 (2016): 21–55.

———. "al-Ḥaqīqa al-tārīkhiyya bayna al-ḍawābiṭ al-'ilmiyya li-al-dawla wa-al-mujtama'." Paper presented at *Nadwat mafhūm al-ḥaqīqa*, Tangiers, September 17–18, 2004.

———. "Historiens, journalistes et essayistes." In *Temps présent et fonctions de l'historien*, edited by Mohammed Kenbib, 35–90. Rabat: Publications de la Faculté des Lettres et des Sciences Humaines, 2009.

———. "À propos de l'histoire contemporaine du Maroc." *Perspectives Universitaires* 1 (2008): 99–107.

Kenbib, Mohammed, ed. *Du Protectorat à l'indépendance: Problématique du temps présent*. Rabat: Publication of the Faculty of Literatures and Human Sciences, 2006.

———. *Temps présent et fonctions de l'historien*. Rabat: Publications de la Faculté des Lettres et des Sciences Humaines, 2009.

Ketelaar, Eric. "Archival Temples, Archival Prisons: Modes of Power and Protection." *Archival Science* 2, no. 3–4 (2002): 221–38.

Khatibi, Abdelkébir. *Le Scribe et son ombre*. Paris : Éditions de la Différence, 2008.
Khatibi, Abdelkébir, and Jacques Hassoun. *Le Même livre*. Paris : Éditions de l'Éclat, 1985.
Kilani, Leïla. *Nos lieux interdits*. Paris: INA, Socco Chico, 2008.
Korostelina, Karina. "History Education and Social Identity." *Identity* 8, no. 1 (2008): 25–45.
Kosansky, Oren, and Aomar Boum. "The 'Jewish Question' in Postcolonial Moroccan Cinema." *International Journal of Middle East Studies* 44, no. 3 (2012): 421–42.
Ksenja Bilbija and Leigh A. Payne, eds., *Accounting for Violence: Marketing Memory in Latin America*. Durham: Duke University Press, 2011.
Lachmann, Renate. "Cultural Memory and the Role of Literature." *European Review* 12, no. 2 (2004): 165–78.
Lafuente, Gilles. "Dossier marocain sur le dahir berbère de 1930." *Revue de l'Occident Musulman et de la Méditerranée* 38, no. 2 (1984): 83–116. DOI: 10.3406/remmm.1984.2047.
Lakmahri, Sami. "'Afwu 1994, al-ṣafḥ al-'aẓīm." *Zamane*, July 9, 2018, https://zamane.ma/ar/blog/2018/07/09/%D8%B9%D9%81%D9%88-1994%D8%8C-%D8%A7%D9%84%D8%B5%D9%81%D8%AD-%D8%A7%D9%84%D8%B9%D8%B8%D9%8A%D9%85/.
Landsberg, Alison. *Engaging the Past: Mass Culture and the Production of Historical Knowledge*. New York: Columbia University Press, 2015.
———. *Prosthetic Memory: The Transformation of American Remembrance in the Age of Mass Culture*. New York: Columbia University Press, 2004.
Laroui, Abdallah. *Le Maroc et Hassan II: Un témoignage*. Québec: Presses Inter Universitaires, 2005.
———. *Les Origines sociales et culturelles du nationalisme marocain, 1830–1912*. Paris: F. Maspero, 1977.
Laskier, Michael M. *The Alliance Israelite Universelle and the Jewish Communities of Morocco, 1862–1962*. Albany: SUNY series in Modern Jewish Literature and Culture, 1984.
———. "Jewish Emigration from Morocco to Israel: Government Policies and the Position of International Jewish Organizations, 1949–56." *Middle Eastern Studies* 25, no. 3 (1989): 323–62.
Leprince, Chloé. "Une Lanceuse d'alerte au placard: L'archiviste qui avait raconté le massacre du 17 octobre 1961." *Franceculture*, November 16, 2018, https://www.franceculture.fr/histoire/une-lanceuse-dalerte-au-placard-larchiviste-qui-avait-raconte-le-massacre-du-17-octobre-1961.
Leveau, Rémy. *Le Fellah marocain défenseur du trône*. Paris: Presses de la Fondation Nationale des Sciences Politiques, 1976.
Levi, Giovanni. "On Microhistory." In *New Perspectives on Historical Writing*, edited by Peter Burke, 93–113. Cambridge: Polity Press, 1991.
Levy, André. *Return to Casablanca: Jews, Muslims, and an Israeli Anthropologist*. Chicago: University of Chicaho Press, 2015.

Lévy, Joseph. "*Juifs du Maroc: Identité et Dialogue*. Grenoble: Éditions la Pensée Sauvage, 1980.
Levy, Lital. "The Arab Jew Debates: Media, Culture, Politics, History." *Journal of Levantine Studies* 7, no. 1 (2017): 79–103.
———. "Self and the City: Literary Representations of Jewish Baghdad." *Prooftexts* 26, no. 1 (2006): 163–211.
Lévy, Simon. *Essais d'histoire*. Rabat: Centre Tarik Ibn Zyad, 2001.
———. "Professor Simon Levy." In *al-Maghrib wa-al-zaman al-rāhin*, edited by Mohammed Kably and Abderrahmane El Moudden, 49–53. Rabat: Manshūrāt al-Maʿhad al-Malakī li-al-Baḥth fī Tārīkh al-Maghrib, 2013.
Lorcin, Patricia M. *Imperial Identities: Stereotyping, Prejudice and Race in Colonial Algeria*. London: I.B. Tauris Publishers, 1995.
Lotfi, Mustapha. "al-Mudhakkirāt laysat tārīkhan." *Assabah*, January 14, 2014, https://assabah.ma/61624.html.
Lovejoy, Paul E. "Introduction: Slavery, Memory, Citizenship." In *Slavery, Memory, Citizenship*, edited by Paul E. Lovejoy and Vanessa S. Oliveira, XIX–XXVIII. Trenton: Africa World Press, 2016.
Maddy-Weitzman, Bruce. *The Berber Identity Movement and the Challenge to North African States*. Austin: University of Texas Press, 2011.
———. "Berber/Amazigh Memory Work." In *The Maghreb in the New Century: Identity, Religion, and Politics*, edited by Bruce Maddy Weitzman and Daniel Zisenwine, 50–71. Gainsville: University Press of Florida, 2007.
Maghraoui, Driss. "Histoire et mémoire: Quels enjeux politiques au Maroc." In *Temps présent et fonctions de l'historien*, edited by Mohammed Kenbib, 17–27. Rabat: Publications de la Faculté des Lettres et des Sciences Humaines, 2009.
Malka, Victor. *La Mémoire brisée des Juifs du Maroc*. Paris: Editions Entente, 1978.
Mansouri, Otmane, and Mohammed Yasir El Hilali, eds. *al-ʿUnf fī tārīkh al-maghrib: Ashghāl al-ayyām al-waṭaniyya al-ḥādiyya wa-al-ʿishrīn li-al-jamʿiyya al-maghribiyya li-al-baḥth al-tārīkhī*. Casablanca: Manshūrāt Multaqā al-Ṭṭuruq, 2015.
Marglin, Jessica M. *Across Legal Lines: Jews and Muslims in Modern Morocco*. New Haven, CT: Yale University Press, 2016.
"Maroc: L'amnistie royale pourrait décrisper la vie politique." *Le Monde*, July 23, 1994, https://www.lemonde.fr/archives/article/1994/07/23/maroc-l-amnistie-royale-pourrait-decrisper-la-vie-politique_3818417_1819218.html.
Marshall, Thomas H. "Citizenship and Social Class." In *Inequality and Society*, edited by Jeff Manza and Michael Sauder, 148–54. New York: W. W. Norton and Co., 2009.
Marzouki, Ahmed. *Tazmamart: Al-zinzāna raqm 10*. Casablanca: Editions Tarik, 2003.
———. *Tazmamart: Cellule 10*. Casablanca: Tarik Editions, 2001.
Mbembe, Achille. "The Power of the Archive and Its Limits." In *Refiguring the Archive*, edited by Carolyn Hamilton et al., 19–27. Cape Town: David Philip, 2002.
McKemmish, Sue, and Michael Piggott. "Recordkeeping, Reconciliation and

Political Reality." *Australia Society of Archivists [ASA] 2002 Annual Conference*, Sydney, Australia, August 13–17, 2002.

Mdidech, Jaouad. *La Chambre noire ou Derb Moulay Cherif.* Casablanca: Eddif, 2002.

Melman, Yossi. "Assassination, Bribes and Smuggling Jews: Inside the Israeli Mossad's Long Secret Alliance with Morocco." *Haaretz*, December 17, 2020, https://www.haaretz.com/israel-news/.premium.HIGHLIGHT-assassination-bribes-smuggling-jews-inside-mossad-s-secret-alliance-with-morocco-1.9372580.

Menin, Laura. "'Descending into Hell': Tazmamart, Civic Activism and the Politics of Memory in Contemporary Morocco." *Memory Studies* 12, no. 3 (2019): 307–21.

Messari, Mohammed Larbi. *Muḥammad al-Khāmis min sulṭān ilā malik.* Rabat: Manshūrāt al-Ma'had al-Malakī li-al-Baḥt fī Tārīkh al-Maghrib, 2013.

Mestaoui, Mohammed. *Smmūs idlisn n tmdiāzīn.* Rabat: IDG, 2010.

"Mi'āt al-jam'iyyāt al-amāzīghiyya tastaghīthu bi-al-malik muḥammad al-sādis al-ḥāmī al-tārīkhī li-al-amāzīghīyya lughatan wa taqāfatan wa hawīyyatan." *Al Maghreb Alaan,* September 8, 2016, https://www.maghrebalaan.com/archives/25315.

Midhat Bourequat, René. *Mort Vivant.* Paris: Pygmalion, 2000.

Miliani, Driss. *Casanfa.* Al-Iskandarīyya: Dār al-'Ayn li-al-Nashr, 2016.

Mohammed VI. "Khitāb ṣāhib al-jalāla al-malik muḥammad al-sādis naṣarahu al-lāh bi-munāsabat waḍ' al-ṭāba' al-sharīf 'alā al-ẓhīr al-muḥdith wa-al-munaẓẓm li-al-ma'had al-malakī li-al-thaqāfa al-amāzīghiyya." IRCAM, October 17, 2001, http://www.ircam.ma/?q=ar/node/4662.

———. "Naṣ khiṭāb jalālat al-malik bi-munāsabat intihā' muhimmat hay'at al-inṣāf wa-al-muṣālaḥa wa-taqdīm al-dirāsa ḥawla al-tanmiya al-bashariyya bi-l-maghrib." *Maghress*, January 6, 2006, https://www.maghress.com/attajdid/22414.

Monjib, Maâti. *La Monarchie marocaine et la lutte pour le pouvoir: Hassan II face à l'opposition nationale, de l'indépendance à l'état d'exception.* Paris: L'Harmattan, 1992.

———. "Professor Maâti Monjib." In *al-Maghrib wa-al-zaman al-rāhin*, edited by Mohammed Kably and Abderrahmane El Moudden, 129–32. Rabat: Manshūrāt al-Ma'had al-Malakī li-al-Baḥth fī Tārīkh al-Maghrib, 2013.

Mounir, Omar. *Nécrologie d'un siècle perdu: Essai sur le Maroc.* Casablanca: Marsam, 2003.

Mouride, Aziz. *On affame bien les rats.* Casablanca: Tarik, 2000.

Muhammad Bin al-Hasan Bin Muhammad. "I'ādat tanẓīm acādimīyyat al-mamlaka al-maghribiyya," *al-Jarīda al-Rasmiyya*, February 9, 2021, accessed July 10, 2021, http://www.sgg.gov.ma/Portals/1/BO/2021/BO_6959-bis_Ar.pdf?ver=2021-02-09-150856-173.

Munīb, Muḥammad. *al-Ẓahīr al-barbarī akbar ukdhūba fī tārīkh al-maghrib al-mu'āṣir.* Rabat: Dār Abī Rāqrāq, 2002.

Munif, Abdulrahman ['Abd al-Raḥmān Munīf]. *al-'Ān hunā, aw, sharq al-mutawassiṭ marrah ukhrā*. Beirut: Al-Mu'assasah al-'Arabiyya li-al-Dirāsat wa-al-Nashr, 1991.

———. *Sharq al-mutawassiṭ: Riwāya*. Beirut: Dār al-Ṭalī'a, 1975.

Murray, Heather. "Literary History as Microhistory." In *Home-Work: Postcolonialism, Pedagogy and Canadian Literature*, edited by Cynthia Sugars, 405–22. Ontario: University of Ottawa Press, 2004.

Nadrani, Mohammed, and Abderrahmane Kounsi. *La Capitale des roses*. Casablanca: Éditions Alayam, 2009.

Nataf, Félix. *Juif maghrébin: Une vie au Maghreb (racontée à ma fille)*. Paris: Fayolle, 1978.

Nora, Pierre. "Between Memory and History: Les lieux de mémoire." *Representations* 26, no. 1 (1989): 7–24.

Nora, Pierre, and Lawrence D. Kritzman. *Realms of Memory: Conflicts and Divisions*. New York: Columbia University Press, 1996.

Nordman, Daniel. "Of Space and Time: On a History of Morocco." *Annales* (English ed.) 71, no. 4 (2016): 583–607.

Nouda, Abderrahman. "Pourquoi Christine Daure Serfaty [sic] mérite la considération du peuple." *LivresChaud* (blog), June 2014, https://livreschauds.files.wordpress.com/2014/06/article-pourquoi-christine-daure-serfaty-mc3a9rite-la-considc3a9ration-du-peuple-marocain-par-a-nouda.pdf.

Nuhoğlu Soysal, Yasemin, and Hanna Schissler, eds. *The Nation, Europe, and the World*. New York: Berghahn Books, 2005.

Nuttall, Sarah. "Literature and the Archive: The Biography of Texts." In *Refiguring the Archive*, edited by Carolyn Hamilton, et al., 283–99. Dordrecht, Netherlands: Kluwer Academic Publishers, 2002.

O'Grady, Megan. "Why Are We Living in a Golden Age for Historical Fiction?" *The New York Times*, July 5, 2019, https://www.nytimes.com/2019/05/07/t-magazine/historical-fiction-books.html.

Organisation Tamaynut. "Le Statut de Tamaynut." TAMAYNUT.org, accessed September 20, 2020, https://wayback.archive-it.org/org-304/20090619212549/http://tamaynut.org/article.php3?id_article=16;.

Orlando, Valérie. *Francophone Voices of the "New" Morocco in Film and Print: (Re)presenting a Society in Transition*. New York: Palgrave McMillan, 2009.

Ouazzi, El Houcine. "Tifinagh: Al-abajadiyya al-aṣlaḥ li-kitābat al-amāzīghiyya." In *Min ajli tarsīm abajadiyyat Tifinagh li-tadrīs al-amāzīghiyya: Taḥālīl wa wathāiq wa ārā'*, edited by AMREC, 33–45. Rabat: al-Jam'iyya al-Maghribiyya li-al-Baḥth wa-al-Tabādul al-Thaqāfī, 2002.

Palazzoli, Claude. *Le Maroc politique: De l'indépendance à 1973*. Paris: Sindbad, 1973.

Perrault, Gilles. *Notre ami le roi*. Paris: Gallimard, 1990.

Plenel, Edwy. "Christine Daure-Serfaty (1926–2014): Résistante et Juste, entre France et Maroc." *Europe Solidaire Sans Frontières*, May 27, 2014, http://www.europe-solidaire.org/spip.php?article32044.

Pomian, Krzysztof. *Sur l'histoire*. Paris: Gallimard, 1999.

Pouessel, Stéphanie. "Écrire la langue berbère au royaume de Mohamed VI: Les enjeux politiques et identitaires du tifinagh au Maroc." *Revue des Mondes Musulmans et de la Méditerranée* 124 (2008): 219–39. DOI: 10.4000/remmm.6029.

"Quffāz amāzīghī fīhi yadun faransiyya." *Al-Tajdīd*, October 25, 2002, https://www.maghress.com/attajdid/13673.

Rabi, Mubarak. *Gharb al-mutawassiṭ*. Beirut: al-Mu'assasa al-'Arabīyya li-al-Dirāsāt wa-al-Nashr, 2018.

Raïss, Mohammed. *Mina al-Skhirāt ilā Tazmamārt tadhkiratu dhahāb wa iyyāb ilā al-jaḥīm*. Casablanca: Afriqia al-Sharq, 2001.

Raissouni, Mustapha. "Taqdīm." In *Hay'at al-taḥkīm al-mustqilla li-ta'wīḍ ḍaḥāyā al-ikhtifā' al-qasrī wa-al-i'tiqāl al-ta'assufī: Al-labina al-ūlā fī masār al-'adāla al-intiqāliyya bi-al-maghrib*, 9–11. Rabat: Manshūrāt al-Majlis al-Istishārī li-Ḥuqūq al-Insān, 2010.

Rancière, Jacques. *The Politics of Aesthetics*. New York: Continuum, 2004.

Rboub, Amin "'Visages et paysages du cœur du Maroc': L'autre Maroc raconté par un reporter." *L'Economiste*, March 27, 2017, http://leconomiste.com/article/1010170-visages-et-paysages-du-coeur-du-maroc-l-autre-maroc-raconte-par-un-reporter.

Recelma, Kaci. "Dissolution du Parti démocrate amazigh marocain: La communauté berbère condamne." *Afrik.com*, April 22, 2008, https://www.afrik.com/dissolution-du-parti-democrate-amazigh-marocain-la-communaute-berbere-condamne.

Reis, Harry T., and Phillip Shaver. "Intimacy as an Interpersonal Process." *Handbook of Personal Relationships* 24, no. 3 (1988): 367–89.

Renouard, Maël. *L'Historiographe du royaume*. Paris: Grasset, 2020.

Rhani, Zakaria. "The Inmate's Two Bodies: Survival and Metamorphosis in a Moroccan Secret Prison." *Revista Crítica de Ciências Sociais* 120 (2019): 183–208. DOI: 10.4000/rccs.9884.

Rivet, Daniel. *Histoire du Maroc*. Paris: Fayard, 2012.

———. *Le Maghreb à l'épreuve de la colonisation*. Paris: Hachette Littératures, 2003.

———. "Pour une histoire du Maroc revisitée." *Revue Historique*, no. 670 (2014): 377–84.

"Le Rôle des Juifs dans l'édification de l'État marocain." *Al Bayane*, July 27, 2020, http://albayane.press.ma/le-role-des-juifs-amazighs-dans-ledification-de-letat-marocain.html.

Rollinde, Marguerite. *Le Mouvement marocain des droits de l'homme: Entre consensus national et engagement citoyen*. Paris: Karthala; Saint-Denis, [France]: Institut Maghreb-Europe, 2002.

———. "Le Mouvement amazighe au Maroc: défense d'une identité culturelle, revendication du droit des minorités ou alternative politique?" In "Mouvements sociaux, mouvements associatifs." Special issue, *Insaniyat / إنسانيات* 8 (1999): 63–70. https://doi.org/10.4000/insaniyat.8325.

Rosen, Lawrence. *Two Arabs, a Berber, and a Jew: Entangled Lives in Morocco*. Chicago: University of Chicago Press, 2015.
Rothberg, Michael. *Multidirectional Memory: Remembering the Holocaust in the Age of Decolonization*. Stanford, CA: Stanford University Press, 2009.
Rousso, Henry. *The Latest Catastrophe*. Chicago: University of Chicago Press, 2016.
Royaume du Maroc. "Bulletin officiel, no. 5484." December 21, 2006, http://www.habous.gov.ma/fr/files/insitut_bo.pdf.
Ruchti, Jefri J. "Morocco's Constitution of 2011." *Constituteproject*, February 4, 2020, https://www.constituteproject.org/constitution/Morocco_2011.pdf.
Schroeter, Daniel J. "The Changing Landscape of Muslim-Jewish Relations in the Modern Middle East and North Africa." In *Modernity, Minority, and the Public Sphere: Jews and Christians in the Middle East*, edited by S.R. Goldstein-Sabbah and H.L. Murre van Den Berg, 39–67. Leiden: Brill, 2016.
Sebti, Abdelahad. "Bayna al-tārīkh wa-al-dhākira al-jamā'iyya: Tashakkulāt wa-rihānāt." *La Recherche Historique* 1 (2003): 27–33.
———. *al-Māḍī al-muta'addid: Qirā'āt wa muḥāwarāt tārīkhīyya*. Rabat: Dār Tubqāl li-al-Nashr, 2016.
———. *al-Tārīkh wa-al-dhākira: Awrāsh fī tārīkh al-maghrib*. Casablanca: al-Markaz al-Thaqāfī al-'Arabī, 2012.
———. "'Unf al-dawla: Taṣawwurāt wa-mumārasāt wa-munṭalaqāt." Paper presented at *'Unf al-dawla*, Marrakesh, June 11–12, 2004.
Serels, Mitchell. "Carlos de Nesry." In *Encyclopedia of Jews in the Islamic World*, edited by Norman A. Stillman (2010), http://referenceworks.brillonline.com/entries/encyclopedia-of-jews-in-the-islamic-world/nesry-carlos-de-SIM_0016700?s.num=0&s.f.s2_parent=s.f.book.encyclopedia-of-jews-in-the-islamic-world&s.q=Carlos+de+nesry.
Serfaty, Abraham. *Le Maroc, du noir au gris*. Paris: Éditions Syllepse, 1998.
Serfaty, Abraham, and Christine Daure-Serfaty. *La Mémoire de l'autre*. Paris: Au Vif Stock, 1993.
Serfaty, Abraham, and Mikhaël Elbaz. *L'Insoumis: Juifs, Marocains et rebelles*. Paris: Desclée de Brouwer, 2001.
Serhane, Abdelhak. *La Chienne de Tazmamart*. Paris: Éditions Paris-Méditerranée, 2001.
———. *Kabazal: Les emmurés de Tazmamart, mémoires de Salah et Aïda Hachad*. Casablanca: Tarik Editions, 2004.
"Shāhid 'alā al-'aṣr—Aḥmad al-Marzūqī." Al Jazeera Channel. Episode no. 1. YouTube video, 50:36, February 24, 2009, https://www.youtube.com/watch?v=1-MhOJIZeNY;
"Shāhid 'alā al-'aṣr—Salah Hachad." Al Jazeera Channel. Episode no. 1. YouTube video, 50:10, May 5, 2009, https://www.youtube.com/watch?v=Uo_bTD7IGAo&list=FLQOE534ak5pSKpaE_JeU4_A&index=50.
Sharpe, Jim. "History from Below." In *New Perspectives on Historical Writing*, edited by Peter Burke, 25–41. State College: Penn State University Press, 1991.
Shaw, Rosalind. "Afterword: Violence and the Generation of Memory." In

Remembering Violence: Anthropological Perspectives on Intergenerational Transmission, edited by Nicolas Argenti and Katharina Schramm, 251–60. New York: Berghahn Books, 2010.

Sidi Hida, Bouchra. *Mouvements sociaux et logiques d'acteurs: Les ONG de développement face à la mondialisation et à l'Etat au Maroc; L'altermondialisme marocain*. Louvain: Université catholique de Louvain, 2007.

Sidqi Azaykou, Ali. "al-Aṣāla wa-al-'umq fī al-'awda ilā al-thaqāfa al-sha'biyya." In *Ma'ārik fikrīyyah ḥawla al-Amāzīghīyya*, ed. Markaz Tarik Ibn Ziad, 15. Rabat Markaz Tarik Ibn Ziad, 2002.

———. "Fī sabīl mafhūm ḥaqīqī lithqāfatina al-waṭaniyya." In *Ma'ārik fikrīyyah ḥawla al-amāzīghiyya*, ed. Markaz Tarik Ibn Ziad, 35–41. Rabat: Markaz Tarik Ibn Ziad, 2002.

———. *Izmuln: Majmū'a shi'riyya amāzīghiyya*. Casablanca: Maṭba'at al-Najāḥ al-Jadīda, 1995.

———. "Min mashākil al-baḥt fī tārīkh al-maghrib." In *Ma'ārik fikrīyyah ḥawla al-amāzīghiyya*, ed. Markaz Tarik Ibn Ziad, 19–21. Rabat: Markaz Tarik Ibn Ziad, 2002.

———. *Namādhij min asmā' al-a'lām al-jughrāfiyya wa-al-bashariyya al-maghribiyya*. Rabat: Manshūrāt al-Ma'had al-Malakī li-al-Thaqāfa al-Amāzīghiyya, 2004.

———. *Tārikh al-maghrib aw al-ta'wīlāt al-mumkina*. Rabat: Markaz Ṭāriq Ibn Ziyyād, 2001.

———. "Tārikh al-maghrib bayna mā huwwa 'alayh wa mā yanbaghī an yakūna 'alayh." *Majallat al-Kalima* 1 (1971): 16–18.

———. "al-Ta'wīl al-nasabī (al-jiniālūjī) hal yumkinu tajāwuzuhu?" *Majallat Kulliyat al-'Ādāb wa-al-'Ulūm al-Insāniyya al-Ribāṭ* 15 (1989–90): 9–34.

———. *Timitār: Majmū'a shi'riyya amāzīghiyya*. Rabat: 'Ukāẓ, 1988.

Silverstein, Paul. "Masquerade Politics: Race, Islam and the Scale of Amazigh Activism in Southeastern Morocco." *Nations and Nationalism* 17, no. 1 (2011): 65–84.

———. "The Pitfalls of Transnational Consciousness: Amazigh Activism as a Scalar Dilemma." *The Journal of North African Studies* 18, no. 5 (2013): 768–78.

Silverstein, Paul, and David Crawford. "Amazigh Activism and the Moroccan State." *Middle East Report*, no. 233 (2004): 44–48. DOI: 10.2307/1559451.

Sloboda, Marién, et al. "The Policies on Public Signage in Minority Languages and Their Reception in Four Traditionally Bilingual European Locations." *Media and Communication* 63 (2012): 51–88.

Slyomovics, Susan. "Abraham Serfaty: Moroccan Jew and Conscious Pariah." *Hesperis-Tamuda* 51, no. 3 (2016): 113–38.

———. "The Moroccan Equity and Reconciliation Commission: The Promises of a Human Rights Archive." *Arab Studies Journal* 24, no. 1 (2016): 10–41.

———. "New Moroccan Publics: Prisons, Cemeteries and Human Remains." In

Knowledge, Authority and Change in Islamic Societies, edited by Allen James Fromherz and Nadav Samin, 125–56. Leiden: Brill, 2021.
———. *The Performance of Human Rights in Morocco*. Philadelphia: The University of Pennsylvania Press, 2005.
Smith, Stephen. "Des Vies de revenants." *Libération*, October 5, 2000, http://www.liberation.fr/planete/2000/10/05/des-vies-de-revenants_339598.
Smolin, Jonathan. "Foreword." In Youssef Fadel, *A Rare Blue Bird Flies with Me*, translated by Jonathan Smolin, VII–XI. Cairo: AUC Press, 2016.
Soulaimani, Dris. "Writing and Rewriting Amazigh/Berber Identity: Orthographies and Language Ideologies." *Writing Systems Research* 8, no. 1 (2016): 1–16. DOI: 10.1080/17586801.2015.1023176.
Soulet, Jean François. *L'Histoire immédiate: Historiographie, sources et méthodes*. Paris: Armand Colin, 2009.
Steedman, Carolyn. *Dust: The Archive and Cultural History*. New Brunswick: Rutgers University Press, 2002.
Sternberg, Joseph. "The Origin of the Libyan Alphabets Revisited." *Scientific Cultures* 1, no. 2 (2015): 7–11.
Stoler, Ann Laura. *Along the Archival Grain: Epistemic Anxieties and Colonial Common Sense*. Princeton, NJ: Princeton University Press, 2009.
———. "Colonial Archives and the Arts of Governance." *Archival Science* 2, no. 1–2 (2002): 87–109.
Stora, Benjamin. "Maroc, le traitement des histoires proches." *Esprit*, no. 266–267 (2000): 88–102.
Southgate, Beverly. *History Meets Fiction*. New York: Routledge, 2009.
Tartakowsky, Ewa. *Les Juifs et le Maghreb: Fonctions sociales d'une littérature d'exil*. Tours: Presses Universitaires François Rabelais, 2016.
Taussig, Michael T. *Defacement, Public Secrecy, and the Labor of the Negative*. Stanford, CA: Stanford University Press, 1999.
Tazi, Mohammad Ezzeddine. *Anā al-mansī*. Casablanca: Al-Markaz al-Thaqāfī al-ʻArabī, 2015.
Thompson, Paul. *The Voice of the Past: Oral History*. Oxford: Oxford University Press, 2000.
Tilmatine, Mohand. "Du Berbère à l'amazighe: De l'object au sujet historique." *AlAndalus Maghreb* 14 (2007): 225–47.
Tirra. "Alliance des Écrivains en Amazighe." Accessed June 6, 2020, http://tirra.net/web/.
Trace, Ciaran B. "On or Off the Record? Notions of Value in the Archive." In *Currents of Archival Thinking*, edited by Terry Eastwood and Heather MacNeil, 47–68. Santa Barbara, CA: Libraries Unlimited, 2010.
Trevisan Semi, Emanuela, and Hanane Sekkat Hatimi. *Mémoire et représentations des Juifs au Maroc: Les voisins absents de Meknès*. Paris: Publisud, 2011.
Trouillot, Michel Rolph. *Silencing the Past: Power and the Production of History*. Boston, MA: Beacon Press Books, 1995.

Tsur, Yaron. "Les Dirigeants du judaïsme marocain." In *Perception et réalités au Maroc: Relations judéo-musulmanes*, edited by Robert Assaraf and Michel Abitbol, 225–36. Paris: Editions Stavit, 1997.

Tual, Joseph. "Polémique autour de livres sur Tazmamart." *Ina.fr*, January 17, 2001, https://www.ina.fr/video/CAC01004329.

Uḍmīn, Muḥammad. *Urfān*. Rabat: Réseau Amazigh pour la Citoyennté-Azêtta, 2005.

'Uthmān, 'Ālā'. "Yūsuf Fāḍil: 'Ṭā'ir azraq nadir yuḥalliqu ma'ī' tu'arrikhu li-jīl al-thamānīnāt fī al-maghrib'." *Youm 7*, March 16, 2014, https://www.youm7.com/story/2014/3/16/.

Valensi, Lucette. "Le Roi chronophage: La construction d'une conscience historique dans le Maroc postcolonial." *Cahiers d'Études Africaines*, no. 119 (1990): 279–98.

Van Dyke, Ruth M., and Susan E. Alcock, eds. *Archaeologies of Memory*. Malden, MA: Blackwell, 2003.

Vermeren, Pierre. *Histoire du Maroc depuis l'indépendance*. Paris: La Découverte, 2006.

———. "Histoire récente, histoire immédiate: L'historiographie française et le cas du Maghreb." In *Temps présent et fonctions de l'historien*, edited by Mohammed Kenbib, 119–26. Rabat: Publications de la Faculté des Lettres et des Sciences Humaines, 2009.

Wainscott, Ann Marie. *Bureaucratizing Islam: Morocco and the War on Terror*. New York: Cambridge University Press, 2017.

Wazana, Kathy, dir. *They Were Promised the Sea*. 2013.

Weintraub, Karen. "Race to the Vaccine: Deliver a Safe, Effective COVID-19 Vaccine in Less than a Year? Impossible. Meet Moncef Slaoui." *USA Today*, December 1, 2020, https://www.usatoday.com/in-depth/news/health/2020/12/01/operation-warp-speeds-moncef-slaoui-guided-covid-19-vaccine-creation/6375043002/.

White, Hayden, and Robert Doran, eds. *The Fiction of Narrative: Essays on History, Literature, and Theory, 1957–2007*. Baltimore, MD: Johns Hopkins University Press, 2010.

Whitney, Craig R. "Popular New King Has a Goal: A Modern Morocco." *The New York Times*, November 12, 1999, http://www.nytimes.com/1999/11/12/world/popular-new-king-has-a-goal-a-modern-morocco.html.

Wizārat al-Awqāf wal-Shu'ūn al-Islāmiyya. "Al-Khiṭāb al-malakī al-sāmī al-ladhī wajjahahu ṣāḥib al-jalāla al-malik al-ḥasan al-thānī ilā al-umma bi-munāsabat thawrat al-malik wal-sha'b." *Habous*, August–September 1994, http://www.habous.gov.ma/daouat-alhaq/item/7773.

Wyrtzen, Jonathan. *Making Morocco: Colonial Intervention and the Politics of Identity*. Ithaca, NY: Cornell University Press, 2015.

Yuba Amdjar, Abderrahim. "al-Thulātī al-amāzīghī 'akāl,' 'afgān,' 'awāl,' awwal

shi'ār li-al-insāniyya . . . !" Amazighworld.org, December 15, 2016, http://www.amazighworld.org/arabic/history/index_show.php?id=572.
Yudice, George. "Testimonio and Postmodernism." *Latin American Perspectives* 18, no. 3 (1991): 15–31.
Zaki, M'barek. *Résistance et Armée de Libération: Portée politique, liquidation, 1953–1958*. Tangiers: E.T.E.I., 1987.
———. *Un Roi et deux républicains: Dialogues de l'au-delà: Hassan II, Ben Barka, Oufkir et les autres*. Rabat: Omega Communication Edition & Distribution, 2006.
Zaki, M'barek, and Ahmed Beroho. *Hassan II ou Confessions d'outre-tombe: Tragicomédie*. Tangiers: Corail, 2005.
Zemon Davis, Natalie. *The Return of Martin Guerre*. Cambridge, MA: Harvard University Press, 1984.
Zerubavel, Yael. *Recovered Roots: Collective Memory and the Making of Israeli National Tradition*. Chicago: University of Chicago Press, 1995.

Index

Note: Figures are indicated by page numbers in *italics.*

Aqlām (journal), 200n65
Arab Uprisings, 22
Arbitration Commission, 3
Archibald, Robert, 82
archives, 1, 12–14, 201n88. *See also* history; other-archives
Argentina, 3
Ashour, Radwa, 117, 144–145, 147–148
Assmann, Aleida, 13, 200n81
Association Marocaine de Recherche et d'Echange Culturel [Moroccan Association for Research and Cultural Exchange] (AMREC), 28–29, 36–37, 48, 50–51, 217n133
Atkinson, Meera, 18
authoritarianism, 8, 21, 82, 91, 113, 115, 121, 172, 178–179, 182, 186–187
autochthony, 39–41
Ayache, Freha, 108
Ayache, Germain, 16, 45, 108, 153–154
Azaykou, Ali Sidqi, 41–42, 44–47, 59–61, 212n44

Bāb tāza (al-Shāwī), 11
Bahloul, Joëlle, 71, 92, 105
Bahnini, Mohammed, 197n48
Baïda, Jamaâ, 154, 220n27
Ballas, Shim'on, 104
bearing witness, 127
Bédarida, François, 152
Belkbir, Abdellatif, 126–127
Belouchi, Belkassen, 116, 138–141
Ben Barka, Mahdi, 8–10, 163–166, 200n67, 250n25
Benjelloun, Hassan, 155, 222n62
Ben Jelloun, Tahar, 116, 134–138, 145–146, 185, 238n154
Ben-Layashi, Samir, 65
Ben Mlih, Abdellah, 241n30
Bennouna, Rabéa, 126–127, 131–132, 239n8
Bensouda, Ahmed, 239n10
Benyoub, Ahmed Chaouqi, 17, 132, 181
Benzaquen, Leon, 106
Berber Dehir, 28
Beroho, Ahmed, 150–151, 164–165
Berque, Jacques, 41
Bessaoud, Mohand Aarav, 37
Bilmuqaddim, Hafiḍa, 154, 241n26
BineBine, Aziz, 126, 134, 136, 187, 229n9, 232n37, 234n132
BineBine, Mahi, 136, 238n154
BineBine, Mohamed, 232n37
Blatterer, Harry, 91
bookstore, 59–61
Borneman, John, 3–4
Bouaziz, Mostafa, 154, 173, 239n7, 244n63, 244n68
Bouderka, M'barek, 132
Boudhan, Mohammed, 34, 39, 211n24
Boukhari, Ahmed, 240n15
Boulter, Jonathan, 200n77
Boum, Aomar, 6, 100, 195n31, 249n19
Boutaleb, Ibrahim, 66, 162, 220n16
Brazil, 3
Brouksy, Lahcen, 196n37
Burton, Antoinette, 68–69
Butler, Judith, 18
Buttin, Maurice, 200n67

Cambodia, 13
Captif de Mabrouka, Le (Mabrouka's Captive) (Aït Moh), 66, 68–71, 83
Casanfa (Miliānī), 66, 71, 75–76, 87
Casanfabar (Abitbol), 76–79, 87
CBRM. See *Comités de lutte contre la repression au Maroc, Les* (Committees Battling against Repression in Morocco [CBRM])
CCHR. See *Conseil consultatif des droits de l'homme* (Consultative Council on Human Rights [CCHR])
Centre de Recherche sur le Temps Présent (Center for the History of the Present, CHP), 161, 163
Centre National de la Recherche Scientifique (National Center for Scientific Research, NCSR), 152
Cette aveuglante absence de lumière (This Blinding Absence of Light) (Ben Jelloun), 116, 134–138, 145–146
Chafik, Mohammed, 49, 59
Chambre noire ou Derb Moulay Cherif, La (The Black Chamber or Derb Moulay Cherif) (Mdidech), 155
Chberreq, Driss T., 126
Chellat, Mohamed, 230n18
Chienne de Tazmamart, La (The Bitch of Tazmamart) (Serhane), 143–144
childhood, 97–106
CHP. See *Centre de Recherche sur le Temps Présent* (Center for the History of the Present, CHP)
Chtatou, Mohamed, 217n133
CICM. See *Conseil des Communautés*

Israélites du Maroc (Council of Israelite Communities of Morocco [CICM])
Cintra (Aourid), 66, 71, 75–77, 79–81, 86–87, 89, 107–109, 112–113, 153
citizenship, 6–7, 52, 92–93, 99, 102–103, 107–110, 177, 180, 184
CMCLA. See *Conseil de la Communauté Marocaine à l'Etranger* (The Council of the Moroccan Community Living Abroad, CMCLA)
Cold War, 2
colonialism, 7, 28, 44, 79, 109, 221n34
Comités de lutte contre la repression au Maroc, Les (Committees Battling against Repression in Morocco [CBRM]), 2–3, 116, 120–121
Communism, 153, 199n56, 221n34
Conseil consultatif des droits de l'homme (Consultative Council on Human Rights [CCHR]), 2–3, 168–169, 181, 194n11, 194n16
Conseil de la Communauté Marocaine à l'Etranger (The Council of the Moroccan Community Living Abroad, CMCLA), 168
Conseil des Communautés Israélites du Maroc (Council of Israelite Communities of Morocco [CICM]), 9
coups, 28, 117–118, 230n11
COVID-19 pandemic, 187
cultural activism, 29–30

Dada l'yakout (Fihri), 185
Dahan, Jacques, 9
Dale, Ignace, 164
Daoud, Zakya, 78, 117, 197n44
DAP. See *Parti Démocratique Amazigh* (The Democratic Amazigh Party, [DAP]
Darouiche, Omar, 216n117
Daure-Serfaty, Christine, 116–117, 119, 121, 123–124, 138, 221n34, 231n21, 232n41, 232n43, 234n67
Della Sudda, François, 116, 232n43
democracy, 8, 29–31, 90–91, 112, 115, 126, 151, 162, 168, 170, 186, 197n48
Democratic Front for the Defense of Constitutional Institutions (DFDCI), 8, 10, 78, 198n50
Demsiri, Mohammed, 212n44
de Nesry, Carlos, 7, 197n41
Derrida, Jacques, 1
DFDCI. *See* Democratic Front for the Defense of Constitutional Institutions (DFDCI)
di Masso, Andrés, 52
Dlimi, Ahmed, 118
Donohoe, Janet, 82
Dwelling in the Archive: Women Writing House, Home, and History in Late Colonial India (Burton), 68–69

Easterman, Alexandre, 7, 9, 199n56
education, 8, 21, 28, 49, 53, 98, 128, 158, 171, 207n139
Einaudi, Jean-Luc, 201n87
Ekbaz, Mikhaël, 106
El Adnani, Jilali, 153
Elinson, Alexander, 234n132
equality, 29–30, 91
ERC. See *Hay'at al-inṣāf wa-al-muṣālaḥa* (Equity and Reconciliation Commission [ERC])
Erll, Astrid, 67
Errahoui, Mohammed, 142
Esposito, Claudia, 136

Fadel, Youssef, 116–117, 141–145, 234n132
Fahli, Asmaa, 14
Farag (Blue Lorries) (Ashour), 117, 144–145, 147–148
Fāsī, Allāl al-, 158
Fassi Fihri, Nouzha, 185
fictionalized microhistories, 68–82
flag, Amazigh, 38–39
Foucault, Michel, 1
Frank, Michael, 63
French Berber Policy, 228n78
French War of Pacification, 101–102
Friedlander, Saul, 161
Front démocratique pour la défense des institutions constitutionelles, Le (The Democratic Front for the Defense of Constitutional Institutions [DFDCI]). *See* Democratic Front for the Defense of Constitutional Institutions (DFDCI)
Front pour la défense des institutions constitutionnelles, Le (The Front for the Defense of Constitutional Institutions), 210n16

Ghallab, Saïd, 8, 78, 198n50
Ghalou, Mohammed El, 129
Gharb al-mutawassiṭ (Rabi), 185
Ghazali, Ismail, 185
Ghiwane, Nass El, 232n41

Giddens, Anthony, 91
Gilson Miller, Susan, 15, 21, 150, 155, 157, 162, 170, 238n1, 244n69, 245n73, 246n95
globalization, 70, 125–126, 135, 148
Goodman, James, 219n13
Gordon, Avery, 133
Gottreich, Emily, 65
gray literature, 1, 36, 59, 218n153
Guessous, Mohamed, 108

Hachad, Aïda, 11–12, 120, 131–132, 231n21, 232n37
Hachad, Salah, 120, 131, 155
Hammoudi, Abdellah, 133, 173, 196n37, 226n48
Hariri, Ibrahim, 89, 93–96
Ḥārith al-nisyān (Tiller of Forgetfulness) (Khamlichi), 89, 97–100, 113
Harrafi, Abdeslam, 4–5
Harrus, Elias, 226n48
Ḥasan, Mawlāy al-, 165
Hassan II: coups against, 28, 117–118; democracy and, 8; Easterman and, 199n56; in end of Cold War, 2; Imazighen and coups against, 28; Jewish emigration and, 8–9; Years of Lead and, ix
Hassan II ou Confessions d'outre-tombe: Tragicomédie (Hassan II or Confessions from beyond the Grave: Tragicomedy) (Zaki and Beroho), 164–165
Hassoun, Jacques, 23
Hatimi, Mohammed, 158, 220n27, 239n7
Hawzālī, Muḥammad, 59
Hay'at al-inṣāf wa-al-muṣālaḥa (Equity and Reconciliation Commission [ERC]), 3–5, 14–15, 19–22, 132–133, 155, 160–161, 167–171, 174, 177–178, 181–182, 185–186, 195n22, 202n91, 244n62, 250n34
Herzenni, Ahmed, 168
historical fiction, 64–65
histories, fictionalized micro-, 68–82
Historiographe du royaume (The Historiographer of the Kingdom) (Renouard), 187
historiographical research, 167–170
historiography, 30, 44–48, 65–66, 82–83, 90–91, 96–97, 133, 151–163, 180
history, 19–20, 41–49, 69, 73, 151–166, 240n15, 241n30
history of the present *(tārīkh al-zaman al-rāhin)*, 150, 152–154, 161–162
Hobsbawm, Eric, 34
Houbaida, Mohammed, 153,162
Hrach Errass, Ali, 216n117
human rights, 2–4, 11, 41, 49, 125–126, 130, 132, 137–138, 144–148, 160–161, 163, 168–174, 179–180, 182–183, 232n45

Iggout, Abdelahdi, 38
IHP. See *Institut d'Histoire du Temps Présent* (Institute of the History of the Present, IHP)
I'zzā, Brahīm, 59
Ilā al-Amām, 10, 122–123
Imazighen, 5, 11, 28, 228n78. *See also* Amazigh
Independent Arbitration Commission for the Compensation of Moral and Material Harm Suffered by Victims of Disappearance and Arbitrary Detention, and by their Beneficiaries. *See* Arbitration Commission
India, 68–69
indigeneity, 15, 36, 37, 39–41,56, 76
In Morocco, "Exploring Remnants of Jewish History" (Frank), 63
Institut d'Histoire du Temps Présent (Institute of the History of the Present, IHP), 152
Institut Royal de la Culture Amazigh (Royal Institute for Amazigh Culture [RIAC]), 27, 30–32, 37, 48, 50, 53, 56–58
Institut Royal pour la Recherche sur l'Histoire du Maroc (Royal Institute for Research on the History of Morocco [RIRHM]), 19–20, 151, 157, 159, 167–168, 170–175, 246n100
intimacy, 91–97, 100–101, 103, 106–112, 225n10
Iskla n yiḍ (I'zzā), 59
Islam, 42–44. *See also* Muslims
Israel, 5, 9, 39, 69, 83, 85, 90, 93–97, 100, 108, 112–113, 183–184, 196n38
Istiqlal party, 7, 10, 154, 159, 199n62
al-Ittiḥādn al-Waṭanī li-al-Quwwāt al-Sha'bīyya (The National Union for Popular Forces) (NUPF), 7, 10, 78
"Iyya" (Ballas), 104
Izenzaren, 38, 213n61

Jaafar, Said, 216n117
Jaafari, Mohammed al-, 59
Jam'iyyat al-Wifāq (the Concord Association), 6

Jamieson, Lynn, 91
Jedamus, Julith, 147
Jewish World Congress, 198n54
Jews, 5–6, xi–xii; autochthony of, 39–41; border crossings with Muslims, 101–105; in Boum, 195n31; citizenship of, 6–7, 184; decrease in population of, 64–65; emigration of, 8–9, 89–91, 112–113; fictionalized microhistories and, 68–82; history of, literature and, 67–68; indigeneity of, 39–41; intimacy between Muslims and, 91–97, 106–112; in Khatibi, 23–24; language and, 37; as leftists, 8–9; mnemonic literature and, 63–64, 66–68, 71–72; nationalism and, 158; population of, 9; public micro-places and history of, 71–82; in Vichy France, 158–159; Zionism and, 77, 81, 84, 90, 95, 105, 114, 198n54
Jil Jilala, 38
Jmāhrī, ʻAbd al-Ḥamīd, 164
Jouhadi, El Houssaine, 42–44
Jouiti, Abdelkarim, 89, 101–105, 109
Juif de Tanger et le Maroc, Le (de Nesry), 7, 197n41
June War, 72, 85

Kabazal: Les Emmurés de Tazmamart (Kazabal: The Prisoners of Tazmamart) (Serhane), 126, 234n95
Kably, Mohammed, 74, 160, 173
Kabyle myth, 28
Kaddouri, Abdemajid, 159
Kazanjian, David, 18
Kenbib, Mohammed, 154, 157, 160, 220n27, 239n7, 240nn11–12
Khaïr-Eddine, Mohammed, 212n44
Khamlichi, Kamal El, 89, 97–100, 113
Khatib, Abdelkarim El, 210n15
Khatibi, Abdelkébir, 23, 101
Khattabi, Muhammad ibn Abd al-Karim al-, 12, 183
Khattabi, Omar El, 12
Kiche, Ahmed, 216n117
Kilani, Leila, 4–5
Kosansky, Oren, 6

Laâbi, Abdellatif, 10, 236n116
LaCapra, Dominic, 161
Lachmann, Renate, 84
Lamalif (journal), 199n65
Landsberg, Alison, 161
landscape, 73–74
language, 23, 27, 29–36, *32–33*, 37, 39, 42–44, 47, 49–52, *53*, 53–58, 202n94, 211n28
Laroui, Abdallah, 23, 78, 90, 122, 133, 161
Latin script, 50
Levi, Giovanni, 68
Levy, André, 39
Levy, Lital, 104
Lévy, Simon, 65, 78–79, 94, 108, 158–159
Liberation Army, 2
Ligue des droits de l'homme, La (Human Rights League), 116
literature, 44; gray, 1, 36, 59, 218n153; historical fiction, 64–65; history and, 163–166; Jewish history and, 67–68; mnemonic, 63–68, 71–74, 82–84, 93–97, 102–103, 105, 112, 179; Tazmamart prison and, 133–148
Lmrabet, Ali, 239n10, 240n10
Lorcin, Patricia, 28
loss, 4–12, 18

MACM. *See* Moroccan Amazigh Cultural Movement (MACM)
Madbouh, Mohamed El, 28
Maddy-Weitzman, Brice, 42, 65, 210n19
Madini, Ahmed El, 91
Maghraoui, Driss, 243n61
Maʻṭī, al-Ḥājj al-, 5
Makhzen, 22
Maktabat al-Alfiyya al-Thalitha (Third Millennium Bookstore), 59–61
Maleh, Edmond Amran El, 94, 108
Malka, Victor, 9, 73, 199n60
March 23 Organization, 199n63, 230n10
Maroc et Hassan II, Le (Morocco and Hassan II) (Laroui), 122
Marriage de plaisir, Le (Ben Jelloun), 185
Marshall, Thomas Humphrey, 92
Marzouki, Ahmed, 119, 129, 136–137, 155, 164, 230n16, 231n21, 232n43, 237n148
Mbembe, Achille, 15
Mdidech, Jaouad, 155
Medbouh, Mohamed, 117
Meknes Declaration, 50, 217n133
Melman, Yossi, 249n25
Même livre, Le (Khatibi and Hassoun), 23
memory, 34–41, 67, 82–87, 100, 151–163
Mernissi, Fatema, 108
Messari, Mohamed Larbi, 108
Mestaoui, Mohammed, 59–61
micro-places, 71–82
Miliānī, Drīs al-, 66, 71, 75–76, 87

Min Skhirāt ilā Tazmamart, tadhkiratu dhahāb wa iyyāb ilā al-jaḥīm (From Skhirat to Tazmamart: A Roundtrip Ticket to Hell) (Raïss), 115, 126, 136–137, 142, 155
Misa'dī, 'Abbās al-, 166
Mīythāq Agadir [the Agadir Charter], 49, 52
mnemonic literature, 63–68, 71–74, 82–84, 93–97, 102–103, 105, 112, 179
Mohammed V, 7–8, 158, 198n53
Mohammed VI, 3–4, 30–31, 50
Monarchie marocaine et la lutte pour le pouvoir, La (The Moroccan Monarchy and the Battle for Power) (Monjib), 7–8
Monjib, Maâti, 7, 154, 174, 241n27
Montagne, Robert, 45–46
Moroccan Amazigh Cultural Movement (MACM), 15–16, 27–31, 35–38, 41, 47–52, 55–58, 61–62
Moroccan Marxist-Leninist Movement (MMLM), 2, 10, 221n34, 227n59, 244n68
Moudden, Abderrahmane El, 154, 171
Mounir, Omar, 64–65
Mouroirs: Chronique d'une disparition forcée (Necroplaces: The Chronicle of an Enforced Disappearance) (Errahoui), 142
Moussadik, Abdeslam, 5
Mouvement National Populaire (The National Popular Movement [NPM]), 29
Mouvement Populaire (The Popular Movement, [PM]), 29, 210n15
al-Muḥarrir, 199n65
Munīf, 'Abd al-Raḥmān, 145
Munaẓẓamat Tamaynūt, 28–29
music, 37–38, 213n61
Muslims: border crossings with Jews, 101–105; citizenship of, 6–7; intimacy between Jews and, 91–97, 106–112; place and, 87. *See also* Islam
Mzirek, Ahmed, 230n18

Naïmi, Farid, 108
Nājī, Muḥammad al-, 241n30
Namādhij min asmā' al-a'lām al-jughrāfiyya wa-al- bashariyya al-maghribiyya (Samples of Names of Moroccan Geographic and Human Landmarks) (Azaykou), 47
Nas El Ghiwane, 38
National Council for Human Rights (NCHR), 6, 14, 163, 169, 195n22
nationalism, 28, 39, 45, 77, 106–112, 122, 158, 198n54
NCHR. *See* National Council for Human Rights (NCHR)
NCSR. See *Centre National de la Recherche Scientifique* (National Center for Scientific Research, NCSR)
neoliberalism, 70
Nora, Pierre, 66–67, 200n78
Nordman, Daniel, 173
Nos lieux interdits (Our Forbidden Places) (documentary), 4
Notre ami l'écrivain (Our friend the novelist) (BineBine and BineBine), 136
Notre ami le roi (Perrault), 121–124
NUPF. See *al-Ittiḥādn al-Waṭanī li-al-Quwwāt al-Sha'bīyya* (The National Union for Popular Forces) (NUPF)

Ochna, Omar, 216n117
O'Grady, Megan, 64
OPDA. See *Organisation de l'action démocratique populaire* (Organization of Popular Democratic Action [OPDA])
Opération Boraq F15: 16 août 1972, l'attaque du Boeing royal (Operation Boraq F15: August 16, 1972, The Attack against the Royal Boeing) (Ouafi and Ouafi), 126, 164
Operation Florence, 118
Organisation de l'action démocratique populaire (Organization of Popular Democratic Action [OPDA]), 124
other-archives: defined, 1, x; embodied, 126–133; fictionalized, 133–148; in public sphere, 1; reimagination of Morocco and, 20–25; scandalous, 118–126; theory of, in Morocccan cultural production, 14–20; traditional archives *vs.,* 1
Ouafi, Ahmed El, 126, 164, 231n21
Ouafi, Kalima El, 126, 164
Oufkir, Mohamed, 2, 5, 28, 117–118, 198n48

Palestine, 5, 9, 24, 39, 69, 77, 83, 85, 90, 93–97, 100, 108, 112–113, 144, 183–184, 196n38
Papon, Maurice, 201n87
Parti authenticité et modernité, Le (Authenticity and Modernity Party), 210n16
Parti Démocratique Amazigh (The Democratic Amazigh Party, [DAP]), 29
Pascon, Paul, 23
Performance of Human Rights in Morocco, The (Slyomovics), 3
Perrault, Gilles, 116, 121–124
place, 73–74, 80–87, 92

Place to Remember, A (Archibald), 82
Plenel, Edwy, 122
pluralism, 28, 45–46, 172–173, 186, 211n24
PM. See *Mouvement National Populaire* (The National Popular Movement, [NPM])
poetry, 44, 59–61, 146–147
Political Crime and the Memory of Loss (Borneman), 4
Pomian, Kzysztof, 242n42, 244n67
publication, 56–58
public sphere, 52–56

Quran, 42–44

Rabi, Mubarak, 185
ra'īyya, 6–7
Raïss, Mohammed, 115, 126, 136, 155, 164, 231n21
Rancière, Jacques, 17
Rapt de voix (Voice Theft) (Belouchi), 116, 138–141
Recherche Historique, La (journal), 155
Renouard, Maël, 187
Résistance et armée de libération: Portée politique, liquidation, 1953–1958 (Resistance and Liberation Army: Political Significance, Liquidation, 1953–1958) (Zaki), 164
RIAC. See *Institut Royal de la Culture Amazigh* (Royal Institute for Amazigh Culture [RIAC])
Rif War, 12, 198n48
Rigney, Ann, 67
RIRHM. See *Institut Royal pour la Recherche sur l'Histoire du Maroc* (Royal Institute for Research on the History of Morocco [RIRHM])
Rivet, Daniel, 162
Rocard, Michel, 122
Roi et deux républicains, Un: Dialogues de l'au-del.: Hassan II, Ben Barka, Oufkir et les autres (One King and Two Republicans: Dialogues of the Hereafter: Hassan II, Ben Barka, Oufkkir, and Others), 165
Rosen, Lawrence, 111–112
Rousso, Henry, 152

Sabbah, Marc, 9
Ṣāḥa al-sharafiyya, al- (The Square of Honor) (al-Shāwī), 11
Sand War, 166
Ṣawt al-Janūb (journal), 44
Schroeter, Daniel, 65
Sebti, Abdelahad, 156, 242n42, 244n67
Seddik, Miloudi, 124
Sekkat Hatimi, Hanane, 100
Semi, Emanuela Trevisan, 100
Serels, Mitchell, 197n41
Serfaty, Abraham, 9–10, 106, 123, 198n53, 227n59, 227n64
Serhane, Abdelhak, 126, 143–144, 164, 234n95
Shāhid 'alā al-'aṣr (Witness of an Era) (television), 155
Shāmma aw Shtrīt (Shamma or Shirit) (Hariri), 89, 93–100, 104–106, 113
Sharq al-mutawassiṭ (East of the Mediterranean) (Munīf), 145
Shāwī, 'Abd al-Qādir al-, 11–12, 236n116
Sheikh al-'Arab, 4–5
signage, *53*, 53–54. *See also* Tifinagh script
Skhirat coup, 10
Skiredj, Boubker, 118
Slaoui, Moncef, 187
Slyomovics, Susan, 3, 14–15, 29, 127, 130, 190
Smmūs idlisn n tmdiazin (Mestaoui), 59
solidarity, 25, 89, 98, 102, 105–106, 111, 118, 139, 145
Souffles/Anfās (journal), 10, 199n65
South Africa, 3, 13, 73, 194n16
Stora, Benjamin, 152
Sūsī, Mukhtār al-, 36–37

Taghūyt n tīn hinān (Aourid), 59
Tamazight language, *53*, 53–58, 202n94, 211n28. *See also* language
Tarikh al-maghrib aw al-ta'wīlāt al-mumkina (Morocco's History and the Possible Interpretations) (Azaykou), 47
"Tārīkh al-maghrib bayna mā huwwa 'alayhi wa mā yajibu an yakūna 'alayhi" ("The History of Morocco between What It Was and What It Should Be") (Azaykou), 44
tārīkh al-zaman al-rāhin (history of the present), 150, 152–154, 161–162
Tauss, Mbark, 216n117
Taussig, Michael, 119
Tawfiq, Aḥmad al-, 171, 173, 226n48
Tazi, Mohamed Ezzeddine, 66, 70–82, 89, 109–111

Tazmamart: 18 Years in Morocco's Secret Prison (BineBine), 187
Tazmamart: Cellule 10 (Tazmamart: Cell Number 10) (Marzouki), 119, 136–137, 142, 155, 164
Tazmamart côté femme: Témoignage (Tazmamart from a Woman's Perspective: A Testimony) (Bennouna), 127, 131
Tazmamart prison, 18, 115–148; birth of, 117–118; Consultative Council on Human Rights and, 2; coups and, 10–11, 230n11; denial of existence of, 115, 118–119; embodied other-archives of, 126–133; Equity and Reconciliation Commission and, 19; families and, 130–132; fictionalization of, 133–148; historicization of, 129–130; human rights and, 125–126, 232n45; whistleblowing on, 124–125
Tazmamart: Une prison de la mort au Maroc (Daure-Serfaty), 123
Tazmamort: Dix-huit ans dans le bagne de Hassan II (Tazmadeath: Eighteen Years in Hassan II's Jail) (BineBine), 126
"Tazmmamart" [sic] (Uḍmīn), 147
Ṭā'ir azraq nādir yuḥalliqu ma'ī (A Rare Blue Bird Flies with Me) (Fadel), 116–117, 141–145, 147–148
Thalāthat ayyām fī Casablanca (Ghazali), 185
al-Thaqāfa al-Jadīda (journal), 200n65
Tifinagh script, 24, 30–31, 34–37, 48–52, 53, 53–58, 211n28
Tirra, 37, 213n51
Tolédano, Meyer, 8–9, 198n54
traditions, 34–41
Train fou: Mémoires d'un rescapé de Tazmamart, 10 juillet 1971 au 29 octobre 1991 (The Mad Train: Memoirs of a Survivor of Tazmamart, July 10, 1971 to October 29, 1991) (Chberreq), 126
transitional justice commissions, 146
Trotet, François, 164
Trouillot, Michel Rolph, 13
Two Arabs, a Berber, and a Jew: Entangled Lives in Morocco (Rosen), 111–112
"Two Ghazals for Aziz" (Jedamus), 147

Uḍmīn, Muḥammad, 146–147
UIA. See *Alliance Israélite Universelle* (Universal Israelite Alliance [UIA])
Usmān, 37–38

Valensi, Lucette, 198n49
Van Dyke, Ruth, 85
Vermeren, Pierre, 162
Vie des hommes infâmes, La (Lives of Infamous Men) (Foucault), 13
Vigreux, Philippe, 238n158

War of Pacification, 101–102
Where Are You Going Moshé? (film), 222n62
women, 105–106, 131–132

Yacine, Kateb, ix
Yazami, Driss El, 6, 14, 168, 202n91
Yemen, 36, 46

Zaghārīd al-mawt (Ululations of Death) (Jouiti), 89, 101–105, 109
Zaki, M'barek, 150–151, 164–165
al-Zaman al-Maghribī (journal), 200n65
Zamane (magazine), 238n1, 239n10
Zerubavel, Yael, 35
Zionism, 77, 81, 84, 90, 95, 105, 114, 198n54

www.ingramcontent.com/pod-product-compliance
Lightning Source LLC
Chambersburg PA
CBHW020356080526
44584CB00014B/1045